HERODAS

*MIMIAMBS*

Aris & Phillips Classical Texts

# HERODAS
# *MIMIAMBS*

*Edited with a Translation, Introduction and Commentary by*

**Graham Zanker**

Aris & Phillips Classical Texts
are published by
Oxbow Books, Oxford



ISBN 978-0-85668-883-6 cloth
ISBN 978-0-85668-873-7 paper

*A CIP record for this book is available from the British Library*

*Cover image: Terracotta group of two women, c. 100 BC*
*© The Trustees of the British Museum*

Printed and bound by CPI Group (UK) Ltd, Croydon, CR0 4YY

*For Ruth again*

# CONTENTS


Acknowledgements ix
Abbreviations xi

Introduction 1
The *Mimiambs* and the Question of Performance 4
Herodas' Metre 6
Herodas' Dialect 7

Herodas *Mimiambs* 13

*Mimiamb* 1 14
Characters and characterization 32
*Mimiamb* 1 and Theokritos' *Idylls* 2, 14 and 15 36

*Mimiamb* 2 42
The characterization of Battaros 66

*Mimiamb* 3 72
Characters and interactions in *Mimiamb* 3 95

*Mimiamb* 4 98
Constructing the scene 122
Constructing the works of art in the scene 124
*Mimiamb* 4 and Hellenistic art criticism 128

*Mimiamb* 5 132
Characters and characterization 153
Setting 156

*Mimiamb* 6 158
Characters and chararacterization 181
The objectivity of Herodas 184

*Mimiamb* 7 188
Mêtrô and Kerdôn 214
Kerdôn's salesmanship 215

*Mimiamb* 8 218
*Mimiamb* 8 as a statement of Herodas' literary programme 233

The Fragments 236

Bibliography 240

Index 249

## ACKNOWLEDGMENTS

Herodas has seen a resurgence in scholarly interest in recent years. The question how his *Mimiambs* were performed, for example, fits in fairly and squarely with the current and exciting study of performance in Classical literature in general. On the other hand, the poems' combination of realistic and even vulgar subject-matter with sophisticated and self-conscious literariness – and the humour that arises out of the fusion – has perhaps a more perennial fascination.

Part of the challenge in writing this commentary has been to communicate the typically Hellenistic humour of the *Mimiambs* to the diverse audience that the Aris & Phillips series aims to address. These are, broadly speaking, students of literature who have no knowledge of Greek, those whose Greek is nascent to fairly advanced, and those who would like original contributions to our thinking about Herodas' poetry. To the more advanced reader I might seem to have been over-generous in the help I have offered, particularly in my referencing of works with which a less advanced student will not be familiar; but what author cannot feel for the young scholar who has wasted an honest morning's work puzzling over what is meant by, for example, '*AB* 298.5' without further help being given? So I have used the Harvard system's 'Bekker (1814) 298.5', by which the student can easily get the full details of the reference by looking up Bekker's *Anecdota Graeca* in the Bibliography.

The works of two scholars in particular have been of enormous value in my attempt to open out the readership of Herodas. The various studies by I. C. Cunningham are outstanding in their meticulous incisiveness, and the recent two-volume edition of the poems by L. Di Gregorio is invaluable in its comprehensive scholarly doxography. It is a pleasure to record my thanks to both scholars.

I have been helped by many colleagues and friends. I am indebted to the former chief editor of this series, the late Malcolm Willcock, who originally accepted the idea of an edition of Herodas, and commented wisely on sections of it in draft. At all stages, however, it has been Chris Collard who has provided exceptional hospitality and support, improving the manuscript and the first proofs beyond my hopes; few editors can have entered into the spirit of such a venture with such acumen and sense of fun, for which I am profoundly grateful and by which I have been hugely entertained.

I owe much besides to institutions, and to the audiences in them who helpfully commented on sections of this work delivered in both seminar and lecture-format: to Heinz Hoffmann and the Philologisches Seminar at Tübingen; to Annette Harder's Hellenistic Poetry Workship in Groningen; to Andrew Ford and the Princeton Classics Department's seminar series; to Dee Clayman and her CUNY graduate and faculty contingent; to David Sider and Stephen Kidd at the NYU graduate seminar; to Gyburg Radke's (now Uhlmann) Seminar at the Freie Universität, Berlin; and to my colleagues at the University of Canterbury. A Fellowship on the Oxford-Canterbury Exchange Scheme provided me with a precious three-month stay at University College and Christ Church, Oxford, which was graciously orchestrated by Chris Pelling, and which enabled discussion with kindly experts in fields where I am an unabashed interloper. A Visitorship at the Institute for Advanced Study in Princeton in the autumn of 2007 permitted me to finish the commentary in ideal circumstances.

I am delighted to acknowledge the assistance of individual members of these institutions and other friends: Alan Bowman, Pat Easterling, Widu-Wolfgang Ehlers, Valtin von Eickstedt, Denis Feeney, Christian Habicht, Josh Katz, Emily Kearns, Nino Luraghi, Sophie Minon, John Oakley, Olga Palagia, Elpida Skerlou, Heinrich von Staden, and Andrew Stewart. I am particularly obliged to Peter Parsons, who has over a long period of time been heroically generous with his time and advice (and his own special sense of humour) in connection with papyrological and related matters. I am solely responsible for all the faults that remain in what I have written.

Finally, I owe a signal debt to my wife, Ruth, who during our stays in Oxford, Athens, Kos and Princeton during my sabbatical in 2007 put up with Herodas as a third, often cantankerous, travelling companion.

GZ, March 2009, Christchurch, NZ

## ABBREVIATIONS

- *BNP* Cancik, H. and Schneider, H. (eds) 2002–. *Brill's New Pauly Encyclopaedia of the Ancient World: Antiquity*, English edition (Salazar, C.F., and Orton, D.E. [eds]) (Leiden)
- *DkP* Ziegler, K. and Sontheimer, W. (eds) 1964–1975 *Der kleine Pauly: Lexikon der Antike*. 5 vols (Stuttgart)
- *FGrH* Jacobi, F. 1923–. *Fragmente der griechischen Historiker* (Berlin)
- GP Gow, A.S.F. and Page, D.L. 1968. *Hellenistic Epigrams* (Cambridge)
- LSJ$^9$ Liddell, H.G., Scott, R. and Jones, R.M. 1996. *A Greek–English Lexicon*, with a Revised Supplement (Oxford)
- *LIMC* *Lexicon Iconographicum Mythologiae Classicae*. 1981–99. 8 vols, with 2 index vols. (Zurich)
- *OGIS* Dittenberger, W. 1903. *Orientis Graeci Inscriptiones Selectae*, 2 vols (Leipzig; repr. 1986 Hildesheim, Zurich, New York)
- *RE* Wissowa, G., Kroll, W., Mittelhaus, K. and Ziegler, K. (eds) 1894–. *Paulys Real-Encyclopädie der classischen Altertumswissenschaft* (Stuttgart)
- *SH* Lloyd-Jones, H. and Parsons, P.J. 1983. *Supplementum Hellenisticum* (Berlin and New York)

## THE USE OF BRACKETS IN THIS EDITION

- [ ] Square brackets indicate *either* a supplement in the Greek text, which will be similarly indicated in the English translation; *or*, in the translation, the connotation implied in the Greek; *or*, again in the translation, stage directions.
- ( ) Round brackets denote speaker-names indicated by the scribe's insertion of a paragraphos (a line under the first few letters of a new speaking part).
- ⟨ ⟩ Triangular brackets enclose conjectured speaker-names.
- † † Obelisks indicate Greek text which is irretrievably corrupt.

## INTRODUCTION

Before the publication of the second-century A.D. papyrus containing eight and a fragmentary ninth of the *Mimiambs* of Herodas in 1891 by F.G. Kenyon, Herodas was known only through approximately twenty lines which had survived in quotations to be found principally in Athenaios' *Scholars at Dinner* and in the fourth book of Stobaios' *Anthology*. Otherwise, the only extant ancient comment on the poet was – and still is – the remark by Pliny the Younger around 100 A.D. about his friend Arrius Antoninus' epigrams in Greek and his iambic poems, possibly in fact mimiambs, if we trust the reading of one manuscript. The passage places Herodas on a level with Kallimachos (as the author of the *Iambs*): 'How much cultured elegance and charm can be found there, how sweet they are, how pleasing, how clear, and how correct. I thought I was holding Callimachus or Herodes, or anything better if it exists.'[1]

Even after the publication of the papyrus and subsequent work on it scarcely anything is known of their author. Even the spelling of his name remains uncertain, given the loss of the papyrus' label. The form Herondas, Ἡρώνδας, occurs only in Athenaios 68b, and is predominantly Boiotian, but there is no evidence that our poet was connected with the Boiotian dialect-area. Moreover, Zonaras 1.957[2] at one place confuses him with Herodotos (παρὰ Ἡροδότῳ), and without a ν this is hard to explain as a corruption of Herondas. Zenobios 6.10[3] has the Ionic-Attic Herodês, Ἡρώδης, but there is no convincing argument that Herodas was connected with that dialect-area either. The Doric form, Herodas, Ἡρώδας, is favoured by Stobaios,[4] and would fit into the locations of the poems where known: the first poem, *The Go-between* or *The Temptress*, has traces of a Koan location,[5] *The Brothel-Keeper* is explicitly set on the island,[6] and the identification of the Asklêpieion of *Mimiamb* 4 with the famous Koan sanctuary now seems beyond reasonable doubt.[7] The evidence would therefore suggest that Herodas is the correct form of the poet's name, and that he lived in the Doric-speaking area of Kos and perhaps the mainland off which it lies.

We have evidence that Herodas lived during the reign of Ptolemy Philadelphos (285–247 B.C.). The fourth poem can be dated to between 285 and 265 B.C.,[8] and the first to after 272–271 B.C.,[9] with the second to be placed after 266 B.C.[10] He was therefore a contemporary of the greatest of the Hellenistic poets, Kallimachos, Theokritos and Apollonios. And that is the sum total of our knowledge of Herodas' life.

The poems themselves fit in strikingly well with the concerns and strategies of the poetry of the period. First, there is the matter of reviving obsolete metres. Herodas' choliambs, or 'lame iambics', iambic verse with a long syllable in place of the last expected short, are a revival of the metre of the sixth-century Hippônax of Ephesos, whom Herodas acknowledges, even if with some qualification, in the eighth *Mimiamb*. Kallimachos also invokes Hippônax, at the beginning and end of his book of *Iambs*. But while Kallimachos and others remained in the tradition of Hippônax in using the metre for invective or moral instruction (however moderated in tone), it is Herodas' innovation to have deployed the metre as a vehicle for the dramatic mode of mime: up till then, even literary mime like that of the fifth-century Sophrôn of Syracuse was in prose. Similarly, Theokritos, Herodas' contemporary, put his urban mimes, *Idylls* 2, 14 and 15, and his pastorals into hexameters, though the exalted pedigree of that metre brought about different effects from Herodas' 'lower' choliambs: for example, Theokritos could experiment with the clash of the grand metre and the low subject-matter. In Herodas, on the other hand, both the metre and subject-matter would have been classified as 'low', and the two components would have reinforced their 'realistic' effect, artfully offset as they were by the artificiality of the revived metre and language.[11] Herodas is therefore a typical Hellenistic poet in his 'crossing of genres' as well, deploying the subject-matter of one genre in the form of another.[12] This was a vital technique in the resuscitation of poetry, which in the fourth century had experienced a sense of exhaustion, except in the case of comedy; for epic, we have the complaint offered by Choirilos of Samos at the close of the fifth century, 'Ah, blessed the man who was skilful in song at that time, / the attendant of the Muses, when the meadow was pure. / But now, when all has been divided up and the poetic skills have their fixed limits, / we are left last as if in a race, nor is there any direction / in which a man, though he look everywhere, can fetch a newly yoked chariot.'[13]

Experimentation with dialect as a source of novel effects was another typical strategy of the poetry of the period, again probably through a desire to combat the pessimism evidenced by Choirilos. The dialect of the *Mimiambs* is East Ionic, despite the fact that the most likely form of Herodas' name is Doric, and that he therefore probably spoke Doric. In terms of realism, Herodas' East Ionic was totally out of place in (at least) *Mimiamb* 2, but arguably in poems 1 and 4 as well, all very likely set in Doric-speaking Kos. The apparent inconsistency is because the poet writes in the tradition of Hippônax, whose choliambs are in Ionic. The tradition of Ionic dialect in choliambs has therefore prevailed over local realism.

But the picture is even more complicated, because, if we are to trust the papyrus, Herodas was remarkably inconsistent in his handling of the dialect. For example, at *Mimiamb* 6.40–5 the papyrus reads as follows:

> ἐγὼ δὲ τούτων αἰτίη λαλεῦσ' εἰμι
> πόλλ', ἀλλὰ τήν μευ γλῶσσαν ἐκτεμεῖν δεῖται.
> ἐκεῖνο δ' οὗ σοι καὶ μάλιστ' ἐπεμνήσθην,
> τίς ἔσθ' ὁ ῥάψας αὐτόν; εἰ φιλεῖς μ', εἶπον.
> τί μ' ἐνβλέπεις γελῶσα; νῦν ὁρώρηκας
> Μητροῦν τὸ πρῶτον; ἢ τί τἀβρά σοι ταῦτα;

The most significant feature of Ionic, η for α, is represented in the first line, and the feminine participle λαλεῦσα is also Ionic. Yet the scribe soon writes the Attic form for 'tongue', γλῶσσαν, which he elsewhere writes as γλάσσαν, the Ionic form.[14] And within the passage quoted above he gives the aspiration, as in ἔσθ' ὁ, but two lines later observes psilosis with τἀβρά. The Ionic ευ spelling in μευ is by no means consistently used. For instance, while we have at 5.20 and 6.62 ὀτεύνεκα, at 7.45 the scribe gives us the Attic ὀτούνεκα (though Attic would require a θ instead of the τ). In *Mimiamb* 4 the papyrus has χοἰ Λεωμέδοντος (7), οὐχ ἕλκος (60), and χὠ ἀνάσιλλος (67), but employs psilosis with οὐκ ὥρηκας (40). At 6.32 we have χἠτέρην but at 7.124 κἠτέρων. Even more confusingly, while the scribe has written at 2.97 the Attic χὠσκληπιός, in line 96 someone else has crossed out his ν in εἶχεν Ἡρακλῆς, and put a χ above it, giving what I read as εἶχε χἠρακλῆς; and it appears that at line 96 the scribe has corrected his own original κ by writing χ over it to give us χὠ Θεσσαλός.[15] Finally, the Ionic trademark κ for Attic π, as in κοτε, found for example at 4.33 and 53 other times, is sometimes ignored, so that in the papyrus we have ποτε at, for example, 6.27.[16] Hippônax' choliamb fragments by contrast evidence only κ.[17]

What is the reason for this inconsistency within a generally Ionic dialect? Sometimes the π for κ can be explained on the grounds of sound-effects, as at 2.28–9, κἀκ ποίου / πηλοῦ πεφύρητ'. In elision or crasis psilosis occurs in the papyrus at most 29 times and otherwise aspiration 49 times (e.g. ἔσθ' ὁ, as in 6.43 above), and aspiration is found universally in composition (e.g. ὑφῆψεν at 2.36). It is true that in Eastern Ionic inscriptions psilosis is the rule in elision or crasis,[18] but, given the papyrus' vast preference for aspiration in this context, Herodas seems likely to have broken with the rules of pure Eastern Greek. I have hesitantly and simply for the sake of consistency regularised aspiration in the place of psilosis, but if we retain the instances of psilosis we would only make the inconsistency of Herodas' dialect even more obvious. I have also tended to Ionicize the papyrus' π for, κ as at 6.27, but have retained π in the alliteration of e.g. 2.28–9.

On any reconstruction, then, nobody spoke Herodas' version of East Ionic Greek. Furthermore, because the papyrus and its correctors did not iron out the inconsistencies, I think we must conclude that they tended to refrain from doing so out of respect for Herodas' text as they had it in front of them. Therefore, the inconsistencies were probably for the most part Herodas', and intentional. The only conclusion to be drawn is that Herodas intended his dialect to be artificial, one effect being variety, and another being to create a clash between the artificiality of the dialect of his characters and the realistic nature of his subject-matter, just as his use of it in Doric-speaking regions must have come as an amusing surprise.

This situation is scarcely unparalleled in Hellenistic poetry. The clearest demonstration that the poets of the age proceeded along exactly the same lines is the explicit statement by Kallimachos that his literary enemies complained that he wrote 'in Ionic and Doric and a mixture of both', Ἰαστὶ καὶ Δωριστὶ καὶ τὸ σύμμεικτον (*Iamb* 13.18 *Fr.* 203.18 Pfeiffer [1949] 206), in addition to writing his choliambic poems in Ionic without having visited Ephesos (*Iamb* 13.11–14 *Fr.* 203.11–14 Pfeiffer [1949] 206). The effects that Kallimachos aimed at were no doubt many and various, but among them will have been formal artificiality.[19] Herodas again emerges as a typical Hellenistic poet.

Herodas shares with his contemporaries another marked tendency, the reflective and explicit self-positioning and defence of his poetry. Kallimachos has his polemic proem to the *Aitia* and his thirteenth *Iamb*, or the coda to the *Hymn to Apollo*; Theokritos has Simichidas and Lykidas' proclamation of their poetic programme in the seventh *Idyll*; and Herodas has the *Dream*, in which he seems to be defending his genre-mixing. Never before in Greek poetry do poets seem to have reached the degree and intensity of the Hellenistic poets' self-conscious and aggressive proprietoriness over their work, not even Pindar.[20]

## *The* Mimiambs *and the Question of Performance*

In what sense did Herodas intend his poems to be 'dramatic', or 'mimic'? The question has fascinated commentators since the discovery of the papyrus,[21] and the main modes of presentation have been seen to be fully-staged performance, recitation by a number of actors, solo recitation, and private reading.

In more recent years, proponents of actual performance have pointed to moments in the text when the situation is not clear, and have argued that these unclarities can only have been resolved by presentation on the stage.[22] For example, the text of *Mimiamb* 4 is inexplicit over when the the cockerel is handed to the priest for sacrifice.[23] But these imprecisions are generally quite insignificant, and against the arguments based on them we have real problems imagining *how* the poems were staged. It is very hard to envisage how *Mimiamb* 4, with its continuing changes of place within the Asklêpieion and its references to specific details of the art works the women are viewing, could have have been represented on a stage, no matter how little in the way of stage-scenery and props was perhaps required in subliterary mime.[24] Then there are the silent parts. In *Mimiamb* 7 two speaking characters and at least six non-speaking parts can be counted.[25] How plausible, or indeed dramatically effective, is that as a basis for staging? On top of this, there is the problem that, if the poems were staged, a good deal of the functions that the silent actors would have had to perform would have been simply boring, as when a bench and a shoe-box must be fetched in *Mimiamb* 7.[26] A further consideration against actual staging is that in the case of *The Brothel-Keeper* a staged version would presumably necessitate the presence of several silent actors taking the part of the jurors, whereas recitation would give the audience the part of the jury whom Battaros is addressing, and would therefore include them in the 'action'. Likewise, in *The Dream* a solo reciter could relate the dream and its interpretation to the audience taking the part of Annas during the extensive monologue: Herodas' *sphragis* is after all meant to be heard by more than a slave, and why not 'directly' by the audience?

We are left with the possibilities of group or solo recitation. Without stage-props and through the human voice alone (though presumably with as much mimic skill in voice-projection and facial expression as the reciters could bring to bear), the whole scene can be hinted at in the text and visually supplemented in the audience's mind's eye. This is an easily assimilated process in the case of the fourth *Mimiamb*,[27] and there is no reason why the technique cannot have been general to all of the poems.[28] This would fit in with the remarkably enthusiastic way in which Hellenistic readers of poetry were prepared to supplement images of visual elements mentally.[29] The advantages of this, and therefore, one presumes, the arguments in favour of recitation, are many. For example, certain unanswered questions like when the girls hand over their bird for sacrifice in *Mimiamb* 4 need not be answered if there is no stage, though they would have to be if the poems were staged. At the same time, when Herodas chooses he can write into his text sufficient cues for the visual imagination of matters of more consequence, like the movement of the women through the Asklêpieion or the *objets d'art* which they inspect. And the element of interpretation which the human voice can contribute undoubtedly makes a text more vivid.

Whether recitation involves a group of voices or a solo voice is perhaps harder to judge, but we do well not to underestimate the capability of a single voice to carry more than one part.[30] Moreover, in no mimiamb do more than four speaking parts feature, and four different voices are well within the range of a skilled mimic: *Mimiamb* 5 alone has four, 2, 6 and 7 have two, 1, 3 and 4 three. In a careful study of the ability of ancient reciters and audiences to differentiate between the voices performed by a single reciter, W.-W. Ehlers[31] has drawn attention to the existence of reciters in the employ of wealthy Greeks and Romans, and they are dated from Alexander the Great's nephew Kallisthenes onwards.[32] He also argues that recitation by more than one speaker is unlikely, given the brevity of the pieces.[33] Performance of the *Mimiambs* by a solo reciter in fact turns out to be the most convincing scenario. Moreover, given for example the evidence of the close of Xenophon's *Symposion* 9.2–7, in which the guests are entertained by a soft-porn mime of the story of Ariadne and Dionysos, the symposion should be regarded as a highly probable performance-venue.[34]

As texts for private reading, finally, the *Mimiambs* simply leave readers the task of interpreting on their own, without the guidance of a prior interpreter in the human voice. It is a measure of Herodas' skill that he can place even private readers, as most of us are, 'in the picture'.

### *Herodas' Metre*[35]

Herodas' metre is the type of the iambic trimeter known as the choliamb ('lame iamb') or *skazôn* ('the iamb with a limp'). Its schema is as follows:

1 2 3 4 5 6 7 8 9 10 11 12<br>
x – ⏑ –|x||– ⏑ –|x – – ⏓

Here the metra are demarcated with the sign |. The syllable-lengths possible in all positions are indicated by the longs and shorts, and variable syllables with x. The positions in the line are located by the suprascript numerals; these normally coincide with the syllables. The most frequent caesura, 'a place in the verse where word-end occurs more than casually',[36] is marked with ||.

As can be seen, the line divides up into three metra, each normally containing four syllables. The idea of a limp derives from the regular occurrence of a long syllable as the penultimate syllable of each line, instead of the short which is invariable in the third metron of the iambic trimeter pure; this gives the verse a dragging feel. The ending of the line in two long syllables occurs in 65% of all lines; otherwise, the ending is in a long and short.

The first variable syllable, or *anceps*, at position 1, is long two thirds of the time, the second *anceps*, at position 5, is long over two thirds, and the third, at position 9, is short in over 95% of the cases. When the third *anceps* is long, it gives the ending –– –⏓, which increases the feel of a drag, and was therefore honoured by the ancient grammarians with the epithet 'broken-hipped,' ('ischiorrhôgic'), thus maintaining the metaphor of limping.

Long or *anceps* syllables can be 'resolved' into two shorts. Resolution can occur in the first *anceps*, giving ⏑⏑– (an anapaest); in the first long, giving ⏑⏑⏑ (a tribrach) if the *anceps* is short, or, if it is long, –⏑⏑ (a dactyl); in the second long, giving ⏑⏑⏑ in the latter half of the first metron; in the third long, giving ⏑⏑⏑ in the first half of the second metron if the *anceps* is short, or –⏑⏑ if the *anceps* is long; in the fourth long, giving ⏑⏑⏑ in the second part of the second metron. None of these types of resolution occurs in more than 2.5% of their several positions. Resolution is not possible in the third *anceps*.

The caesura is found in Herodas chiefly (75%) after the fifth syllable ('penthemimeral'), and secondarily after the seventh syllable ('hephthemimeral'). At *Mimiamb* 5.32 and 74 a diaeresis, or coincidence of a word-end with a metron-end, occurs after the second metron (or fourth foot).[37] Herodas does not observe Porson's law, which forbids –|– ⏓ ⏑ (the | denoting the division between two words) in the final metron (or feet five and six).

The differences in the metrical practices of Herodas, Hippônax, and Kallimachos are not great, though e.g. Kallimachos avoids the broad effect of ischiorrhôgic verse-endings, and is stricter than Herodas over resolution.

## *Herodas' Dialect*

As we have seen, Herodas' dialect, at least as represented by the papyrus, is essentially Eastern Ionic, but inconsistent within itself and including other dialect-forms, especially from Attic. The following is a list of the major characteristics of Herodas' Ionic, as far as it can be recovered from the papyrus. It is based on the appendix on Herodas' dialect and prosody in Cunningham (1971) 211–7, who should be consulted for statistical comparisons with Hippônax and Kallimachos, though I disagree with him on the matter of psilosis; see also Schmidt (1968).

1. η for original long α (e.g. πρῆγμα, 4.40).

2. ι is omitted from the diphthongs in γλυκέας (6.23), Κλεοῦς (3.92), ἀλοᾶν (2.34), ποεῖν (6.9). The first element of a diphthong is shortened in Θρέισσα (1.1, 79), λείη (8.45), χρεΐζειν (1.49, 7.64).

3. Quantities can be exchanged ('metathesis'), as in ἵλεως (4.11, 25), Λεωμέδων (4.7), νεωκόρος (4.41, 45, 90), and in the genitive plural of α-stem nouns (e.g. ἀστροδιφέων, 3.54), and the genitive singular of ευ-stem nouns (e.g. γναφέως, 4.78).

4. Contraction.
α+*e*-vowel = long α; α+*o*-vowel = ω. No contraction in -άω verbs.
ε+α = εα (scanned as two shorts), εα (scanned as one long); η in ἤν and ἔπην (also ἐπέαν, -έαν scanned as one long).
ε+ο (ου) = εο (two shorts) (εου, short and long); εο (one long) (εου, one long); ευ.
ε+ω = εω (short and long); εω (one long)
ε+οι = οι.
ε+ε (ει) = ει. No uncontracted forms in -έω verbs.
ε+η (ηι)= εη (short and long), εῃ (short and long) in δωρέην (2.19), ἐκχέῃ (7.7); η (ηι) in γενῇ (2.1, 32; 4.84), and in -έω verbs.
ι+ει = long ι in ὑγίη (4.86).
ο+α = ω, as in κατασβῶσαι (5.39).
ο+ο = οο (two shorts) in βοός (3.68); ου in other contracted *o*-stem nouns, in the genitive singular of ω-stem nouns, and in -όω verbs.
ο+ε = οε (two shorts), as in εὐνοέστερον.
ο+ει = οι in -όω verbs.
ο+η = ω, as in βῶσον (4.41).

5. Elision.
Short vowels are generally elided; -αι is elided in verbal endings, -οι in μοι and σοι.

6. Vowel Collision.
(1) In Herodas ε is the only vowel elided from the initial position of a word ('aphaeresis'): e.g. κοῦ 'στι (5.9).
(2) Amalgamation of vowels, especially when indicated in writing ('crasis'), often involves καί. When it elides initial ε, the result is κἀ- (long) or κἠ-. When it elides initial εἰ, the result is κεἰ or κἠ. Amalgamation also occurs with the definite article, as in τοὔνομ' (2.75), though οἱ ὀ- gives ὡ-, as in ὡρνιθοκλέπται (6.102). Note also ὦνδρες (2.61), μἤλασσον (3.58), ἐγὦδε (1.3), ἐγῷμι (5.15), and ᾦ (4.75).
(3) Instances of elision of a vowel when there is no written indication ('synekphônêsis', or 'synizêsis') involve mainly the article, καί, ἤ, μή, εἰ, and pronouns, but there are many other types, as at 5.4 ἐγὼ Ἀμφυταίῃ (cf. 2.72, 3.8, 21).

7. Hiatus between words, where two contiguous vowels do not affect one another, is rare; see e.g. μηδὲ εἷς (1.43).

8. Compensatory lengthening, whereby a vowel is lengthened because an original consonant has been lost, is characteristic of Ionic and occurs in Herodas in the words οὐδός, καλός (long α), οὖλος, γοῦνα, μοῦνος, εἴριον, κούρη, and νοῦσος. However, when the metre requires it, Herodas writes καλός (short α), μόνος, ἴσος (short ι), and yet offers ὅλος, ἔριον, and ὅρος when they are not required metrically but might have been expected in an Ionic text.

9. On κ for π see above, p. 3.

10. Ionic σσ is present in ὅσσος and τόσσος, but is more often presented as ὅσος and τόσος, together with μέσος, sometimes out of metrical necessity. The papyrus occasionally has Attic ττ, which I retain at 6.97, λαιμάτ[τε]ι.

11. On psilosis, the absence of aspiration, and my avoidance of it see above, pp. 3–4.

12. Movable ν occurs at the end of verbal forms, dative plurals and adverbs mainly before a vowel. Final ς in ἄχρις, μέχρις and οὕτως occurs before vowels, and only once (7.7) before a consonant (μέχρις τὸν ὕπνον).

13. The combination of the plosive consonants π β φ, τ δ θ, κ γ χ with the liquid consonants λ ρ is used by Herodas to lengthen or keep the quantity of a preceding short vowel for metrical convenience.

14. Declension.
(1) *a*-stems: the genitive singular of masculine nouns is -εω (one long); the genitive plural is -εων (one long); in the papyrus, the dative plural appears as -ῃσιν, -ῃσι, -ῃς, -αισι, -αις, but I have regularised the last two Attic forms to -ῃ-.
(2) *o*-stems: for the hyperionicism πυρέων at 2.80 see the note there; dative plurals appear in -οισιν, -οισι and -οις.
(3) *i*-stems: the genitive singular ends in -ιος, as in πόλιος which can be scanned as ⏑⏑⏑ and as –⏑; the dative singular is long -ι; the accusative plural is long -ις.
(4) For a long *o*-stem accusative singular in -οῦν see 2.98n.
(5) *s*-stems: the neuter genitive singular ends in -ευς, the masculine in -εω (short and long syllables); the neuter nominative and accusative plural is -εα (two shorts) or just -εα; the genitive plural is -εων, scanned either as a short and long or as one long.
(6) personal pronouns: ἐγώ, ἐμέ, με, μευ, ἐμοί, μοι; ἡμεῖς, ἡμέας, ἡμῖν, ἧμιν; σύ, σέ and σε, σευ, σοί and σοι; ὑμεῖς, ὑμέας, ὑμῶν, ὑμῖν and ὗμιν; οἱ, μιν, νιν, the last of which is Doric.
(7) reflexive pronouns: ἐμαυτόν, ἐμαυτήν, σαυτόν, σαυτοῦ, σαυτῆς, and σεωυτόν, σεωυτοῦ; ἑαυτόν, ἑωυτόν, and ὡὐτῆς.
(8) interrogative pronouns: genitive singular τέο, τεῦ.
(9) relative pronouns: the genitive singular of ὅς is οὗ or εὗ; for the genitive singular of ὅστις the papyrus has ὅτου but ὅτευ must replace it; the papyrus has ὅτεῳ and ὅτῳ once each for the dative singular of ὅστις but the latter Attic form should probably be regularised to fit the former Ionic.
(10) diminutives: frequently employed, especially with the -ίσκος ending.

15. Conjugation.
(1) 'Attic reduplication' is represented by ἀκήκουκα, ἄρηρε, ἐλήλουθα, ὀρώρηκα, the last as well as ὤρηκα.
(2) augment: for its omission at 8.45 and 73 see 8.73n.
(3) endings: in the second person singular indicative middle the papyrus offers both Attic -ει and Ionic -ῃ; the Attic forms have been brought into line with the Ionic.
first person plural indicative middle: -όμεθα and -όμεσθα.
second person singular imperative middle: -εο and -ευ, though κάθησο at 6.1.
subjunctive active: first person singular -ω and -ωμι; third person singular -ῃ.
optative active: second person singular in -αις, third person singular in -αι and -ειε(ν).

(4) in -άω verbs, α becomes ε before ο and ου, forming ευ; it also becomes ε before ω, giving εω; it is retained before ε and ει, forming long α and long αι; ὁρῆν, χρῆσθαι and ψῆν are not exceptions, but instances of Ionic *e*-stems, ὁρέω, χρέομαι, ψέω.
(5) for εἰμί, the papyrus has both Ionic εἰς and Attic εἶ in the second person singular present indicative, and I have replaced the Attic form with the Ionic; the first person plural is presumably Ionic εἶμεν at 6.70 (see n.); the participle has ὤν and ἐών, but otherwise ἐ- appears as a separate syllable or contracted to εὐ-; epic ἔασι and ἔσσεται are also found.

16. Prepositions.
(1) the second syllable of a prepositional prefix is 'knocked off' ('apokôpê') in ἄστηθι at 8.1.
(2) Herodas uses ἐς and εἰς as metrically required, otherwise indifferently.

17. Particles.
Herodas uses οὖν, not Ionic ὦν.

### *Notes*

1. *Letters* 4.3.3: *quantum ibi humanitatis, uenustatis, quam dulcia illa, quam amantia, quam arguta, quam recta. Callimachum me uel Heroden uel si quid melius tenere credebam.*
2. = *Etymologicum Magnum* 411.33 Gaisford (1848).
3. Leutsch-Schneidewin (1839) 1 164, 6.
4. E.g. Stobaios 4.23.14 Wachsmuth-Hense (1909) 4.575.
5. See p. 21.
6. See lines 95–8.
7. See p. 106.
8. See p. 105.
9. See p. 21.
10. See *Mim.* 2.16n.
11. For 'high', 'low' etc. as ancient literary terms see the Discussion of *Mim.* 8, below, p. 234.
12. See the Discussion of *Mim.* 8, below, pp. 234–5.
13. ἆ μάκαρ, ὅστις ἔην κεῖνον χρόνον ἴδρις ἀοιδῆς,
Μουσάων θεράπων, ὅτ' ἀκήρατος ἦν ἔτι λειμών·
νῦν δ' ὅτε πάντα δέδασται, ἔχουσι δὲ πείρατα τέχναι,
ὕστατοι ὥστε δρόμου καταλειπόμεθ', οὐδέ πῃ ἔστι
πάντῃ παπταίνοντα νεοζυγὲς ἅρμα πελάσσαι.
*Fr.* 317 *SH* (1983) 147–8
14. 3.84, †93, 5.8, 37, 6.16, 7.77, 110. Likewise, at 3.24 we have from his hand the Attic τριθημέρᾳ, but at 6.21 τριτημέρη (minus the usual ι-adscript).

15. The same thing happens at *Mim.* 4.3, χὠπόλλων, though I restore the κ.
16. Note also 2.28, 56, 7.22, 44.
17. Cunningham (1971) 213.
18. As Cunningham (1971) 214 points out.
19. See in general Kerkhecker (1999) 256–7 on the aim of πολυείδεια, 'variety of form'; Acosta-Hughes (2002) 5, 63 n. 18.
20. See e.g. the conspectus in Hopkinson (1988) 86–91.
21. See the convenient history of the inquiry in Mastromarco (1984) 1–19.
22. Mastromarco (1984).
23. *Mim.* 4.12n., and note the vagueness of the spatial arrangement of *Mim.* 5, discussed below, pp. 156–7.
24. Cf. Hunter (1993) 39.
25. See below, p. 200.
26. Puchner (1993) 29, Stanzel (1998) 160–2.
27. See *Mim.* 4.56b–78n. and pp. 122–8.
28. This has recently also been argued by Stanzel (1998) esp. 162.
29. See Zanker (2004) 72–102.
30. Cunningham (1981) 161–2.
31. Ehlers (2001).
32. Ehlers (2001) 19 with n. 24, citing Ploutarchos, *Alexandros* 54, on Stroibos, the slave who read aloud (*anagnôstês*) to Kallisthenes.
33. Ehlers (2001) 27.
34. For symposion-performance of Hellenistic poetry see in general Cameron (1995) 71–103, with pp. 89–90 on Herodas.
35. The following sketch is indebted to the appendix on metre in Cunningham (1971) 218–21, though I have opted in favour of 'metron' and 'metra' as the basic verse-unit(s). Many readers will be more familiar with 'feet' as the unit of analysis; for their benefit I have in what follows given the names dactyl, spondee, tribrach and so on in brackets after the metrical values. Using feet is a convenient way of specifying a particular place in the verse, but it does not accommodate certain phenomena like the choriambic anaclasis mentioned below, n. 37.
36. West (1983) 192.
37. Cunningham's (1971) 220 acceptance of choriambic anaclasis, whereby the metron becomes –⏑⏑– instead of ⏓–⏑–, is challenged by West (1983) 161.

# HERODAS

*MIMIAMBS*

## 1. ΠΡΟΚΥΚΛΙΣ Η ΜΑΣΤΡΟΠΟΣ

*(ΜΗΤΡΩ)* Θρέισσ', ἀράσσει τὴν θύρην τις· οὐκ ὄψῃ
μή τις παρ' ἡμέων ἐξ ἀγροικίης ἥκει;
*(ΘΡΕΙΣΣΑ)* τίς τὴν θύρην;
*⟨ΓΥΛΛΙΣ⟩* ἐγὦδε.
*⟨ΘΡ.⟩* τίς σύ; δειμαίνεις
ἆσσον προσελθεῖν;
*⟨ΓΥ.⟩* ἢν ἰδού, πάρειμ' ἆσσον.
*⟨ΘΡ.⟩* τίς δ' εἰς σύ;
*⟨ΓΥ.⟩* Γυλλίς, ἡ Φιλαινίδος μήτηρ.
ἄγγειλον ἔνδον Μητρίχῃ παρεῦσάν με.
*⟨ΘΡ.⟩* καλεῖ -
*⟨ΜΗ.⟩* τίς ἐστιν;
*⟨ΘΡ.⟩* Γυλλίς.
*⟨ΜΗ.⟩* ἀμμίη Γυλλίς.
στρέψον τι, δούλη. τίς σε μοῖρ' ἔπεισ' ἐλθεῖν,
Γυλλίς, πρὸς ἡμέας; τί σὺ θεὸς πρὸς ἀνθρώπους;
ἤδη γάρ εἰσι πέντε κου, δοκέω, μῆνες
ἐξ εὖ σε, Γυλλίς, οὐδ' ὄναρ, μὰ τὰς Μοίρας
πρὸς τὴν θύρην ἐλθοῦσαν εἶδέ τις ταύτην.
*(ΓΥ.)* μακρὴν ἀποικέω, τέκνον, ἐν δὲ τῇς λαύρῃς
ὁ πηλὸς ἄχρις ἰγνύων προσέστηκεν,
ἐγὼ δὲ δραίνω μυῖ' ὅσον· τὸ γὰρ γῆρας
ἡμέας καθέλκει χἠ σκιὴ παρέστηκεν.
*⟨ΜΗ.⟩* ....].ε καὶ μὴ τοῦ χρόνου καταψεύδεο·
.......]. γάρ, Γυλλί, χἠτέρους ἄγχειν.
*(ΓΥ.)* σίλλαινε· ταῦτα τῇς νεωτέρῃς ὗμιν
πρόσεστιν. ἀλλ' οὐ τοῦτο μή σε θερμήνῃ.

2 ἀποικίης, γρ supra π P

## 1. THE GO-BETWEEN *OR* THE TEMPTRESS

(*Mêtrichê*) Threissa, someone's knocking at the door. Go and see
whether it isn't one of our folk come from the country.
(*Threissa*) Who's knocking? <*Gyllis*> Me, here. <*Th.*> Who are you? Are
you frightened to come nearer? <*Gy.*> Here I am, nearer: look.
<*Th.*> Who are you? <*Gy.*> Gyllis, Philainis' mother.
Tell Mêtrichê inside that I'm here.
<*Th.*> The caller's – <*Mê.*> Who? <*Th.*> Gyllis. <*Mê.*> Nanny Gyllis!
Leave us a while, slave. What destiny persuaded you to visit us,
Gyllis? What's a goddess like you doing among mere mortals?
I reckon it's now about five months, Gyllis,
by the Fates it is,
since anyone saw you coming to this door, even in a dream.
(*Gy.*) I live a long way away, child, and in the lanes
the mud comes up to your knees,
and I'm as weak as a fly. Old age
drags us down and its shadow stands near us.
<*Mê.*> ...], and don't blame your old age.
[You've got] plenty more hugs left in you yet.
(*Gy.*) Have your laugh! That sort of thing's for you young girls.
But this [joking] certainly isn't going to get you warmed up.

ἀλλ᾽ ὦ τέκνον, κόσον τιν᾽ ἤδη χηραίνεις
χρόνον μόνη τρύχουσα τὴν μίαν κοίτην;
ἐξ εὗ γὰρ εἰς Αἴγυπτον ἐστάλη Μάνδρις
δέκ᾽ εἰσὶ μῆνες, κοὐδὲ γράμμα σοι πέμπει,
ἀλλ᾽ ἐκλέλησται καὶ πέπωκεν ἐκ καινῆς.
κεῖ δ᾽ ἔστιν οἶκος τῆς θεοῦ· τὰ γὰρ πάντα,
ὅσσ᾽ ἔστι κου καὶ γίνετ᾽, ἔστ᾽ ἐν Αἰγύπτῳ·
πλοῦτος, παλαίστρη, δύναμις, εὐδίη, δόξα,
θέαι, φιλόσοφοι, χρυσίον, νεηνίσκοι,
θεῶν ἀδελφῶν τέμενος, ὁ βασιλεὺς χρηστός,
Μουσῆιον, οἶνος, ἀγαθὰ πάνθ᾽ ὅσ᾽ ἂν χρῄζῃ,
γυναῖκες, ὁκόσους οὐ μὰ τὴν Ἅιδεω Κούρην
ἀστέρας ἐνεγκεῖν οὐρανὸς κεκαύχηται,
τὴν δ᾽ ὄψιν οἷαι πρὸς Πάριν κοθ᾽ ὥρμησαν
.... κρ]ιθῆναι καλλονήν – λάθοιμ᾽ αὐτάς
......] . κοίην οὖν τάλαινα σὺ ψυχήν
ἔχουσα θάλπεις τὸν δίφρον; κατ᾽ οὖν λήσεις
γηρᾶσα] καί σευ τὸ ὥριον τέφρη κάψει.
........ ἄλλῃ χἠμέρας μετάλλαξον
τὸ]ν νοῦν δύ᾽ ἢ τρεῖς, χἰλαρὴ κατάστηθι
........ ἄλλον· νηῦς μιῆς ἐπ᾽ ἀγκύρης
οὐκ] ἀσφαλὴς ὁρμεῦσα· κεῖνος ἢν ἔλθῃ
..........]ν[.] μηδὲ εἷς ἀναστήσῃ
ἡ]μέας ....τοδινα δ᾽ ἄγριος χειμών
..[.............].. κοὐδὲ εἷς οἶδεν
......]ν ἡμέων· ἄστατος γὰρ ἀνθρώποις
.....]..η[. ]. ἀλλὰ μήτις ἕστηκε
σύνεγγυς ἧμιν;
⟨*ΜΗ.*⟩ οὐδὲ εἷς.
⟨*ΓΥ.*⟩ ἄκουσον δή
ἅ σοι χρεΐζουσ᾽ ὧδ᾽ ἔβην ἀπαγγεῖλαι·
ὁ Ματαλίνης τῆς Παταικίου Γρύλλος,
ὁ πέντε νικέων ἆθλα, παῖς μὲν ἐν Πυθοῖ,
δὶς δ᾽ ἐν Κορίνθῳ τοὺς ἴουλον ἀνθεῦντας,
ἄνδρας δὲ Πίσῃ δὶς καθεῖλε πυκτεύσας,
πλουτέων τὸ καλόν, οὐδὲ κάρφος ἐκ τῆς γῆς
κινέων, ἄθικτος ἐς Κυθηρίην σφρηγίς,
ἰδών σε καθόδῳ τῆς Μίσης ἐκύμηνε

Come on, child, how long are you going to put up with the separation,
wearing out your solitary bed on your own?
It's ten months since Mandris went off to Egypt,
and he doesn't send you even a word,
but has forgotten all about you and has drunk out of a new cup.
The Goddess has her own house there. Everything
you can find anywhere else is there in Egypt –
wealth, the wrestling-club, power, the peaceful life, reputation,
shows, philosophers, money, young lads,
the temple of the brother and sister gods, the King is good,
there's the Museum, wine, all the good things he could want,
women, so many of them that the sky can't boast it's got as many stars
– no, by Persephonê –,
as beautiful as [the goddesses] who once visited Paris
....] for their beauty to be judged, begging their ladyships' pardon,
......] So my poor darling, what sort of attitude is this
when you're just keeping your chair warm? So before you know it
you'll [have grown old], and ash will consume your youthful charms.
Look] elsewhere, and try a new approach
for two or three days, and be cheerful
......] someone else: a ship which lies at only one anchor
isn't safe. If Death comes
.................................. not even one could raise
us up again ... but a dreadful storm
.................................. not even one of us
frail, unstable creatures knows [the future] for mortals
................ –But there isn't anyone
near us, is there? <*Mê.*> No one at all. <*Gy.*> Well, listen
to what I came here wanting to tell you.
Gryllos, the son of Pataikion's daughter Matalinê,
the five-time winner at the games, as a lad at the Pythian games,
twice winning in the adolescent division at the Isthmian games,
twice beating men at boxing at the Olympics,
nicely well-off, wouldn't hurt a fly,
an untouched seal as far as sex is concerned, –
he spotted you at the procession of the Descent of Misê and felt a surge

τὰ σπλάγχν' ἔρωτι καρδίην ἀνοιστρηθείς,
καί μευ οὔτε νυκτὸς οὔτ' ἐφ' ἡμέρην λείπει
τὸ δῶμα, τέκνον, ἀλλά μευ κατακλαίει
καὶ ταταλίζει καὶ ποθέων ἀποθνῄσκει.
ἀλλ', ὦ τέκνον μοι Μητρίχη, μίαν ταύτην
ἁμαρτίην δὸς τῇ θεῷ· κατάρτησον
σαυτήν, τὸ γῆρας μὴ λάθῃ σε προσβλέψαν.
καὶ δοιὰ πρήξεις· ἡδέω[ν τεύξῃ καί σοι]
δοθήσεταί τι μέζον ἢ δοκεῖς· σκέψαι,
πείσθητί μευ· φιλέω σε, ναὶ μὰ τὰς Μοίρας.
*(ΜΗ.)* Γυλλί, τὰ λευκὰ τῶν τριχῶν ἀπαμβλύνει
τὸν νοῦν· μὰ τὴν γὰρ Μάνδριος κατάπλωσιν
καὶ τὴν φίλην Δήμητρα, ταῦτ' ἐγὼ ἐξ ἄλλης
γυναικὸς οὐκ ἂν ἡδέως ἐπήκουσα,
χωλὴν δ' ἀείδειν χώλ' ἂν ἐξεπαίδευσα
καὶ τῆς θύρης τὸν οὐδὸν ἐχθρὸν ἡγεῖσθαι.
σὺ δ' αὖτις ἔς με μηδὲ ἕνα, φίλη, τοῖον
φέρουσα χώρει μῦθον· ὃν δὲ γρῄῃσι
πρέπει γυναιξὶ τῆς νέῃς ἀπάγγελλε·
τὴν Πυθέω δὲ Μητρίχην ἔα θάλπειν
τὸν δίφρον· οὐ γὰρ ἐγγελᾷ τις εἰς Μάνδριν.
ἀλλ' οὐχὶ τούτων, φασί, τῶν λόγων Γυλλίς
δεῖται· Θρέισσα, τὴν μελαινίδ' ἔκτριψον
χἠκτημόρους τρεῖς ἐγχέασα τοῦ ἀκρήτου
καὶ ὕδωρ ἐπιστάξασα δὸς πιεῖν.
*(ΓΥ.)* καλῶς.
*(ΜΗ.)* τῆ, Γυλλί, πῖθι.
*⟨ΓΥ.⟩* δεῖξον ου[.] .........πα.[
πείσουσά σ' ἦλθον, ἀλλ' ἕκητι τῶν ἱρῶν.
*⟨ΜΗ.⟩* ὧν οὕνεκέν μοι, Γυλλί, ὠνα[..........
*⟨ΓΥ.⟩* .....γένοιτο, μᾶ, τέκνον ...........
ἡδύς γε· ναὶ Δήμητρα, Μητρίχη, τούτου
ἡδίον' οἶνον Γυλλὶς οὐ πέπωκέν κω.
σὺ δ' εὐτύχει μοι, τέκνον, ἀσφαλίζευ δέ
σαυτήν· ἐμοὶ δὲ Μυρτάλη τε καὶ Σίμη
νέαι μένοιεν, ἔστ' ἂν ἐμπνέῃ Γυλλίς.

64 ἡδέω[ν τεύξῃ καί σοι] Headlam (1922) 7

in his insides as his heart was stung by love,
and he doesn't leave my house either by day or by night, child,
but wails at me
and calls me dearest and is dying with longing.
So, Metrichê my child,
grant the Goddess this one little peccadillo; dedicate yourself to her
in case you don't all of a sudden notice old age staring you in the face.
You'll win two ways: [you'll gain a life of pleasure, and]
more will be given to you than you can imagine. Think about it,
and follow my advice. By the Fates, it's all because I love you.
(*Mê.*) Gyllis, your grey hairs are dulling your wits.
I swear by Mandris' voyage home to me
and by dear Demeter,
I wouldn't willingly have put up with all this from any other woman:
I'd have taught her to sing her lame songs with a limp
and not to expect a welcome on the threshold of my door.
Don't you ever again come to me, my dear,
with even one more story like that. Tell your young girlfriends
a story that old women ought to be telling.
Let me, Metrichê, the daughter of Pytheês, keep
my chair warm. No one makes jokes against Mandris.
But Gyllis doesn't need this kind of talk at all, they tell me.
Threissa, clean out the black cup,
pour out a half measure of the neat wine,
mix in a drop of water and give it to her to drink. (*Gy.*) Lovely, but I really couldn't.
<*Mê.*> There, Gyllis, drink up. <*Gy.*> Show [..............
I came to persuade you; it was because of the rites of Aphrodite.
<*Mê.*> On account of which to me, Gyllis, [............
<*Gy.*> .....]may it be. My, child, [.........
pleasant. By Demêter, Metrichê,
Gyllis hasn't ever drunk a sweeter drop!
Farewell, child, and do look after yourself.
I still have Myrtalê and Simê who I hope will
remain young, as long as Gyllis is breathing.

## COMMENTARY

Synopsis The hour of day is unspecified, but it is possibly winter (13–14). The scene is the house of Mêtrichê, who is probably a former hetaira, and the town may be Kos-city. An old woman named Gyllis knocks on the door of the house of her young friend, and after some comic business while the identity of the caller is established (1–7), Mêtrichê expresses her surprise at seeing Gyllis after such a long time (8–12). Gyllis blames this on the distance she lives from Mêtrichê, complains about the mud in the lanes, and laments her old age (13–16). After Mêtrichê has offered ribald consolation (17–18), Gyllis warms to her task. She tells Mêtrichê that the latter's lover Mandris, who has been away in Alexandria for ten months, has clearly fallen prey to the city's enormous attractions, so Mêtrichê's fidelity is misplaced, and she is going to grow old without a partner (19–47). She ascertains from Mêtrichê that they are alone (48a), and proceeds to recommend the services of a young man of her acquaintance named Gryllos, whose athletic prowess, gentleness, wealth, availability and devotion to Mêtrichê since he saw her at a festival Gyllis she details (48b-66). Mêtrichê retorts that all old age is doing to Gyllis is dulling her wits, and that she would not have put up with such pimping from anyone else. She asserts her continuing devotion to Mandris, but then changes the subject and offers Gyllis a cup of wine (67–81a). Gyllis accepts after some feigned reluctance, savours the wine enthusiastically, bids Mêtrichê farewell, and talks of two other young hetairai whose company she hopes to enjoy for as long as she lives (81b-90).

Text The part-distributions, where they are not indicated by a paragraphos (a short horizontal line on the papyrus under the first few letters of a new speaker's words), can generally be assigned securely. A consensus seems to be emerging over the attributions in the passages where more than one person speaks in one line (*antilabê*), especially at lines 1–7, 48 and 82–5, and here I follow the most recent editors, Di Gregorio (1997) and Cunningham (2004), except that I differ from Cunningham in giving all of line 20 to Gyllis. The left-hand sides of lines 32–47 (column 3 of the papyrus) are the most damaged; my policy here has been to give at least some information about what remains, principally to avoid the impression that the complete words are the only (miraculous) survivals.

DATE The mention of 'the temple of the brother and sister gods' at line 30 secures a dating no earlier than 272–271 B.C., the year in which we first have attestation of the office of the 'priest of Alexander and the Theoi Adelphoi'; this evidence comes from the Hibeh papyrus (P. Hibeh 199, lines 16–17). Fraser (1972) 2, 876–8 n. 30, followed e.g. by Sherwin-White (1978) 94–5 n. 60, shows that, at least theoretically, a date during the reign of Ptolemy Euergetes (246–21) cannot be ruled out. But so late a dating is at least twenty years after what seems likely in the case of *Mimiambs* 2 and 4: see the introductory remarks on those poems.

SETTING Weil (1891) 671 and (1892) 518 was the originator of the thesis that *Mimiamb* 1 is set on Kos because of the oaths by the Moirai at lines 11 and 66. He observed that oaths by the Moirai are elsewhere used by Simaitha in Theokritos' second *Idyll* (160) and by Kokkale in *Mimiamb* 4, poems whose setting is almost certainly Koan: see Gow (1952) 1 xx, and below, p. 51 for *Idyll* 2, and below, p. 106 for *Mimiamb* 4. He therefore concluded that the rare oath was specifically Koan. See further Sherwin-White (1978) 106 n. 122, who moreover refutes the dismissal of Weil's argument by Cunningham (1971) 2, 61. Reinach (1891) 215 first pointed out that relations between Kos and Alexandria were close at this period, and that the praise of Alexandria at lines 26–35 therefore sits very well in a Koan setting. His arguments have been restated by Fraser (1972) 2, 877–8, and see now Sherwin-White (1978) 90–131 on the connections between Kos and Alexandria. Weil and Reinach's position has been accepted by the majority of scholars ever since. The setting is therefore probably Kos, in all likelihood Kos-city. Mêtrichê's house may be fairly modest but not desperately so: she seems to be a former hetaira, and, if my suggestion at line 2n. is correct, she will have a country-property and retainers as well as her city-house servants. Her circumstances will in that case be much less humble than, for example, Simaitha's in Theokritos' second *Idyll*.

SOURCES Go-betweens figured in the *magoidiai*, a genre related to mime, in which, as Athenaios (*Scholars at Dinner* 621c) records the second-century B.C. Aristokles as saying, the (apparently sole) performer wore women's clothing, and accompanied himself with drums and cymbals; more particularly, the *magoidos* acted out different roles, 'sometimes women as adulteresses and go-betweens, and at others times a man in a drunken state and serenading his lady-love'. The *Etymologicum Gudianum* s.v. μαστροπός says that the commentary on Sophrôn (probably the one by Apollodôros of Athens) defines the word as 'a woman who procures the services of prostitutes', so at least the word appeared in Sophrôn. Go-betweens figure in extant comedies, like Syra in Terence's *Hecyra* (I.1–2), Cleaereta in Plautus' *Asinaria* (I.3, III.1) and Syra and Melaenis in Plautus' *Cistellaria* (I.1–2, III, IV.1). At *Amores* 1.15.17–18 Ovid's list of stock types fixed by Menander includes an *improba lena*. But, as we shall see in the Discussion, Herodas' poem also has striking connections with the second, fourteenth and fifteenth *Idylls* of Theokritos, which have nothing to do with go-betweens, and Herodas may be the debtor.

PURPOSE The primary aim of the *Mimiamb* is the characterization of Gyllis. Secondary are the praise of Alexandria (placed in the mouth of an unlikely source as is common in the court-poetry of the Ptolemies), the characterization of Mêtrichê, and, possibly, emulation of Theokritos, as we shall again see in the Discussion.

**1. knocking, ἀράσσει:** here of loud knocking, typical of comedy; see Aristophanes, *Women at the Assembly* 977. Theokritos' second *Idyll* has Simaitha twice referring to Delphis knocking on a door in an agitated state, in one case her own (6), in the other the gates of Hades (160), not that this similarity is likely to have been something either poet was consciously aiming for.
**2. one of our folk, παρ' ἡμέων:** if the reading is correct, the phrase's meaning 'someone in our service' is possible; cf. τὴν παρ' ἐμοῦ, 'mine', at Menandros, *The Bad-Tempered Man* 375.
**from the country:** in the papyrus the original reading is ἀποικίης, 'from the colony', but this meaning is hard to fit into the context; and the scribe wrote γρ over the π by way of correction. Mêtrichê's first thought as to the identity of the noisy caller is therefore that it is a rustic who is in her service. This is most naturally explained if she has some sort of property in the country. The difficulty editors have seen in Mêtrichê's having a country property is obviated if we follow Di Gregorio (1995) 677–83, 690–2, who suggests that Mandris has left a piece of country real estate in Mêtrichê's hands during his absence.
**3. τίς τὴν θύρην;:** supply ἤραξεν or ἀράσσει. The ellipse is common in colloquial speech.
**ἐγῷδε:** = ἐγὼ ἥδε (crasis; see above, p. 9).
**4. ἦν:** an interjection: 'see!'
**5. εἶς:** the Ionic form of Attic εἶ.
**Philainis:** The papyrus has Φιλαιν[ί]ου in the main text, but another hand has written Φιλαινίδος in the right margin; the names amount to the same thing, Philainion being simply a pet name for Philainis. Philainis of Leukadia was the authoress of a treatise on sexual positions; see Headlam-Knox (1922) 13 and Gow-

Page (1965) 2, 3–4 for the evidence. That Gyllis has a daughter of this name (if she is not Philainis herself) gives us a broad hint about her profession and prepares us for her proposition. If Gyllis is Mêtrichê's foster-mother (see 7n.), Philainis will be Mêtrichê's foster-sister. The historical Philainis' name became common among prostitutes, and it is interesting that in Plautus' *Asinaria* Philaenium is the daughter of the go-between Cleaereta.

**6. here, ἔνδον:** after a verbal form like ἄγγειλον, εἴσω would be the normal adverb ('bring the announcement inside that…'; see Euripides, *Helen* 447, ἄγγειλον εἴσω δεσπόταισιν σοῖς …). But ἔνδον after verbs implying motion can be found at e.g. Menandros, *The Arbitrators* 354, 754–5.

**7.** The distribution of speakers in this line is disputed. The arrangement printed here is that of, most recently, Cunningham (1971) and (2004) and Di Gregorio (1997). The papyrus has a paragraphos at the beginning of the line, which means that the speaker will be different from the one immediately preceding, Gyllis. The slave-girl Threissa tries to say 'Gyllis is calling you' (καλεῖ σε Γυλλίς), but is interrupted by Mêtrichê's 'Who is it?', and then manages to get in 'Gyllis'. This would fit in with the space after ἐστιν in the papyrus, and with the fact that Gyllis has just given Threissa her name; it is natural that Mêtrichê should then express her surprise by repeating Gyllis' name, adding a title which betokens at least affection, if not Gyllis' role in her life as her nurse. An alternative, maintained e.g. by Headlam-Knox (1922), is to read κάλει (imperative), and attribute it and 'Who is it?' to Mêtrichê, giving the rest of the line to Gyllis, but Groeneboom (1922) 39 points out that the logical and usual procedure is to ask the guest's name first and then to invite him or her in. The fact that a single verse-line could be divided so greatly is no necessary obstacle to thinking that the *Mimiambs* were performed by one actor; see above, pp. 4–6.

**Nanny, ἀμμίη:** Hesychios α 3699 Schmidt (1858) 1 148 gives the word the meaning of 'mother' or 'nurse'. It was probably a children's word. Clearly, Gyllis is not Mêtrichê's mother, and she is likely to have been Mêtrichê's nurse or foster-mother, though it cannot be ruled out of court entirely that the term is only one of endearment; see further Di Gregorio (1995) 686.

**8. leave us a while, στρέψον τι:** literally 'turn away a little'; στρέφω is here used intransitively.

**μοῖρα:** Mêtrichê employs ironically highflown phraseology.

**9. What's a goddess like you doing among mere mortals?, τί σὺ θεὸς πρὸς ἀνθρώπους;:** τί is adverbial, 'why?'; supply ἥκεις, giving the sense 'Why have you, (as) a god, come to mortals?', which explains why σύ and θεός are both nominatives. Mêtrichê continues with her irony. Headlam-Knox (1922) 16 aptly cite Apollonios' *Argonautika* 3.52–4, where Aphrodite teases Hera and Athene: 'Ladies, what intention and need can have brought you after such a long time? Why can you have come, you who have not at all been frequent visitors in the past, since you are pre-eminent among goddesses?', based on *Il.* 18.385–7. For further epic allusions, see below, pp. 33–4.

**10. κου:** 'about', in approximations.
**11. even in a dream, οὐδ' ὄναρ:** literally 'not even in a dream', a common idiom for 'not at all'; see e.g. Plato, *Theaitêtos* 173d οὐδ' ὄναρ πράττειν προσίσταται αὐτοῖς, '[such things] do not enter their minds even in a dream.'
**by the Fates:** for this oath as evidence that the poem is set on Kos see above, p. 21. Whereas in its rare occurrences elsewhere the oath's significance lies in appropriateness of the functions of the Moirai (for example, as avengers of wrongdoing), in Herodas it seems to have no such specific reference.
**13. a long way away, μακρήν:** an adverb.
**lanes, λαύρης:** originally an Ionic word, attested in Hippônax, *Frr.* 63, 95.10 Degani (1991) 81, 105; the scholiast on Aristophanes' *Peace* 99 stresses the narrowness and filth of the alleys denoted by the word.
**14. ἰγνύων:** from ἰγνύς, which actually refers to the back of the knee.
**15. I'm weak, δραίνω:** literally, 'I am able to do', from δράω with -αίνω (so also at *Mim.* 2.95); Schwyzer (1939) 1 694.
**15–16.** For Gyllis' strategy in emphasizing old age as support for her proposition see below, pp. 32–3.
**its shadow, χὴ σκίη:** there is no support in Greek literature for σκία meaning 'the shadow of death'; it seems reasonable to follow Di Gregorio (1997) 59 and take σκίη as referring to the shadow of old age, a pivotal ploy in Gyllis' strategy for Mêtrichê.
**17. don't blame your old age, μὴ τοῦ χρόνου καταψεύδεο:** literally 'don't speak falsely of your age', i.e. 'don't blame your age for lessening your physical capabilities.' For χρόνος in the sense of a person's age see LSJ$^9$ s.v. II.
**18. hugs, ἄγχειν:** 'squeeze', here in an erotic sense. Mêtrichê teasingly opines that Gyllis is not past her days of active sex, and Gyllis seizes on the mild sexual joke to turn the conversation to her own ends (see below, pp. 32–3).
**19–20:** part-distribution and meaning disputed. I follow Di Gregorio (1997) 60–4: with ταῦτα, Gyllis refers to the lovemaking mentioned by Mêtrichê ('That sort of thing's for you young girls'), but her τοῦτο refers to Mêtrichê's joking, which, however, will not keep her warm (οὐ μή plus the aorist subjunctive usually expresses strong negation: Kühner-Gerth [1955] 2 221–2); and so Gyllis can proceed seamlessly to her question how long Mêtrichê intends to sleep alone. This reading makes a fluent sense of the lines which is not forthcoming in the reconstructions by the other editors. That the same speaker should use ἀλλά twice is no objection, since the first is adversative, the second hortative, equivalent to ἀλλ' ἄγε (the combination occurs later in the poem at lines 59 and 61, again spoken by Gyllis).
**21. ἤδη χηραίνεις:** the first two syllables of the third metron (-η χηρ-) are long, giving a spondee (an 'ischiorrhôgic choliamb': West [1982] 41, 161, 175; above, p. 7), which Bo (1962) 12–14 notes that Herodas often uses to give emphasis to a word, here obviously χηραίνεις, 'put up with the separation'. χηραίνω (=χηρεύω) is not attested elsewhere.

**24. even a word, οὐδὲ γράμμα:** actually, 'not even a letter of the alphabet'; 'a letter' (ἐπιστολή) would demand γράμματα. If Gyllis has not darkened Mêtrichê's doorstep for five months (10–12), how can she know that Mandris has not written during that period of Mandris' ten-month absence? It is quite in accord with Herodas' characterization of Gyllis that the 'slip' is in fact part of his presentation of her hard sell.
**23. Mandris:** against Cunningham's statement (1971) 64 that the name is otherwise unknown, Sherwin-White (1978) 106 n. 122 notes that it occurs on an inscription on Kalymnos, the island lying north west of Kos; she is followed by Di Gregorio (1997) 64–5. The Koan connection is thereby strengthened.
**25. has drunk out of a new cup, πέπωκεν ἐκ καινῆς:** a marginal note on the papyrus gives us κύλικος, 'cup', which seems to be the correct supplement, the phrase meaning that Mandris has found a new girlfriend. The metaphor is attested elsewhere; see e.g. Plautus, *The Truculent Slave* 43, *si semel amoris poculum accepit meri*, 'if once he has accepted the cup of undiluted love'...
**26. κεῖ:** = ἐκεῖ; see Schwyzer (1939) 1 613 (*c*).
**The Goddess has her own house there:** coming from Gyllis, this can only refer to Aphrodite. Gyllis has no particular 'house' or temple of the goddess in mind. She is merely saying that all pleasure is concentrated in Egypt, specifically in Alexandria, its major city (cf. γάρ, 'for', in the following clause).
**Everything you can find anywhere else is there in Egypt, τὰ γὰρ πάντα ... Αἰγύπτῳ:** literally 'all things such as exist and are produced anywhere (κου, Ionic for που) exist in Egypt.'
**28–32:** Herodas has intentionally arranged Gyllis' catalogue of the attractions of Alexandria in a comic disorder; particularly amusing, perhaps, are the juxtapositions of 'shows', 'philosophers' and 'money' (29), 'the Museum' and 'wine' (31). The disorder characterizes the old reprobate. The 'encomium' of Ptolemaic achievement is an instance of the strategy common among the Alexandrian poets whereby praise of the rulers is put in the mouths of unlikely and unexpectedly humble, if not downright low people; to judge by the frequency with which the technique is used, and by the contrast with poetic approaches to other Hellenistic regents like Theokritos' to Hierôn of Syracuse (*Id.* 16), which is far more that of a courtier, the Ptolemies seem to have found such humour congenial; see the Discussion, pp. 37–8.
**28. wealth:** Egypt was proverbial for its wealth from Homer on (*Od.* 3.301, 14.263, 285–6).
**power:** as the capital of the Ptolemaic empire, Alexandria is a politically and militarily powerful centre.
**the peaceful life:** εὐδία denotes 'good climate' and Alexandria was renowned for its climate, but the Rosetta stone (*OGIS* 90.11) tells how Ptolemy V Epiphanes tried to lead Egypt to εὐδία, denoting settledness or tranquillity. Gyllis, who is listing Alexandria's attractions, might seem more likely to refer to climate, but perhaps both senses are present here.
**29. shows:** Alexandria was lavish in its festivals, as we know from Theokritos,

*Idyll* 15, and from Kallixeinos' description of Philadelphos' procession recorded by Athenaios, *Scholars at Dinner* 196a–203c, on which see Rice (1983).

**philosophers:** this probably refers to philosophers in our sense, like the Peripatetic Demetrios of Phaleron and Stratôn of Lampsakos whom Soter attracted to Alexandria; see Pfeiffer (1968) 99–104, Fraser (1972) 114.

**young lads:** young men as companions for Mandris, though we cannot rule out a homosexual reference: Mandris' counterpart in Theokritos, Delphis, is clearly bisexual, if we can trust Simaitha's despairing recollection of her informant's words, 'She said she didn't know for certain whether [Delphis] was possessed by love for a man or a woman' (*Id.* 2.150–1).

**30. the temple of the brother and sister gods:** Philadelphos and Arsinoe, his sister and second wife, were deified and given a precinct in their own lifetime in 272/1 B.C.: see in general Fraser (1972) 215–17. On the significance of this line for the dating of *Mim.* 1 see above, p. 21.

**χρηστός:** predicative, with ἐστι understood. The sentence interrupting the catalogue is striking, but characterful.

**31. Museum:** i.e. 'place of the Muses', the famous Museum at Alexandria, instituted by Soter, was a residential 'college' for scholars in the fields of literature, philosophy, natural history, science, mathematics, astronomy and medicine; see Pfeiffer (1968) 96–102, Fraser (1972) 312–19.

**wine:** Athenaios, *Scholars at Dinner* 33d–f is testimony to the excellence and plentifulness of Egyptian wine (see further Nairn [1904] 6 and Groeneboom [1922] 48). When Herodotos 2.77.4 states that there was no viticulture 'in the land', he is only referring to Upper Egypt and the South Delta (see Lloyd [1976] 334); at 2.37.4 he talks of the wine given to the Egyptian priests.

**32. Persephonê:** in the Greek, 'Kourê, [wife] of Hades'. Korê (Herodas' spelling, Kourê, is the Ionic version, in accordance with Herodas' use of the Ionic dialect; see above, pp. 2–4) originally meant 'daughter of Demeter', but here the goddess' alternative name is used. It should be noted that Korê was a prominent figure in cult on Kos: Sherwin-white (1978) 28, 305–7, 311–12, 362. This would fit with the location of the poem on Kos advanced above, p. 21.

**34. τὴν δ' ὄψιν:** accusative of respect, 'in appearance'.

**35. κριθῆναι:** infinitive of purpose; see Schwyzer (1950) 2 362–5.

**begging their ladyships' pardon:** Gyllis tries to avert the goddesses' anger at being compared with mortal women. This is part of Gyllis' superstitiousness parading as piety. The construction with λανθάνομαι, 'may I escape the notice of x deity', is also used at *Mim.* 6.35 by Korittô, but λάθειν θεούς is a common idiom; see e.g. Pindar, *Olympian* 1.64, Euripides, *Medea* 332.

**36–48:** having done her enthusiastic and graphic best to picture the temptations to which she alleges Mandris will surely have succumbed, Gyllis turns to Mêtrichê, on whom she unleashes a portentous display of platitudes on the insecurity of solitary life, in preparation for her real proposal.

**36. what sort of attitude is this…?:** literally, 'having what sort of mind do you…?' Cf. Euripides, *Orestês* 519 τίν' εἶχες, ὦ τάλας, ψυχὴν τότε; For the meaning of ψυχή here, see LSJ[9] s.v. IV.3, 'of the emotional self'.
**37. you're just keeping your chair warm:** Gyllis taunts Mêtrichê with the charge of inaction. There was a proverb 'a woman's bottom', which Suidas says referred to lazy people, or to women in general, because a woman's place was in the home (Suidas Γ 499 Adler [1928] 1 548, 17–18). This leads to the possibility that Gyllis is at once admitting that Mêtrichê is doing the right thing in Mandris' absence, but also saying that her inactivity has been excessive, and that she should now take matters into her own hands.
**38. you'll [have grown old]:** literally, 'you will not notice that you have grown old.' γηρᾶσα is the supplement proposed by Rutherford (1891), and seems likely. If it and the restoration of the end of the previous line are correct, we have an interesting case of tmesis. Tmesis with οὖν is a characteristic of Ionic, and conveys a sense of liveliness, but here a main verb (and a line-end) also separates the compound participle καταγηρᾶσα.
**κάψει:** from κάπτω, 'devour', 'gulp down'; 'the ashes of decay will gulp down her youthful beauty' (Cunningham [1971] 69).
**39. Look]:** with 'elsewhere', a verb of looking seems required, and most editors favour πάπτην]ον.
**40. cheerful:** ἱλαρή does mean 'cheerful', but here has the common connotation 'alluring', 'come-hitherish'; cf. Meleagros 108.6 Gow-Page, ἢν δ' ἱλαρὸν βλέψῃς ἡδὺ τέθηλεν ἔαρ, 'if you have an enticing look, spring flourishes sweetly.' Cf. English 'give someone the glad eye'.
**41. at only one anchor:** 'It is good to have two anchors fastened from the ship in a stormy night', Pindar tells us at *Olympian* 6.100, in case the one drags; and Euripides, *Phaithôn* 125–6 has Merops say that a single ruler of a city is dangerous, while the presence of a supporting second is a safer bet. Mêtrichê needs more than one string to her bow given the state of her love-life.
**42. κεῖνος:** lines 43–4 seem to presuppose an earlier mention of death, which Gyllis does not mention directly, preferring the word 'that' (meaning Thanatos or Hades) in order to avert evil omen.
**43. μηδὲ εἷς:** hiatus, which occurs in this phrase elsewhere at lines 45, 48 and 73 of this poem alone.
**47. there isn't anyone … is there?, μήτις:** as usual, this introduces a question to which a negative answer is expected. The motif of the fear of eavesdroppers seems to have been common in New Comedy: see Plautus, *The Braggart Soldier* 955–7, *The Ghost* 472–4 etc.
**48–66:** Gyllis at last comes out with her proposition. She devotes six lines (50–5) to describe what a catch Gryllos is: a star boxer at sub-junior, junior and senior levels in the major Greek games, he has nonetheless a 'sensitive' side, being well-off, gentle and, Gyllis claims, as yet inexperienced in sex. She then balances this outstandingly

attractive profile by detailing in five lines (56–60) how madly in love Gryllos is with Mêtrichê: he has fallen in love with her at first sight at a festival, and is continuously besetting Gyllis with his outpourings and, implicitly, with requests that Gyllis perform the function of her profession. The speech, thus analyzed, is designed to advertise Gryllos' attractions, but also to flatter Mêtrichê and make her pity Gryllos for the suffering she has caused him through her own instantaneously effective charms. All this from a go-between who will profit financially if her words win Mêtrichê over.

**48–9. χρεΐζουσ':** = Attic χρῄζουσα. Normal word-order would put ἀπαγγεῖλαι before χρεΐζουσ'.

**50. the son of Pataikion's daughter Matalinê:** Pataikion and Matalinê are both women's names, instead of the more usual patronymics; the women are presumably more familiar to Gyllis and Mêtrichê's circle. The ancients associated the name 'Gryllos' with γρυλλίζειν, 'to grunt', so it has the meaning 'Grunter' or 'Pig', which undercuts Gyllis' picture of the lovelorn gallant. The name also has athletic associations, because a Gryllos won the stadion-race at Olympia in 332 B.C.; Gyllis may be opportunistically capitalising on them for promotional purposes.

**51. at the Pythian games:** Pythô was a poetic name for Delphi, the site of the Pythian games; the name was thought to have originated in the name of the serpent, Pythôn, slain by Apollo as his first adventure.

**52. at the Isthmian games:** literally, 'at Korinth', the site of the Isthmian games.

**τοὺς ἴουλον ἀνθεῦντας:** ἴουλον is an accusative of respect from ἴουλος, 'first down'; the phrase means literally 'blossoming in their first down'. τοὺς ἀνθεῦντας is governed by νικέων in the previous line (just as in line 53 ἄνδρας is the direct object of καθεῖλε), ἆθλα being an internal accusative: 'defeating [in terms of] five prizes ... adolescent competitors'.

**53. at the Olympics:** literally, 'at Pisa', a synonym for Olympia. Gyllis conludes her catalogue of Gryllos' victories on an emphatic note, the Olympic games being the most important athletic festival.

**καθεῖλε:** 'brought down'; the construction with the finite verb now replaces the participial construction with νικέων at 51, a common type of anacoluthon.

**54. τὸ καλόν:** adverbial, 'nicely'. For the use of the article in such a context compare Kallimachos, *Ep.* 6.1 GP τὸν τὸ καλὸν μελανεῦντα, referring to a young man '[whose chin is] nicely darkening', and e.g. Theokritos, *Id.* 3.3, 18.

**wouldn't hurt a fly, οὐδὲ κάρφος ἐκ τῆς γῆς / κινέων:** literally, 'not even moving a straw from the ground': anyone who doesn't even move an inconsequential twig must be very quiet indeed; it is the equivalent of the English 'wouldn't harm a fly.' The phrase, used of modest maidenly behaviour (see Aristophanes, *Lysistrata* 474), is also found at *Mim.* 3.67, where see n. Coming so soon after the reference to his prowess at boxing, it is probably an instance of Gyllis' tendency to stretch the limits of credibility.

**55. an untouched seal:** this probably refers to the seal-ring which leaves an impression; it is untouched because it has so far not yet left a mark, and therefore has not been touched by wax. It is clearly a double-entendre for 'phallus'; see Henderson (1975) 124. It is true that athletes in training abstained from sex, but we are meant to assume that Gyllis is again exaggerating.

**56. at the procession of the Descent of Misê:** the dative in καθόδῳ is standard for expressing the festival at which something occurs. 'Descent' implies a procession celebrating a descent to Hades; 'Descent of Korê' was the name of the second day of the Thesmophoria. Misê, perhaps originally a Phrygian goddess, is mentioned here for the first time; she was introduced into the cult of Demeter as the hostess who persuaded Demeter to eat after mourning for Korê (even though Baubô was more usually credited with this service). To judge by this passage, Misê must have descended to Hades as a copy of the descent of Korê, and a procession seems to have celebrated Misê's *kathodos*. In literature and no doubt in life festivals were a common scenario for love-encounters, since they were one of the few occasions on which women could appear in public, as happens with Simaitha when she falls in love with Delphis in Theokritos' second *Idyll*; see Gow (1952) 2 49. The cliché may suggest that Gyllis is fabricating the whole story of Gryllos' infatuation.

**felt a surge, ἐκύμηνε:** 'seethe', 'swell', of passion (see also Plato, *Laws* 930a, though there it refers to the passion of hatred), an image from a wave of the sea (κῦμα).

**57. in his insides, τὰ σπλάγχνα:** accusative of respect. This may be the first instance of the word to refer to the seat of love, as also at Theokritos, *Id.* 7.99; see below, p. 41 n. 18. However, at *Mim.* 3.42 (where see n.) it denotes anxiety.

**stung, ἀνοιστρηθείς:** οἶστρος and οἰστρῶ in compounds are not dead metaphors in the Hellenistic period: see especially Apollonios of Rhodes, *Argonautika* 3.276. Gyllis is intentionally emphasizing Mêtrichê's effect on Gryllos.

**59. wails at me, μευ κατακλαίει:** = κατά μευ κλαίει. If, as is likely, the implication in these words is 'he blames me' (for his predicament), Gyllis is imputing to Gryllos a lover's contradictory states of mind: the next minute, he is fawning on her, and then he is on the point of dying because of his passion.

**60. calls me dearest:** at 6.77 Korittô tells how she wheedled the dubious shoemaker Kerdôn to grant a certain request, using the same verb (ταταλίζουσα). At 5.69 the slavegirl Kydilla addresses her mistress Bitinna with the word τατί, obviously an endearment when you want to ingratiate yourself to gain a favour. Gryllos' fawning therefore implies that he is asking a favour, specifically coaxing Gyllis to act as go-between for him and to approach Mêtrichê.

**61. Mêtrichê, my child, ὦ τέκνον μοι Μητρίχη:** as Cunningham (1971) 74 notes, μοι here is the so-called 'possessive' dative, which was originally used for the genitive as well as the dative; it survived into Classical Greek, occurring in the solemn tragic phrase ὦ τέκνον μοι. Gyllis' diction intensifies as she finally announces her precise proposition to Mêtrichê. An alternative explanation of μοι is that it is an 'ethic' dative, giving the meaning 'Please'.

**62. grant:** as if the indiscretion were a dedicatory offering.

**dedicate yourself to her, κατάρτησον:** literally, 'hang yourself down [from the

goddess' statue]' as was done with dedicatory offerings to a deity, so, metaphorically, 'dedicate yourself [to Aphrodite]', continuing the image of the previous sentence.
**63. staring you in the face, προσβλέψαν:** aorist participle, attracted as standardly into the tense of λανθάνω; Mêtrichê must make the best of her opportunities before old age creeps up on her.
**64. you'll win, πρήξεις:** 'you will accomplish, gain': LSJ[9] s,v, III.1.
**65. δοθήσεται:** the donor will be Gryllos gratified.
**think about it, σκέψαι:** second person singular aorist middle imperative of σκέπτομαι, drawing people's attention to a matter; see LSJ[9] s.v. II.1.
**66. follow my advice, πείσθητι μευ:** πείθομαι sometimes takes the genitive instead of the more normal dative, possibly when it is felt to be the approximate equivalent of a verb of hearing and obeying, like (ὑπ)ακούειν.
**By the Fates:** for this as a specifically Koan oath see above, p. 21, line 11n., and below, 4.30n.
**67–81.** Mêtrichê's reaction is firm and decisive, but after her well-measured scolding of Gyllis for her impudence, she shows with her offer of a cup of wine the good-natured irony with which she had treated Gyllis at 7–18.
**67. your grey hairs, τὰ λευκὰ τῶν τριχῶν:** 'the whiteness of your hair'; the construction with a neuter singular or plural and a genitive emphasizes the abstract quality; cf. also in Herodas *Mim.* 3.52.
**68. by Mandris' voyage home to me:** by this oath Mêtrichê simultaneously demonstrates her trust that Mandris will return and her fidelity to him.
**71. I'd have taught her to sing her lame songs with a limp:** i.e., she would have made her limp to suit her 'lame' songs. This is an ironically disparaging reference to Herodas' *chol*iambic metre: cf. Kallimachos, *Fr.* 203.13–14, 65–6 Pfeiffer (1949) 206, 209, where choliambic poets are called οἱ τὰ μέτρα μέλλοντες / τὰ χωλὰ τίκτειν, 'those intending to give birth to limping measures'. The heavily obvious repetition ('polyptoton') is thus explained.
**74–5.** Literally, 'tell to young women [a story] which it is appropriate for old [women] to tell,' i.e. 'talk decorously to your juniors'. γρῄη (= Attic γραῖα) can, like γέρων, act as an adjective, here going with γυναιξί, which also serves τῆς νέῃς.
**76. the daughter of Pytheês:** by using her patronymic Mêtrichê stands on her dignity as she throws Gyllis' words back in her face (cf. 37). Pytheês is Ionic for Attic Pytheâs.
**77. No one makes jokes about Mandris, οὐ γὰρ ἐγγελᾷ τις εἰς Μάνδριν:** for εἰς meaning 'against' with verbs of laughing see Sophokles, *Aias* 79 οὔκουν γέλως ἥδιστος εἰς ἐχθροὺς γελᾶν, 'Isn't it the sweetest mockery to mock at one's enemies?'
**78. they tell me:** Mêtrichê changes the subject, subtly suggesting that she knows of Gyllis' reputation as a tippler, and that Gyllis will therefore be more interested in a cup of wine than a dressing-down.
**79. the black cup, μελαινίδ':** the cup was named after its shape, which resembled that of a (presumably black) shell; the word occurs in the fragments of Sophrôn's mimes (*Fr.* 96 Kassel-Austin [2001] 1 231).

**80. a half measure:** literally, 'three sixth-parts', i.e. half a χοῦς, *chous*, whose volume varied in different regions of Greece.
**81. mix in a drop of water, ἐπιστάξασα:** Threissa is to let the water only 'drip on' the wine, while the wine is to be poured in; Gyllis is in for a stiff drink, and Mêtrichê knows that that is what Gyllis prefers.
**I really couldn't, καλῶς:** 'no, thank you' (cf. Aristophanes, *Frogs* 888–9), but her resistance is only token. For καλῶς as a refusal formula see especially Quincey (1966) 136–8.
**82–5.** The text, speaker-attribution, and meaning of these lines are all insecure. **show, δεῖξον** (82) in the sense of 'show me' is hard to accommodate. The 'rites' of 83 are most likely to be Aphrodite's, continuing the language of dedication to the goddess at 61–3. **My, μᾶ** (85) is an exclusively female exclamation expressing admiration, surprise or indignation; the word originally seems to have meant 'mother'; Kynno uses it at 4.33 and 43, Korittô and Mêtrô at 6.4, 22, 47, and Praxinoa at Theokritos, *Id.* 15.89.
**86. pleasant, ἡδύς γε:** the adjective clearly refers to the wine: Gyllis goes on to say she hasn't drunk any 'sweeter' wine, and that statement accords naturally with the intensive γε here.
**87. ἡδίον':** the ι is long here, in accordance with Attic usage, but at *Mim.* 2.91 it is short in βέλτιον, the form expected of Herodas' Ionic.
**88. εὐτύχει:** this was a common way to say 'farewell', and is frequently attested in both literary and real letters.
**μοι:** an ethic dative.
**ἀσφαλίζευ:** in Ionic -εο(υ)- contracts to -ευ- (cf. Attic -ου-); for other instances in the *Mimiambs*, see e.g. 2.66 (αἰσχύνευ), 77 (ἐπορνοβόσκευν), 3.40 (τέγευς), 4.10 (κατοικεῦσιν), 39 (ἕπευ), 69 (ἐδόκευν), 5.29 (πληκτίζευ), 7.82 (ὠνευμένης), 92 (σκέπτευ), 8.22 (ἐσύλευν), 25 (ἐποίευν), 73 (δόκευν); μευ and σευ are the predominant forms of the genitives of the first and second personal pronouns; see above, p. 10.
**89. Myrtalê and Simê:** Myrtalê is a name associated with hetairai, as at 2.65 and elsewhere, the myrtle being sacred to Aphrodite: see e.g. Virgil, *Eclogues* 7.62, *gratissima ... formosae Veneri myrtus*, 'the myrtle most favoured by beautiful Venus'. Simê itself is not elsewhere attested as the name of a hetaira, but other names with the 'flat-nose' component are. By being put on a par with Myrtalê and Simê, Mêtrichê is likely to be a hetaira too, or perhaps more probably an ex-hetaira, given her stable attachment to Mandris.

## DISCUSSION

### *1. Characters and characterization*

Herodas' first *Mimiamb* admirably illustrates Herodas' technique of characterization. This is especially the case with the figure of Gyllis, who speaks over two thirds of the poem's lines. In the prefatory remarks to the poem[1] we saw that the character of the more or less professional go-between was a special feature of Sophrôn's mimes, the *magoidiai* and New Comedy. Despite Aristophanes' jibe at *Frogs* 1079 about go-betweens like the nurse of Euripides' *Phaidra*, they were amateurs, so with Gyllis we have come even further down the social scale, into the proper province of mime.[2] Gyllis is therefore a representative of a stock type in mime and comedy. Herodas takes the type and individualises it with particular traits, in what has been called the 'mosaic' technique.[3]

Gyllis is endowed with multiple attributes that individualise her character. Some, like her drunkenness, seem to come with the literary type to which she belongs,[4] and it was presumably a temptation in real life for a nurse to act as a go-between. But there her typicality really ends. Her garrulity over her old age at lines 15–16 is a disarming *captatio beneuolentiae*, but is in fact a disingenuous prelude to her appeal to Mêtrichê not to waste her youth by her fidelity to Mandris at lines 36–47. There Gyllis uses arguments from old age and death, together with proverbial-sounding wisdom about the dangers of depending on only one lover for security and happiness, to get Mêtrichê to seize the day. When she issues the general advice to Mêtrichê to give in and not let old age catch up on her at lines 61–6, she uses the theme of old age as a scare-tactic to round off her whole outrageous proposition, in what almost amounts to a peroration. So she cleverly capitalises on her own old age, which she takes care to represent as a highly undesirable condition, to secure her ends.

Her determined eye for business can be seen in her appearance at this particular moment: Mandris has been away for ten months (24), and it is five months since Gyllis' last visit (10), so her timing is strategic: Mêtrichê, she might think, would be at her most vulnerable. She is also quick to take up a useful cue, as when Mêtrichê jokingly makes her comment that Gyllis still has lots of cuddles left in her yet; when Gyllis replies that joking about sex is in effect cold comfort for a young woman in Mêtrichê's position, she uses the mild sexual remark to her advantage, turning the conversation to her real purpose (18–20). She shamelessly loads her case, first by painting the pleasures of Alexandria so vividly, to induce Mêtrichê to believe that Mandris has forgotten her, then by her hyperbolic praise of Gryllos' athletic accomplishments. She takes great care to allay any fear that such an athlete, whose sports include the notoriously physical ancient boxing, is going to be a rough hearty (54–5). Her account of how he fell in love at first sight when he saw Mêtrichê at the festival is no doubt motivated to flatter Mêtrichê,[5] as is the description of Gryllos' lovelorn state as he pines away in Gyllis' house (55–60). And of course she is doing all this pleading purely out of her love for Mêtrichê (66).[6] However, Gyllis reveals her true intentions and game-play at the conclusion of the poem. She tells Mêtrichê to look after herself and, it is hinted, to remain firm in her celibacy, but, as her parting shot, she names two other young women, Myrtalê and Simê, whom she wishes will stay young for her as long as she breathes (88–90). It is hard to resist the inference that these are girls from Gyllis' brothel, that her wish that they remain young is ultimately based on financial considerations (but it also implies rather cattily that, after all, Mêtrichê isn't so young), and that the old harridan has had them lined up from the beginning as her fall-back position to take on the job if Mêtrichê turns it down: Gyllis' commission depends on a sale! As a comment to close off the poem, this is a masterstroke on Herodas' part.[7]

Gyllis makes a great display of piety when she mentions the goddesses of the Judgment of Paris (35), and presents herself as a repository of homespun wisdom in her build-up to her proposal. But this reassuring impression of piety, reliability and good sense is undercut when she asks rather abruptly whether she and Mêtrichê are alone (47–8). Respectability is a mask which she can drop when she wants to get down to business. On the other hand, she can resume it at will when it is expedient. When she has received her dressing-down from Mêtrichê, she claims that she acted as she did out of reverence for the holy rites due to Aphrodite (83).

The reconciliatory cup of wine given by Mêtrichê is of course prompted by Gyllis' reputation as a tippler. Gyllis at first coyly declines the offer (82), but once she has protested the reverence of her mission she devotes herself to praising the wine extravagantly, finally taking her farewell, not without a touch of spite when she mentions her other young friends, who, she implies, are more compliant than Mêtrichê (86–90).

It is not only by the superimposition of these human traits that Herodas characterizes Gyllis, however. As a true poet of the Alexandrian school, he also enlists the aid of earlier literature to enrich the texture of his characterizations. Elena Esposito has recently shown how much Herodas has used motifs and phraseology from Homer in his characterization of Gyllis.[8] For example, when Gyllis says 'I'm as weak as a fly', she is using a once-off Homeric word, δραίνω, from *Iliad* 10.96, when Agamemnon refers to the indomitable spirit of the old Nestor; the contrasting contexts add to the humour. We can talk of bathos of the most potent kind when Gyllis excuses her not having visited Mêtrichê by saying 'Old age drags us down and its shadow stands near us' (15–16), because her phraseology in χἠ σκιὴ παρέστηκεν is so close to Thetis' sad warning to Achilles that ἄγχι παρέστηκεν θάνατος at *Iliad* 18.132. Gyllis is also compared with the ancestor of all literary nurses, Eurykleia in the *Odyssey*, when Mêtrichê sends her packing at lines 68–78, this time because Mêtrichê's turn of phrase so closely echoes Penelope's rebuke of *her* old nurse at *Odyssey* 23.11–14, 20–4. For instance, Penelope says she would have dismissed any other of her maidservants if she had come bearing such news about Odysseus as Eurykleia's, εἰ … τίς μ' ἄλλη γε γυναικῶν, αἵ μοι ἔασι, / ταῦτ' ἐλθοῦσ' ἤγγειλε … (*Od.* 23.21–2), while Mêtrichê claims that she would have been upset if she had heard 'these things from any other woman', ταῦτ' ἐγὼ ἐξ ἄλλης / γυναικός (69–70); but an ironic common element is, more generally, the homecoming of Odysseus – and the bourgeois Mandris. And Penelope's claim that the gods have crazed Eurykleia's wits (*Od.* 23.11) is answered more prosaically by Mêtrichê's statement that old age has dulled Gyllis' mind (67), while Penelope can excuse Eurykleia on the grounds of her advanced years (*Od.* 23.24).

In summary, Gyllis is evidently a literary stereotype, but it is a sign of Herodas' considerable skill in comic characterization that she assumes much more than merely typical proportions, taking on an individuality of her own, even when literary techniques like Homeric allusion are employed.

If, as seems likely, Mêtrichê is an ex-hetaira,[9] she comes close to the type familiar especially from New Comedy called the 'gold-hearted hetaira', of which Habrotonon in Menander's *The Arbitrators* is a good example.[10] But she too is individualised beyond typicality.

Her greeting to Gyllis as 'Nanny Gyllis' shows a spontaneous willingness to acknowledge their relationship, which was probably that of a hetaira and her go-between, if not that of child and nurse as well.[11] The tone of her address is affectionately ironical, as she asks what 'destiny' has brought her, and what business a 'goddess' like Gyllis has with mere mortals like Mêtrichê and her household. Indeed, the whole exchange reminds the audience of the meeting of Thetis and Charis in *Iliad* 18 (quite apart from Apollonios' reworking of that passage at *Argonautika* 3.52–4, cited at 9n.), with Gyllis making an unlikely Thetis-double. Her response to Gyllis' first complaint about her old age – '[You've got] plenty more hugs left in you yet' (18) – is a good-natured attempt to jolly Gyllis along, though Gyllis turns it to her own purposes, as we have seen. After Gyllis has crowned her proposal with yet another argument from old age, Mêtrichê's firm rejection is preluded by her testy remark that all old age is doing to Gyllis is dulling her brain (67–8), and she reprises the theme when she says Gyllis should tell young women what it is appropriate for old women to tell, thus using the argument from seniority to her own ends and against Gyllis' (74–5). She quotes Gyllis' words back at her when she says Gyllis should let her keep her chair warm (76–7; cf. Gyllis' entreaty at 37), and the firmness of her stand is emphasized by her statement of her family-lineage, 'me, Mêtrichê, the daughter of Pytheês'. When she swears by Mandris' return, she is asserting that his return is a sure thing, and her comment that no one is going to make a laughing-stock of Mandris shows how deeply her feelings are running.

When she says she wouldn't have put up with any other woman saying the kind of things Gyllis has said (69–72), Herodas may indeed be making her voice a metatheatrical comment. On the surface her words can be taken as meaning 'I would have taught a limping woman limping things', but, given the pun of 'lame', *chôlên*, on 'choliambic poetry', another meaning can be attached to her words: the old and limping Gyllis would have received a real lesson in 'limping', or choliambic, abuse. This may be Herodas' way of nailing his colours to the mast,[12] but it does not detract from the intensity of Mêtrichê's indignation. Indeed, as Esposito[13] remarks, there is something of the Odyssean Penelope about Mêtrichê, as we saw from the way that she reproves Gyllis, though there is gently humorous deheroization in the downscaling of the absence of the two women's husbands from ten years to ten months.

However, when she recognizes that she has made her point, she offers Gyllis her conciliatory cup of wine, knowing her old friend's *faiblesse*, does so with the minimal proportion of water, which she knows will be to Gyllis' taste, and coaxes Gyllis out of the sham coyness she shows over accepting the wine (78–82). She even softens the fact that she knows of Gyllis' fondness for drink by saying that 'they say' Gyllis has no need for reproof, that is that she will respond to other stimuli. She therefore displays affection, firmness, insight and tact in dealing with her old friend's importunity. All this is quite impressive in a character given so few lines.

### *2.* **Mimiamb** *1 and Theokritos'* **Idylls** *2, 14 and 15*

There can be no doubt that there are points of contact between Herodas' first *Mimiamb* and three of Theokritos' *Idylls*. Who is indebted to whom is a difficult question, though the admittedly slight evidence suggests Herodas as the debtor. However that may be, it adds significantly to our appreciation of the two poets' techniques and skill if we consider their shared motifs and formal devices.

In *Idyll* 2, Simaitha's infatuation with Delphis begins when she sees him at a festival of Artemis (76–86) and is driven to send her maid, Thestylis, to bring Delphis home (94–103). For his part, Delphis claims that in fact he was already smitten by her, and just about to force entry into her house, such was his desperation (114–38). This is evidently simple flattery. In *Mimiamb* 1 it is Gryllos who, Gyllis says, fell in love with Mêtrichê at the festival of the Descent of Misê, and he is the one who is in the lovelorn state (56–60); here it is Gyllis who is applying the flattery. The common motifs are embedded perfectly in each poem. Simaitha's story combines with Delphis' ingratiating tone to convey the themes in intimate and extensive detail in the *Idyll*, while Gyllis' speech conveys them quite briefly in the *Mimiamb*. The disparate space allotted to them is explicable on the grounds that the *Mimiamb*'s prime concern is the characterization of Gyllis, while for the *Idyll* the meeting is a major moment in Simaitha's narrative. Similarly, Delphis' claim that he is driven to such lengths by love is backed up by his statement that love has the same effect both on virgins, who lose their status because of love's frenzy, and married women, who leave their husband's bed while it is still warm (133–8). Of course, this thought is not particularly relevant to his own case, but perfectly appropriate to Simaitha's, and tells us that he is playing with her, and that she is indeed 'easily won', as she puts it herself (138). Gyllis uses the idea in her plea for Mêtrichê to give up on Mandris (21–47), especially when she asks her how long she is intending to wear out the same bed on her own (21–2), and to give in to Aphrodite (61–2). Delphis' gratuitous and ironical use of the thought can therefore be contrasted with the vital and explicit part it plays in Gyllis' argument.

Again, there is the motif of Delphis' and Gryllos' athletic prowess. Delphis stresses his own with mock modesty: he claims that he had wanted to visit Simaitha anyway, and now she has beaten him with her summons by the narrow margin by which he beat Philinos at running 'the other day' (πρᾶν ποκα, 114–6). Whether this is the famous Koan runner or another of the same name,[14] Delphis is advertising his track record in a tempting manner. So is Gyllis with what one feels is a hyperbolic report of Gryllos' five panhellenic victories in boxing (51–3), but the report is by proxy, and humility would not have been so necessary. And, while Gyllis, on Gryllos' behalf, can offset the image of the man as a hideous ruffian by emphasizing his wealth, gentleness and non-promiscuity (54–5), Delphis can protest his charm only by another show of modesty when he says he is called genial and handsome by the other lads (124–5). One or the other poet is transposing the motif to a different voice, but the result is equally successful in both instances. The dénouement of Simaitha's and Mêtrichê's stories is of course a total contrast, Mêtrichê turning out to be anything but 'easily won', and yet the very contrast seems to have been pointedly intentional, whichever the direction of influence. Both women swear an oath by the Fates, μὰ τὰς Μοίρας in Mêtrichê's case (11, though Gyllis also says ναὶ μὰ τὰς Μοίρας at line 66), ναὶ Μοίρας in Simaitha's (160), but where there is no particular appropriateness to Mêtrichê's use of it (nor to Gyllis', for that matter), Simaitha uses it when she swears that her magic will make Delphis beat on the gates of Hades; in her case, the oath is quite powerful, whereas in Herodas' poem the impression seems to be one of mere colloquiality. But, again, the common feature is deployed perfectly in either context.

In the case of our poem and *Idyll* 14, the praises of Alexandria (*Mim*. 1.26–35, *Id*. 14.58–68) are obvious points of contact, even if their strategies are very different, or, rather, present reverse images. Gyllis, true to her purpose of unsettling Mêtrichê, stresses the hedonistic aspects of the city, though she does make a flattering remark about the regent and briefly mentions the precinct of the Theoi Adelphoi. Thyonichos' praise of Ptolemy is far more lavish, appropriately so, since Thyonichos is trying to coax his friend out of his moping mood by suggesting that he become a mercenary and go to Alexandria where he will find a sympathetic and excellent paymaster in Ptolemy. So Ptolemy's personal virtues are detailed, including his affability and openness to affairs of the heart (ἐρωτικός), as well as his generosity as a ruler, and his shrewd ability to know who are his friends and who are his enemies.[15] Praise of the Ptolemies in incongruously low contexts is a feature of encomiastic poetry written in their honour, and should not be taken as distancing poet from patron.[16] But whereas Gyllis represents Alexandria as the 'problem', Thyonichos presents it as the solution. The two encomiastic passages are therefore inversions of one another, but it is impossible to tell who has done the inversion given the appropriateness with which each encomium is suited to its context.

Similarly, the situations of the main characters are reversed. Aischinas is the lovelorn one, and his graphic story of how his girlfriend Kyniska ran out on him at a party (*Id.* 14.12–53) is the centre-piece of Theokritos' poem. In *Mimiamb* 1, Mêtrichê is confident that Mandris is faithful, and is level-headed and in total control of herself. Aischinas in fact resembles Gryllos, whom Gyllis portrays to Mêtrichê as pining away so desperately – and flatteringly for Mêtrichê. Here it is just possible that we have an indication of the direction of influence. It is perhaps more likely that Herodas should have relegated the motif of the pining lover and replaced it with a more buoyant figure than that Theokritos should have foregrounded the motif as he found it in Herodas in miniature. If this possibility is accepted, we might be entitled to the conclusion that Herodas has attempted to outdo Theokritos in 'low' detail, with the confidante-figure now a go-between and the protagonists now both women, which would have given an even more 'low' context to the praise of Ptolemy.

Another common theme is that of old age. Thyonichos urges Aischinas to take positive and immediate steps towards employment as a mercenary on the grounds that they are both turning grey (*Id.* 14.68–70). Gyllis' deployment of the topos is far more extensive (*Mim.* 1.21–47, 89–90), and Mêtrichê picks up on it very effectively herself when she turns it on its head (*Mim.* 1.67–8, 74–5). Here it seems more likely that Herodas is expanding a theme in Theokritos' poem than that Theokritos is telescoping one that he found in Herodas. If so, we have a further possible piece of evidence for Theokritos' priority.

A formal similarity between the two poems is the allocation of one line of verse to two or more speakers, the *antilabê*, of their openings, when the characters meet. There is the commonplace amazement over how long it's been since they've met; in Theokritos we have the agreement between the two friends on the matter (ΘΥ. ὡς χρόνιος. ΑΙ. χρόνιος, *Id.* 14.2), but in Herodas the idea is expanded to Mêtrichê's teasing comment on Gyllis' appearance after these five months (*Mim.* 1.8–12), which is moreover woven into the poem's context and the presentation of Gyllis' motives for the visit. If the commonplace is more than just a commonplace, the likelihood is that Herodas is again expanding on a motif in Theokritos. But, apart from that motif and the *antilabê*, the openings of the two poems have in fact little in common.

The resemblances between *Mimiamb* 1 and *Idyll* 15 are clear. Their personnel and situation are quite similar: a friend, Gyllis/Gorgô, visits a friend, Mêtrichê/Praxinoa, after some time; a slave, Threissa/Eunoa, facilitates the visitor's welcome; there is subversive talk of their menfolk, Mandris/Dinôn; the visitor makes a proposal, Gyllis that Mêtrichê take up with Gryllos, Gorgô that they all go to the Adonis-festival in Arsinoê's palace. Only the baby Zôpyriôn has no counterpart in Herodas' poem, but that is situational. The verbal correspondences between the two opening passages of *antilabê* are much more extensive than is the case with *Idyll* 14. Gorgô and Praxinoa both use the word 'within' (ἔνδοι, *Id.* 1.1; cf. *Mim.* 1's ἔνδον, 6), and Praxinoa briefly remarks how long it's been (ὡς χρόνῳ, *Id.* 1.1), though she expands on this by adding that she is amazed that Gorgô has come 'even now' (*Id.* 1.2); this is less perfunctory than with Aischinas and Thyonichos, but Herodas gives Mêtrichê far more to say in this vein, with her own ironical tone.

Moreover, Gyllis' 'I live a long way away' (μακρὴν ἀποικέω, *Mim.* 1. 13) leads to her complaints about the mud in the streets and her old age (*Mim.* 1.13–16), but Gorgô's comment that Praxinoa lives further and further away (τὺ δ' ἑκαστέρω αἰὲν ἀποικεῖς, *Id.* 15.7) is motivated by her experience of negotiating the crowds and the soldiers everywhere. This in turn leads to Praxinoa's grumbling about Dinôn, her husband, and to Gorgô's complaints about hers, and to the business with the baby, who grows nervous on hearing his mother complaining about his father (*Id.* 15.4–21). The motif is therefore more elaborately embedded in Theokritos, where it feeds into the suburban lives of both women. It is perhaps significant that, while Gyllis complains about the mud and her own old age, Gorgô's talk is of busy soldiers and chariots in the streets; after all, this is Alexandria! But it would fit in with the general impression that when Theokritos and Herodas have passages and themes in common Herodas prefers to emphasize the 'realistic' or 'low' detail.[17] If so, this would further suggest that Herodas had Theokritos before him.[18]

## NOTES

1. Above, pp. 21–2.
2. The definition of mime preserved by the grammarian Diomedes, that mime is a 'representation of life admitting things permissible and not permissible' (συγκεχωρημένα καὶ ἀσυγχώρητα), appears to have been coined by Theophrastos; see Zanker (1987) 144–5, followed e.g. by Gutzwiller (1991) 135 and Fantuzzi-Hunter (2002) 247–8 n. 23.
3. See Arnott (1971) for an analysis of this technique through the examples of *Mimiambs* 5 and 6. Headlam (1922) xxxi–xxxvi has a typically learned discussion of it, though perhaps he overstresses the stock typicality of Herodas' characters, as is noted by Cunningham (1971) 15. On characterization in Herodas see in general Ussher (1985).
4. Headlam (1922) xxxiii lists for example Leaena the *lena* in Plautus' *Curculio* (I.2). Gyllis also belongs to the literary type of the nurse, which was regularly associated with drunkenness in the Hellenistic period too; see e.g. the epigrams on Marônis by Antipatros of Sidon (27 GP) and Leonidas of Tarentum (68 GP), on Seilênis by Dioskorides (29 GP), and Ampelis by Ariston (2 GP).
5. Di Gregorio (1997) 90–1.
6. Di Gregorio (1997) 94–5 well analyzes Gyllis' emphasis on personal and professional ties: Gyllis is attempting thereby to remind Mêtrichê of their old familiarity while trying to distance Mêtrichê from Mandris.
7. Cf. Di Gregorio (1995) 687.
8. Esposito (2001) 150–9.
9. Di Gregorio (1995) 683–7 assembles the main evidence: Gyllis' arguments include the waning of Mêtrichê's beauty with the approach of old age (37–8), and the enticement of Gryllos' wealth (41–2, 54, 65), which make more sense if addressed to a hetaira than to a married woman with an assured security in old age; the very fact that Gyllis visits Mêtrichê militates against the latter's being a married woman; Gyllis puts Mêtrichê on the same level as her other hetaira-protégées (89–90); the name of Gyllis' daughter, Philainis, immediately suggests the famous hetaira who wrote the treatise on sexual positions (see 5n.), and therefore the world in which we are moving. See also Di Gregorio (1997) 45, 60, 77, 91, 94, 111, who at (1995) 688n. 75 and (1997) 101 moreover argues that Mêtrichê is not a particularly young woman.
10. See Wehrli (1936) 40–5, Di Gregorio (1995) 689–90.
11. There is, moreover, good reason to think that Herodas has defined her social position quite precisely, apart from her being an ex-hetaira now in a stable relationship with (though not married to) Mandris. See above, on line 2 for the possibility that τις παρ' ἡμέων ἐξ ἀγροικίης ('one of our folk from the country', 2) implies that Mêtrichê has been put in charge of countryside property belonging to Mandris in his absence.
12. See Di Gregorio (1997) 99–100 with lit.
13. Esposito (2001) 156–7.
14. See Gow (1952) 2 55 on line 115.
15. The stirring martial allusion at *Id.* 14. 66–7 to Tyrtaios, *Frr.* 10.31–2, 12.16–17 West (1998) 2 155, 157, firmly sets off Theokritos' picture of Alexandria from Gyllis'.

16. See Zanker (1987) 24–7, 84, 179–82, (1989) 88–91.
17. This is often felt to be the case particularly with *Idyll* 15 and *Mimiamb* 4's artistic programme in which Herodas makes Kynnô express aggressive admiration for the realism of Apelles (72–8); the thesis is pressed most vigorously by Luria (1963), but see also especially the more moderate and persuasive account by Gelzer (1985) 106–16, see further below, 4.75n. and pp. 128–9.
18. The similarity of the phrases ἐκύμηνε / τὰ σπλάγχν' at *Mim.* 1.57 and ὑπὸ σπλάγχνοισιν ἔχει πόθον at *Id.* 7.99 seems unlikely to have been intentional, though the two passages are the earliest attested uses of the intestines as the seat of love; see e.g. Cunningham (1971) 73.

## 2. ΠΟΡΝΟΒΟΣΚΟΣ

*(ΒΑΤΤΑΡΟΣ)* ἄνδρες δικασταί, τῆς γενῆς μὲν οὐκ ἐστέ
ἡμέων κριταὶ δήκουθεν οὐδὲ τῆς δόξης,
οὐδ' εἰ Θαλῆς μὲν οὗτος ἀξίην τὴν νηῦν
ἔχει ταλάντων πέντ', ἐγὼ δὲ μηδ' ἄρτους,
δικῇ] ὑπερέξει Βάτταρόν τι πημήνας·
πολλοῦ γε καὶ δεῖ·] [τ]ὠλυκὸν γὰρ [ἂν] κλαύσαι
†....].ιησομαστοσηιασ[..]νχωρη†
χοὖτος μέτοικος] ἐστὶ τῆς πόλιος κἠγώ,
καὶ ζ]ῶμεν οὐχ ὡς βουλόμεσθ' ἀλλ' ὡς ἡμέας
ὁ και]ρὸς ἕλκει. προστάτην ἔχει Μεννῆν,
ἐγὼ δ' Ἀριστοφῶντα· πὺξ νενίκηκεν
Μεννῆς, Ἀριστοφῶν δὲ κ[ἤτι] νῦν ἄγχει·
κεἰ μ]ὴ ἐστ' ἀληθέα ταῦτα, το[ῦ ἡ]λίου δύντος
ἐξε]λθέτω[...]ων, ἄνδρες, [ἣν εἶ]χε χλαῖναν
καὶ γ]νώσε[θ' ο]ἵῳ προστάτῃ τεθώρηγμαι.
ἐρεῖ τάχ' ὑμῖν] 'ἐξ Ἄκης ἐλήλουθα
πυρ]οὺς ἄγων κἤστησα τὴν κακὴν λιμόν.'
ἐγὼ δ]ὲ πόρνας ἐκ Τύρου· τί τῷ δήμῳ
τοῦτ' ἔστι;] [δ]ωρεὴν γὰρ οὔθ' οὗτος πυρούς
δίδωσ' ἀλή]θε[ι]ν οὔτ' ἐγὼ πάλιν κείνην.

5 δικῇ] Crusius (1892)[2] 174
6 πολλοῦ γε καὶ δεῖ] Milne ap. Knox (1926)[2] 78, [τ]ὠλυκὸν γὰρ [ἂν] κλαύσαι Knox (1922) 62
8 χοὖτος μέτοικος] F.D. (1892) 72
9 καὶ ζ]ῶμεν Headlam (1892) 89
10 ὁ και]ρὸς Stadtmüller (1894) 457
12 κ[ἤτι] Bücheler (1892) 9
13 κεἰ μ]ὴ Blass (1892)[2] 861–2
14 ἐξε]λθέτω Knox (1926)[2], [ἣν εἶ]χε χλαῖναν Blass (1892)[2] 862
15 γ]νώσε[θ' ο]ἵῳ Knox (1922) 75
16 ἐρεῖ τάχ' ὑμῖν] Crusius (1894) 15
17 πυρ]οὺς F.D. (1892) 72
18 ἐγὼ δ]ὲ Headlam (1899) 151
19 τοῦτ' ἔστι;] Headlam (1899) 151
20 δίδωσ' ἀλή]θειν F.D. (1891) 409

## 2. THE BROTHEL-KEEPER

(*Battaros*) Gentlemen of the jury, of our birth
or reputation you are, of course, not judges,
nor, if Thalês here has a ship worth
five talents, while I don't even have bread,
will he win [in this case] after harming Battaros.
[Far from it,] [for he would weep salty tears]
*(sense of whole line irretrievable)*
[and he is a metic] of the city like me,
[and] we live not how we want to but however
[the moment] draws us on. He has Mennês as his sponsor in town,
while I have Aristophôn. Mennês has had victories in boxing,
while Aristophôn is still an active wrestler even now.
If this is not true, when the sun has set
[let him come out], gentlemen, [with?] [the cloak he used to have]
and he will see what kind of sponsor I am armed with.
[Perhaps he will say to you,] 'I have come from Akê
with wheat on board and I stopped the dreadful famine',
[but I] have arrived from Tyre with prostitutes. What is this to
the people? For neither does the defendant [give] his wheat [to grind] for free
nor in my turn do I give that girl there for free.

εἰ δ' οὕνεκεν πλεῖ τὴν θάλασσαν ἢ χλαῖναν
ἔχει τριῶν μνέων Ἀττικῶν, ἐγὼ δ' οἰκέω
ἐν γῇ τρίβωνα καὶ ἀσκέρας σαπρὰς ἕλκων,
βίῃ τιν' ἄξει τῶν ἐμῶν ἔμ' οὐ πείσας,
καὶ ταῦτα νυκτός, οἴχεθ' ἡμῖν ἡ ἀλεωρή
τῆς πόλιος, ἄνδρες, κἀφ' ὅτεῳ σεμνύνεσθε,
τὴν αὐτονομίην ὑμέων Θαλῆς λύσει.
ὃν χρῆν ἑαυτὸν ὅστις ἐστὶ κἀκ ποίου
πηλοῦ πεφύρητ' εἰδόθ' ὡς ἐγὼ ζώειν
τῶν δημοτέων φρίσσοντα καὶ τὸν ἥκιστον.
νῦν δ' οἱ μὲν ἐόντες τῆς πόλιος καλυπτῆρες
καὶ τῇ γενῇ φυσῶντες οὐκ ἴσον τούτῳ
πρὸς τοὺς νόμους βλέπουσι κἠμὲ τὸν ξεῖνον
οὐδεὶς πολίτης ἠλόησεν οὐδ' ἦλθεν
πρὸς τὰς θύρας μευ νυκτὸς οὐδ' ἔχων δᾷδας
τὴν οἰκίην ὑφῆψεν οὐδὲ τῶν πορνέων
βίῃ λαβὼν οἴχωκεν· ἀλλ' ὁ Φρὺξ οὗτος,
ὁ νῦν Θαλῆς ἐών, πρόσθε δ', ἄνδρες, Ἀρτίμμης,
ἅπαντα ταῦτ' ἔπρηξε κοὐκ ἐπῃδέσθη
οὔτε νόμον οὔτε προστάτην οὔτ' ἄρχοντα.
καίτοι λαβών μοι, γραμματεῦ, τῆς αἰκείης
τὸν νόμον ἄνειπε, καὶ σὺ τὴν ὀπὴν βῦσον
τῆς κλεψύδρης, βέλτιστε, μέχρις εὖ 'νείπῃ,
μὴ πρός τε κῦσος φῇ τι χὠ τάπης ἦμιν,
τὸ τοῦ λόγου δὴ τοῦτο, ληίης κύρσῃ.
*(ΓΡΑΜΜΑΤΕΥΣ)* ἐπὴν δ' ἐλεύθερός τις αἰκίσῃ δούλην
ἢ ἕκων ἐπίσπῃ, τῆς δίκης τὸ τίμημα
διπλοῦν τελείτω.
*(ΒΑ.)* ταῦτ' ἔγραψε Χαιρώνδης,
ἄνδρες δικασταί, καὶ οὐχι Βάτταρος χρῄζων
Θαλῆν μετελθεῖν. ἢν θύρην δέ τις κόψῃ,
μνῆν τινέτω, φησ'· ἢν δὲ πὺξ ἀλοιήσῃ,
ἄλλην πάλι μνῆν· ἢν δὲ τὰ οἰκί' ἐμπρήσῃ
ἢ ὅρους ὑπερβῇ, χιλίας τὸ τίμημα

If, just because he sails the sea or because he wears
a cloak worth three Athenian minas, while I live
on land dragging a threadbare coat and rotten shoes,
he can take one of of my girls by force and without my assent –
all this by night, what's more! –, the safety of our city is done for,
gentlemen, and the very thing you pride yourselves on,
your autonomy, will be destroyed by Thalês.
He ought to know who he is and from what
clay he's been made, and to live like me,
in trembling awe and respect of even the least of the townsfolk.
As things are, the people who are the city's upper crust
and who can give themselves a puff of pride in their birth
have a greater regard for the laws than the defendant, and no citizen has given me,
the foreigner, any thrashing, nor has he come to
my doors by night, nor, with torches in his hands,
set my whole household alight, nor violently made off
with any of my prostitutes. But this Phrygian here,
who is now Thalês, but formerly, gentlemen, bore the name Artimmês,
has done all of these things, and has shown no respect at all
either for the law or for his sponsor or for the ruler.
So now, clerk of court, take and read out the law
concerning assault, and you, my dear chap, plug the spout
of the water-clock until he has finished reading,
so its arse-hole doesn't say something as well, and we find the bedclothes
reaping the reward, as in fact the saying goes.

(*Clerk of Court*) 'Any free man who assaults a female slave
or willingly harasses her must pay double the fine
set for the crime.'

*Ba.* That is what Chairôndas wrote,
gentlemen of the jury, not a mere Battaros intending
to prosecute a Thalês. 'If anyone batters down a door,
let him pay a mina', he says, and 'If anybody gives another a beating with his fists,
let him pay another mina again.' If anyone burn the house of another
or trespass, he set the fine at one thousand drachmas,

ἔνειμε, κἢν βλάψῃ τι, διπλόον τίνειν.
ᾤκει πόλιν γάρ, ὦ Θάλης, σὺ δ’ οὐκ οἶσθας
οὔτε πόλιν οὔτε πῶς πόλις διοικεῖται,
οἰκεῖς δὲ σήμερον μὲν ἐν Βρικινδήροις
ἔχθες δ’ ἐν Ἀβδήροισιν, αὔριον δ’ ἤν σοι
ναῦλον διδοῖ τις, ἐς Φασηλίδα πλώσει.
ἐγὼ δ’ ὅκως ἂν μὴ μακρηγορέων ὑμέας,
ὦνδρες δικασταί, τῇ παροιμίῃ τρύχω,
πέπονθα πρὸς Θάλητος ὅσσα κὴν πίσσῃ
μῦς· πὺξ ἐπλήγην, ἡ θύρη κατήρακται
τῆς οἰκίης μευ, τῆς τελέω τρίτην μισθόν,
τὰ ὑπέρθυρ’ ὀπτά. δεῦρο, Μυρτάλη, καὶ σύ·
δεῖξον σεωυτὴν πᾶσι· μηδέν’ αἰσχύνευ·
νόμιζε τούτους οὓς ὁρῇς δικάζοντας
πατέρας ἀδελφοὺς ἐμβλέπειν. ὁρῆτ’ ἄνδρες,
τὰ τίλματ’ αὐτῆς καὶ κάτωθεν κἄνωθεν
ὡς λεῖα ταῦτ’ ἔτιλλεν ὡναγὴς οὗτος,
ὅθ’ εἷλκεν αὐτὴν κἀβιάζετ’ – ὦ γῆρας,
σοὶ θυέτω ἐπεὶ τὸ αἷμ’ ἂν ἐξεφύσησεν
ὥσπερ Φίλιστος ἐν Σάμῳ κοθ’ ὁ Βρέγκος.
γελᾷς; κίναιδός εἰμι καὶ οὐκ ἀπαρνεῦμαι,
καὶ Βάτταρός μοι τοὔνομ’ ἐστὶ χὠ πάππος
ἦν μοι Σισυμβρᾶς χὠ πατὴρ Σισυμβρίσκος,
κἠπορνοβόσκευν πάντες, ἀλλ’ ἕκητ’ ἀλκῆς
θαρσέων λέ[οντ’ ἄγχ]οιμ’ ἂν εἰ Θαλῆς εἴη.
ἐρᾷς σὺ μὲν ἴσως Μυρτάλης; οὐδὲν δεινόν·
ἐγὼ δὲ πυρέων· ταῦτα δοὺς ἐκεῖν’ ἕξεις.
ἢ νὴ Δί’, εἴ σευ θάλπεταί τι τῶν ἔνδον,
ἔμβυσον εἰς τὴν χεῖρα Βατταρίῳ τιμήν,
καὐτὸς τὰ σαυτοῦ θλῆ λαβὼν ὅκως χρῄζεις.
ἓν δ’ ἔστιν, ἄνδρες – ταῦτα μὲν γὰρ εἴρηται
πρὸς τοῦτον – ὑμεῖς δ’ ὡς ἀμαρτύρων εὔντων
γνώμῃ δικαίῃ τὴν κρίσιν διαιτᾶτε.
ἢν δ’ οἷον ἐς τὰ δοῦλα σώματα σπεύδῃ
κἠς βάσανον αἰτῇ, προσδίδωμι κἀμαυτόν·

78 λέ[οντ’ ἄγχ]οιμ’ ἂν Bücheler (1892) 13

and if anyone cause any damage, he ruled that he had to pay double.
For he was founding a city, Thalês, but you have no idea
either of a city or of how a city is governed,
but today you live in Brikindêra,
yesterday in Abdêra, and tomorrow, if someone
gives you the fare, you'll sail to Phasêlis.
But as for me, in order not to exhaust you by long speechifying
and with digression, gentlemen of the jury,
I have suffered at the hands of Thalês the proverbial fate of the mouse
in tar: I was punched about; the door of my establishment,
for which I pay a third of its value in rent, was battered down;
my lintel got a roasting. – Myrtalê, you must come here, too.
reveal yourself to all; don't be ashamed before anyone;
consider that in the jurymen whom you see judging this case
you are looking upon your fathers, your brothers. Gentlemen, look
at her plucked skin, above and below,
how smooth this 'innocent' plucked it
when he dragged her and forced her. – O, Old Age,
he should offer you a sacrifice in thanks, since he would have spat up blood
like Philistos the Brenkos once upon a time on Samos.
– You laugh? I'm a queer, I won't deny it,
and my name is Battaros, Sisymbrâs was my
grandfather and my father was Sisymbriskos,
and they were all brothel-keepers, but as far as strength goes
I'd confidently [strangle a lion] – if it were Thalês.
Perhaps you're in love with Myrtalê? Nothing odd about that:
I like my bread. Give me the one and you shall have the other.
Or, by Zeus, if you've got the hots for her anywhere in you
just press her price into your dear little Battaros' hand,
and you can take and maul your own property however you like.
There is one particular matter, gentlemen – for so far I've been addressing
the defendant: there being no witnesses, you must
decide the case before you with just judgment.
If all he's after is the bodies of slaves
and demands they be put to torture, then I offer myself as well.

λαβών, Θαλῆ, στρέβλου με· μοῦνον ἡ τιμή
ἐν τῷ μέσῳ ἔστω· ταῦτα τρυτάνῃ Μίνως
οὐκ ἂν δικάζων βέλτιον διῄτησε.
τὸ λοιπόν, ἄνδρες, μὴ δοκεῖτε τὴν ψῆφον
τῷ πορνοβοσκῷ Βαττάρῳ φέρειν, ἀλλά
ἅπασι τοῖς οἰκεῦσι τὴν πόλιν ξείνοις.
νῦν δείξεθ' ἡ Κῶς χὠ Μέροψ κόσον δραίνει
χὠ Θεσσαλὸς τίν' εἶχε χἠρακλῆς δόξαν,
χὠσκληπιὸς κῶς ἦλθεν ἐνθάδ' ἐκ Τρίκκης,
κἤτικτε Λητοῦν ὧδε τεῦ χάριν Φοίβη.
ταῦτα σκοπεῦντες πάντα τὴν δίκην ὀρθῇ
γνώμῃ κυβερνᾶθ', ὡς ὁ Φρὺξ τὰ νῦν ὗμιν
πληγεὶς ἀμείνων ἔσσετ', εἴ τι μὴ ψεῦδος
ἐκ τῶν παλαιῶν ἡ παροιμίη βάζει.

Take me, Thalês, and put me on the rack; just place the compensation-money
before the court. If Minôs were judging this case
with his scales he wouldn't have decided it better.
For the rest, gentlemen, don't think that you're casting your vote
for Battaros the brothel-keeper, but for
all the foreigners living in the city.
Now is the moment for you to show the might of Kôs and Merops,
and the reputation of Thessalos and Heraklês,
and how Asklêpios came here from Trikkê
and the reason why Phoibê gave birth to Lêtô here.
With all this in your minds steer the case
with straight judgement, since this Phrygian, you will find,
will be the better for a beating, unless
the proverb from men of old tells a lie.

## COMMENTARY

Synopsis Battaros, a brothel-keeper resident in Kos as a metic, delivers a speech accusing the captain of a merchant ship, Thalês, another metic, of having abducted a prostitute from his establishment, and of damaging the premises in the process (33–40, 60–5). He begins with the rhetorical commonplace that the jury should treat him and Thalês as equals before the law (1–10), and proceeds to establish the credentials of his sponsor on the island (10–15). He weighs the benefits to Kos of his having imported prostitutes against Thalês' inevitable defence that he has stopped a famine by importing wheat from Akê (16–20). Acquittal, he claims, would be tantamount to the island's loss of autonomy (21–7); unlike Thalês, he is a law-abiding and respected resident foreigner (28–40). He asks the clerk to read out the law concerning unprovoked physical assault, demanding, with recourse to the most vulgar imagery, that the attendant put a stopper in the bottom of the clepsydra so that Battaros might not lose a minute of the time allocated for his accusation (41–8). He interrupts the clerk, pointing out that the law was introduced by the famous lawgiver, Chairôndas, and continues by filling in the details of the law by himself (48–54). He repeats his accusation against Thalês, whose life he characterizes as shiftless and seedy (55–65), and then produces his first exhibit, the blushing prostitute Myrtalê, whose depilation he absurdly argues to have been the result of Thalês' rough treatment rather than standard practice in her profession (65–71). To Thalês' amusement he claims that it was only because of old age that he hadn't given Thalês a beating, and, admitting that he is a *kinaidos* and that his family have been brothel-keepers for generations, asserts that his physical strength is nonetheless overwhelming (71–8). He changes tack, making the impudent suggestion that Thalês pay for Myrtalê and take her away in an out-of-court settlement (79–83), and with equal impudence offers his own body for torture prior to giving evidence as if he were a slave, since there were no witnesses of the crime apart from Myrtalê – provided that Thalês place the compensation-money before the court (84–91). His peroration is a mixture of rhetorical clichés – the case concerns not only Battaros but all foreign residents, and the Koan jury should live up to its exalted past – and a resoundingly banal proverb in conclusion (92–102).

Text Since the poem is almost entirely a speech by one person, and since the beginning and end of the clerk's reading out of the law is clearly marked out by the sense of the lines and attendant paragraphoi, there are no problems of line-allocation. The left margin of the papyrus' seventh column (lines 5–20) is damaged, but I have admitted what seem to be the most likely supplements for each line, except for the unintelligible seventh.

Date Some time before 266 B.C.; see 16n.

Setting Lines 95–100, in which Battaros asks the jury to show the mettle of the ancient heroes and heroines of Kos, secure the location of the poem to a lawcourt on the island.

Sources The name Battaros is attested in inscriptions from Magnesia, Miletos and Samos; it is therefore not an invention of Herodas. However, the first known occurrence of the verb βατταρίζειν, 'to stutter', is in Hippônax (*Fr.* 155 Degani (1991) 152), and Herodas may well have intended to give his speaker a name which would be humorously inappropriate to the special skills required of an orator, and at the same time within the iambic tradition; see further 75n. Perhaps the figure of a hopeless orator was part of the tradition of mime as well, for we know that Sophrôn depicted a character named Boulias who delivers a speech which is internally inconsistent (Sophrôn, *Fr.* 104 Kassel-Austin [2001] 1 233). The brothel-keeper was also a stock figure in comedy: in Middle Comedy, for example, Euboulos wrote a Πορνοβοσκός (*Frr.* 87–8 Kassel-Austin 5 241), and, in New Comedy, Poseidippos wrote a play of the same name (*Frr.* 23–4 Kassel-Austin 7 572). Plautus and Terence supplement the picture for New Comedy, endowing the character with stock characteristics of greed (Terence, *The Self-Tormentor* 39), impudence (Plautus, *Curculio* 58), brazen dishonesty (Plautus, *The Captives* 57) and old age (Plautus, *The Rope* 125, 317), all shared by Battaros in our poem. The structure of Battaros' speech follows actual procedure in the lawcourts, and Herodas draws on Attic oratory for many details and stock-in-trade arguments and expressions.

Purpose It has often been supposed that the poem's point is the parody of Attic oratory. Yet the rhetorical commonplaces used by Battaros are on closer inspection subservient to the real aim, which is the characterization of the outrageous old brothel-keeper. See the Discussion.

**1–10.** The thought that birth, reputation and wealth are irrelevant in the eyes of the law is often to be found in the Attic orators; see e.g. Demosthenes 21 (*Against Meidias*) 143 and Isokrates 20 (*Against Lochites*) 19. By exaggerating Thalês' wealth and his own poverty, Battaros is also fishing for the jurors' sympathy, and possibly suggesting that Thalês will be able to pay compensation easily.
**1. γενῆς:** this form, used also in line 32, is probably a contraction of γενέης, and is found in poetry, e.g. Hippônax, *Fr.* 75.5 Degani (1991) 89, and Kallimachos, *Fr.* 511 Pfeiffer (1949) 375.
**2. δήκουθεν:** Attic δήπου(θεν) was considered a mannerism of the Attic orators, and Loukianos ridiculed the Atticists of his day for their use of it: 41 (*The Rhetoric Teacher*) 18, 46 (*Lexiphanes*) 21. With it and γενῆς Battaros is probably striving for the grand manner. The contrast is comic, and part of Battaros' characterization.
**3–4. a ship worth five talents:** Battaros grossly exaggerates the value of the ship, to judge by Lysias 32 (*Against Diogeitôn*) 25, where a merchant ship is valued at two talents, and [Demosthenes] 33 (*Against Apatourios*) 12, where a ship is sold for forty minas.
**8. πόλιος:** scanned as a dissyllable, short followed by long, as at line 31, though at line 26 the word is trisyllabic; the ι is consonantalised between the consonant and the vowel, ο; see West (1982) 14 for this prosody.
**9.** Battaros expresses a proverbial thought which is found frequently; see e.g. Menandros, *Fr.* 47 Kassel-Austin (1998) 6.2 67 (perhaps from *The Girl from Andros*) ζῶμεν γὰρ οὐχ ὡς θέλομεν, ἀλλ' ὡς δυνάμεθα. Herodas uses such proverbs to give the impression of everyday reality, but the technique is studied and literary; see Arnott (1971) 130–131.
**10–15.** The text is seriously damaged. I print what I think to be the most plausible supplements, though I can find no satisfactory solution for [...]ων in line 14, suggesting 'with' in the translation, and the imperfect in [ἣν εἶ]χε in the same line looks very strange: a present seems demanded. The lines concern the fact that metics were required to have a citizen of the city in which they were resident as their sponsor. Battaros claims that his sponsor, an active wrestler named Aristophôn, is as respectable as Thalês', Mennês, a former champion boxer. However, even though the supplements to lines 13 to 15 are very uncertain, the general sense seems to be that Aristophôn is a λωποδύτης, a clothes-thief who stole clothes from people while bathing, or robbed them of their clothing late at night: the word for cloak, χλαῖνα, is not in doubt in the text, and το[ῦ ἡ]λίου δύντος, 'when the sun has set', seems secure. Battaros might therefore be giving his sponsor the profile of such a thief, hinting that Thalês will lose his cloak if he accepts Battaros' challenge to go out in a cloak after sunset. (That Thalês is the subject of 'let him come out' is in accord with Battaros' habit of referring to his opponent in the third person singular: e.g. 10, 15, 16.) In that case, one might be tempted to conclude, Battaros casts a shadow on his own respectability, for it was assumed that a metic revealed his character by his choice of sponsor; see Isokrates 8 (*On the Peace*) 53 τοὺς μὲν μετοίκους τοιούτους

εἶναι νομίζομεν οἵουσπερ ἂν τοὺς προστάτας νέμωσιν, 'we judge the characters of metics by the kind of patrons they choose to sponsor them.' The impertinence would hardly be out of place in Battaros.

**προστάτῃ τεθώρηγμαι:** this is the only known use of θωρήσσω, 'I arm', in an metaphorical sense with an instrumental dative of a person: the more normal practice is with an instrumental dative of a thing, as in Homer, *Od.* 23.369 ἐθωρήσσοντο δὲ χαλκῷ, 'they were armed in bronze.' Perhaps Battaros is comically presented as echoing and extending the high-sounding formula, as Di Gregorio (1997) 131 suggests.

**16–20.** Battaros tries to anticipate a possible argument from Thalês in a rhetorical figure called προκατάληψις; the figure was commonly used by the orators, e.g. by Demosthenes at 21 (*Against Meidias*) 160 and 38 (*Against Nausimachos*) 25.

**16. Akê:** The Phoinikian trading city of Akê passed into Ptolemaic hands in around 290 B.C., and was re-named Ptolemais. To judge by numismatic evidence the renaming occurred sometime in the period between 286 and 266 B.C., so the poem was probably written before 266: Reinach (1909). Though the old name may have persisted in local usage till after 266 (as is argued most recently by Di Gregorio [1997] 134), the dating of this poem to the period before that year at least tallies with the dating of *Mimiambs* 1 and 4.

**17. I stopped the dreadful famine:** this was one of the benefactions to the state standardly adduced to strengthen a case; see e.g. Demosthenes 20 (*Against Leptines*) 33 and 34 (*Against Phormiôn*) 38.

**18. Tyre:** Like Akê, Tyre was an important Phoinikian trading city. After it was sacked by Alexander in 332 B.C., it quickly re-established itself and came under Ptolemaic control in 295/4 B.C.

**19. prostitutes:** the counter-benefaction offered by Battaros to the service he alleges Thalês will quote is of course ridiculous. It is even more comic in that Battaros seriously proposes it as an equal to Thalês', or at least has the affrontery to pretend that it is so.

**δωρέην:** this is an instance of an original accusative of apposition which developed into an adverb; Schwyzer (1950) 2 86–7. Battaros outrageously argues that his and Thalês benefactions are on a par because Thalês charges for his wheat as much as Battaros does for his girls.

**20. that girl, κείνην:** this will refer to Myrtalê, of whom Battaros alleges Thalês wanted to make free avail. That would constitute another dig at Thalês: not only are his benefactions no greater than Battaros', but he wants Battaros' merchandise gratis while demanding payment for his own.

**21–7. If, just because he …, while I …, he can …, the safety of our city is done for, and the very thing …, your autonomy, will be destroyed …:** the brothel-keeper essays the solemn, periodic style of the orators. Moreover, quite apart from perverting several rhetorical commonplaces, Battaros brazenly repeats his claim about his poverty and Thalês' wealth from lines 3–4.

**21. he sails the sea, πλεῖ τὴν θάλασσαν:** θάλασσαν is a kind of internal object, from a noun related in sense to but not cognate with the intransitive verb. The phrase is possibly borrowed from the orators, who use it frequently: see e.g. Demosthenes 4 (*First Philippic*) 34.

**22. three Athenian minas:** this seems to be another gross exaggeration: at *Mim.* 5.21 three minas is the price of a slave, and a himation costs only twenty drachmas in Aristophanes, *Wealth* 982–3.

**Athenian:** the Attic silver standard prevailed in the third-century Greek world except for the Ptolemaic empire, which adopted the Rhodian silver standard in about 310 B.C., so defining the denomination as 'Attic' would be superfluous in any region except the Ptolemaic empire.

**23. threadbare coat:** this was worn by poor men, Spartans and ascetics.

**ἀσκέρας:** the word is possibly a reminiscence of Hippônax 34.3 Degani (1991) 65. This type of shoe was said to be good for use in winter (Pollux 7.85 Bethe [1931] 2 76, 5–6); since Battaros' shoes are rotten, they cannot offer the protection they would normally have done, and that is also the reason why they have to be dragged along. Again the brothel-keeper tries to win the jury's sympathy.

**25. all this by night, what's more!:** as if the brothel-keeper were a solid citizen who worked normal day-time hours: Groeneboom (1922) 75.

**the safety of our city is done for:** a commonplace in oratory; see e.g. Isokrates 20 (*Against Lochites*) 9–11 and [Demosthenes] 25 (*Against Aristogeitôn*) 18–19. The claim is hopelessly out of proportion to the circumstances.

**ἧμιν:** dative of disadvantage. Though a metic, Battaros ingratiatingly makes common cause with the Koans.

**27. autonomy:** at this time Kos was an independent ally of the Ptolemaic empire; see Sherwin-White (1978) 95–7, with 175–223 on the Koan constitution. The idea that Egypt might end the Koans' autonomy because the court allows a brothel-brawler to go free is of course ridiculous.

**28–40.** After all this bombast Battaros affects his true humility, but his line of argument is associative and confused: 'Thalês should know his place like me, and respect the lowliest citizens; as it is, the noblest of Koan society obey the laws, and no citizen has ever harmed me by trying to burn down my establishment and run off with any of my girls; but Thalês, who is incidentally a crypto-barbarian, has done precisely these things, and has no respect for the law and the state officials.'

**28. He:** the relative ὅν refers to the subject of l. 24, Thalês.

**28–9.** The construction is, literally: 'It is necessary that (χρῆν) he (ὅν; see previous n.), having recognised (εἰδότα) himself (ἑαυτόν) [for] who he is (ὅστις ἐστί), … live (ζώειν; from the Ionic present ζώω) as I (ὡς ἐγώ)…'

**ποίου:** the papyrus' non-Ionic form (π- instead of Ionic κ-) gives marked alliteration, which conveys Battaros' righteous indignation; cf. *Mim.* 5.9.

**29. clay:** Herodas seems to know a version of Prometheus' creation of man from clay according to which the Titan made different men out of different qualities of clay; cf. Kallimachos, *Fr.* 493 Pfeiffer (1949) 366, εἴ σε Προμηθεύς / ἔπλασε, καὶ πηλοῦ μὴ ’ξ ἑτέρου γέγονας, ‘if Prometheus moulded you, and you are not made of another clay…’ (on which see Pfeiffer [1949] 366 for further references), Juvenal 14.34–5, *iuuenes, quibus arte benigna / et meliore luto finxit praecordia Titan*, ‘young men, whose hearts the Titan has moulded with kindly skill and from a better clay’. Thalês should remember his lowly status, as the exemplary Battaros does.

**30. townfolk, δημοτέων:** ‘ordinary citizens’, not in the Attic sense of ‘belonging to the same deme’. The –έων ending is scanned as one long syllable (‘synizesis’).

**in trembling awe and respect, φρίσσοντα:** the verb denotes terror or dread (so also at *Mim.* 6.64): Battaros is ingratiatingly exaggerating the respect due to the lowliest of the citizenry.

**the least, ἥκιστον:** here used as a superlative adjective, the adverbial ἥκιστα being the much more usual form.

**31. upper crust:** καλυπτῆρες are the tiles which cover the roof, and the word easily becomes a metaphor for the upper echelons of society; Battaros is forever tugging his forelock. The usage is not precisely paralleled elsewhere, though note Euripides, *Fr.* 703.1 (Kannicht [2004] 2 692) ἄνδρες Ἑλλήνων ἄκροι, ‘topmost men of the Greeks’; perhaps it was suggested to Herodas by the mention of clay two lines earlier.

**32. puff of pride, φυσῶντες:** the verb, taken metaphorically from the way a fluteplayer puffs up his or her cheeks, has connotations of arrogance (see e.g. Menandros, *Fr.* 219 Kassel-Austin [1998] 6.2 153). People hearing the word applied to them might justifiably feel aggrieved, but Battaros has self-revealingly lost any sensitivity to the nuance. The dative is instrumental, denoting cause; see Kühner-Gerth (1955) 1 438–40.

**greater… than, οὐκ ἴσον τούτῳ:** ‘not equally to this man’ means ‘more than he’ (‘meiosis’).

**34. thrash, ἠλόησεν:** ‘thresh’ to ‘thrash’, as in English. The form of the verb is epic and Ionic, ἀλοιάω (Attic ἀλοάω); Herodas avoids a spondee to close the second metron, and so avoids the diphthong -οι- here, though at 51, again for metrical reasons, he uses the epic form ἀλοιήσῃ.

**35–7:** here, and at 50 and 63–5, Battaros reveals the circumstances of the crime. Thalês has made away with one of Battaros’ girls in the course of a *kômos*, a revel. Appropriately inebriated after a party and still wearing their garlands, young men, alone or in the company of fellow-revellers and often flute-girls, made their way through the dark with torches to the house of a boyfriend or girlfriend, to whom they begged admittance, singing a *paraklausithyron* (παρακλαυσίθυρον), a serenade designed to announce their presence to the beloved. To press home their point, they knocked at the door. If the lover were still not admitted, he would stay ostentatiously at the beloved’s door, hanging his garland from it, leaving his burnt-out torch in front of it, or *in extremis* trying to knock or burn it down. The *kômos* is a common theme in the poetry of Herodas’ time: Delphis in Theokritos’ second *Idyll* is a habitual reveller; the third has the Goatherd performing a country version of the serenade; the so-called *Maiden's Lament* (Powell [1925] 177–80) is a serenade, this time by a woman; and the motif is frequently found in Hellensitic epigram, as at Asklepiades 11–13 and Kallimachos 8 GP.

**35. μευ:** Ionic form of Attic μου, as also at e.g. line 64.

**36. set my whole household alight:** an exaggeration, for Battaros later (65) specifies that only the door's lintel was burnt.

**prostitutes, τῶν πορνέων:** this partitive genitive (governed by λαβών) denotes a certain number of girls, and may suggest that Battaros has only an impersonal regard for his workers. In that it leaves open the conclusion that Thalês abducted more than one of the girls, it is another case of Battaros' typical exaggeration, since he has just stated that only one girl was involved (24).

**37. οἴχωκεν:** the ω in the perfect of οἴχομαι is formed on the analogy with μέμβλωκα from βλώσκω; see Schwyzer (1939) 1 721.

**37–8:** Casting doubt on one's opponent's ethnicity or respectable origins is a standard ploy among the orators, the best example being when Demosthenes 18 (*On the Crown*) 130 claims that Aischines changed his father's name from Τρόμης ('Trembler', a foreign name) to Ἀτρόμητος ('Intrepid'), and his mother's from Ἔμπουσα (a bogey-woman) into Γλαυκοθέα ('Grey Goddess'); for his part, Aischines 2 (*On the False Legation*) 78 claims that Demosthenes came from Skythian nomadic stock. Battaros calls Thalês a Phrygian because Phrygia was a common source of slaves, and Phrygians became a by-word for worthlessness. Thalês, Battaros claims, has dropped the name Artimmês, which is attested as that of a Persian satrap in Xenophon's *Anabasis* (7.8.25), for the name of one of the region's most famous figures, Thalês of Miletos.

**39. has shown no respect, ἐπηδέσθη:** the aorist passive form of ἐπαιδέομαι can take a direct accusative; see e.g. Plato, *Laws* 921a.

**40. sponsor, προστάτην:** Cunningham (1971) 89 sees here a reference not to Thalês' sponsor Mennês at line 10, but, with ἄρχοντα, to magistrates so named in Koan inscriptions. It seems equally possible, however, that the word refers to Mennês: Thalês has no regard for his obligation to his sponsor, though he has taken on a public responsibility that Thalês be on good behaviour. ἄρχων is, in that case, probably general in meaning.

**41–5.** In best rhetorical manner, Battaros requests the clerk of court (γραμματεύς) to read out the relevant law, and asks the official in charge of the clepsydra (ὁ ἐφ' ὕδωρ) to stop its flow so as not to lose the time he has been allocated to address the jury. He still manages to put his own outrageously vulgar spin on the procedure.

**41. So now, ... take and read out the law, καίτοι... / τὸν νόμον ἄνειπε:** the particle denotes a change of subject; see Denniston (1954) 557 ii, who notes that it is not found in the orators, so Battaros may be guilty of using a non-rhetorical locution just when he avails himself of a standard phrase from the lawcourts.

**assault, αἰκείης:** unprovoked physical assault: see *RE* 1 (1894) 1006–7 s.v. (Thalheim).

**42–5.** The text and interpretation of these lines are hotly debated. The reading offered here takes it that Battaros wants the clepsydra official to plug (βύω) the water-clock's spout so the 'anus' will not 'say' anything 'in addition' [to the clerk's recitation of the law], πρός being used adverbially and the τε preceding the καί in χὠ; the talking spout will of course only express water, but the brothel-keeper seizes on the obvious association with a human anus, and suggests with typical grossness that it will defecate; the bedclothes (τάπης) will receive the result, ληίη, 'booty', being used ironically, much as English would say 'reap the benefit' (cf. German 'Da haben wir die Bescherung!'). The motif of a talking anus is comic; see e.g. Aristophanes, *Frogs* 238. The standard formula in oratory was σὺ δ' ἐπίλαβε τὸ ὕδωρ, 'But you, stop the water-clock' (so e.g. Demosthenes 45 [*Against Stephanos* 1] 8 and 54 [*Against Konôn*] 36), but Battaros is more precise in order to set up his joke. Addressing the clepsydra official with the familiar βέλτιστε would never have been permitted in court, but it is consonant with Battaros' impudence.

**44. we find:** from ἦμιν as dative of interest.

**45. as in fact the saying goes, τὸ τοῦ λόγου δὴ τοῦτο:** one of several similar idiomatic expressions using the accusative adverbially with the general meaning 'as the saying goes', lit. ' the [matter] of the expression [being] in fact *this*'; see for further examples Headlam-Knox (1922) 87–8, Fraenkel (1950) 2 277–8. For δή, 'in fact', in quoting phrases like this see Denniston (1954) 235. The actual proverb is otherwise unknown.

**46–54.** The clerk reads out the law concerning physical assault, but Battaros, after an ostentatious show of impartiality, has the effrontery to interrupt the clerk and to recite laws unrelated to assault but fitting his own alleged circumstances.

**46. δέ:** the particle perhaps indicates that the clause has been taken out of its full context.

**free man ... female slave, ἐλεύθερος ... δούλην:** doubling the fine seems to have ensued if a free person was harmed; see e.g. Lysias 1 (*On the Murder of Eratosthenes*) 32 ἐὰν δέ τις ἄνθρωπον ἐλεύθερον ἢ παῖδα αἰσχύνῃ βίᾳ, διπλῆν τὴν βλάβην ὀφείλειν, 'If anyone forcibly violates a free male adult or child, [he shall be] liable to double damages', and the Demosthenes passage cited in the next note. Herodas may therefore be humorously inverting the actual state of affairs. He may also have stipulated a female slave in order comically to suit the law more closely to the situation. Myrtalê is a slave at least in origin; see lines 82 and 87 with nn.

**47. willingly, ἕκων:** laws often specified whether crimes were committed voluntarily or involuntarily; see e.g. Demosthenes 21 (*Against Meidias*) 43 [all the laws of damage] ἂν μὲν ἑκών βλάψῃ, διπλοῦν, ἂν δ' ἄκων, ἁπλοῦν τὸ βλάβος κελεύουσιν ἐκτίνειν, 'they demand that, if a man willingly cause damage, he should give compensation for twice the amount, whereas, if he does so unwittingly, for the equivalent amount.'

**harrasses, ἐπίσπῃ:** the aorist of ἐφέπω, which besides 'pursue' can mean 'harry', or 'molest': see e.g. *Il.* 11.177 and LSJ[9] s.v. A.II.4.

**48. Chairôndas, Χαιρώνδης:** Chairôndas, or (more usually) Charôndas, who probably lived in the sixth century B.C., was the revered author of the law-codes of cities in Magna Graecia like Katana in Sicily; see *BNP* 3 (2003) 204–5 s.v. Charondas (Hölkeskamp). The form of his name with Χαιρ- is attested in the manuscripts of Stobaios 4.2.24, and may therefore be a genuine alternative. In any case, Battaros cites a venerable legal figure (not that Charôndas is known to have influenced Koan law) for the law on assault, and can claim that he himself cannot be criticized for any self-interest or part in making the law. He goes on to assert that Charôndas was also the author (φησ', 51; ἔνειμε, 54) of the other laws that he cites piecemeal, not all of them related to the law of physical assault that he has requested of the clerk (41–2) – on door-breaking, punching, burning a house down, trespass and damaging property – all tailored to suit his own situation. He is being impudently opportunistic to say the least.

**50. θύρην ... κόψῃ:** usually of simple knocking at the door, but here even rougher than Gyllis' knocking at *Mim.* 1.1.

**51. τινέτω:** first syllable scanned long, as in Homer; see also τίνειν at line 54.

**52. πάλι:** = πάλιν, not so used before the Hellenistic period, when it is selected for the sake of metre, or, as here, for euphony, to lighten the consonant-group -ν μν-.

**53. trespass, ὅρους:** usually of boundary-stones between two pieces of land (e.g. *Il.* 21.405), but here naturally extended to the walls of a house.

**one thousand drachmas, χιλίας:** idiom omits the denomination, here δραχμάς.

**54. τίνειν:** the infinitive functions just as a noun in the accusative (Schwyzer [1950] 2 365), and is governed by ἔνειμε, supplied from the previous clause.

**55–9:** Battaros' emphasis on Charôndas' civilized legislation suggests to Battaros a gratuitous outburst on the theme of Thalês' allegedly uncivil and shiftless life spent in dubious localities. The brothel-keeper proceeds by association and contrast rather than logic.

**55. οἶσθας:** a ς has been added to the more normal οἶσθα, which consequently looks more like an ordinary second person singular. The form occurs in comedy; see e.g. Menandros, *The Arbitrators* 480.

**56. πῶς:** this Attic form for the Ionic κῶς is the papyrus reading; it is probably an attempt at alliteration as at line 28 (ποίου for κοίου); cf. ὅκως at line 60.

**57. Brikindêra, Βρικινδήροις:** The correct quantity of the ending was -δᾰρα; Herodas has created assonance by assimilating the name to that of Ἄβδηρα in the next line. Brikindêra was a port in Rhodes. Its name evidently sounded foreign to Greek ears: Lynkeus of Samos, Duris' brother and a pupil of Theophrastos, described figs from the port as τῷ μὲν ὀνόματι βαρβαριζούσας, ταῖς δ' ἡδοναῖς ... ἀττικιζούσας (Athenaios, *Scholars at Dinner* 652d), 'speaking a barbarian language in terms of their name, ... but Attic in terms of their tastiness'.

**58. Abdêra:** this city in Thrace was prosperous, but known for the uncivilized nature of its inhabitants: [Demosthenes] 17 (*On the Treaty with Alexandros*) 23 attacks a political faction at Athens for bullying tactics associated with places like Abdêra rather than Athens. Its citizens were also known for dullness (despite Demokritos!), which seems to be implied in our passage, though the evidence is otherwise no earlier than Cicero at e.g. *On the Nature of the Gods* 1.120 and *Letters to Atticus* 7.7.4; however, Cicero clearly regards Abdêra as proverbial for the quality, and the city must have been stigmatized in this way for some time; see also Juvenal, *Satire* 10.50, Martial, *Epigrams* 10.25.4.

**59. διδοῖ:** a form of the subjunctive δίδῳ based on the analogy with –οω verbs.

**Phasêlis:** a city on the coast of Lykia said by Stratonikos to be inhabited by the most base of any people in Pamphilia (Athenaios, *Scholars at Dinner* 350a); admission to its citizenship could be purchased for a mina, according to the paroemiographer Makarios 8.26 Leutsch-Schneidewin (1851) 2 217, 16 – 218, 2. All the cities that Battaros suggests Thalês might frequent therefore have negative connotations.

**πλώσει:** a future from πλώω, an epic and Ionic form of πλέω.

**60–5a:** Battaros cuts short his digressive attack on Thalês, and at last returns to the charge of assault and related damages that he started to detail at lines 33–40; Thalês has committed offences against all the laws leveled against him by the law as read out by the clerk and selected by Battaros himself.

**60. by long speechifying, μακρηλογέων:** Battaros again adopts a tone in grand the manner of the Attic orators: cf. Demosthenes 14 (*On the Symmories*) 41 ἵνα δ', ὦ ἄνδρες Ἀθηναῖοι, μὴ μακρὰ λίαν λέγων ἐνοχλῶ, 'so as not to give annoyance, gentlemen of Athens, by talking at excessive length'; the tag ἵνα μὴ μακρολογῶ, 'so as not to draw out my speech', is common in the orators.

**61. with digression, παροιμίῃ:** dative of instrument; the word is most convincingly understood as used in its literal sense, 'digression', which is attested in the ancient lexica; see e.g. Hesychios π 966 Schmidt (1861) 3 287.

**αἰσχύνευ:** for the Ionic contraction in -ευ- see *Mim.* 1.88n.

**62–3:** literally 'as many things as the mouse in tar [suffered] as well'. The actual proverb was ἄρτι μῦς πίσσης γεύεται, 'the mouse is just now tasting the tar,' which Diogenianos 2.64 Leutsch-Schneidewin (1839) 1 206, 3–5 said was used 'of those who have had recent experience of trouble, for the animal falling into tar suffers terribly'. It is indeed used in oratory ([Demosthenes] 50 [*Against Polykles*] 26), but closer to Herodas in intention and tone is its appearance in Theokritos' *Idyll* 14.51, a poem which, though the direction of influence is uncertain, is related to Herodas' first *Mimiamb*; see above, pp. 37–8. The juxtaposition of Battaros' citation of the orators in line 60 and the lowly proverb results in pure bathos.

**64. a third, τρίτην:** supply e.g. μοῖραν; it is most convincingly taken as a third of the value of the house (so e.g. Cunningham [1971] 93). This might seem a high rent, but Battaros is a hardened exaggerator, and his kind of establishment was exposed to precisely the occupational hazards that Battaros is describing.

**of its value, μισθόν:** in apposition with τρίτην; literally, 'the third [of the value] of which I pay as rent'.

**65b-71:** Battaros produces – nude – his prize exhibit, Myrtalê, the hetaira whom Thalês has tried to make away with, and whose alleged injuries Battaros displays as his hard evidence. Similarly, the orator Hypereides is said to have paraded the hetaira Phrynê before the jury with her breasts bared, despite her needing defence against the charge of ἀσέβεια (Athenaios, *Scholars at Dinner* 590e). The majority of the editors see a parody of the orator here (though cf. Cunningham [1971] 95): the orator is replaced by a brothel-keeper, and a high-class hetaira is replaced by a much lowlier sister. The passage is at the very least one of the most successful comic moments in Herodas: we can only imagine, for example, the look on the jurors' faces when they hear themselves put in the place of Myrtalê's father or brothers. And Battaros, whose real interest in Myrtalê is purely financial, with impudent hypocrisy assumes the role of her tender father.

**65. Myrtalê:** the name, derived from the word for myrtle, appears as a hetaira's also at *Mim.* 1.89, where see n.

**66. σεωυτήν:** Ionic form of Attic σεαυτήν.

**67–8:** the construction is 'Consider that you are looking upon' (nominative and infinitive) 'these men … as your fathers …' (in predication). The motif of claiming such family affinities is found in oratory; see Andokides 1 (*On the Mysteries*) 149 ὑμεῖς τοίνυν καὶ ἀντὶ πατρὸς ἐμοὶ καὶ ἀντὶ ἀδελφῶν καὶ ἀντὶ παίδων γένεσθε, 'You, therefore, act as both my father and my brothers and my children.'

**69. plucked skin, τίλματα:** any prostitute practised depilation for her clients' pleasure, the normal verb being παρατίλλω, as at Aristophanes' *Frogs* 516 where Xanthias is offered dancing girls who have recently been depilated (ἄρτι παρατετιλμέναι). Battaros' claim that Myrtalê's depilation is the result of any rough treatment by Thalês is outrageous. The fact that the jury is invited to inspect the 'exhibit' in such detail means that Myrtalê is nude.

**70. ὡναγής:** = ὁ ἀναγής. Cunningham (1971) 96 rightly takes this word as being used sarcastically, with the meaning 'he who is not subject to ἄγος, divine punishment', i.e. 'pure'.

**71. dragged, εἵλκεν:** from Homer onwards ἕλκω carries a connotation of rape; see e.g. *Il.* 22.62, 65.

**71–8.** Battaros puts his failure to give Thalês a beating down to his old age, but is nettled by Thalês' laughter into claiming that despite his hereditary effeminacy he could throttle a lion. He thereby makes nonsense of his excuse for not fighting Thalês, his old age, and simultaneously obliges the jury with a parade of his pedigree which is spectacularly irrelevant to the case. Self-consistency and relevance, however, are clearly not things that the brothel-keeper values highly.

**71. O, Old Age:** Battaros personifies old age, as happens commonly enough in Greek drama (Euripides, *Suppliant Women* 1108, Menandros, *Fr.* 867 Kassel-Austin [1998] 6.2 410, and also in *Mim.* 1.63), and the personification comes close to a deity, which suggests to Battaros the image of sacrificing in gratitude. However, at *Mim.* 6.10 Korittô says θῦέ μοι ταύτῃ, 'Be grateful to this woman', to a slave, and so perhaps the idea of simple thanks is in the foreground.

**72. ἐπεὶ … ἂν:** a word like 'otherwise' or a phrase like 'if I weren't old' has been

omitted, as is common in such sentences; see e.g. *Mimiambs* 4.15 and 6.11.
**he would have spat up, ἐξεφύσησεν:** the verb is used when a wound has admitted blood into the lungs or windpipe; see Sophokles, *Aias* 918 'spitting up (φυσῶντ' ἄνω) to his nostrils the blackened blood from the crimson wound'.
**73.** This line alludes to the proverb τὸν ἐν Σάμῳ κομήτην, 'the long-haired man on Samos', explained by ps.-Ploutarchos, *Alexandrian Proverbs* 2.8 Leutsch-Schneidewin (1839) 1 337, 5–12 as referring to the story of how a long-haired boxer was taunted on Samos by his rivals with the effeminacy signalled by his hair, and defeated them all. ὁ Βρέγκος is difficult: Βρίγκος is an attested name, and even if the meaning is uncertain (though LSJ[9] s.v. βρέγκος conjectures βρεῦκος, i.e. βροῦχος, 'locust') Brenkos might be taken as a sobriquet (Di Gregorio [1997] 157); otherwise, it could be taken as the genitive of Βρέγξ, giving 'son of Brenx' (Cunningham [2002] 213), but the name is unattested. Battaros compares himself with the long-haired boxer, whose name is said to have been Pythagoras in some sources, in that he is only externally effeminate, and he compares Thalês with Philistos, a surprised victim. Battaros' implication that his effeminacy is only external helps explain why Thalês laughs, and leads naturally into Battaros' defiant admission of his true character and calling.
**74. You laugh?, γελᾷς;:** the singular surely proves that Thalês is doing the laughing: the jury was addressed in the plural at line 68.
**queer, κίναιδος:** this vague term (most fully documented by Kroll *RE* 10.1 (1921) 459–62) seems originally to have denoted a performer of a type of lascivious Ionian dance, the dominant characteristic of which was lewd effeminate bottom-movement. It was early applied to effeminates and pathic homosexuals, and became a favourite insult in oratory. Aischines 1 (*Against Timarchos*) 131, for example, casts the slur of κιναιδεία on Demosthenes. The modern English 'queer' perhaps closest approximates to the Greek word's meaning and connotation; see further 75n.
**I won't deny it, καὶ οὐκ ἀπαρνεῦμαι:** Battaros brazenly boasts of what society regarded as shameful. The motif is found in tragedy, at e.g. [Aischylos], *Prometheus* 266, but also comedy; see e.g. Terence, *Adelphi* 188 *leno sum, pernicies communis, fateor, adulescentium*, 'I'm a pimp, the common downfall, I admit, of young men'. In the comic usages, as here in Herodas, a sense of sham heroic defiance seems implied. For the Ionic contraction in -ευ- see *Mim.* 1.88n.
**75. Battaros:** the name is connected with βατταρίζειν, 'to stammer', but it could also be related to βάταλος, which was a word for 'arse': Aischines 1 (*Against Timarchos*) 131 reveals that Demosthenes had the nickname Βάταλος as a result of his alleged ἀνανδρία and κιναιδεία, 'unmanliness' and 'being a queer'.
**76. Sisymbrâs** and **Sisymbriskos** are names taken from a type of mint, σισύμβριον. Hetairai commonly had flower names (as at line 65 of this poem and at *Mim.* 1.89), and the comic poet Theophilos, *Fr.* 11.2 Kassel-Austin (1989) 7 706 introduces one named precisely Sisymbrion. This adds colour to the effeminacy of the clan: their very names are modelled on feminine lines.

**77. they were all brothel-keepers:** cf. Plautus, *The Persian* 57–8, where the parasite Saturio says *pater, auos, proauos, atauos, tritauos / quasi mures semper edere alienum cibum*, 'My father, grandfather, greatgrandfather, great-greatgrandfather, great-great-greatgrandfather, have, like mice, always eaten the food of others'. The progression from *kinaidos* (on the meaning see above, 74n.) in youth to brothel-keeper in old age was a natural career-move. For the Ionic contraction in -ευ- in ἐπορνοβόσκευν see *Mim.* 1.88n.
**as far as strength goes:** the preposition, originally meaning 'by the will of', here has a limiting force, 'as far as strength is concerned'.
**78. I'd ... [strangle a lion], λέ[οντ' ἄγχ]οιμ' ἂν:** Bücheler's supplement fits the traces and gives good sense: Battaros is by implication contrasting himself with Thalês, who can only exercise his strength on women, and comparing himself with Herakles in his defeat of the Nemean lion.
**79–83:** Battaros suggests an out-of-court settlement: if Thalês really loves Myrtalê, all he needs to do is pay Battaros for her, and he can treat her as roughly as he likes. He thereby reveals that his fatherly concern for Myrtalê (65–71) and his orator's high moral tone are pure hypocrisy.
**80. πυρέων:** a hyperionicism: in *o*-stem words the genitive plural is -ῶν in Ionic as well as Attic. The genitive is dependent on an ἐρῶ, 'I love', supplied from ἐρᾳ̃ς in the previous line.
**give me one and you shall have the other, ταῦτα δοὺς ἐκεῖν' ἕξεις:** Battaros' variation on the proverb ἅμα δίδου καὶ λάμβανε, 'Give and receive at the same time.' Battaros is fond of proverbs; see also 9n., 45n., 62–3n., 73n., 100–2n.
**81. by Zeus, νὴ Δί':** νή in oaths is Attic, and Herodas elsewhere has ναί, the Ionic form, but the oath νὴ Δί' is so common in comedy and prose that Herodas may have preferred the Attic form here.
**if you've got the hots for her anywhere in you, σευ θάλπεταί τι τῶν ἔνδον:** literally 'anything of your things within is heated [by love]'; τὰ ἔνδον = τὰ σπλάγχνα at *Mim.* 1.57.
**82. her price:** Myrtalê is therefore a slave, as was most commonly the social background for prostitutes, though there were exceptions; see *DkP* 4 (1972) 1192 s.v. Prostitution (Krenkel).
**dear little Battaros:** the diminutive denotes that Battaros is crawling, after all his fire and brimstone. The diminutive -ίω̣ ending, scanned as one long syllable, is perhaps another example of synizesis; see above, 30n.
**83. maul:** θλάω means 'to bruise', with the connotation of rough sex. After the wheedling tone of the the proposal of the previous two lines, Battaros becomes vulgar.
**84–91:** Battaros now turns to the jury and begins his peroration, only to interrupt it with an impudent offer of 'help' to the jurymen in their deliberations.
**84. There is one particular matter, ἓν δ' ἐστιν:** expressions like this often serve in rhetoric (but the usage is not confined to rhetoric) to introduce a final point; see e.g.

Aischines 2 (*On the Embassy*) 159 ἓν δὲ πρὸς τοῖς εἰρημένοις εἰπεῖν ἔτι βούλομαι, 'I wish to say one more thing in addition to what has been said.'
**ταῦτα μέν:** answered by ὑμεῖς δ' in the next line: 'these remarks have been made to *him*, … but *you* …'
**85. there being no witnesses, ἀμαρτύρων εὔντων:** there are no other witnesses apart from the complainant and Myrtalê, who apparently being a slave (see 82 and 87nn.) cannot give evidence except after torture (cf. 87–8), so especial just judgment is required from the jurors.
**86. with just judgment, γνώμῃ δικαίῃ:** dikasts swore to judge γνώμῃ τῇ δικαιοτάτῃ 'with most just judgment': see e.g. Demosthenes 23 (*Against Aristokrates*) 96.
**decide the case, τὴν κρίσιν διαιτᾶτε:** the more common phrase is κρίσιν κρίνειν, as at Plato, *Republic* 360e; Battaros has opted for the less obvious verb, which actually had come to mean 'to arbitrate'; see LSJ[9] s.v. διαιτάω II.2, and cf. Theokritos, *Id.* 12.34.
**87. if, ἢν δ':** having reminded the jury that the crime had no witnesses, Battaros suggests that Thalês will want to torture Myrtalê before she gives evidence as was customary with slaves giving evidence, but the brothel-keeper opportunistically offers himself for torture *in addition*, so that he will win compensation for possibly both Myrtalê and himself if they are harmed: the accuser had to pay the value of the slave for damage done him in the course of torture if the charge turned out to be false. Strictly, however, the accuser is Battaros. Moreover, as a metic he was a free man, and could not be subjected to torture except in grave cases like crimes against the state. The offer is also motivated by the prospect of financial gain. It is therefore triply outrageous, and a tribute to Herodas' skill in comic exaggeration.
**οἶον:** adverbial neuter singular of the adjective οἶος, 'only', as when Hesiod, *Theogony* 26 makes the Muses address him and his like as γαστέρες οἶον, 'nothing but stomachs.'
**88. torture:** βάσανος originally meant a touchstone which proved the authenticity of gold, and was transferred to the process of questioning a slave after torture.
**προσδίδωμι κἀμαυτόν:** the combination of the prefix of the verb and the καί reinforce the idea that Battaros is offering his body for torture *as well* [as Myrtalê's].
**89. put me on the rack, στρέβλου:** 'stretching' was done on a ladder (Aristophanes, *Frogs* 620) or on a wheel (Aristophanes, *Lysistrata* 846).
**compensation-money:** this was to be put in advance before the court for the damages done to Battaros when Thalês' 'charge' fails, not that Thalês is the accuser or that Battaros is a slave. The brothel-keeper displays both financial greed at any cost to his person, and preposterous confidence in his cause.
**90. Minôs:** the great mythological legislator while alive, and, after his death, judge of the disputes of the dead in the afterworld, along with Aiakos and Rhadymanthos; see *Od.* 11.568–71. The figure of Minôs was a motif in Attic oratory (see Demosthenes 18 [*On the Crown*] 127), and Battaros may again be availing himself of oratory's stock-in-trade. The thought that the jurors would be serving justice better than Minôs if they follow Battaros' suggested procedure is comically ludicrous.

**91. βέλτιον:** the ι in comparatives is short in dialects other than Attic, where it is normally, but not exclusively, long; at *Mim.* 1.87, however, ἥδίον' has the ι long. See further e.g. Collard (1975) 2 386, and Arnott (1996) 827.
**διήτησε:** for variation's sake, as at 86.
**92–102:** Battaros resumes his peroration: the jurors must realize that they are making a judgment with repercussions for all foreign residents, and must live up to the noble example of Kos' heroes.
**92–4:** the argument that the jurors' ruling will have wider implications than the present case is a commonplace in the Attic orators; see e.g. Demosthenes 56 (*Against Dionysodôros*) 48 μίαν δίκην δικάζοντες νομοθετεῖτε ὑπὲρ ὅλου τοῦ ἐμπορίου, 'while you are deciding one case alone, you are laying down a law for the whole port.' Battaros has a particular interest in the gambit because he is trying to divert the jurors' attention from the fact that they have in front of them such a disreputable figure as a brothel-keeper.
**you're casting your vote, τὴν ψῆφον ... φέρειν:** the phrase refers to the way jurymen literally carried their voting pebble, ψῆφος, to the voting-urns, but is here used metaphorically.
**95–100:** Attic orators frequently exhort their audience to act and judge worthily of the state's glorious past; see e.g. Demosthenes 18 (*On the Crown*) 208. Moreover, Battaros' words and examples are echoed in the ninth pseudo-Hippokratic letter (Littré [1861] 9 320), dated to the first century A.D., Κῷοι οὐδὲν ἀνάξιον πρήξουσι οὔτε Μέροπος οὔτε Ἡρακλέους οὔτε Ἀσκληπιοῦ, 'Koans will do nothing unworthy of either Merops or Herakles or Asklêpios.' Perhaps, therefore, Battaros is using a form of this kind of appeal that was traditional on Kos. It is just possible that by singling out Herakles, Asklêpios and Phoibê Battaros is reinforcing his argument at lines 92–4, that the Koans should respect him just as much as they do these illustrious visitors to their island: Massa Positano (1971) 70–1, followed by Di Gregorio (1997) 169.
**95. Kos and Merops:** the pre-Dorian inhabitants of Kos were called Meropes after the autochthonous founder and king of Kos, Merops, whose daughter was Kos. Another daughter of Merops was the Klytia mentioned by Theokritos at *Id.* 7.5 whose child by Eurypylos was Chalkôn, the creator of the spring Bourina (for which see *Id.* 7.6–7, with Zanker [1980] and [2006] 374); these were the illustrious Koan ancestors of Theokritos' hosts at the harvest festival, Phrasidamos and Antigenes. See in general Sherwin-White [1978] 47–50.
**the might:** the verb δραίνω is used also by Gyllis at *Mim.* 1.15; the close association of Kos and Merops as eponymous heroes of the island probably explains the singular; cf. εἶχε at line 96 and *Mim.* 4.6, where the verbs are attracted into the singular by their immediate antecedent subject.
**96. Thessalos and Herakles:** when Herakles returned from Troy after capturing it Hera forced him to land on Kos by sending adverse winds. There he killed the king, Eurypylos, and had Thessalos as a son by Eurypylos' daughter, Chalkiopê. See further Sherwin-White (1978) 317–20.

**97. Trikkê:** for this Thessalian town, which was viewed as the origin of the cult of Asklêpios on Kos, see *Mim.* 4.1–2n.
**98:** another source for the belief that Leto's birthplace was Kos is Tacitus, *Annals* 12.61.1, where the legend is cited as one of the reasons why Claudius gave the island freedom from taxation; see further Sherwin-White (1978) 300–1. Leto's father was the Titan Κοῖος, Koios (Hesiod, *Theogony* 404–8); his name was at some juncture modified to Κῷιος, Kôios, which opened up the association with the island.
**Λητοῦν:** the Ionic form of the accusative of names ending in -ω, the final -ν bringing the accusative into line with the characteristic ending of that case. The nominative and accusative of Λητώ are elsewhere (as at e.g. Hesiod, *Theogony* 406) the same in form.
**ὧδε:** in its locative meaning, as opposed to its familiar modal sense, this adverb earlier meant 'to this place', but in this passage, as also at *Mim.* 3.96, it has become 'here'.
**99. straight, ὀρθῇ:** changed from the δικαίῃ of line 86 because of the image of steering present in κυβερνᾶτε, 'steer'.
**100–2. this Phrygian:** oratory often talks of a just punishment's ability to make a defendant better; see e.g. Isokrates 20 (*Against Lochites*) 16 and Lysias 24 (*For the Disabled Man*) 27. But here Battaros refers back to his claim at line 37 that Thalês is a Phrygian, the lowest form of barbarian or slave, and redeploys the orators' motif by putting it in the phraseology of the proverb Φρὺξ ἀνὴρ πληγεὶς ἀμείνων καὶ διακονέστερος, 'Once given a beating, a Phrygian is better and more manageable.' The banalisation of a standard rhetorical argument is typical of our Battaros.
**100. ὗμιν:** dative of interest.
**101. ἔσσεται:** Battaros uses the epic form of Ionic ἔσται in an attempt at high-flown diction, but in the context of a common proverb it merely increases the bathos of his concluding words. Something similar happens when Kynnô uses the same epicism at *Mim.* 4.50, where see note.
**102. tells, βάζει:** another epic verb to enrich the bathos, the peroration's very last word.

## DISCUSSION

### *The characterization of Battaros*

As we have already seen (p. 51), Battaros is a representative of a type in Middle and New Comedy, the brothel-keeper. He may also be related to a type in mime, the bad orator exemplified by Sophrôn's Boulias. It is therefore possible that he would have been understood as a composite type by Herodas' original audiences or readership, though the component indicated by the title will have been the dominant one. In comedy, the brothel-keeper (Latin *leno*) had stock attributes of greed, impudence, dishonesty and old age, and all these traits find rich expression in Battaros.

Greed is in evidence throughout. Apart from the impersonal way he speaks about the girls in his employ (see 36n.), we have the hard financial motives underlying his hypocritical show of fatherly concern for Myrtalê before the jury (65–71), his suggestion to Thalês of an out-of-court settlement (79–93), which is purely designed to extract money from the merchant-captain by the path of least resistance, and his quest for potential double compensation when he offers himself as well as Myrtalê for torture (87–90).

Impudence is also abundantly present. There is his perversion of a rhetorical commonplace when he equates Thalês' saving the state by his shipment of wheat and his own service to the state by his shipload of prostitutes, claiming that he can charge for his wares as surely as Thalês does for his (16–20). There is the inappropriately familiar address to the clepsydra-operator (43), his grubby joke about stopping up the clepsydra (42–5), and his interruption of the clerk of court's reading of the law on assault when he hijacks the reading by citing laws he claims are particularly pertinent to his own case (48–54). Part of his strategy in offering his body up for torture prior to giving evidence is to display how sure he is of his case. As we shall see, his arrogation of the commonplaces, style and tone of law-court rhetoric is in itself an act of the most impertinent presumption.

Battaros' dishonesty consists largely of gross exaggeration, and distorted and sometimes self-contradictory description of the facts. He exaggerates shamelessly when he would have the jury believe that Myrtalê's depilation is a result of Thalês' rough treatment of her rather than a condition of her employment (69–72). He exaggerates both the value of Thalês' ship and clothes (3–4, 21–2), and his own poverty and threadbare apparel (3, 22–3) in his bid for the jurors' sympathy. He contradicts himself when at one moment he suggests that Thalês has burnt down Battaros' whole establishment and forcefully abducted more than one prostitute (34–7), while at the next he reveals that only the door-lintel of the house was burnt and one girl was involved (63–5). He therefore opportunistically overstates the circumstances of the very crime which Thalês has committed against him and which is the cause of the whole case he is bringing.

He gets considerable mileage out of his old age in his outburst at lines 71 to 78, where he says on the one hand that Thalês can be thankful that old age prohibited Battaros from retaliating, and admits that he comes from a long line of 'queers' (*kinaidoi*) from whom such feats of strength are hardly to be expected, but on the other hand claims that he is strong enough to throttle a lion if it is Thalês. His second claim contradicts his first, but Battaros seizes on any argument that suits his immediate needs.

If these are the standing characteristics of the comic brothel-keeper type, Battaros displays them all, but we have already gone much further than getting to know a stock type. He possesses considerable individuality, and the typical traits have been skilfully individualised. But his character is individualised by other means as well which are sometimes quite unparalleled in what we know of comedy and mime.

Akin to his impudence is the defiance that he exhibits in his parade of his ancestral calling (74–7), though that defiance is ridiculously punctured by the feminine names of his grandfather and father which he is carried away enough to cite explicitly (see 76n.). The quality is evidenced for sycophants and brothel-keepers in Comedy (see 75, 77nn.), but in Herodas it is set in amusing contrast with Battaros' shameless wheedling, as when he proceeds to use an incongruously familiar diminutive inviting Thalês simply to buy Myrtalê – 'your dear little Battaros' (Βατταρίῳ, 83). Throughout the poem his effrontery in even bringing the case against Thalês makes a glaring contrast with the crawling obsequiousness with which he refers to the jury. He flatters Koan pride in saying that he has nothing but the deepest respect for the least of the citizenry (30) and in talking of how the 'upper crust' of society treat him well (31), though in his eagerness to please he overdoes it when he says that they 'can give themselves a puff of pride in their birth' (32). And with a sickeningly ingratiating tone he makes common cause with the jury when he claims that 'the safety of *our* city' (ἡμῖν, 25) is under threat.

The most interesting way in which Battaros is characterized, however, is the way in which Herodas plays off the disreputable figure against the sententious orator. Throughout the speech there is an ironical incongruity, in that the lofty rhetorical sentiments, language and expressions are put in the mouth of a brothel-keeper, who is moreover bringing an action at law with the sole motive of financial profit from a relatively harmless if colorful incident that has occurred in his establishment. This becomes most pointed at the end of the harangue, when Battaros urges the jury to realize that their ruling has a bearing not only on Battaros the brothel-keeper, but on all metics resident in the city (92–4). The idea is a commonplace in oratory, but Battaros uses it to shift the jurors' focus from himself to the wider implications of the case. It is clear at this point that Battaros is aware of the tension between the high-mindedness of his appeal and his own precarious bargaining power. Part of the humour is that he immediately persists with his high moralising in his closing and again commonplace exhortation to the jury that they live up to the grand past of their island and its heroes (95–100; see 95–100n.). Another example of this kind of tension is the moment when Battaros exhibits Myrtalê, and invites her to look upon the jurors as fathers and brothers (67–8). The appeal to the consanguineity of the jury may be yet another commonplace in oratory (see 67–8n.), but the jury whose nobler feelings Battaros has consistently appealed to will hardly have relished the association he has implied that they have with his sex-worker. This situational irony may be a result that Herodas himself intended by crossing the stock comic character of the brothel-keeper with the figure of the orator who contradicts himself as evidenced for mime by Sophrôn's Boulias.

The humour of this underlying tension is compounded by Battaros' irrepressible vulgarity, which is found in his lame deployment of hackneyed motifs and expressions from the lawcourts, his confused and self-serving mode of argumentation, the inappropriateness and bad taste of his jokes, and the bathos he achieves by his use of that repository of folk-wisdom, the proverb.

His very exordium illustrates the majority of these elements, though not his attempts at humour, for he is bent on establishing a serious tone (1–10). The passage is a standard orator's *captatio beneuolentiae*, as Battaros tries to secure the jurors' sympathy. This he does by using the rhetorical topos where the jurors are reminded that all citizens are equal before the law, but he grafts on to the motif a statement of his opponent's wealth and his own poverty. The value he puts on Thalês' ship is clearly however an exaggeration (see 3–4n.), and so is his description of his own poverty: if he can pay a third of the value of his property as rent (see 64n.), it is unlikely that he will be without bread, though admittedly it is difficult to decide which claim is the more exaggerated. The element of exaggeration thus already undercuts his high moral tone. So does the way he expresses himself. His statement that both he and Thalês are metics who are driven from pillar to post according to where their opportunities lie is proverbial, and has a hackneyed feeling to it (see 9n.), and his ostentatious use of the overworn particle δήκουθεν (see 2n.), also suggests that he is merely aping the more obvious features of the rhetorical style. Far from what Battaros has intended, his comic unmasking has already begun.

Battaros' nomination of his patron Aristophôn (10–15) involves his first foray into humour. It is hard to see what the point of his peculiar means of evaluating Aristophôn's credentials could be otherwise, for he can't be serious when he invites Thalês to face Aristophôn after dark when he practises his skill at robbing people of their clothes. And, if a metic's choice of patron was thought to reveal the metic's own character (see 10–15n.), Battaros' joke has dangerous consequences for his case. When he attempts in standard rhetorical mode (see 16–20n.) to anticipate Thalês' potential claim that he has benefited Kos by his import of wheat (itself a theme of oratory), his counter-claim that he has been an equal benefactor in supplying the island with whores is comically ridiculous, and his insistence that he is under no more obligation to offer his merchandise for free than Thalês reveals his comically greedy motives (16–20). The incongruity of Battaros' appeal to the grand style of oratory and the seedy reality of his character is made evident through his own words.

Nor do matters improve much when the brothel-keeper makes his build-up to the absurd claim that Koan civic safety and autonomy depend on whether Thalês is brought to book (21–7). Battaros' repetitiveness is displayed as he insists that he and Thalês are equal before the law and simultaneously uses the opportunity to make his exaggerated estimates of Thalês' cloak and the poverty of his own clothing. His complaint that Thalês committed the alleged crime at night is equally perverse, since his own hours of maximal business dictated when Thalês might have visited the brothel. We have already noted the toadying way he puts himself on the same level as the jurors by calling the state 'our city'. All this while Battaros makes his most sustained attempt at the learned periodic prose of Attic oratory (see the analysis at 21–7n.).

In the following section, in which he asserts that he has lived life as a metic among the best sort of Koans in mutual respect, unlike Thalês, he undercuts any claim to a convincing rhetorical style (28–40). There is logical confusion in his attack on Thalês for not respecting him as do the citizens of Kos, who have never done such a thing to him as stage a rowdy serenade at his brothel: in what way is it relevant, for example, for the jurors to know that none of their fellow-citizens have maltreated Battaros, except possibly to feel somehow flattered (see 28–40n.)? His statement that Thalês doesn't know 'from what clay he's been made' seems to be a reference to a myth that Prometheus used different grades of clay when originally making humans (see 29n.), and it may well have been yet another piece of folk-wisdom. Exaggeration is evident in his claim to live 'in trembling awe' of the lowliest Koan citizen, and in his overstatement of Thalês' 'crime' (34–7). His aspersions on Thalês' origins and name are perfectly consonant with rhetorical practice (see 37–8n.), even if the claim that Thalês was a Phrygian is a little hackneyed. In fact, this is the one bit of rhetorical claptrap in which the brothel-keeper seems completely at home.

The tension between the orators' standard motifs and Battaros' banalisation of them is present throughout the reading of the pertinent law and the command to stop the clepsydra (41–54), for Battaros offsets his allusions to oratory by his rude familiarity with the clepsydra-official, and by his crude joke. But adding to his characterization is the way he perversely broadens out the case for physical assault, for which the clerk reads out the law, from damage to property, back to assault, to arson and trespassing, all the time precisely detailing the value of the fines to which he sees himself entitled (50–4). Moreover, his claim of impartiality, that it wasn't he but Chairôndas who wrote the law, is contradicted by his tailor-made list of the other grievances. His charge that Thalês, unlike Chairôndas, is shiftless and will go to the seediest cities if the right money is involved (55–9) is self-evidently hypocritical. The time-honoured orators' promise to keep the speech short (60–5) is reduced to bathos by the proverb about the mouse in the tar, and his claim that his door was knocked down and its lintel scorched contradicts his earlier report of the damage. Producing Myrtalê as an exhibit may have had a famous precedent in oratory (see 65b–71n.), but the argument that her state of depilation must be ascribed to Thalês and his gaffe over Myrtalê's relationship to the jurors are nothing less than masterpieces of comic inappropriateness.

We have seen how inconsistent Battaros is over his physical strength (71–8), but there is the further hypocritical inconsistency that he is so brazenly advertising his own shameful means of employment after repeatedly decrying Thalês' profession and origins. And all this is underlined by the inevitable quotation of a proverb, this time the one about the long-haired Samian boxer. His offer of his own body for torture is motivated principally by the hope of financial gain, and is a perversion of actual judicial practice (see 87n.), but this doesn't stop Battaros from solemnly invoking the authority of Minôs. Indeed, when he asks the jury to judge the case 'with just (literally 'straight') judgment' (ὀρθῆι / γνώμηι), he echoes the phraseology of the dikasts' actual oath to judge 'with most just judgment' (see 86n.). The solemn tone thus established is shattered immediately, when Battaros closes his speech with the proverb about a Phrygian being the better for a beating, and attributes the piece of folk-wisdom to the hoary authority of 'men of old'. The bathos resonates down the centuries.

## 3. ΔΙΔΑΣΚΑΛΟΣ

(*ΜΗΤΡΟΤΙΜΗ*) οὕτω τί σοι δοίησαν αἱ φίλαι Μοῦσαι,
Λαμπρίσκε, τερπνὸν τῆς ζοῆς τ' ἐπαυρέσθαι,
τοῦτον κατ' ὤμου δεῖρον, ἄχρις ἡ ψυχή
αὐτοῦ ἐπὶ χειλέων μοῦνον ἡ κακὴ λειφθῇ.
ἔκ μευ ταλαίνης τὴν στέγην πεπόρθηκεν
χαλκίνδα παίζων· καὶ γὰρ οὐδ' ἀπαρκεῦσιν
αἱ ἀστραγάλαι, Λαμπρίσκε, συμφορῆς δ' ἤδη
ὁρμᾷ ἐπὶ μέζον. κοῦ μὲν ἡ θύρη κεῖται
τοῦ γραμματιστέω – καὶ τριηκὰς ἡ πικρή
τὸν μισθὸν αἰτεῖ κἢν τὰ Ναννάκου κλαύσω –
οὐκ ἂν ταχέως λήξειε· τήν γε μὴν παίστρην,
ὅκουπερ οἰκίζουσιν οἵ τ' προύνεικοι
χοἱ δρηπέται, σάφ' οἶδε χἠτέρῳ δεῖξαι.
χἠ μὲν τάλαινα δέλτος, ἣν ἐγὼ κάμνω
κηροῦσ' ἑκάστου μηνός, ὀρφανὴ κεῖται
πρὸ τῆς χαμεύνης τοῦ ἐπὶ τοῖχον ἑρμῖνος,
ἢν μήκοτ' αὐτὴν οἷον Ἀΐδην βλέψας
γράψῃ μὲν οὐδὲν καλόν, ἐκ δ' ὅλην ξύσῃ·
αἱ δορκαλῖδες δὲ λιπαρώτεραι πολλόν
ἐν τῇσι φύσῃς τοῖς τε δικτύοις κεῖνται
τῆς ληκύθου ἡμέων τῇ ἐπὶ παντὶ χρώμεσθα.
ἐπίσταται δ' οὐδ' ἄλφα συλλαβὴν γνῶναι,
ἢν μή τις αὐτῷ ταὐτὰ πεντάκις βώσῃ.
τριθημέρᾳ Μάρωνα γραμματίζοντος
τοῦ πατρὸς αὐτῷ, τὸν Μάρων' ἐποίησεν
οὗτος Σίμων' ὁ χρηστός· ὥστ' ἔγωγ' εἶπα
ἄνουν ἐμαυτήν, ἥτις οὐκ ὄνους βόσκειν
αὐτὸν διδάσκω, γραμμάτων δὲ παιδείην,
δοκεῦσ' ἀρωγὸν τῆς ἀωρίης ἕξειν.
ἐπεὰν δὲ δὴ καὶ ῥῆσιν οἷα παιδίσκον

## 3. THE TEACHER

(*Mêtrotimê*) As I hope the dear Muses may grant you pleasure,
Lampriskos, and the enjoyment of your life,
flay this boy over his shoulders until his soul
is only just left hanging on his lips, the evil thing.
He has utterly ruined my house, poor me,
by playing spin-the-coin. Knucklebones aren't anywhere enough for him,
Lampriskos, but now things are heading
for some greater disaster. Where the door
of the primary teacher is to be found – and the awful end of the month
is demanding his fees even if I weep the tears of Nannakos –
he'd have difficulty in telling. As for the casino,
where the ruffians
and the runaways hang out, he knows it well enough to show to anybody.
His poor wax writing-tablet, which I wear myself out
waxing every month, lies neglected
in front of his bedpost nearest the wall,
except for when he looks at it as if it were Hades,
writes rubbish on it, and then scrapes it all clean.
Meanwhile, his dice lie much shinier
in their pouches and nets
than the oil-flask we're always using.
He can't even recognise the letter *alpha*
unless you shout the same thing at him five times.
The day before yesterday when his father was teaching him to spell *Marôn*,
this fine boy made Marôn
*Simôn*, so that I thought
I was mad for not teaching him
how to feed asses rather than reading and writing,
kidding myself I'd have some support for my old age.
What's more, whenever – as one does with a lad –

ἢ ’γώ μιν εἰπεῖν ἢ ὁ πατὴρ ἀνώγωμεν,
γέρων ἀνὴρ ὠσίν τε κὤμμασιν κάμνων,
ἐνταῦθ’ ὅκως νιν ἐκ τετρημένης ἠθεῖ
‘Ἄπολλον … Ἀγρεῦ …’. ‘τοῦτο’ φημὶ ‘χἠ μάμμη,
τάλης, ἐρεῖ σοι – κἠστὶ γραμμάτων χήρη –
χὠ προστυχὼν Φρύξ.’ ἢν δὲ δή τι καὶ μέζον
γρῦξαι θέλωμεν, ἢ τριταῖος οὐκ οἶδεν
τῆς οἰκίης τὸν οὐδόν, ἀλλὰ τὴν μάμμην,
γρηῢν γυναῖκα κὠρφανὴν βίου, κεῖρει,
ἢ τοῦ τέγευς ὕπερθε τὰ σκέλεα τείνας
κάθηθ’ ὅκως τις καλλίης κάτω κύπτων.
τί μευ δοκεῖς τὰ σπλάγχνα τῆς κακῆς πάσχειν
ἐπεὰν ἴδωμι; κοὐ τόσος λόγος τοῦδε·
ἀλλ’ ὁ κέραμος πᾶς ὥσπερ ἴτρια θλῆται,
κἠπὴν ὁ χειμὼν ἐγγὺς ᾖ, τρί’ ἥμαιθα
κλαίουσ’ ἑκάστου τοῦ πλατύσματος τίνω·
ἓν γὰρ στόμ’ ἐστὶ τῆς συνοικίης πάσης,
‘τοῦ Μητροτίμης ἔργα Κοττάλου ταῦτα’,
κἀληθίν’ ὥστε μηδ’ ὀδόντα κινῆσαι.
ὅρη δ’ ὁκοίως τὴν ῥάκιν λελέπρηκε
πᾶσαν, καθ’ ὕλην, οἷα Δήλιος κυρτεύς
ἐν τῇ θαλάσσῃ, τὠμβλὺ τῆς ζοῆς τρίβων.
τὰς ἑβδόμας δ’ ἄμεινον εἰκάδας τ’ οἶδε
τῶν ἀστροδιφέων, κοὐδ’ ὕπνος νιν αἱρεῖται
νοεῦνθ’ ὅτ’ ἦμος παιγνίην ἀγινῆτε.
ἀλλ’ εἴ τί σοι, Λαμπρίσκε, καὶ βίου πρῆξιν
ἐσθλὴν τελοῖεν αἵδε κἀγαθῶν κύρσαις,
μὴ λασσον αὐτῷ –
(ΛΑΜΠΡΙΣΚΟΣ) Μητροτίμη, μὴ ἐπεύχεο·
ἕξει γὰρ οὐδὲν μεῖον. Εὐθίης κοῦ μοι,
κοῦ Κόκκαλος, κοῦ Φίλλος; οὐ τάχεως τοῦτον
ἀρεῖτ’ ἐπ’ ὤμου τῇ Ἀκέσεω σεληναίῃ
δείξοντες; αἰνέω τἄργα, Κότταλ’, ἃ πρήσσεις·
οὔ σοι ἔτ’ ἀπαρκεῖ τῇσι δορκάσιν παίζειν
ἀστράβδ’ ὅκωσπερ οἵδε, πρὸς δὲ τὴν παίστρην
ἐν τοῖσι προυνείκοισι χαλκίζεις φοιτέων;
ἐγώ σε θήσω κοσμιώτερον κούρης
κινεῦντα μηδὲ κάρφος, εἰ τό γ’ ἥδιστον.

either I or his father ask him to recite a speech,
him an old man with his ear and eye troubles,
then he then lets it dribble out like water from a hole in a cup
'Apollo ... Hunter...' 'This', I say, 'even your grandma,
you wretch, can recite to you – and she's illiterate –,
and any old Phrygian.' What's more, if we decide
to grumble any more loudly, either he doesn't want to know
the doorstep of his own home for three days, and fleeces his grandma,
an old woman with absolutely no means,
or he stretches his legs on the roof
and sits there bending down like a monkey.
How do you think my heart suffers because of his wickedness
when I see it? And I'm not so concerned with him:
all the tiling is shattered like wafers
and when winter's near, I weep
as I pay three half obols for each tile,
for the whole block of flats is of one accord:
'This is the work of Kottalos, Mêtrotimê's son',
and they're right, so we can't loosen even a tooth [on food].
Look at how his back is all peeled with sunburn,
dragging out his boring, aimless life in the woods
like a Delian cray-fisherman on the sea.
He knows the school-holidays on the seventh and twentieth better
than the astronomers, and he can't even sleep
while he's thinking of when you're on holiday.
But if these Muses here are to grant you any fine success in life
and you are to meet with blessings,
don't give him any less –
(*Lampriskos*) Metrotimê, stop asking,
for he'll get nothing less. Where's Euthiês?
Where's Kokkalos? Where's Phillos? Quickly
lift this boy on your shoulders to reveal him to the moon of Akesês.
I admire your achievements, Kottalos.
Isn't it enough for you any more to play with knucklebones
with lightning reactions like these boys, but you go to the casino
and play spin-the-coin among the ruffians?
I'll make you better behaved than a girl,
you won't harm a fly, if that's what you'd really like.

κοῦ μοι τὸ δριμὺ σκῦτος, ἡ βοὸς κέρκος,
ᾧ τοὺς πεδήτας κἀποτάκτους λωβεῦμαι;
δότω τις εἰς τὴν χεῖρα πρὶν χολῇ βῆξαι.
(ΚΟΤΤΑΛΟΣ) μή μ' ἱκετεύω, Λαμπρίσκε, πρός σε τῶν Μουσέων
καὶ τοῦ γενείου τῆς τε Κόττιδος ψυχῆς,
μὴ τῷ με δριμεῖ, τῷ 'τέρῳ δὲ λώβησαι.
⟨ΛΑ.⟩ ἀλλ' εἰς πονηρός, Κότταλ', ὥστε καὶ περνάς
οὐδείς σ' ἐπαινέσειεν, οὐδ' ὅκου χώρης
οἱ μῦς ὁμοίως τὸν σίδηρον τρώγουσιν.
(ΚΟ.) κόσας, κόσας, Λαμπρίσκε, λίσσομαι, μέλλεις
ἔς μευ φορῆσαι;
⟨ΛΑ.⟩ μὴ 'μέ, τήνδε δ' εἰρώτα.
⟨ΚΟ.⟩ ταταῖ, κόσας μοι δώσετ';
⟨ΜΗ.⟩ εἴ τί σοι ζῴην,
φέρειν ὅσας ἄν ἡ κακὴ σθένῃ βύρσα.
⟨ΚΟ.⟩ παῦσαι· ἱκαναί, Λαμπρίσκε.
(ΛΑ.) καὶ σὺ δὴ παῦσαι
κακ' ἔργα πρήσσων.
⟨ΚΟ.⟩ οὐκέτ', οὐχί [τι] πρήξω,
ὄμνυμί σοι, Λαμπρίσκε, τὰς φίλας Μούσας.
(ΛΑ.) ὅσσην δὲ καὶ τὴν γλάσσαν, οὗτος, ἔσχηκας·
πρός σοι βαλέω τὸν μῦν τάχ' ἢν πλέω γρύξῃς.
(ΚΟ.) ἰδού, σιώπω· μή με, λίσσομαι, κτείνῃς.
(ΛΑ.) μέθεσθε, Κόκκαλ', αὐτόν.
(ΜΗ.) οὐ δεῖ σ' ἐκλῆξαι,
Λαμπρίσκε· δεῖρον ἄχρις ἥλιος δύσῃ.
(ΛΑ.) ἀλλ' ἐστὶν ὕδρης ποικιλώτερος πολλῷ.
⟨ΜΗ.⟩ καὶ δεῖ λαβεῖν νιν κἀπὶ βυβλίῳ δήκου,
τὸ μηδέν, ἄλλας εἴκοσίν γε, καὶ ἢν μέλλῃ
αὐτῆς ἄμεινον τῆς Κλεοῦς ἀναγνῶναι.
⟨ΚΟ.⟩ ἰσσαῖ.
⟨ΛΑ.⟩ λάθοις τὴν γλάσσαν ἐς μέλι πλύνας.
⟨ΜΗ.⟩ ἐρέω ἐπιμηθέως τῷ γέροντι, Λαμπρίσκε,
ἐλθοῦσ' ἐς οἶκον ταῦτα, καὶ πέδας ἥξω
φέρουσ' ὅκως νιν σύμποδ' ὧδε πηδεῦντα
αἱ πότνιαι βλέπωσιν ἃς ἐμίσησεν.

82 ουκετουχι P τι suppl. Kenyon (1891) 23

Where's that scorcher of a strap of mine, the bull's tail,
the one with which I thrash the boys I've put in fetters and separated off.
Someone put it in my hand before I cough with bile.
(*Kottalos*) Lampriskos, don't, I beg you by the Muses
and by your beard and your dear little Kottalos' life,
Not the scorcher! Beat me with the other one.
<*La.*> But you're wicked, Kottalos, so that
no one would praise you even if he were selling [you] in the slave-market,
not even in places where mice eat iron like [any other food].
(*Ko.*) How many, how many, please Lampriskos, are you going
to land on my …?
<*La.*> Don't ask me, ask your mother here.
<*Ko.*> Ouch, how many will you give me?
<*Mê.*> As I hope to live dear to you,
as many as your wicked hide can stand.
<*Ko.*> Stop, that's enough, Lampriskos.
(*La.*) And you can stop
your wicked behaviour.
<*Ko.*> I won't do anything naughty any longer,
I swear to you by the precious Muses, Lampriskos.
(*La.*) What a big tongue you've grown, too, you rascal.
I'll soon put the gag on you if you keep complaining.
(*Ko.*) Look, I'm quiet! Please don't kill me.
(*La.*) Let him go, Kokkalos.
(*Mê.*) You mustn't stop,
Lampriskos. Flay him till the sun sets.
(*La.*) But he's much more black and blue than a water-snake.
<*Mê.*> – And, even if he's into his books, he ought to get
at least another twenty – the absolute wretch! –, even if he's going
to read better than Kleô herself.
<*Ko.*> Hooray!
<*La.*> I hope your tongue gets washed in honey, even if you don't notice it.
<*Mê.*> On second thoughts, Lampriskos, I'm going to go home
and tell the old man all this, and I'll bring fetters
so that the Lady Muses whom he has hated
will see him hopping to school here with his feet tied together.

## COMMENTARY

Synopsis The scene is the classroom of a primary teacher (see below, 9n.) named Lampriskos, to whom a desperate mother, Mêtrotimê, complains about the unruliness of her son, Kottalos, who is in Lampriskos' charge. Mêtrotimê implores the teacher to give Kottalos a sound beating for his gambling, keeping bad company, neglect of his reading and writing, his sponging off his grandmother when his parents try to bring him in line, his retreat to the roof in the same circumstances, his subsequent damage to the roof-tiles which gets Mêtrotimê into trouble with her tenement neighbours, and his eternal dreaming of the holidays (1–58a). Lampriskos interrupts the harangue by ordering three boys to hold Kottalos on their shoulders while he administers the flogging with one of his favourite straps, Kottalos pleading for mercy (58b-86). A promise is extracted from the boy to be better behaved (82–3), and, despite his mother's pleas that the teacher continue the session, Lampriskos orders the other boys to let Kottalos go. Kottalos expresses his delight, possibly with a rude gesture like poking out his tongue, and Mêtrotimê hits on the idea of refining Kottalos' punishment by hobbling him with chains (87–97).

Text The major crux is the distribution of parts at lines 89–92, on which see nn.

Date There is no internal evidence.

Structure The poem divides into two parts. The first is Mêtrotimê's monologue (1–58a), which starts and ends with appeals to Lampriskos (1–4, 56–58a) and with appeals in the name of the Muses (1, 57). These appeals flank Mêtrotimê's description of Kottalos' true preoccupations (5–13, 53–5). The central section (14–52) contains Mêtrotimê's description of the boy's rebellious antics. The speech is therefore a ring-composition. The second part portrays Kottalos' beating, and is itself divided into two parts, Lampriskos' reply (58b–70) and the actual beating (71–93). The whole poem begins and ends with the references to the Muses of the schoolroom, Mêtrotimê first calling them 'dear' (1), and then saying that Kottalos 'has hated' them (97), while the last words of her monologue appeal to the Muses as Lampriskos' special deities (57). The framing-patterns give the poem a sense of authorial control and objectivity which contrasts with the violent emotion and action depicted.

Setting The schoolroom of Lampriskos, decorated as usually in schoolrooms with statues of the Muses (1, 57, 97). We must imagine the presence of a desk for Lampriskos and seats for the boys. There is no direct evidence for the location of the school, but scholars have proposed Kos on the very slight grounds that the names Nannakos (10) and Marôn (24, 25) are attested on the island (Fraser and Matthews [1987] 299, 323); it is argued that, although Nannakos here refers to a proverbial king, he was a king of Phrygia, and the actual name was originally from Asia Minor, with which Kos had connections (Sherwin-White [1978] 245–9). See also 59–60n.

Sources The flogger-schoolmaster seems to have been a comic type. The first appearance of the type may have been as early as Epicharmos' play *Agrôstînos* (*Fr.* 1 Kassel-Austin [2001] 1 17), in which a teacher named Kolaphos ('Flogger') appeared. In Aristophanes' *Clouds* 972 we have the Just Argument mentioning the beatings inflicted in the schools of the Marathon generation. The presence of the type in New Comedy may be inferred from Plautus' *The Two Bacchises* 432–4. From Herodas' own time, the epigrammatist Phanias 2 GP (= *AP* 6.294) describes the dedication of a schoolmaster named Kallôn on his retirement: Kallôn dedicates to Hermes among other things the staff he used to beat his charges about their temples, and the flogging strap and the cane he kept by his side in the classroom. And of course there is *Orbilius plagosus*, 'Orbilius the Flogger', immortalised by Horace at *Letters* 2.1.70–1. The type also figures in art. We have the famous fresco from Pompeii which depicts a thrashing, one boy holding the victim over his shoulders and another holding his legs down while the teacher administers the punishment, a picture which corresponds with lines 60–1 of our poem. In life, the profession of the *grammatistês*, the 'primary teacher', was generally regarded as one of the lowest of the low: Marrou (1956) 145–7.

The name Μητρότιμος occurs in Hippônax (*Fr.* 193 Degani [1991] 167), and may have influenced Herodas' choice of the otherwise unattested name Mêtrotimê for his poem's protagonist. The irony inherent in the name, 'honoured in motherhood', may also have been a factor. Her loquacity puts her in the type of the garrulous women of New Comedy, as in Alexis' *Thrasôn* (*Fr.* 96 Kassel-Austin [1991] 2 71), or Plautus' *Casina* 498 and *Rope* 905.

Purpose The principal purpose of the piece is the characterization of Mêtrotimê, who is at her wits' end with frustration and disappointment over her son's underperformance at school when she has set high hopes on his success.

Despite the title, which merely indicates the context, the characterization of Lampriskos is a secondary aim, though it is by no means superficial.

**1–4.** Mêtrotimê begs Lampriskos to give her son a thrashing.
**1. as, οὕτω:** 'on this condition', the condition being explained in the imperative δεῖρον in line 3; for the syntax and idiom of the whole command cf. Menandros, *The Arbitrators* 88–90 ... οὕτω τί σοι / ἀγαθὸν γένοιτο ... / ἐμοὶ τὸ παιδίον δός, literally 'on the condition that you gain something good, give me the child.' τι goes with τερπνόν in line 2.
**2. the enjoyment of your life, τῆς ζοῆς τ' ἐπαυρέσθαι:** for the infinitive as the equal of a noun see 2.54n.
**3. over his shoulders, κατ' ὤμου:** 'down on his shoulders'; see Demosthenes 19 (*On the False Legation*) 197 ξαίνει κατὰ νώτου πολλὰς [πληγάς], 'he inflicts many lacerating blows over his shoulders.' Some scholars interpret the phrase as 'hanging from the shoulders of someone else', as in the punishment detailed at 60–1; but κατά + genitive does not have this meaning. A third explanation is worth noting: starting from *Il.* 15.352 and 23.500, where chariot-drivers are said to whip their horses κατωμαδόν, and accepting the scholiasts' explanation of the adverb as 'down from the shoulder', i.e. 'with full swings of their arms', Di Gregorio (1997) 184 revives the old suggestion that that is what is meant here; I would add that at *Il.* 23.431 the weight used in the weight-throwing contest is called δίσκος κατωμάδιος, i.e. '[thrown] from the shoulder', which gives the same sense. In that case, Mêtrotimê would be asking Lampriskos to 'put his shoulder' into the whipping. I hesitantly opt for the first interpretation in my translation, while conceding the attractiveness of the third.
**ἄχρις:** as with other authors, Herodas uses the conjunction with the subjunctive without ἄν; see also e.g. line 88.
**4. on his lips:** Mêtrotimê envisages the soul as a breath, which passes the lips on death. She is therefore asking Lampriskos to beat Kottalos so hard that the boy will only just be able to hang on to his life. This view of the soul is common in Greek culture (and others); see e.g. the amusing deployment of the motif by Meleagros 23.5–6 GP: βαιὸν ἔχω τό γε λειφθέν, Ἔρως, ἐπὶ χείλεσι πνεῦμα· / εἰ δ' ἐθέλεις καὶ τοῦτ', εἰπὲ καὶ ἐκπτύσομαι, 'Scanty is the remaining breath that I have on my lips, Eros, but if you want that as well, tell me and I'll spit it out.' The postponement ('hyperbaton') of ἡ κακή, so far from ἡ ψυχή, is a nice psychological touch: the furious mother adds her qualification as an angry afterthought.
**5–21.** Mêtrotimê comes to the point: Kottalos' passion is for gambling, not school.
**5. has utterly ruined, ἐκ ... πεπόρθηκεν:** to be taken together, in 'tmesis', the 'cutting' of the prefix from the stem of a compound verb, here ἐκπορθεῖν. Here the two components are placed at each end of the line, and this is the maximal distance that Herodas allows; see also *Mim.* 4.18. Cunningham (1971) 104 shows that Herodas is going beyond the practice of the older choliamb poets like Hippônax in his use of

tmesis separating preposition and verb by several words and placing the components at the beginning and the end of the verse. He suggests that the intention may have been to heighten the diction. ἐκπορθεῖν is often found in tragedy: see e.g. Sophokles, *Women of Trachis* 1104 and Euripides, *Trojan Women* 95, 142. It means 'ransack', and is here an exaggeration. **μευ ταλαίνης**, an exclamation in an oblique case in a constructed sentence, is also common in tragedy, and in Homer: see e.g. Sophokles, *Elektra* 450, 812 and *Il.* 19.287, with Headlam-Knox (1922) 120 for further examples in the accusative and dative as well, though the nominative is common. **στέγη**, properly 'roof', is frequent in tragedy meaning 'house', as here, by the figure of speech in which a part of a thing is named but the whole is intended ('synekdochê'). Though ἐκπορθεῖν and στέγη also occur in prose, there seems no good reason to deny to the line as a whole the *color tragicus* that Groeneboom (1922) 99 saw in it. The point of the elevated tone is to characterize Mêtrotimê's heightened emotional state (perhaps also hinting at an element of self-dramatization), and to set up a contrast with the unexpectedly banal tone of the next line, with its reference to Kottalos' children's gambling game; the bathos is nicely brought out by the extended instance of tmesis.

**6. playing spin-the-coin, χαλκίνδα παίζων:** this is echoed by χαλκίζεις at line 65. Pollux 9.110–17 Bethe (1931) 2 178, 1–179, 29 has a list of children's games ending in –ίνδα, which is the ending of adverbs denoting exclusively playing *at* a game; see Schwyzer (1939) 1 627. Pollux 9.118 Bethe (1931) 2 179, 32–180, 1 also tells us that χαλκισμός involved spinning a coin and stopping it with the finger so that it remained upright.

**καὶ γάρ:** 'for in fact': Denniston (1954) 108–9; the particle-combination is not found elsewhere in Herodas.

**οὐδέ:** going with and emphasizing ἀστραγάλαι: Denniston (1954) 199; for similar separation of οὐδέ from the word it qualifies in Herodas, see *Mim.* 6.51, 60.

**7. knucklebones, αἱ ἀστραγάλαι:** the feminine form is the old Ionic form of Attic ἀστραγάλοι. Knucklebones was the standard game for boys and girls, and did not involve a stake apart from the bones themselves; see Apollonios of Rhodes, *Argonautika* 3.117–26, where Eros beats Ganymêdês at the game and makes off with his haul.

**7–8. things are heading / for some greater disaster, συμφορῆς δ' ἤδη / ὁρμᾷ ἐπὶ μέζον:** συμφορῆς is a genitive dependent on μέζον, 'to a greater extent of'. The subject of ὁρμᾷ is τὸ πρᾶγμα, which is commonly left unexpressed in this kind of phrase; see e.g. Plato, *Laws* 839c εἰς τοῦτο προβέβηκε νῦν ὥστε …, 'it has now come to this, that …'. ὁρμᾷ ἐπί is a case of 'synekphônêsis' or synizêsis'; see above, p. 9.

**9. the primary teacher, γραμματιστέω:** the γραμματιστής was the first teacher in the the Hellenistic Greek child's education outside the family, and, as his name implies, he taught reading and writing; see Marrou (1956) 142–59. Since this is the area in which Kottalos is so deficient (22–6, 32–4), 'the door of the primary teacher' must refer to Lampriskos.

**end of the month, τριηκάς:** the thirtieth and last day of the month (= Attic ἕνη καὶ νέα, 'the last and the new [moon]', referring to the change of the old for the new moon; see West [1978] 351), when all financial accounts had to be settled, including the payment of the primary schoolteacher: Marrou (1956) 146.

**10. the tears of Nannakos:** Nannakos, who was a legendary king of Phrygia from before the time of Deukalion, asked his people to gather in the temples and weep in order to stop the gods from sending the flood: Zenobios 6.10 Leutsch-Schneidewin (1839) 1 164, 1–8; thus the phrase τὰ Ναννάκου κλαύσομαι was proverbial for useless pleading, and Herodas adapts it to fit his syntax. It seems astonishing that Mêtrotimê should voice her implied criticism in front of him for her having to pay him, even if she makes the complaint indirect by saying that the end of the month 'demands' his payment. Di Gregorio (1997) 176, 190–1 offers the explanation that Mêtrotimê is upset at not getting value for her money given that her son spends so little time in the school and therefore derives no profit from her financial sacrifice, but it is hard to extract this from the text. More likely, perhaps, we are simply to assume that in her exasperation Mêtrotimê has forgotten her place when she adds her parenthesis: she and her family are hardly wealthy, and her resentment over the burden of school-fees seems, naturally enough, to have tumbled out along with her infuriation with Kottalos.

**11. λήξειε:** this, the reading of the papyrus, is the first aorist form of λάσκω, and is unique (LSJ⁹ s.v. λάσκω takes ἔληξα at *Mim.* 8.65 as the sole occurrence of the form, though it is there far more easily derived from λήγω, 'I cease'); the usual form is ἔλακον. The meaning of the verb when used of humans ranges from the original 'scream' to merely 'say', 'utter' (e.g. Euripides, *Iphigeneia among the Taurians* 461), as here. The word has elevated associations, occurring in epic and tragedy; the fact that Aristophanes parodies its use (*Frogs* 97, *Wealth* 39) only proves that it was felt to be high-flown. Mêtrotimê's use of it is therefore likely to be a continuation of the tragic diction of line 5, and with the same bathetic effect: Kottalos couldn't 'utter' where his common-or-garden school is. The verb comes as something unexpected, παρὰ προσδοκίαν.

**γε μήν:** this answers the μέν of line 8; see Denniston (1954) 347–9.

**12. hang out, οἰκίζουσιν:** only here and in Hesychios ο 252 Schmidt (1861) 3 184 in the intransitive sense.

**ruffians, προύνεικοι:** derivation, spelling and accentuation uncertain, but Pollux 7.130–2 Bethe (1931) 2 87, 22–88, 10 informs us that the word denoted porters who carried goods from the agora or the harbour for hire (so also e.g. Hesychios π 4034 Schmidt (1861) 3 396); thereafter, it came to carry connotations of roughness; see Diogenes Laertios 4.6.

**13. to show to anybody, χἠτέρῳ δεῖξαι:** χἠτέρῳ = καὶ ἑτέρῳ; he knows clearly how 'to show the casino also to another person' because he knows the location so well. This use of 'another', more commonly with ἄλλος, is quite idiomatic; see e.g. Xenophon, *Oikonomikos* 12.4 κἂν ἄλλον δήπου δυναίμην διδάξαι ἅπερ αὐτὸς ἐπίσταμαι, 'I would be able to teach another also what I myself know' (also at *Oikonomikos* 15.10, 18.9,

20.24: Headlam-Knox [1922] 127). For οἶδα in the sense 'I know how to' see LSJ[9] s.v. εἴδω B.2; δεῖξαι has as its direct object τὴν παίστρην from line 11.

**14. poor, τάλαινα:** the adjective again has tragic associations; cf. line 5. The wax-board, on which schoolchildren wrote and erased their exercises with a pencil-shaped instrument (sharp at one end, rounded for erasing at the other), is personified. κάμνω + participle also has an elevated tone; see e.g. Homer, *Il.* 1.168. Mêtrotimê's solemnity, lavished on the humble wax-board, again humorously undercuts itself.

**16. bed, χαμεύνης:** a low bed, often associated with poor people. A ἑρμίς or ἑρμίν is a bed-post, and Odysseus uses the word to describe the base of his and Penelope's bed at *Od.* 23. 198. The construction is πρὸ τοῦ ἐπὶ τοῖχον ἑρμῖνος τῆς χαμεύνης.

**17. ἢν μήκοτε:** the equivalent of πλὴν ὅτε. αὐτήν is the object of βλέψας. The scansion of Ἀΐδην is Ionic; for Hades as a traditional object of hatred see e.g. Agamemnon's comment about the god at *Il.* 9.159, βροτοῖσι θεῶν ἔχθιστος ἁπάντων, 'most hated of all the gods to mortals'.

**18. writes ... on it, ... scrapes it clean, γράψῃ ... , ἐκ ... ξύσῃ**: logically, 'writes' should be subordinate to 'rubs out', and γράψας might have appeared instead of γράψῃ ('*having* written something, he rubs it out'), but Herodas uses the more paratactic style of μέν...δέ for greater immediacy and vividness. The suppressed subordination explains why οὐδέν and not μηδέν is used in an if-clause.

**19. dice, δορκαλῖδες:** dice were made from deer-horn (the word usually means 'deer'), and the word, like δορκάδες at line 63, seems to have been a popular abbreviation of δορκάδειοι ἀστράγαλοι, which is found in Theophrastos, *Characters* 5.9.

**shinier, λιπαρώτεραι:** this governs the genitive of comparison τῆς ληκύθου at line 21. Mêtrotimê refers to the proverb λιπαρώτερος ληκυθίου, 'shinier than an oil-flask' (Diogenianos 6.31 Leutsch-Schneidewin [1839] 1 274, 17–18), referring to something brighter even than the most frequently used household utensil.

**20. pouches and nets, φύσῃς ... δικτύοις:** some critics take these words literally, thinking they refer to the bellows and nets of Mêtrotimê's husband, but bellows and nets as implements of a blacksmith and a fisherman can hardly refer to a single profession, and in any case why would Kottalos leave his well-used dice lying around in the midst of his father's tools? Other scholars, like Cunningham (1971) 108, therefore argue that the words refer to containers for the dice, 'leather pouches' because of the similarity to the shape and materials of a bellows, and 'nets' in the sense of the Latin word *reticulum*. Chris Collard points out to me that φύσα can mean 'wineskin' (see LSJ[9] s.v. I 4) and δικτύον 'bottom of a sieve' (see LSJ[9] s.v. 5), and so suggests that Mêtrotimê is referring to kitchen utensils; but, again, why would Kottalos leave his beloved dice in such a place?

**21. always, ἐπὶ παντί:** literally 'on every occasion.'

**22–36a.** Mêtrotimê describes Kottalos' lack of progress in reading and writing.

**22. the letter *alpha*, ἄλφα συλλαβήν:** Dionysios Thrax 16.6–17, 2 Uhlig (1883) says that συλλαβή can be used to mean a single vowel. This militates against the idea (for which see most recently Di Gregorio [1997] 199) that Mêtrotimê uses the wrong grammatical term, characterizing herself as an uneducated person.

**23. βώσῃ:** the contracted form of βοάω, common in Ionic.

**24. τριθημέρᾳ:** the papyrus offers the Attic form here, though at *Mim.* 6.21 the Ionic form τριτημέρῃ (with psilosis) appears.

**teaching him to spell *Marôn*, Μάρωνα γραμματίζοντος:** this is the only attested use of γραμματίζω meaning 'teach to write', but an analogy is provided by the noun γραμματιστής, 'one who teaches how to write'. Though Kottalos' father will have tried to teach Kottalos to write 'Marôn' in the nominative, the proper name is governed by 'teaching him to spell', and therefore appears in the accusative, as standardly in this sort of construction. Greek primary-school children were first taught the names of the letters of the alphabet, then how to write them singly, then single syllables, then single words and phrases, then two-syllable words, then multiple-syllable words, and finally full texts from the classics, which were also recited by heart; see Marrou (1956) 150–3. Ma-rôn and Si-môn are examples of two-syllable words. Marôn was a common name in the Eastern Aegean (including Kos) and Asia Minor (see Fraser and Matthews [1987] 299), and, as Treu (1981) shows, it was frequently used as a name in teaching reading and writing; Kottalos might have been expected to get it right.

**25. his father, τοῦ πατρός:** this seems most naturally to refer to Kottalos' father, Mêtrotimê's husband, but, given what we learn of his old age (line 32) and given that mention is made of Kottalos' grandmother (lines 34, 38), scholars have suggested that Mêtrotimê is referring to *her* father; see e.g. Di Gregorio (1997) 178–9. Herzog (1927) 31–2 argued that lines 5, 9, 29 and 46 show that Mêtrotimê is a widow, but her independent actions can in each case be explained on the grounds of her husband's age and infirmity, as Cunningham (1971) 110 points out.

**26. Simôn, Σίμων':** a name of a throw of dice; see Pollux 7.205 Bethe (1931) 2 108, 17. On hearing a two-syllable name ending in ων, Kottalos' mind turns immediately to one with which he is more familiar. The name of the throw, which is probably a bad one, perhaps derives from the Simôn of Aristophanes, *Clouds* 351, who is called a 'snatcher of public funds', and whose thieving became proverbial.

**this fine boy:** ironic.

**27. how to feed asses:** the base and brutish associations that muleteers had in antiquity are well brought out at Aristophanes, *Women at the Assembly* 491–2.

**28. reading and writing, γραμμάτων παιδείην:** that this phrase means literally 'education in letters of the alphabet' rather than 'book-learning' (Cunningham [1971] 110) is secured by the use of γράμματα at line 35, where the reference is to Kottalos' grandmother's illiteracy, and by the elementary stage of education that Kottalos is at, on which see 30n.

**29. support for my old age, ἀρωγὸν τῆς ἀωρίης:** ἀωρία in the sense of 'old age' is not attested elsewhere, and means 'generally bad times'; however, the specific meaning of 'old age' seems defensible here, given the context of a mother addressing her son and given the universal Greek expectation that children will support parents in their declining years; see e.g. Euripides, *Medea* 1032–3 ἦ μήν ποθ' ἡ δύστηνος εἶχον ἐλπίδας / πολλὰς ἐν ὑμῖν γηροβοσκήσειν τ' ἐμέ, 'Indeed, I once much hoped in you, poor wretch, to support me in my old age.'

**30. δὲ δή:** the combination of particles 'stresses an addition' (Denniston [1954] 259, 460), and recurs at line 36; here the meaning is further emphasized by καί.

**a speech:** for the role of learning poetic texts in the Greek primary education see above, 24n. Amusing attestation of the practice is found in the epigram of Kallimachos, 26 GP, in which the 'yawning' tragic mask of Dionysos, dedicated by a pupil in the hope of progress in learning, has to listen to lines of a speech of Dionysos' from Euripides' *Bakchai* recited by schoolboys.

**as one does with a lad, οἷα παιδίσκον:** supply 'τις ἀνώγει ῥῆσιν εἰπεῖν,' i.e., literally, 'as [one asks] a lad [to recite a speech]'. Children started school at seven years of age; see Marrou (1956) 142–3; hence παιδίσκος here.

**31. ἀνώγωμεν:** an Ionic verb (cf. the form ἄνωγα of other dialects). The first person plural is used to convey concerted action, the singular being more normal after ἢ … ἤ or οὔτε … οὔτε.

**32. κάμνων:** normally with accusative of the part affected, but here with the dative.

**33. ἐκ τετρημένης:** for the ellipse of κύλικος, 'cup', cf. *Mim.* 1.25 with n.

**lets it dribble out, ἠθεῖ:** elsewhere 'strain' or 'filter' a liquid, here used metaphorically.

**34. Apollo ... Hunter:** the speech from which this comes is unknown; it is *Fr.* 197b Kannicht-Snell (1981) 2 70. The epithet is used of Apollo in Aischylos' *Prometheus Unbound*, *Fr.* 200 Radt (1985) 3 318.

**φημί:** the vivid present.

**35. τάλης:** τάλας is the proper Ionic form, and τάλης is therefore a hyperionicism, whereby the ending has been formed by the false analogy with Ionic forms like νεηνίης, but we cannot say whether the error is Herodas' or the scribe's. The vocative seems to be an interjected expletive.

**illiterate, γραμμάτων χήρη:** 'devoid of letters', i.e. of reading and writing.

**36. any old Phrygian, ὁ προστυχὼν Φρύξ:** προστυχών = ὁ τυχών, 'the first x who comes across you'. For Phrygians see *Mim.* 2.37, 100–2nn.

**36b–49.** When Mêtrotimê and her husband apply the pressure on Kottalos, he resorts to destructive and embarrassing behaviour.

**36. δὲ δὴ καί:** in her agitation, Mêtrotimê introduces her next complaint with the same particle construction as at line 30, where see n.

**37. grumble, γρῦξαι:** γρύζω was originally associated with the sound γρῦ, the grunting sound of pigs (γρύλλη, Hesychios γ 942 Schmidt [1858] 1 447), and it is frequent in Aristophanes in this sense; see e.g. *Wealth* 17; cf. the name of Mêtrichê's suitor, Gryllos, at *Mim.* 1.50. But here it has come to mean little more than 'say' (note its usage in this sense at Kallimachos, *Fr.* 194.60 Pfeiffer [1949] 181), at most 'grumble'. Hesychios γ 937 Schmidt (1858) 1 447 glosses γρύζειν with φθέγγεσθαι and λέγειν. An analogous weakening appears in the use of λάσκω at line 11.

**for three days, τριταῖος:** for the predicative adjective used adverbially ('for three days') see Schwyzer (1950) 2 179. The usage is found in Theokritos, *Idylls* 2.4 and 10.12 ἔραμαι σχεδὸν ἐνδεκαταῖος, 'I've been in love for almost eleven days.'

**he doesn't want to know, οὐκ οἶδεν:** literally, 'is unacquainted with', as elsewhere only at [Theokritos], *Id.* 25.27, where reference is made to the gardeners who 'know' (ἴσασι) the boundaries of Augeias' huge property.

**39. an old woman:** corresponding with γέρων ἀνήρ, 'an old man', at line 32; Mêtrotimê emphasizes their old age to make her point that Kottalos is stretching the limits.

**fleeces, κείρει:** literally 'to shear'; here metaphorically meaning the same as the English 'fleece'.

**40. roof, τέγευς:** since Kottalos breaks the tiles of this 'roof', we must picture him on the sloping part of the roof of the house, which was tiled, not on 'the flat roof' (Headlam-Knox [1921] 139) where there were no tiles and people could walk; see Boter (1990), followed by Di Gregorio (1997) 207, both of whom take τὰ σκέλεα τείνας as meaning that Kottalos is sitting astride the top of the roof. For the Ionic contraction in -ευ- see *Mim.* 1.88n.

**41. monkey:** monkeys were kept as household pets; see e.g. Euboulos, *Fr.* 114.4 Kassel-Austin (1986) 5 257–8, Theophrastos, *Characters* 5.9. The pet was considered mischievous (Cicero, *De Divinatione* 1.34.76), and Mêtrotimê may be be implying that Kottalos is not only looking down at her but also making fun of her.

**42. my heart, σπλάγχνα:** literally, 'the inward parts', the seat of anxiety, as also at Aischylos, *Libation Bearers* 413, but any passion can be implied; cf. *Mim.* 1.57 with n. for the association with love. Mêtrotimê's anxiety for Kottalos' welfare seems to be amusingly undercut in the following lines, where she is concerned more for her having to pay for the repairs and for her social embarrassment.

**τῆς κάκης:** causal genitive, as at *Mim.* 4.26.

**43. ἴδωμι:** a form of the subjunctive first person singular common in Homer; see Chantraine (1942–53) 1 461–2. Cf. the third person singular form used by Herodas at *Mim.* 4.63.

**I'm not so concerned with him, κοὐ τόσος λόγος τοῦδε:** λόγος in the sense of 'concern' (LSJ[9] I.4); the verb, which is commonly omitted in this construction, is either γίνεται or ἐστί; τοῦδε implies that Mêtrotimê points at Kottalos, or that we are to imagine her doing so. For the whole sentence cf. Sophokles, *Aias* 264 φρούδου γὰρ ἤδη τοῦ κακοῦ μείων λόγος, 'there is immediately less concern for an evil that is past.'

**44. the tiling, ὁ κέραμος:** the singular is used collectively, as often with expressions for roof tiling; see Aristophanes, *Clouds* 1126–7 …τοῦ τέγους / τὸν κέραμον…

**wafers, ἴτρια:** these were thin biscuits, and therefore easily broken; Athenaios, *Scholars at Dinner* 646d.

**45. when winter's near:** and the roof has to be made watertight.

**three half obols, τρί' ἡμαιθα:** Herodas' contemporary Phoinix of Kolophon (*Fr.*

2.3 Powell [1925] 233) equates an ἡμαιθον with a loaf of bread. It was half an obol, so Mêtrotimê is putting the price of one tile at one and a half obols (= one quarter of a drachma), which seems reasonable for a tile, even if Mêtrotimê has to buy several; see Théodore Reinach's note in Nairn-Laloy (1991) 114.

**46. for each tile, ἑκάστου τοῦ πλατύσματος:** genitive of the thing for which one pays, dependent on τίνω (LSJ[9] I.5); though coming directly after κλαίουσα, the phrase comically suggests that Mêtrotimê laments the tiles one by one. πλάτυσμα is a non-technical term and means anything that is flat; in the sense of 'tile' it is otherwise unattested, and may be a means of characterizing Mêtrotimê as having a limited technical vocabulary.

**47. of one accord, ἓν...στόμα:** literally, 'the entire tenement has one mouth', so, perhaps, 'the talk of the entire tenement'; the more normal idiom for 'with one voice' is ἐξ or ἀπὸ ἑνὸς στόματος with a verb of speaking, as at Aristophanes, *Knights* 670, οἱ δ' ἐξ ἑνὸς στόματος ἅπαντες ἀνέκραγον, 'they all shouted with one voice.'

**48. Mêtrotimê's son:** the matronymic in the place of the usual patronymic can probably be explained on the grounds that Mêtrotimê rules the household, her husband being unable to contribute very much, and the neighbours would see more of her than her husband.

**49. κἀληθινά:** sc. λέγουσιν, 'and they're telling the truth.'

**so we can't even loosen a tooth [on food], ὥστε μηδ' ὀδόντα κινῆσαι:** this difficult phrase has been variously interpreted. Perhaps the most plausible approach is to see in ὀδόντα κινῆσαι a reference to eating, because the phrase is used, notably by Hippônax (*Fr.* 132 Degani [1991] 141–2), of teeth being loosened in their jaws through a blow or old age, and it is possible that one could talk of loosening one's teeth as a slang expression for eating. Alternatively and more straightforwardly, κινῆσαι might have its basic sense, 'to move', and the expression might simply mean 'to use our teeth'. In any case, we would have to understand e.g. ἡμᾶς or τινα(ς) in the accusative and infinitive after ὥστε. μηδέ would then quite naturally mean 'not even a [tooth]', in which case Mêtrotimê is complaining that cleaning up after Kottalos has put such a strain on the family's finances that not even minimal food can be bought. This interpretation is closest to that of Di Gregorio (1997) 211–13 (with lit.).

**50–5.** Kottalos prefers the outdoors to school and study, and his chief intellectual preoccupation is with when the next holiday will come.

**50. back, ῥάκιν:** an otherwise unattested form of ῥάχις; it goes with πᾶσαν, the accusative being one of respect: 'he has become scaly as to his whole back.'

**51. in the woods, καθ' ὕλην:** Kottalos gets overexposed to the sun in the woods just as the fisherman 'on the sea'.

**a Delian cray-fisherman, Δήλιος κυρτεύς:** the κυρτεύς differed from an ordinary fisherman (ἁλιεύς, γριπεύς) in that he fished with a baited pot (κύρτη) rather than e.g. a net. This device became proverbial for people who achieved their ends without effort, because fish got caught in it without any labour on the part of the fisherman (see Zenobios 4.8 Leutsch-Schneidewin [1839] I 86, 4–7), so the κυρτεύς suggests Kottalos' laziness appropriately enough; the life of the ordinary fisherman was considered very laborious (see Theokritos, *Id.* 1. 39–45). It is unclear why the κυρτεύς should be called 'Delian,' though 'a Delian diver' (Δήλιος κολυμβητής) was a proverbial expression for skilled swimmers (Suidas Δ 400 Adler [1931] 2 37, 29–30), and Herodas may be caricaturing Mêtrotimê by making her confuse two proverbs of opposite meaning.

**52. his boring, aimless life, τὠμβλὺ τῆς ζοῆς:** see on *Mim.* 1.67. τρίβω generally has a disparaging connotation; cf. e.g. Sophokles, *Elektra* 602 τλήμων Ὀρέστης δυστυχῆ τρίβει βίον, 'poor Orestês drags on an unhappy life.'

**53. the seventh:** the seventh day of the month was regarded as the day of the birth of Apollo; see Hesiod, *Works and Days* 770–1. Schools were closed on it.

**the twentieth:** this is the collective form, more usual than the ordinal numeral like ἕβδομαι, though the Hesiodic passage just cited has a similar mixture of the two forms of expression. The twentieth of the month was an alternative birthday for Apollo.

**54. astronomers, ἀστροδιφέων:** a unique form for 'astronomer', built with its root in διφάω, 'I seek', on the analogy of e.g. μηχανοδίφης at Aristophanes, *Peace* 790; -έω- is scanned as one syllable, in synizesis. Astronomers would have had a very precise knowledge of the calendar, and Kottalos can outdo them – when it comes to the dates of school-holidays.

**αἱρειται:** the active would be more normal, but the middle is found in similar phrases, like κακά νιν ἕλοιτο μοῖρα, 'may an evil fate take him', at Sophokles, *Oidipous the King* 887. Sleep is supposed to be able to 'all-taming' (πανδαμάτωρ, *Il.* 24.5), hence οὐδέ, 'not even': Kottalos is indeed excited.

**55. when, ὅτ' ἦμος:** this combination of conjunctions is found in Hellenistic epic, at e.g. Apollonios of Rhodes, *Argonautika* 4.267, 452 in the order ἦμος ὅτε; Herodas will have altered the order to fit in with his metre. He seems to use it here as a relative, dependent on νοεῦντα, 'thinking of [the time] when'; the subjunctive ἀγινῆτε (ἀγινέω is an Ionic form of ἄγω) is attested in such relative clauses, as at Aristophanes, *Frogs* 1002 φυλάξεις ἡνίκ' ἂν τὸ πνεῦμα λεῖον καὶ καθεστηκὸς λάβῃς, 'you will look out for when you get a smooth and steady wind.'

**holiday, παιγνίην:** = ἑορτή, 'holiday', as at Aristophanes, *Lysistrata* 700.

**56–8a:** Mêtrotimê seems to have run out of things to say, so she repeats her wish that Lampriskos prosper if he carries out the request she made initially (for the ring-composition see above, p. 78); he seizes the opportunity to stop her harangue.

**56. success, πρῆξιν:** the meaning 'success' is paralleled at Pindar, *Olympian* 1.85 τὺ δὲ πρᾶξιν φίλαν δίδοι, 'grant welcome success.'

**57. τελοῖεν ... κύρσαις:** these optatives, here after a subordinate clause introduced by εἰ, 'if', express a wish in the if-clause, 'if you wish these things to happen'; see Theokritos, *Id.* 15.70, with Gow (1952) 2 284. The construction is paralleled in lines 1–3 above, except that there it is introduced by οὕτω + optative.

**these Muses, αἵδε:** the statues of the Muses in the classroom, as at lines 1, 97; see above, p. 79.

**58. μῆλασσον:** ἔλασσον is more likely to be a neuter accusative rather than an adverb, given Lampriskos' ἕξει in the next line which picks it up. Mêtrotimê would have said something like 'Don't give him less than he deserves', but Lampriskos cuts into her sentence with 'Stop begging me [not to give him less than he deserves], for he'll get nothing less.' Mêtrotimê's μή signals that a negative command is in the offing.

**58b–70:** Lampriskos prepares for the flogging, sarcastically summarizes Kottalos' misdemeanours, and asks for his favourite strap.

**58b. ἐπεύχεο:** a Homeric imperative form; Lampriskos is airing his learning in front of the uneducated Mêtrotimê.

**59–60. Euthiês ... Kokkalos ... Phillos:** Euthiês is a common name, occurring also at *Mim.* 4.24, where a Euthiês is said to have dedicated statues in the Koan Asklêpieion; the latter two are not common, but in the same poem, Kokkalê appears as the name of a free woman (l. 19 etc.; see below, p. 107 for Kokkalê's status). This is possibly a further indication that the present poem has a Koan setting. The boys will be Kottalos' classmates, called in to assist with the beating.

**60–1. lift this boy, οὐ ... ἀρεῖτε:** the negative and future indicative denote an order 'in a forceful and threatening tone, at times with a certain ironical bitterness' (Kühner-Gerth [1955] 1 176–7). The posture that we must visualise is that of Kottalos being held 'over the shoulders' of one of the three other boys, and his legs being held down by a second, as in the famous Herculaneum wall-painting (Baumeister [1888] 1590, fig. 1653); perhaps the third boy was to hold Kottalos' arms. Cf. also Apuleius, *Metamorphoses* 9.28 *uocatis duobus e familia ualidissimis quam altissime sublato puero ferula nates eius obuerberans* ..., 'two of the strongest of the household were summoned and the boy was lifted up as high as possible, while he [the baker], thrashing his buttocks with a rod, ...'

**to the moon of Akesês:** Akesês was the pilot of Nêleus, and was proverbial for waiting for the full moon before setting sail in order to have the best light for the voyage (see e.g. Diogenianos 1.57 Leutsch-Schneidewin [1839] 1 189, 16 – 190, 3); that is, he waited till the moment was ripe. The moment is now ripe for Lampriskos to punish Kottalos, and he has apparently wanted to do so for some time. σεληναίη is a rare form of the usual σελήνη, and Lampriskos may well be characterized as parading his erudition again.

**62. I admire:** the first instance of Lampriskos' mordent sarcasm, found also at lines 65 and 67.

**63–5:** Lampriskos repeats Mêtrotimê's phraseology at lines 6, 11–12. Lampriskos' scolding comes immediately after his instructions to the helpers, so perhaps we are to imagine the boys carrying out his order as he speaks.

**63. knucklebones, δορκάσιν:** see 19n.

**64. with lightning reactions:** the accentuation, derivation and meaning of ἀστράβδα are all in doubt; the least vulnerable derivation is from ἀστράπτειν, 'to flash like lightning' (whence my tentative translation), but the actual meaning is unclear, and the adverb may be a gaming term. For the connotation of quick reactions compare the Latin *micare* [*digitis*], 'to flash with the fingers', referring to the game whereby one player suddenly raised some of the fingers of one hand, and the other had to guess instantly how many fingers were held up.

**65. go, φοιτέων:** again ironical, because the verb φοιτᾶν used absolutely or with ἐς διδασκάλου means 'to go to school'; see LSJ[9] I.5: Kottalos goes to the casino as a boy goes to school.

**66–7.** The κ-alliteration probably emphasizes Lampriskos' controlled sarcasm, which comes out clearly in the phrase at line 6 εἰ τό γ' ἥδιστον, 'if that's what you'd really like'. His show of anger does not appear until line 70.

**67. you won't harm a fly, κινεῦντα μηδὲ κάρφος:** this phrase was proverbial for quiet personalities, and is used at *Mim.* 1.54 in an expanded form; see the n. The phrase is also used by Aristophanes, *Lysistrata* 473–4, a passage with close similarities to the present couplet: ἐπεὶ 'θέλω 'γὼ σωφρόνως ὥσπερ κόρη καθῆσθαι, λυποῦσα μηδέν' ἐνθαδί, κινοῦσα μηδὲ κάρφος, 'since I wish to sit modestly at home like a maiden, not bothering anyone here, stirring not even a twig'. The similarity is probably the result of both poets' deployment of proverbial expressions rather than an actual reminiscence on Herodas' part. **κοσμιώτερον κούρης**, 'better behaved than a girl', draws on the proverbial quietness of a girl, for which see also Xenophon, *The Spartan Constitution* 3.5 αἰδημονεστέρους δ' ἂν αὐτοὺς ἡγήσαιο καὶ αὐτῶν τῶν ἐν τοῖς θαλάμοις παρθένων, 'one would consider them more modest than the very maidens in their bridal chambers', quoted by Headlam (1922) 148 and Cunningham (1971) 119.

**if that's what you'd really like, εἰ τό γ' ἥδιστον:** in this sarcastic expression (of course Kottalos doesn't want to be well behaved!) γε performs the function that it often does in sarcastic exclamations; see Denniston (1954) 128.

**68. scorcher, δριμύ:** the adjective here describes things which produce sharp, piercing feelings, here on the victim's body; cf. *Il.* 11.269–70, where it qualifies the 'arrow' of childbirth as it takes hold of a woman in labour.

**the bull's tail:** Phanias' epigram (2.3 GP) on a retiring schoolmaster includes a κέρκος, 'tail', among the dedications.

**69. separated off, ἀποτάκτους:** 'set apart': Lampriskos puts his recalcitrant charges in fetters in a separate part of the schoolroom where he will deal with them.

**70. I cough with bile, χολῇ βῆξαι:** on this reading (the papyrus does not show the iota adscript, and there have been many conjectures other than merely supplying the iota), a possible interpretation is that Lampriskos' (perhaps feigned) disgust makes his bile rise to his throat and cause him to cough; the dative will in that case be causal. For disgust or anger causing one's bile to rise see the scholiast on Apollonios, *Argonautika* 2.354 Wendel (1935) 156. Cf. Cunningham's (2002) 221 explanation of the phrase: 'He [Lampriskos] fears his shouting may cause bile to accumulate in his lungs and make him ill.' Di Gregorio (1997) 225 also inclines to this view.

**71–87a.** Kottalos desperately tries to get Lampriskos to use a less painful strap and attempts to bargain over the number of strokes he is to receive, Mêtrotimê insisting on the maximum. The punishment begins, and Kottalos immediately promises to mend his ways.

**71. μή με:** on this reading of the papyrus με foreshadows the με in line 73, both being dependent on λώβησαι at the end of line 73. σε is dependent on ἱκετεύω, and is interposed between πρός and τῶν Μουσέων, much as με in line 73 comes between an article and its noun; this idiom is not uncommon in Greek tragedy, conferring solemnity (here mock) on the pronoun; see e.g. Euripides, *Medea* 853–4, *Hekabê* 752, *Alkêstis* 1098; Herodas himself uses it also at *Mim*. 5.12, 19, 7.126.

**72. by your beard:** a supplication was accompanied by the gesture of touching the beard of the person supplicated, as e.g. Thetis does with Zeus at *Il.* 1.501.

**Κόττιδος:** with this accentuation we have a diminutive of the name Kottalos, Κόττις; it is designed to elicit Lampriskos' pity; cf. *Mim*. 2.82, Βατταρίῳ, with n. There is in that case a crescendo in the persons and objects by which Kottalos begs Lampriskos, ending with an appeal by his own life. Others accentuate the name as Κοττίδος from Κοττίς, which is taken to refer to Lampriskos' wife or daughter; this is unlikely, since the woman is otherwise unmentioned, and requires further identification.

**73. μή:** literally, 'not with the scorcher; beat me with the other'. Cunningham (1971) 121 explains this negative as a 'special negative'; this is a standard Greek way of negating one option, and refers to the words immediately following; it does not go with λώβησαι, nor must we understand λωβήσῃ; usually it would be οὐ, but because a command is implied μή is used. The construction is used again at line 78, and in *Mim*. 5.29, 52.

**74. selling, περνάς:** 'selling [you] as a slave', when the seller would normally pile on praise; Kottalos is so bad that not even a slave-trader would praise him if he were on sale.

**75. ἐπαινέσειεν:** a potential without ἄν in a consecutive clause; the particle can be omitted in main sentences, as at *Mim*. 5.76, so, since there is no difference between a potential in a main sentence and a consecutive clause, its omission here is understandable.

**χώρης:** partitive genitive after the adverb of place.

**76.** The motif of a locality so desolate that the mice are forced to eat iron, used especially in reference to the island of Gyaros, is here developed by Lampriskos to add a twist of the knife to the humiliating jibe of the preceding two lines: in such a poor country, I suggest he is saying, a slave-trader would not even praise Kottalos to sell him to the locals, although they would need the all the hype that can be brought to bear to be encouraged to part with their money. Others (starting with Headlam-Knox [1922] 153) take the point to be that in such desolate areas praise of slaves would be cheap.

**like, ὁμοίως:** the meaning 'like [any other food]' (adopted e.g. by LSJ$^9$ s.v. ὅμοιος C.II.2) is not an easy extraction from the Greek word.

**77. how many, how many, κόσας, κόσας:** supply πληγάς, as with κόσας at line 79, ὅσας at line 80 and ἱκαναί at line 81; so also at *Mim*. 5.33–4. For the repetition cf. *Mim*. 4.61.

**78. on my..., ἔς μευ:** supply τὸ νῶτον, as at *Mim.* 5.33. For πληγὰς φορεῖν, in association with εἰς, cf. Polybios 2.33.6 τύπτοντες εἰς τὰ στέρνα καὶ τὰ πρόσωπα καὶ πληγὴν ἐπὶ πληγῇ φέροντες..., 'striking blow after blow on their breasts and faces...'

**μὴ 'μέ, τῆνδε δέ:** see on line 73.

**79. Ouch, ταταῖ:** an expression of pain, found in this form only in Plautus, *Stichus* 771, where *tatae* occurs with other Greek exclamations. The pain will be in anticipation, because the beating does not actually begin until line 81. Some editors read τατᾶ, as if it meant 'Mama'; cf. Gyllis' ταταλίζει at *Mim.* 1.60, used of Gryllos' ingratiating endearments, and *Mim.* 5.69, where Kydilla refers to her mistress Bitinna with the address τατί; but Cunningham (1971) 123 objects that τατᾶ means 'father'.

**ζώῃν:** an optative expressing a wish in a subordinate clause; see 57n. The ethic dative σοι, coming from Mêtrotimê at this juncture, is ironical.

**80. can stand, φέρειν:** taken out of its clause, in 'emphatic hyperbaton'; the infinitive, thus emphasized, gives the implication that Kottalos will be beaten as long as he can put up with it without actually dying.

**81–2:** at line 73 Kottalos had picked up Lampriskos' λωβεῦμαι at line 69 with λώβησαι; now, in response to Kottalos' παῦσαι, Lampriskos commands Kottalos to 'stop' his bad behaviour, and his πρήσσων is picked up by Kottalos' promise not to 'do' anything bad, πρήξω. Through this vivid exchange we see the domineering schoolmaster and the ostentatiously compliant pupil.

**82. I won't do anything naughty any longer, οὐκέτ', οὐχί [τι] πρήξω:** the sentence as reconstructed here consists of two parts: Kottalos means to say firstly that he will 'no longer' do anything, but then seems to think that to be inadequate, and tries to reinforce his assurance, and says 'I won't do anything'; there is therefore no reason to object to the text printed here on the grounds that it breaks the law that a double negation with a compound negative followed by a simple negative betokens affirmation.

**83. by the precious Muses:** here again Kottalos tries to ingratiate himself by picking up a phrase of his superiors, this time Mêtrotimê's wish at line 1 that αἱ φίλαι Μοῦσαι might profit Lampriskos. Mêtrotimê there pretty clearly regards the Muses as 'dear' to Lampriskos, appealing to his pride as an educated man, and Kottalos may be using the same tactic here. It cannot of course be ruled out that he is now saying that the goddesses are dear to *himself*, in which case he would be trying to express his capitulation.

**84. καί:** expressing 'surprise or indignation': Denniston (1954) 316 (iv) and (v), noting e.g. Aristophanes, *Wasps* 900 ὦ μιαρὸς οὗτος· ὡς δὲ καὶ κλέπτον βλέπει, 'The dirty scum! How thievish he looks, too!'

**you rascal, οὗτος:** this form of address is rude, and is used, as here and at *Mim.* 7.66, when one is irritated at someone, or when one is ordering slaves about, as at *Mim.* 4.93.

**γλάσσαν:** this is an Ionic form of γλῶσσα, used also in the papyrus at line 93, and *Mim.* 5.8, 37, 6.16 and 7.77, 110, though at 6.41 we find γλῶσσαν. **οὗτος:** exclamatory nominative. The whole line reappears at *Mim.* 5.8, but the two lines are more likely to be drawing on a common expression than to be a self-citation with no obvious point.

**85. gag, μῦν:** 'mouse', unattested elsewhere in the meaning of a gag, but probably connected with μύω, 'I close'. See also *Mim.* 5.68n.

**87. let him go, μέθεσθε ... αὐτόν:** the middle of μεθίημι normally takes a genitive in the sense of 'get free of', but is assimilated into the role of the active. Kokkalos is one of the boys summoned at line 59–60 to hold Kottalos while he is being beaten. Lampriskos is satisfied that Kottalos has learnt his lesson, and terminates the flogging.

**87b–97.** The distribution of speakers in this passage is one of the most debated in the whole of Herodas. A paragraphos appears before 87, 88 and 89. There also is much in the interpretation of several phrases that is unclear.

**87b–8.** The one-and-a-half lines must belong to Mêtrotimê: she is the one who is relentless in her wish to have Kottalos flogged (80), and Lampriskos has stopped the punishment (87a). The lack of connecting particles in the text printed here is no problem, since the asyndeton can be explained on the grounds of Mêtrotimê's agitation: Denniston (1954) xlv.

**88. sets, δύσῃ:** δύω and its compounds in the first aorist are usually transitive, as in the famous epigram of Kallimachos (34.3 GP) ἠέλιον λέσχῃ κατεδύσαμεν, 'we made the sun set with our conversation', but it appears in an intransitive sense at *Homeric Hymn to Apollo* 443 ἐς ἄδυτον κατέδυσε, 'he entered his shrine'.

**89.** The paragraphos probably gives the line to Lampriskos, who will then be objecting to Mêtrotimê's desire to continue the beating. ποικιλώτερος will in that case mean 'more variegated', i.e. in colour, than a hydra (which is black and white), the English 'black and blue'. This gives natural sense to ἀλλά. Others, e.g. Di Gregorio (1997) 235–7, take the adjective as meaning 'more cunning', and give the whole of lines 89–92 to Lampriskos; but if Lampriskos has already registered satisfaction with the beating, why does he return to the charge here? Moreover, the adversative ἀλλά is difficult to explain. Cunningham (1971) 125 proposes before line 89 a lacuna of a whole line starting with ἀλλά and omitted by haplology; in the missing line, he suggests, Lampriskos expressed his objection, and Mêtrotimê takes over in line 89, ποικιλώτερος meaning 'more cunning.'

**90–2.** Given the speaker's expressed wish for more punishment, these lines are likely to be Mêtrotimê's, though there is no paragraphos. On this reading, καί will connect Mêtrotimê's sentence with what she had said at lines 87b–8, possibly also carrying the sense 'What's more [i.e. over and above a repudiation of Lampriskos' objection] the boy needs another instalment.'

**90. even if he's into his books, κἀπὶ βυβλίῳ δήκου:** a difficult phrase, which Cunningham (1971) 125 perhaps most plausibly takes as 'even over his book ...', i.e. even if he were to feign studiousness; δῆκου will then convey Mêtrotimê's irony over the concept of a studious Kottalos: see Denniston (1954) 267.

**91. the absolute wretch, τὸ μηδέν:** cf. Euripides, *Elektra* 370, with Denniston (1939) 93–4 for the expression; here in apposition with νιν.

**another, ἄλλας:** sc. πληγάς; see line 77n.

**92. Κλεοῦς:** this is the rarer form of Κλειώ, and is found e.g. at Pindar, *Nemean* 3.83; Kleiô is the first Muse mentioned in Hesiod's list of Muses at *Theogony* 77–9, and may have influenced Herodas' choice of her here. She will be one of the statues of the Muses decorating Lampriskos' schoolroom.

**93. Hooray!, ἰσσαῖ:** the lexicographers (e.g. Suidas I 605 Adler [1931] 2 666, 18–19), define the expression ἴσσα, which appears to be a shortened form of ἰσσαῖ, as meaning *Schadenfreude*: if they are referring to Plato the comedian, *Fr.* 68 Kassel-Austin (1989) 7 460, and Menandros, *Fr.* 233 Kassel-Austin (1998) 6.2 161, the word was perhaps especially associated with comedy. The most likely character to be using it in this *Mimiamb* is Kottalos: he would naturally express his delight on triumphing over his mother, who must now, given Lampriskos' refusal to punish him any more, devise her own means of punishing him. The reference to his tongue later in the line moreover makes it quite likely that he sticks it out for good measure.

**I hope your tongue gets washed in honey, λάθοις τὴν γλάσσαν ἐς μέλι πλύνας:** at *Il.* 1.249 Nestor is said to have a voice which flowed more sweetly than honey from his tongue, and Hesiod, *Theogony* 83–4 claims that when the Muses favour a man 'they pour a sweet dew on his tongue, and his words flow sweet from his mouth.' The most likely person to say the words is Lampriskos; as Cunningham (1971) 126 puts it, 'If … K. were to wash his tongue in honey, he would become an orator and a scholar; as he appears unlikely to make any effort in this direction, L. ironically wishes that it may happen without his knowledge.' On this line-attribution, Lampriskos has reverted from his fleeting concern for Kottalos to his old sarcasm.

**94. ἐπιμηθέως:** 'on second thoughts' (cf. the allegorical significance of the names Prometheus, 'Forethought', and Epimetheus, 'Afterthought') because, if she had known that bringing Kottalos to Lampriskos was going to be so unsuccessful, she wouldn't have done so in the first place, and now she must resort to her own devices after all. The translation 'carefully', given by e.g. LSJ[9] s.v. ἐπιμηθής, does not seem to have much point.

**the old man:** the old man, probably Kottalos' father, of lines 31–2.

**96. fetters, σύμποδα:** Strabo 15.1.42 uses σύμπους of tying an elephant's feet together.

**ὧδε:** 'here' rather than 'to this place'; so also at *Mim.* 2.98.

**97. Lady Muses, πότνιαι:** the poem begins and ends with the Muses, whose schoolroom-statues are spoken of as alive.

## DISCUSSION

### *Characters and interaction in* Mimiamb *3*

*Mimiamb* 3 is unique among the poems preserved by the papyrus in that it deals with a family. Though the main aim of the piece is the characterization of Mêtrotimê, her family circumstances are significant for this, and for her attitude to Kottalos (and for his to her).

As we have seen (above, p. 79), Mêtrotimê has affinities with the New Comedy type of the woman chatterbox, and her fifty-seven-and-a-half line monologue, which has to be cut short abruptly by Lampriskos, amply exemplifies it. In fact, however, she is very precisely individualised, far beyond mere typicality. It is pretty clear that Kottalos is the family's only child, and that he is therefore the sole hope for Mêtrotimê's 'superannuation' (26–9). Her bitterness over Kottalos' inattention to his education is therefore well motivated. Moreover, her husband (as the old man at lines 24–5, 31–2 is most likely to be) is apparently next-to useless in helping with family affairs, to the extent that Mêtrotimê's aggrieved neighbours talk of Kottalos as her son rather than using the more usual patronymic (48). She is in effect alone and unsupported in the management of her family. Her frustration is therefore doubly motivated.

Her state of mind is evidenced by the vehemence of her commands that Lampriskos give the boy a sound thrashing, her insistence that the teacher continue the beating after he himself has terminated it (87–92), and her scheme to punish her son by hobbling him with fetters (94–7; see also 1–4, 56–8a, 79–80). Her lack of control over her emotions and sense of proportion is the most natural explanation of her gaffe when she complains about what must be the school-fees due to Lampriskos – as if he were not present (9–10; see 10n.).

Herodas hardly seems to want us to be sympathetic to his heroine because of her difficult situation. True, she makes much of her efforts to further Kottalos' education, for example by complaining that her monthly waxing of the boy's writing-board is a waste of time, but even there her turn of phrase is self-dramatizingly epic (see 14n.; cf. 5n.), and Herodas thereby makes the woman prick her own balloon and us laugh at her. Similarly, when she sees her son on a dangerous part of the tenement-roof, she may indeed express maternal concern (42–3), but immediately states that she is not so worried about him as she is over the expense of replacing the tiles he has broken (43–6; n.b. κλαίουσ', 'weeping', 46), and over the humiliation she is subjected to by her neighbours

(47–9).[1] In fact, Herodas at every turn subverts any reason for our sympathy for a mother under severe stress. He steadfastly presents her in all her ugliness, and his sole aim is the pursuit of a detached, objective version of the humour that we associate with 'slice-of-life' comedy. Although the details of her situation are precisely observed, they are subsidiary to the characterization of Mêtrotimê, and therefore to the potential humour in Herodas' portrayal of her.

Given the pressure Kottalos' family puts on him, it is no wonder that the boy is rebellious, especially since he is the only child, but again Herodas refuses to court any sympathy for him. We know of no literary type to which he belongs: Pheidippides in Aristophanes' *Clouds* is a rebellious son, but at a much later stage of development. His 'model' is probably from everyday life and experience. He is presented to us firstly through his mother's eyes, in the light of all Mêtrotimê's allegations that he taken the housekeeping to service his gambling (5–8), keeps bad company (11–3),[2] neglects his homework (14–26, 30–6), cadges off his grandmother when the going gets tough at home (36–9), or climbs out of reach on the roof where he damages the tiles (40–9), spends too much time out of doors (when he should be diligently studying indoors), and can only think of when the next holidays occur (53–5). Coming from Mêtrotimê's perspective, the negative picture that emerges of Kottalos might be considered exaggerated. But, when Kottalos speaks in his own person, he directly shows himself to be a thoroughly objectionable boy indeed. He makes appeals to Lampriskos for leniency, attempting to ingratiate himself among other things by formal supplication and appeal to the Muses (71), and promises to mend his ways, again in the name of the Muses (87–8), but undercuts all this show of pitiful compliance and repentance by his spitefully triumphant cry ἰσσαῖ (93), in all likelihood accompanied by the gesture of poking out his tongue, when he has secured a cessation of punishment (see 93n.). This exclamation shows his true moral ugliness, which may be motivated by parental pressure (or lack of it in the case of his father-figure), but is not mitigated by consideration of it. Herodas' strategy is the same as with Mêtrotimê: environmental circumstances may motivate human ugliness, but they are not meant to help us condone it. We are meant to remain objective and laugh at the boy's unruly behaviour as indirectly detailed by his mother, and to laugh – with equal objectivity – at his direct display of sneakiness and final jubilation when he has seen that he has foiled his mother's designs. And laughter over him is in the service of Mêtrotimê's comic discomfiture. Part of the humour is conditioned, in other words, by the feeling that mother and son deserve one another.

The figure of Lampriskos performs much the same role in throwing Mêtrotimê's character into sharper relief. We have seen that he belongs to a comic type, but, as the dedicatory epigram by Phanias shows, the type was one perceived in ordinary life as well (see above, p. 79). He shows touches of the superior erudition stereotypically ascribed to schoolteachers in his recourse to Homeric and other elevated diction (see 58b, 61, 93 with nn.), and the sarcasm similarly associated (see 62, 66–7, 74–6 with nn., 93 with n.). He enjoys his moment as he quotes Mêtrotimê's report of Kottalos' gambling (63–5) in his build-up to the punishment. He shows a schoolmasterly tendency to quote his victim against himself at lines 81–2, when he picks up the boy's 'Stop!' with 'And you can stop your wicked behaviour.' Yet for all these more or less unpleasant characteristics, which are as usual designed to create a comic effect, Lampriskos has a sense of fair play, and stops the beating when he thinks it appropriate (87), and, at least on the part-distribution offered here, actually defends Kottalos from Mêtrotimê's demands for further punishment (89, on which see n.).[3] Although Lampriskos has his ugly side, then, his ultimate fairness over Kottalos' punishment has the effect of making Mêtrotimê even more ugly in her obsessiveness. So both the other speaking parts contribute to the comic characterization of the poem's main character.

*Mimiamb* 3 has much to teach us about Herodas' aims generally. We have seen that he presents circumstances in the lives of his characters which help us understand their motives and motivation, and does so quite incisively and observantly, but that this detail is presented with notable objectivity, and is subservient to humour, however edgy this type of humour might seem to modern taste. A modern playwright would almost be expected to field such information as gaining his audience's understanding and sympathy. He would bring out, perhaps, the appalling circumstances against which Mêtrotimê is struggling, and guide us to see the tragic element in her plight. Kottalos would be presented as a child rebelling against impossible parental expectations, and his wickedness would be subject to mitigating circumstances. Lampriskos would become a rallying ground for radical improvement of the education system. We must not expect this sentiment from Herodas, however much his approach goes against modern sensitivities, nor must we blame him for the fact.

## Notes

1. Di Gregorio (1997) 179–80 paints a more sympathetic picture of Mêtrotimê, arguing e.g. that here she is trying to hide her mother's love.
2. This kind of thinking is common in Euripides: for instance, he makes Orestes attest to 'relations in social intercourse' as one of the true guides to character at *Elektra* 383–5; see further Fraenkel (1950) 385–6 on *Agamemnon* 838–40.
3. Di Gregorio (1997) 176 speaks of 'a certain compassion'.

## 4. ΑΣΚΛΗΠΙΩΙ ΑΝΑΤΙΘΕΙΣΑΙ ΚΑΙ ΘΥΣΙΑΖΟΥΣΑΙ

*(ΚΥΝΝΩ)* χαίροις, ἄναξ Παίηον, ὃς μέδεις Τρίκκης
καὶ Κῶν γλυκεῖαν κἠπίδαυρον ᾤκηκας
σὺν καὶ Κορωνὶς ἥ σ' ἔτικτε κὠπόλλων
χαίροιεν, ἧς τε χειρὶ δεξιῇ ψαύεις
Ὑγίεια, χὤνπερ οἵδε τίμιοι βωμοί,
Πανάκη τε κἠπιώ τε κἰησὼ χαίροι,
χοἰ Λεωμέδοντος οἰκίην τε καὶ τείχεα
πέρσαντες, ἰητῆρες ἀγρίων νούσων
Ποδαλείριός τε καὶ Μαχάων χαίροντων,
χὤσοι θεοὶ σὴν ἑστίην κατοικεῦσιν
καὶ θεαί, πάτερ Παίηον· ἵλεῳ δεῦτε
τὠλέκτορος τοῦδ', ὅντιν' οἰκίης τοίχων
κήρυκα θύω, τἀπίδορπα δέξαισθε.
οὐ γάρ τι πολλὴν οὐδ' ἕτοιμον ἀντλεῦμεν,
ἐπεὶ τάχ' ἂν βοῦν ἢ νενημένην χοῖρον
πολλῆς φορίνης, κοὐκ ἀλέκτορ', ἴητρα
νούσων ἐποιεύμεσθα τὰς ἀπέψησας
ἐπ' ἠπίας σὺ χεῖρας, ὦ ἄναξ, τείνας.
ἐκ δεξιῆς τὸν πίνακα, Κοκκάλη, στῆσον
τῆς Ὑγιείης.
*<ΚΟΚΚΑΛΗ>* ἆ, καλῶν, φίλη Κυννοῖ,
ἀγαλμάτων· τίς ἦρα τὴν λίθον ταύτην
τέκτων ἐποίει καὶ τίς ἐστιν ὁ στήσας;
*<ΚΥ.>* οἱ Πρηξιτέλεω παῖδες· οὐχ ὁρῇς κεῖνα
ἐν τῇ βάσι γραμματ'; Εὐθίης δ' αὐτήν
ἔστησεν ὁ Πρήξωνος.
*<ΚΟ.>* ἵλεως εἴη
καὶ τοῖσδ' ὁ Παιὼν καὶ Εὐθίῃ καλῶν ἔργων.
*<ΚΥ.>* ὅρη, φίλη, τὴν παῖδα τὴν ἄνω κείνην
βλέπουσαν ἐς τὸ μῆλον· οὐκ ἐρεῖς αὐτήν
ἢν μὴ λάβῃ τὸ μῆλον ἐκ τάχα ψύξειν;
*<ΚΟ.>* κεῖνον δέ, Κυννοῖ, τὸν γέροντ' – ἆ πρὸς Μοιρέων
τὴν χηναλώπεχ' ὡς τὸ παιδίον πνίγει.

## 4. WOMEN OFFERING A DEDICATION AND A SACRIFICE TO ASKLÊPIOS

(*Kynnô*) Hail, Lord Paiêôn, who rule over Trikka
and have made your dwelling in sweet Kos and Epidauros,
and hail also to Korônis who bore you, and to Apollo, and to Hygieia
whom you touch with your right hand,
and hail to those who own these honoured shrines,
Panakê, Êpiô and Îêsô,
and greetings to those who destroyed the house and walls of Leômedôn,
healers of savage diseases,
Podaleirios and Machaôn,
and as many other gods and goddesses who inhabit your hearth,
Father Paiêôn. Come here and graciously
accept this cockerel, the herald of my house's walls which I sacrifice, for seconds.
For we don't draw water from a well that's at all abundant or ready,
since we might perhaps have been offering an ox or a sow
heaped with lots of crackling, not a cockerel, as offerings
for our cure from sicknesses which you have wiped away,
Lord, as you stretched forth your gentle hands.
Kokkalê, put the tablet down
on Hygieia's right. <*Kokkalê.*> Oh, what beautiful statues, Kynnô dear!
So who was the sculptor who made this marble statue
and who dedicated it?
<*Ky.*> The sons of Praxitelês; can't you see
that writing on the base? And Euthiês,
the son of Prêxôn, dedicated it. <*Ko.*> May Paiêôn be gracious
to both the sculptors and Euthiês for their beautiful work!
<*Ky.*> My dear, look at that girl
looking up at the apple! Wouldn't you say
she'll faint on the spot if she doesn't reach it?
<*Ko.*> And that old man, Kynnô – oh, by the Fates,
how that little boy is squashing the goose!

*<KY.>* πρὸ τῶν ποδῶν γοῦν εἴ τι μὴ λίθος, τοὔργον,
ἐρεῖς, λαλήσει. μᾶ, χρόνῳ κοτ' ὥνθρωποι
κἠς τοὺς λίθους ἕξουσι τὴν ζοὴν θεῖναι.
*(KO.)* τὸν Βατάλης γὰρ τοῦτον οὐχ ὁρῇς, Κυννοῖ,
ὅκως βέβηκεν ἀνδριάντα τῆς Μυττέω;
εἰ μή τις αὐτὴν εἶδε Βατάλην, βλέψας
ἐς τοῦτο τὸ εἰκόνισμα μὴ ἐτύμης δεῖσθω.
*(KY.)* ἕπευ, φίλη, μοι καὶ καλόν τί σοι δείξω
πρῆγμ' οἷον οὐχ ὥρηκας ἐξ ὅτευ ζώεις.
Κύδιλλ', ἰοῦσα τὸν νεωκόρον βῶσον.
οὐ σοὶ λέγω, αὕτη, τῇ ὧδε χὤδε χασκεύσῃ;
μᾶ, μή τιν' ὤρην ὧν λέγω πεποίηται,
ἕστηκε δ' εἴς μ' ὁρεῦσα καρκίνου μέζον.
ἰοῦσα, φημί, τὸν νεωκόρον βῶσον.
λαίμαστρον, οὔτ' ὀργή σε κρηγύην οὔτε
βέβηλος αἰνεῖ, πανταχῇ δ' ἴση κεῖσαι.
μαρτύρομαι, Κύδιλλα, τὸν θεὸν τοῦτον,
ὡς ἔκ με καίεις οὐ θέλουσαν οἰδῆσαι·
μαρτύρομαι, φήμ'· ἔσσετ' ἡμέρη κείνη
ἐν ᾗ τὸ βρέγμα τοῦτο τὤσυρὲς κνήσῃ.
*(KO.)* μὴ πάνθ' ἑτοίμως καρδιηβολεῦ, Κυννοῖ·
δούλη 'στι, δούλης δ' ὦτα νωθρίη θλίβει.
*(KY.)* ἀλλ' ἡμέρη τε κἠπὶ μέζον ὠθεῖται·
αὕτη σύ, μεῖνον· ἡ θύρη γὰρ ᾤκται
κἀνεῖθ' ὁ παστός.
*<KO.>* οὐχ ὁρῇς, φίλη Κυννοῖ,
οἷ' ἔργα; κείνην ταῦτ' ἐρεῖς Ἀθηναίην
γλύψαι τὰ καλά – χαιρέτω δὲ δέσποινα.
τὸν παῖδα δὴ τὸν γυμνὸν ἢν κνίσω τοῦτον
οὐχ ἕλκος ἕξει, Κύννα; πρός γάρ οἱ κεῖνται
αἱ σάρκες οἷα θερμὰ θερμὰ πηδῶσαι
ἐν τῇ σανίσκῃ. τὠργύρευν δὲ πύραυστρον
οὐκ ἢν ἴδῃ Μύελλος ἢ Παταικίσκος

51 τωυσυρες P: τὤσυρὲς: Blass (1891) 730, Danielsson (1891) 1354
57 κοινην (ut uid.) P: κείνην Danielsson (1891) 1354, Di Gregorio (1997) 289–90
61 θερμα P: θερμα alt. sscr. m. rec.

*<Ky.>* At the very least, if it weren't a stone in front of our feet, you'd say
the sculpture's about to speak. Heavens, given time, men
will even be able to put life into stones.
*(Ko.)* Yes, Kynnô, for can't you see how this statue of Batalê,
Myttês' daughter, is standing?
If anybody hasn't seen Batalê herself, let him take a look
at this likeness and not have any need of the real article.
*(Ky.)* My dear, come with me and I'll show you
the most beautiful thing you've seen in your life.
– Kydilla, go and call the attendant.
You, aren't I speaking to you, while you're gawping this way and that?
Grief, she's taken no notice of what I'm saying,
but just stands there staring at me more vacantly than a crab.
Go and call the attendant, I say!
You greedy thing, neither a sacred nor a secular woman
Praises you for being good – you're equally useless anywhere.
May this god here be my witness, Kydilla,
you're inflaming me even though I don't want to flare up!
May he be my witness, I say – there'll come that day
when I'll give you real reason to scratch your disgusting head.
*(Ko.)* Don't get excited so easily over every little thing, Kynnô.
She's a slave, and slow reactions block a slave's ears.
*(Ky.)* But it's day now and the crowd's pushing forward.
You, stay here, for the door has been opened
and the inner temple's curtain has been pulled back. *<Ko.>* Kynnô dear, can't you see
what wonderful works of art? You'd think Athene over there
had chiselled these lovely things. – Greetings, my Lady!
If I scratched this naked boy,
wouldn't he get a wound, Kynnô? The flesh that covers him
pulses like hot, hot springs
in the painting. And the silver tongs!
– If a [fool like] Myellos or [a thief like] Lamprîon's son Pataikiskos

ὁ Λαμπρίονος, ἐκβαλεῦσι τὰς κούρας
δοκεῦντες ὄντως ἀργύρευν πεποιῆσθαι;
ὁ βοῦς δὲ χὠ ἄγων αὐτὸν ἥ θ' ὁμαρτεῦσα
χὠ γρυπὸς χὠ ἀνάσιλλος ἄνθρωπος
οὐχὶ ζοὴν βλέπουσι χἠμέρην πάντες;
εἰ μὴ ἐδόκευν τι μέζον ἢ γυνὴ πρήσσειν,
ἀνηλάλαξ' ἄν, μή μ' ὁ βοῦς τι πημήνῃ·
οὕτω ἐπιλοξοῖ, Κυννί, τῇ ἑτέρῃ κούρῃ.
(*ΚΥ.*) ἀληθιναί, φίλη, γὰρ αἱ Ἐφησίου χεῖρες
ἐς πάντ' Ἀπελλέω γράμματ'· οὐδ' ἐρεῖς 'κεῖνος
ὤνθρωπος ἓν μὲν εἶδεν, ἓν δ' ἀπηρνήθη',
ἀλλ' ᾧ ἐπὶ νοῦν γένοιτο καὶ θεῶν ψαύειν
ἠπείγεθ'. ὃς δ' ἐκεῖνον ἢ ἔργα τὰ ἐκείνου
μὴ παμφαλήσας ἐκ δίκης ὀρώρηκεν,
ποδὸς κρέμαιτ' ἐκεῖνος ἐν γναφέως οἴκῳ.
(*ΝΕΩΚΟΡΟΣ*) κάλ' ὗμιν, ὦ γυναῖκες, ἐντελέως τὰ ἱρά
καὶ ἐς λῷον ἐμβλέποντα· μεζόνως οὔτις
ἠρέσατο τὸν Παιήον' ἤπερ ὑμεῖς.
ἰὴ ἰὴ Παίηον, εὐμενὴς εἴης
καλοῖς ἐφ' ἱροῖς τῇσδε κεἴ τινες τῶνδε
ἔασ' ὀπυιηταί τε καὶ γενῆς ἆσσον.
ἰὴ ἰὴ Παίηον, ὧδε ταῦτ' εἴη.
<*ΚΟ.*> εἴη γάρ, ὦ μέγιστε, χὐγίῃ πολλῇ
ἔλθοιμεν αὖτις μέζον' ἵρ' ἀγινεῦσαι
σὺν ἀνδράσιν καὶ παισί.
<*ΚΥ.*> Κοκκάλη, καλῶς
τεμεῦσα μέμνεο τὸ σκελύδριον δοῦναι
τῷ νεωκόρῳ τοὔρνιθος· ἔς τε τὴν τρώγλην
τὸν πελανὸν ἔνθες τοῦ δράκοντος εὐφήμως,
καὶ ψαιστὰ δεῦσον· τἄλλα δ' οἰκίης ἕδρῃ
δαισόμεθα, καὶ ἐπὶ μὴ λάθῃ φέρειν, αὕτη,
τῆς ὑγιίης· † λῷ † πρόσδος· ἦ γὰρ ἱροῖσιν
† μεω̣ν αμαρτιησηυγιηστι † τῆς μοίρης.

94 δωι, λ supra π P

95 μεθ' ὧν ἁμαρτεῖ ἧσ[ίς ἐ]στι τῆς μοίρης Cunningham (1971) 147, (2004) 17, μέζων ἁμαρτίης ἡ ὑγίη 'στὶ τῆς μοίρης e.g. Massa Positano (1973) 104–5

were to see them, wouldn't they have their eyes standing out on stalks
thinking they're really made of silver?
And the ox, the man leading him, the girl attendant,
the hook-nosed man there, and the fellow with his hair sticking up -
don't they all have the look of life and day?
And if I didn't think it too showy for a woman
I'd have shouted aloud, for fear that the ox would do me some harm:
he's giving me such a sideways glare, Kynnô, out of one eye!
*(Ky.)* That's because the hands of Apellês of Ephesos are true
in all his lines. You couldn't say 'That man
saw one thing and turned down another',
but whatever came into his mind, he strove to touch
[the perfection of] even the gods. If anyone views him or his works without a fair examination
may he be hung up by the foot in a laundry shop.
*(Temple-Attendant)* Ladies, your sacrifice is perfectly favourable
and looking on the auspicious side. No one has more greatly
pleased Paiêôn than you.
Glory, glory to you, Paiêôn, may you look kindly
on these women for their fair sacrifice, and on those
who are related to them by marriage or blood.
Glory, glory, Paiêôn, may this be so.
<*Ko.*> Amen, greatest god, in good health
may we come again bringing greater sacrifices
with our husbands and children. <*Ky.*> Kokkalê, remember
to cut the little leg of the bird off carefully and to give it
to the attendant. Put the cake-coin offering
in the serpent's box in holy silence
and moisten the barley-cakes. We'll eat the rest at home;
you there, don't forget to take away
some of the holy bread. Hand [it] out as much as you like, for certainly at sacrifices
........................................................................ of the share.

## COMMENTARY

Synopsis It is dawn. Two married women, Kynnô and Kokkalê, with Kynnô's slave, Kydilla, visit the temple of Asklêpios, in all likelihood the famous Asklêpieion on the island of Kos, to offer a sacrifice for relief from some unspecified illness. Kokkalê has not visited the temple before. In front of the altar, Kynnô sings a hymn of greeting to the god and others sharing his altar. She apologizes for the smallness of her offering, a cockerel (1–19). A votive tablet is placed at the right of the statue of Hygieia (19–20). The women's attention is immediately caught by the beauty of the altar-statues, which are the work of the sons of Praxiteles, and by the lifelike quality of statues displayed in the plaza (20–38). After Kynnô has promised to show Kokkalê even more wonderful works of art, and has abused Kydilla for her slowness in calling the temple-attendant to open the door to the temple (39–53), the door is opened to admit the gathering crowd (54–6). The women enter the temple, and Kokkalê admires statues in the front porch, or pronaos, to the main room of the temple, the naos (56–8). Then, in the naos, she comments enthusiastically on the painting of a sacrifice by Apelles (59–71), for whose truth to life and versatility Kynnô voices admiration (72–8). Still in the naos, the temple-attendant pronounces the success of the sacrifice (79–85), Kokkalê promises to come again with more impressive offerings and with their families (86–8), and Kynnô gives directions for cutting up the cockerel, giving a money-donation, and taking the rest of the cockerel home to eat (88–95).

Text The main problem with the text of *Mimiamb* 4 is, as so often with our papyrus, the lack of part-attributions. The text offered here follows the majority casting for the poem, represented by Headlam-Knox (1922), Massa Positano (1973) and Di Gregorio (1997), though in several places it goes its own way with line-allocations. Cunningham (1966) 118–21, (1971) 127 argues that Kynnô's companion is called Philê, Kokkalê being a slave. But in that case the reader or listener has to wait till line 27 to be given Philê's name, Φίλη, and in the meantime has heard her saying to Kynnô 'Kynnô dear', φίλη Κυννοῖ (20, repeated at 56); this is unacceptably confusing. Cf. also Arnott (1984). The following is a list of my line-attributions and those in some of the most important editions:

The present edition: 1–20a Kynnô; 20b–2 Kokkalê; 23–5a Kynnô; 25b–6 Kokkalê; 27–9 Kynnô; 30–1 Kokkalê; 32–4 Kynnô; 35–8 Kokkalê; 39–

51 Kynnô; 52–3 Kokkalê; 54–6a Kynnô; 56b–71 Kokkalê; 72–8 Kynnô; 79–85 Attendant; 86–8a Kokkalê; 88b–95 Kynnô.

Di Gregorio (1997): 1–11a Kynnô; 11b–18 Kokkalê; 19–20a Kynnô; 20b–2 Kokkalê; 23–5a Kynnô; 25b–38 Kokkalê; 39–51 Kynnô; 52–3 Kokkalê; 54–6a Kynnô; 56b–71 Kokkalê; 72–8 Kynnô; 79–85 Attendant; 86–8a Kokkalê; 88b–95 Kynnô.

Cunningham (1971, 2002, 2004): 1–20a Kynnô; 20b–2 Philê; 23–5a Kynnô; 25b–6 Philê; 27–9 Kynnô; 30a Philê; 30b–4 Kynnô; 35–8 Philê; 39–51 Kynnô; 52–3 Philê; 54–6a Kynnô; 56b–71 Philê; 72–8 Kynnô; 79–85 Attendant; 86–95 Kynnô.

Massa Positano (1973): 1–18 Kokkalê; 19–20a Kynnô; 20b–2 Kokkalê; 23–5a Kynnô; 25b–6 Kokkalê; 27–9 Kynnô; 30–1 Kokkalê; 32–4 Kynnô; 35–8 Kokkalê; 39–51 Kynnô; 52–3 Kokkalê; 54–6a Kynnô; 56b–71 Kokkalê; 72–8 Kynnô; 79–85 Attendant; 86–8a Kokkalê; 88b–95 Kynnô.

Nairn-Laloy (1928, 3rd edn. 1991): 1–20a Kynnô; 20b–2 Kokkalê; 23–5a Kynnô; 25b–38 Kokkalê; 39–51 Kynnô; 52–3 Kokkalê; 54–6a Kynnô; 56b–71 Kokkalê; 72–8 Kynnô; 79–85 Attendant; 86–95 Kynnô.

Groeneboom (1922): 1–18 Kokkalê; 19–20a Kynnô; 20b–2 Kokkalê; 23–6 Kynnô; 27–38 Kokkalê; 39–51 Kynnô; 52–3 Kokkalê; 54–6a Kynnô; 56b–71 Kokkalê; 72–8 Kynnô; 79–85 Attendant; 86–8a Kokkalê; 88b–95 Kynnô.

Headlam-Knox (1922): 1–20a Kynnô; 20b–2 Kokkalê; 23–5a Kynnô; 25b–38 Kokkalê; 39–51 Kynnô; 52–3 Kokkalê; 54–6a Kynnô; 56b–71 Kokkalê; 72–8 Kynnô; 79–85 Attendant; 86–95 Kynnô.

Date Apelles the painter must have died before 280 B.C., and the sons of Praxiteles, Timarchos and Kêphisodôtos, by 265 B.C., which gives us rough outside limits: so Cunningham (1966) 17–18, (1971) 128; Massa Positano (1973) 29–33 would narrow the period down to 280 to 275. Kokkalê's wish that Paiêôn show his favour to the sons of Praxiteles and the dedicator (25–6) suggests that the sculptors are still alive. This gives us at least the dramatic date. For the suggestion that the poem was written to celebrate the extensions to the Koan Asklêpieion in the first half of the third century B.C. see below, p. 106. If accepted, it would give us a rough date of composition, and the poem's date of composition may not have been been long after the dramatic date. Theokritos' fifteenth *Idyll*, with which *Mimiamb* 4 has some affinities, probably has about 272 B.C. as its dramatic date and is unlikely to have been composed much later than that (Gow [1952] 2 265).

Setting Since Rudolf Herzog's excavations of the Asklêpieion on Kos in the first years of the twentieth century, it has been regarded as highly likely that Temple B on the second terrace of the site is the scene of *Mimiamb* 4. The reasons for accepting the identification are put most cogently by Sherwin-White (1978) 350–2: the epithet 'sweet' applied to Kos by Kokkalê at line 2, and not to the other famous Asklêpieia; the Koan oath 'by the Fates' at line 30; the altar on the site is monumental, and could easily have accommodated the complex statues alluded to in the poem; finally, underground offertory chests (θησαυροί) like the one Kynnô mentions at line 90 are not specific to the worship of Asklêpios nor universally attested for it, and yet Herzog discovered a collection-box precisely in the naos of Temple B; it is the rectangular box in Fig. 2, below, p. 121.

In the light of the identification, Herzog (1903) associated the charming statue of The Boy with an Egyptian Goose in the Vatican with this temple on the strength of lines 30–2 of the poem, and Margarete Bieber (1923–24) used it to identify extant statues found in the course of excavation. Cunningham (1966) 115–17 and (1971) 128 objects that the poem makes no mention of art known to have existed in the Koan Asklêpieion in the third century B.C., especially the Aphrodite Anadyomenê of Apelles himself. Yet by the time Strabo 14.2.19 located the Aphrodite Anadyomenê in the Asklêpieion, the precinct was an extensive complex, and the paintings he names could in fact have been displayed in the large temple built in the first half of the second century on the first terrace, or even housed in the building behind the altar on the second terrace, which is known from extant bases to have displayed at least statues: Sherwin-White (1978) 343, 349 n. 508. The works of art referred to by Cunningham need not have been in the third-century temple at all; and his argument from silence loses its force.

Purpose The first major building phase of the Koan Asklêpieion, especially Temple B and the second terrace, occurred in the first half of the third century B.C. (Sherwin-White [1978] 342–4 ). The objective dating for the composition of the poem is congruent with the suggestion (made by Sherwin-White [1978] 352) that the occasion of the *Mimiamb* was to celebrate the extensive upscaling of the sanctuary and its cult. This would parallel the celebration of the Adonis cult in Alexandria that *Idyll* 15 of Theokritos presents. It also fits the religious beginning and end of the *Mimiamb*.

Herodas' second concern is the characterization of the two women, especially in their role as contrasts. With Kynnô and Kokkalê as the central speaking parts in the line-distribution offered in the text, two clear characters emerge. Kynnô is the more experienced of the two in matters of Asklêpios' cult and the layout of the temple, telling Kokkalê where to put the votive tablet (18–20), giving her directions about the distribution of the cockerel's carcase and the coin-offering (88–95), and giving advice about the names of the sculptors of the altar-statues (23–5) and the best works of art in the temple (39–40, 72–8). She is overbearing with Kydilla (41–51), while it is left to Kokkalê to mediate kindly between the two (52–3). Kokkalê is in fact probably one of the most sympathetic characters in Herodas. Kynnô's excuse for the smallness of the offering places the social status of both women at a quite humble level (1–18; cf. 86–8), though it is significant that Kynnô rather bossily gives all the advice about how her friend's sacrifice should be apportioned (88–90, 92–3). Kokkalê's enthusiasm for the works of art on the precinct is indeed naive (21–6, 30–1, 35–8, 57–71), but not necessarily a parody of uninformed taste. Together, therefore, the characters of Kynnô and Kokkalê contrast with one another, though it should be noted that Kynnô shares Kokkalê's enthusiasm for truth to life in art (27–9, 32–4).

The poem's middle section is concerned with the women's responses to works of art in the precinct. Some scholars like Headlam-Knox (1922) xliii (followed by Cunningham [1966] 114) regard this section as the *raison d'être* of the entire poem. It is rightly placed in the tradition of similar descriptions of works of art starting from Homer, *Iliad* 18 (Achilles' shield), the pseudo-Hesiodic *Shield of Herakles*, Euripides' *Iôn* 184ff., and, in the time of Herodas himself, Theokritos, *Idylls* 1.27–56 (the Goatherd's cup) and 15.100–30 (the tableau at the Adonia). But the other passages directly describe the *objets d'art*, while Herodas presents them indirectly, through the excited reactions of the spectators to them, in such a manner that a surprisingly full image of them can be extracted. A forerunner in the technique of registering viewers' responses to works of art is to be found in Aischylos' satyr-play, the *Isthmiastai or Theôroi*, in which the satyrs admire the life-like quality of the painted votive images of themselves, 'work of art of Daidalos', which 'only needs a voice', and would deceive even their mothers; see the text and discussion of Krumeich-Pechstein-Seidensticker (1999) 131–48. This approach assumes vogue-status in Hellenistic epigram, in which the speaker reacts to works of art but does not directly describe them (cf. the series in the *Palatine Anthology* on Myron's Cow: *AP* 9.713–44, 793–8). It may be Herodas' spin on two approaches to give an indirect but also unexpectedly full presentation of the works of art in the Koan Asklêpieion, though it should be remembered that Theokritos also uses the technique, even if much more briefly, when he makes Gorgô and Praxinoa comment on the tapestries at the Adonia (*Id.* 15.80–6). See below, pp. 124–8.

The description of the works of art seen by the women culminates in Kynnô's praise of the truth to life and versatility of the painting of Apelles. However ironically the women's taste might be presented, that is no argument against thinking that Herodas approved of Apelles' all-inclusive vision, and, perhaps, that he regarded Apelles as a kindred spirit in his willingness to deal with scenes from everyday life, just as the votives in the plaza are admired for doing. See further the Discussion.

**1–20.** In the absence of any firm indication of a change of speaker in these lines (though Di Gregorio (1997) 253–54 identifies a line under καί at 11 as a paragraphos), they are probably best given to one speaker, with the address to Kokkalê at 19 showing that the speaker must be her companion, Kynnô. Moreover, Kynnô will more naturally know the gods represented by the sculptures around the altar because she has been in the temple before (see e.g. 39–40), while it is Kokkalê's first visit. In particular, giving 1–18 to one speaker would bring them into close accord with the form and pattern of a paian or hymn to Asklêpios which was in wide use in Herodas' times. This is the paian printed by Powell (1925) 136–8, versions of which are found in Athens, Erythrai, Dion in Macedonia, and Ptolemais in Egypt. Its sequence is an address to Asklêpios, mention of his family, mention of his divine associates, a prayer, and a closing address to the god. Kynnô's hymn adds the listing of the god's cult-centres, but that is also paralleled in the little hymn to Asklêpios appended to the first-century A.D. Andromachos of Crete's poem on herbal cures preserved by Galênos, *On Antidotes* 1.6 Kühn (1827) 14 32–42. Another addition is Kynnô's excuse for the smallness of the offering, but that could be part of Kynnô's characterization as something of a snob.

The women are standing before the altar in the plaza in front of the temple. As Kynnô sings her hymn, she names the statues of Asklêpios, his parents, his wife, his daughters, his sons, and (for safety's sake) any other deities who share his altar. As will become clear from 20–5, the statues are the work of the sons of Praxiteles, Timarchos and Kêphisodôtos. The statues will probably have been attached to the altar (rather than free-standing). The altar of the Koan Asklêpieion was monumental, and would easily have accommodated all the statues: see Sherwin-White (1978) 351.

**1. Paiêôn:** The *Iliad* (5.401–2, 899–900) shows that he was once a separate divine doctor, but he merged with Apollo and Asklêpios when they acquired their attribute of healing.

**1–2. Trikka ... Kos and Epidauros:** these were the three major cult-centres of Asklêpios. Trikka was the chief town of the area in North Greece whose contingent was led by Podaleirios and Machaôn in the *Iliad* (2.729–33); they appear in line 9 below. Epidauros was the most famous sanctuary of Asklêpios, on the eastern coast of the Peloponnese. The island of Kos lies north of Rhodes, off the coast of modern Turkey. *Mim.* 2.95–8 shows that at least in the third century B.C. Koans believed that their Asklêpios came from Trikka in Thessaly. This is quite compatible with the legend, preserved in Theopompos (*FGrH* 2B, 115 F 103[14]), that Podaleirios, the only son of Asklêpios to survive the Trojan war, settled after it in Syrna in Caria, and gave rise to the Koan Asklêpiadai. This family was also a famous guild of doctors on the island. The gentilicial ending of their name shows that they must go back to the Archaic period, if not before, so the Koan association with Asklêpios will have been equally ancient; see Sherwin-White (1978) 256–63, 339.

**3. σὺν καί:** σὺν is adverbial (see LSJ[9] s.v. C.2, 'besides', 'also'), and, in combination with καί, it is a Hellenistic usage; see also e.g. Apollonios of Rhodes, *Argonautika* 1.74.

**Korônis:** mother of Asklêpios; her story is told in Pindar, *Pythian* 3.8–46.

**5. Hygieia:** this is usually Asklêpios' daughter, but she is presented here as his wife; his wife is standardly Êpionê (here Êpiô, 6). On Kos, Hygieia was accorded a prominent position in the cult of Asklêpios, and a lesser role was accorded to Êpionê (Sherwin-White [1978] 347, 351; so also Bieber [1923–4] 242 n. 1, Cunningham [1971] 129, Di Gregorio [1997] 259), which leads to the conclusion that she was regarded as the god's wife only on the island – another pointer to the Koan Asklêpieion as the scene of our poem. The pose of Asklêpios with his right hand touching Hygieia is attested in extant sculpture: see *LIMC* 5.1 s.v. Hygieia, nos. 80, 232 with p.571 (F. Croissant, who identifies the survivals with the altar-statue of Asklêpios and Hygieia).

**χὤνπερ:** = καὶ ὧνπερ ('crasis'), 'and hail to [Panakê, Êpiô and Îêsô], whose honoured shrines these are.' ὅς and ὅσπερ are often indistinguishable; see LSJ[9] s.v. ὅσπερ.

**6. Panakê, Êpiô and Îêsô:** 'Remedy of All', 'Gentle One', 'Healing One', all daughters of Asklêpios; see 5n. on Hygieia for Êpionê's usual status as Asklêpios' wife. The cumulative connectives are usual in prayers.

**χαίροι:** the verb has been attracted into the number of its immediate antecedent, the singular Îêsô, despite the plurality of the sentence's subjects.

**7. Leômedôn:** the king of Troy who commissioned Apollo and Poseidon to build Troy's walls (Apollodôros 2.5.9); Herodas has Ionicized the name Λαομέδων, Lâomedôn, to Λεωμέδων in metathesis; see above, p. 8.

**9. Podaleirios and Machaôn:** these are known as sons of Asklêpios and master-physicians from Homer's Catalogue of Ships at *Il.* 2.729–33.

**10–11a.** An all-embracing formula to save offending any deity not addressed.

**10. κατοικεῦσιν:** for the -ευ- contraction see above, *Mim.* 1.88n.

**11. goddesses:** archaeologists have used the reference to these deities in order to identify certain extant pieces of statues from the Asklêpieion. Bieber (1923–4) 244–5 identified the girl's head found by Herzog as belonging to a statue of one of Asklêpios' daughters, a proposal followed by Massa Positano (1973) 8; cf. Gelzer (1985) 108 n. 28 and Di Gregorio (1997) 260–1. Bieber (1923–4) 246–7 also

postulated that 'goddesses' includes a reference to the remains of a statuette thought to have been an image of Aphrodite. Morricone (1991) has published two female heads now in the Museum in Kos which she argues belonged to the statue group decorating the Koan altar.
**ἵλεῳ:** nominative masculine plural of ἵλεως -ων.
**Father, πάτερ:** Kynnô had begun her address to the gods by invoking Paiêôn as 'Lord', ἄναξ, and here at the close of the address she calls him 'Father'. Both epithets were liturgical, the latter being most commonly associated with Zeus. Even a Kynnô can indulge in the Hellenistic pleasure in variation.
**12. this cockerel:** the genitive is dependent on τἀπίδορπα (13), 'seconds'. Kynnô means that her offering is so humble that it will not be sufficient to qualify as a full meal for the gods; she is indirectly apologizing for the poverty of the sacrifice. The bird, which was the only sacrifice affordable for poor people, seems to have been regarded as particularly appropriate to the worship of Asklêpios as the god of health, as is also evidenced by Sokrates' dying words to Kritôn not to forget the cockerel they owed the god (Plato, *Phaidôn* 118a).

When is the cockerel handed over to be sacrificed? Some critics (e.g. Massa Positano [1973] 53) argue that when the slave Kydilla is ordered to call the temple-attendant (41), it is in order to hand the cockerel over to him. But the γάρ in Kynno's order αὕτη σύ, μεῖνον· ἡ *γὰρ* θύρη ὤικται (55), 'You, stay here, *for* the door has been opened', strongly implies that the earlier directive is now superfluous and therefore countermanded; that in turn implies that the earlier directive was to get the naos door opened; similarly also Mastromarco (1984) 42–5 and Di Gregorio (1997) 287–8. Precisely when the cockerel was deposited is left open, as Mastromarco (1984) 43–5 notes, but can we not quite naturally imagine the handover to have taken place together with the placing of the votive tablet at the altar (19–20), just after Kynnô has apologetically presented the bird (12) to the statue of Asklêpios on the altar? See also above, pp. 4–7.
**the herald of my house's walls:** the cockerel proclaims its territory. The combination of 'house and walls' already occurs at 7, where it has associations of epic grandeur. It is quite in Herodas' manner to make Kynnô inadvertently quote the epic-sounding phrase in the new, humble context in order to make gentle fun of her through the irony.
**14. πολλὴν ... ἕτοιμον:** these accusatives are instances of the feminine (ἕτοιμος is a two-termination adjective) to denote indefinite abstracts: Fraenkel (1950) on Aischylos, *Agamemnon* 916 (Cunningham [1971] 14n.). The metaphor of the well or spring of wealth is common.
**16. heaped with:** LSJ[9] s.v. νέω (C) II give 'to be stuffed with', but the usage is unparalleled.
**crackling:** then, as now, a delicacy, as we know from the New Comedy poet Diphilos, *Fr.* 90 Kassel-Austin (1986) 5 106.
**17. τάς:** Ionic equivalent of Attic ἅς, feminine accusative plural of the relative pronoun.

**18. ἐπί ... τείνας:** tmesis, on which see *Mim.* 3.5n. The effect here seems to be to heighten the tone as Kynnô concludes her prayer, just as at *Mim.* 3.5.

**19. the tablet:** Strabo 8.6.15 relates that the temples of Asklêpios at Epidauros, Kos and Trikka were full of dedicated tablets which recorded in writing the god's cures. These tablets, made of wood or stone, were commonly leant against the feet or legs of the deity's statue (as here); Kynnô probably specifies the right side of the statue of Hygieia as the place for the tablet because it was the auspicious side. See the n. on 12 for the suggestion that this is the moment when the cockerel is given to a temple-attendant for sacrifice.

**20–6.** The formalities completed, Kokkalê admires the statues on or around the altar that Kynnô has referred to in the hymn. That Kokkalê is talking about the statues of the deities and not, as is often thought, the statues of human subjects under review at 27–38 is made quite unambiguous by her use of the word ἄγαλμα at 21. Before the Imperial period, *agalma* was the specific term for a statue of a god: Zanker (2004) 141–3. There is a very good example of the usage in the sanctuary of Asklêpios and Hygieia in Pheneos. The statue base was found in situ, signed by Attalos of Athens (second century B.C.) and containing an inscription which calls the cult-statues of the two deities *agalmata*: Vanderpool (1959) 280–1. The word for statues of humans like the Girl and the Apple would have been ἀνδριάς, *andrias*, and that is precisely the word used for the statue of Batalê at 36. This information is important for our knowledge of the types of subject treated by the sons of Praxiteles, though it was already known from Pliny (*Natural History* 36.24) that Kêphisodôtos had made a statue of Asklêpios.

**20–1. what beautiful statues, καλῶν ... ἀγαλμάτων:** genitive of exclamation.

**21. τίς ἦρα:** Herodas' Ionic version of the particle has the same meaning here as Attic ἆρα after an interrogative pronoun, 'who, then, ...?', 'so who ...?': Denniston (1954) 45–6.

**23. the sons of Praxiteles:** on Timarchos and Kêphisodôtos see Stewart (1990) 295–7.

**24. that writing:** from at least the early fifth century, private individuals like Themistokles dedicated temples and cult statues, and presumably inscribed their names on their dedications for them to have survived in the tradition: see e.g. Ploutarchos, *Themistokles* 22. In the Hellenistic period the practice is well evidenced, e.g. by the architrave on the Pergamon Altar: Ridgway (2000) 22–3. Cunningham (1966) 114 and (1971) on 20–6 is therefore wrong to argue that the presence of the dedicatory inscription precludes a reference to cult statues. For a parallel for the 'signature' of Kêphisodôtos and Timarchos see above, 20–6n.

**26. for their beautiful work, καλῶν ἔργων:** 'for', 'in return for', 'as a reward for'; the genitive can be used in this sense with any verb; see Schwyzer (1950) 2 128.

**27–38.** Another class of sculptures claims the women's attention. These are statues of human subjects, votive offerings displayed in the plaza in front of the temple, as was standard in Greek sanctuaries. Their subjects are a girl looking longingly at an apple (27–9), an old man (30a), a boy with a goose (30b–4), and a portrait of a local girl named Batalê (35–8). If the Asklêpieion is the Koan one, the votives could have stood on any of the bases before or even on the north side of the temple: Herzog (1932) Plates 16–17, 37–8. We know enough about Greek votives to be sure that they could all have stood outside: bronze and marble are hardy materials. In the case of Batalê, we are dealing with a portrait statue, presumably of bronze, as almost always in the Hellenistic world. This statue, too, is most likely to have stood somewhere outside the temple. One would not expect a run-of-the-mill portrait to be in the pronaos, for example: there is nothing special about it that would merit such an exalted location, and no need to protect it from the elements. Hellenistic sanctuaries were crowded with such portraits, and in the Koan Asklêpieion a semicircular recess dug into the slope of the hill (an 'exedra'), which stood to the side of the altar, could well have housed a group of them: Herzog (1932) 32–3, Plates 14, 37–8. Alternatively, it could have stood on one of the bases at the south-east corner of the temple or along the north side. At line 27, then, the women must be envisaged as moving at least a few steps from the altar en route to the pronaos as they view the votive statues.

Whereas in the case of the altar-embellishments Kokkalê has admired the statues on the criterion of beauty (20), she and Kynnô respond to these *andriantes* (36) on the criterion of their lifelike quality. These were key-concepts in contemporary art-criticism: see the Discussion.

**27–9.** An extant sculpture has been seen as underlying the subject of these lines. Lehman (1945) 430–3, followed by Webster (1964) 158–9, has argued that 27–9 refer to an original statue of a Girl under the Apple Tree, of which there is a copy in the Institute of Fine Arts of New York University. He suggests at p. 432 that the statue 'may well have been produced in Kos, as a copy of the original mentioned by Herondas.' The snake coiled around the tree makes the connection with the Koan Asklêpiadai particularly attractive, as Massa Positano (1973) 65 and Di Gregorio (1997) 273 emphasize: this guild of doctors, originally a family claiming descent from Asklêpios, used their divine ancestor's snake as their symbol. Cunningham (1966) 114 objects that Herodas does not mention the serpent depicted on the tree, but Massa Positano points out that Herodas nowhere offers a complete 'description', but concentrates on what seems most significant, here the evocation of intense longing.

**27. ἄνω:** with βλέπουσαν in the next line; as Headlam (1922) and Cunningham (1971) ad loc. note, the word-order has been disturbed by Kynnô's excitement. To take τὴν ἄνω κείνην as a unit meaning 'that [girl] up there' seems precluded by the fact that the statues are displayed at ground level; note line 32 'If it weren't a stone in front of our feet'.

**28. ἐρεῖς:** we might have expected the optative, εἴποις ἄν, 'you would say'; but the future is idiomatic, and also occurs at 33, 57, 73, 5.56, 6.59, 67, 7.115.

**29. ἐκ ... ψύξειν:** tmesis; see 18n. The lifelike quality of the statue is its chief attraction.

**30. old man:** Kokkalê's self-interruption dramatizes her excitement, and gives more emphatic prominence to the statue of the boy and goose.

**by the Fates:** the oath by the Moirai, which occurs also in *Mim.* 1.11, 66, seems specifically Koan: see above, p. 21 and *Mim.* 1.11n.

**30–4:** This must refer to the the original of the Roman copy of the Boy with an Egyptian Goose in the Vatican, who reaches up with his right hand demanding that the viewer pick him up, and leans to his left to restore his displaced balance, squashing his unfortunate pet just below its neck in the process; his mouth is open, as if voicing his command. So Herzog (1903), and see Cunningham (1966) 115 and (1971) ad loc., who disproves the statue's identification with Boêthos' Boy Strangling a Goose (see Pliny, *Natural History* 34.84), which is upheld e.g. by Headlam-Knox (1922) on 30: Boêthos has now been firmly dated to the second century B.C. (so also Gelzer [1985] 108 n. 28 with his Korrekturzusatz at p. 116). Cf. Massa Positano (1973) on 31 and Di Gregorio (1997) 274. For a discussion of how the group involves the spectator see Zanker (2004) 103–5, 136.

**31. goose:** the χηναλώπηξ (literally 'fox-goose', because of its resemblance to a goose and its alleged fox-like mischievousness; see Ailianos, *On the Characteristics of Animals* 5.30) is the Egyptian goose, briefly mentioned by Herodotos in the book devoted to Egypt in the *Histories* (2.72): 'They say that … among birds the fox-goose is sacred to the Nile.'

**32. in front of our feet:** on a low base, in accordance with Greek practice.

**γοῦν:** 'at least', corroborating Kokkalê's statement.

**33. about to speak:** it is a commonplace Hellenistic response to lifelike statues that they will give voice, as frequently happens in connection with Myron's Cow; see e.g. Antipater of Sidon 40 GP: 'I think the heifer is going to low; so not only Prometheus but you, too, Myron, can fashion living things.'

**34. ἕξουσι:** for ἔχω + infinitive in the sense of 'I am able' see LSJ[9] s.v. A.III.1.

**35. γάρ:** yes, [they will be able to put life into stone,] for [this statue also is lifelike].

**35–6. Batalê, Myttês' daughter:** both names indicate Batalê's position in society as that of a hetaira. The name Batalê, like Battaros in *Mim.* 2.75, is connected with the verb to stammer (βατταρίζειν), which had associations of effeminacy (Demosthenes' enemies nicknamed him Battalos: Aischines 1.131, see above on *Mim.* 2.75). Myttês is related to the noun μύτις, *mytis*, which denoted a man with an unbridled sexual appetite (Hesychios μ 1990 Schmidt [1861] 3 133). See further Cunningham (1971) 135 on 35–38, Di Gregorio (1997) 276–7.

**36. βέβηκεν:** 'is standing', LSJ[9] A.1.2. That her stance is probably wanton can be inferred from her profession; see Headlam-Knox (1922) 186–7 on 36, with Cunningham's (1971) reservations ad loc.; so also Di Gregorio (1997) 277, Skinner (2001) 219.

**statue, ἀνδριάντα:** the specific Greek term for a statue of a human: see 20–6n. Despite her non-respectability in society, Batalê too has offered a votive portrait to thank the god for ridding her of some malady.

**37–8.** The putative person who has not seen Batalê is male, as indicated by the male aorist participle βλέψας, 'having looked'. When Kokkalê says 'let him ... not have any need of the real article', she seems to be suggesting in a rather bourgeois way that the man should be content with Batalê's simulacrum, and not engage with her on any more intimate basis. This might be called 'an inversion of the Pygmalion topos: Batalê is *better* left in [bronze or] stone': Zanker (2006) 369 n. 64.

**39–56.** A domestic intermezzo, featuring Kynnô's abuse of her slave, Kydilla. Kynnô promises to show Kokkalê even greater masterpieces, so orders Kydilla to get the temple-attendant to open the door to the temple (see 12n. 'this cockerel') and so let them see the art-treasures. Kydilla is unresponsive, apparently immersed in her viewing of the statues, and Kynnô launches her tirade. Kokkalê intervenes and succeeds in calming her friend, who notices that the door has opened in response to the breaking of day and the growing crowd; the curtain to the naos has also been drawn back. The spat with Kydilla has proven a storm in a teacup. The bathos must be intentional. The women are still in front of the temple, though now they are approaching it.

**39. ἔπευ:** for the Ionic contraction in -ευ- see *Mim*. 1.88n.

**40. ὤρηκας:** an Ionic form of ἑώρακας; cf. below, 77n.

**41. the attendant:** a *neôkoros* was originally a temple-cleaner like Iôn in Euripides' play (see esp. *Iôn* 102–84), but gained more significant responsibilities like giving information to worshippers; he remained subordinate to the temple-priest.

**You, aren't I speaking to you...?:** perhaps as only to be expected, this almost seems to be a formula in comedy when people are being ordered about: see e.g. Aristophanes, *Wealth* 926–7, Menandros, *The Arbitrators* 718–19.

**42. αὕτη:** common in drama, meaning 'you there!' (as also at lines 55 and 93); see LSJ[9] s.v. C.1.5.

**gawping, χασκεύσηι:** this verb is often used in reference to slaves in comedy, whose attention has wandered from their masters: Aristophanes, *Lysistrata* 426–7, Menandros, *The Bad-Tempered Man* 441.

**43. Grief, μᾶ:** this is is an oath 'by mother'; it is used elsewhere by Herodas (1.85, 4.33, 5.13, 56, 59, 6.4, 21, 47) and Theokritos (15.89), only by women and as little more than an exclamation. Here it seems to have retained sufficient of its original force as an oath to have affected the μή in the statement 'she's taken no notice of what I'm saying': μή + infinitive after a verb of swearing is regular, the μή replacing οὐ, while here the construction seems to have been extended to μή + indicative in strong negative assertion. The parallel at Aristophanes, *Birds* 194–5 is very close: μὰ γῆν, μὰ παγίδας, μὰ νεφέλας, μὰ δίκτυα, / μὴ 'γὼ νόημα κομψότερον ἤκουσά πω ('By earth, by traps, by mist-nets, by nets, / I've never yet heard an idea more clever!'). See Dunbar (1995) ad loc. Headlam (1922) 189, on the line is therefore right to see the English equivalent as 'I'll be damned if …'

**ὤρην:** 'heed' (here Ionic; Attic ὥρα), to be distinguished from ὥρη (ὥρα), 'season', 'time' etc.

**ὧν:** for ἐκείνων ἅ, '[notice] of those things which', by attraction of the relative.

**44. more vacantly than a crab:** because a crab's eyes protrude and appear to have an indeterminate, vacant stare: cf. Sokrates at Xenophon, *Symposion* 5.5.

**46. You greedy thing:** λαίμαστρον is attested only here (though cf. its possible use at *Mim.* 7.18); it functions as general abuse rather than referring to any actual greediness on Kydilla's part.

**46–7. sacred ... secular:** βέβηλος-ον means 'secular', 'profane', and ὀργή must be its opposite here. ὀργή, otherwise unattested, must be an adjective related to ὄργια etc.; opposed to βέβηλος, it most likely means 'sacred'. Emily Kearns suggests to me that it might mean 'religious professional', given its connection with ὄργια, and given the fact that the normal opposition is between ἱερός (or ἁγνός) and βέβηλος in reference to people, as in the 'Cyrene cathartic law' (Rhodes-Osborne [2003] 97.9–10 and 21); she therefore attractively proposes 'neither priestess nor laywoman'; LSJ[9] Supplement s.v. ὀργή (C) offers 'initiated'. Cf. Cunningham (1971) and Di Gregorio (1997) ad loc., who argue for 'pious … impious'. 'Praises' demands a personal subject, so Headlam-Knox (1921) 191–2 seem wrong to suggest that ὠργή is a synonym or error for ὀργάς, 'a tract of land devoted to a god' (LSJ[9] s.v. ὀργάς 2 hesitantly follow Headlam-Knox).

**good, κρηγύην:** this word occurs only once in Homer (*Il.* 1.106), and is therefore something that would have caught the eye of a Hellenistic poet, but the frequency with which it occurs in choliambic poetry (see also *Mim.* 6.39) raises the possibility that it was used by Hippônax (so Cunningham [1971] 137) rather than that Herodas is seeking out recherché vocabulary.

**49. ἐκ … καίεις:** tmesis again (18n.).

**50. ἔσσετ':** epic form of the future of εἰμί; here the final -αι is elided.

**there'll come that day:** a reminiscence of Hektor's famous prediction to Andromachê at *Il.* 6.448 (= 4.164), ἔσσεται ἦμαρ ὅτ' ἄν ποτ' ὀλώλῃ Ἴλιος ἱρή, 'There will come a day when holy Troy will perish.' Through the epic reminiscence, whether we are meant to think that Kynnô knows she is citing Homer or not, Herodas is putting Kynnô's domestic concerns in a humorously ironic light, rather as he had done, though less aggressively, with Kynnô at 12 (see note there).

**51. disgusting, τὠσυρές:** = τὸ ἀσυρές: Blass and Danielsson's emendation is generally accepted, though Cunningham (1971) 39 obelizes the word. Kynnô is most likely saying that Kydilla will scratch her head because Kynnô will brand it by way of punishment, and the unhealed scar will itch; βρέγμα properly means 'forehead', which is where brands were inscribed.

**52. Don't get excited, καρδιηβολεῦ:** if this is the correct reading, it is the present passive imperative (with Ionic –ευ for Attic –ου) of a verb καρδιηβολέομαι, 'to be stricken in heart'. In this form the verb is unattested elsewhere, though Hesychios gives us καρδιοβολεῖσθαι, and καρδιο- and καρδια- are are interchangeable spellings; cf. Schwyzer (1939) 1 438.

***πάντα:*** adverbial.

**53. slow reactions, νωθρίη:** Ionic form of νωθρεία, 'sluggishness'. Kokkalê is trying to calm Kynnô by saying that the slave's stereotypical indolence has made her unable even to hear what is said to her.

**54–6a.** Kynnô notices that the temple has been opened now that the crowd is growing. Thus there is no necessity for Kydilla to call the temple-attendant after all.
**54. ὠθεῖται:** impersonal passive, 'there is a crush'.
**56. ἀνεῖθ':** perfect middle or passive of ἀνίημι. The inner temple is separated from the outside by a curtain as well as a door; see Vatin (1970) esp. 214–16.
**56b-78.** Kokkalê expresses awe at sculptures, of which one must be of Athene, whom Kokkalê addresses. The women are therefore passing at this point through the pronaos, where more significant statues were displayed. But, somewhat abruptly (59), Kokkalê's attention turns to a painting by the great Apelles of a sacrifice, which must be part of the decoration of the naos. The sudden change of focus can be explained by the fact that we must imagine the women as first passing through the pronaos and then into the naos where the painting is revealed. This progression would have been easily pictured by ancient audiences familiar with the layout of a temple, if not of the Koan Asklêpieion itself; see below, pp. 127–8. We may compare this with what is required when Theokritos in *Id.* 15, which has affinities to *Mim.* 4, makes Gorgo and Praxinoa change scene from the house to the street (44), and then from the street to the palace interior (77). Kokkalê responds to the lifelike quality of the painting, just as she and Kynnô had done with the statues in the plaza, and Kynnô praises the painter for the accuracy of his draftsmanship, whatever the subject, and for his versatility.
**57. κείνην:** text uncertain; I follow the reading and punctuation of Danielsson and Di Gregorio, which gives 'Athene over there' as the sense of the adjective.
**58. chiselled, γλύψαι:** specifically of sculpture. Athene was the goddess of handicrafts in general; see also *Mim.* 6.65 and 7.116, where however the workmanship is lavished on objects very different from statues. She is invoked at Theokritos, *Id.* 15.80 in her particular role as goddess of spinning and weaving.
**καλά:** long first α (epic and lyric).
**Greetings, my Lady, χαιρέτω δὲ δέσποινα:** third-person imperative of χαίρειν, which is used to greet a person (see e.g. Theokritos, *Id.* 14.1, χαίρειν πολλὰ τὸν ἄνδρα Θυώνιχον) or a statue of a god (see e.g. Menandros, *The Bad-Tempered Man* 401, τὸν Πᾶνα χαίρειν). We can easily imagine Kokkalê addressing a statue of Athene at the entrance to the naos, especially if we accept κείνην in 57.
**59–71:** we know that Kokkalê is no longer referring to a sculpture or frieze when she admires the sacrifice-scene, because of ἐν τῇ σανίσκῃ, 'in the painting', or 'panel' (62), and because Apelles is the artist. The painting of the sacrifice involving the boy with the sacrificial tongs, the ox and the attendants is comparable in general subject-matter with a painting which Pliny, *Natural History* 35.93 attributes to Apelles, the 'procession of a *megabyzos*, a priest of Diana of Ephesos', though it cannot be identified as the same as the one mentioned by Pliny. Kokkalê's criterion is, as with the statues outside the temple, the lifelike quality and *trompe-l'oeuil.*
**59–62a** The painting of the boy is so lifelike its flesh will bleed if it is scratched; the silver sacrificial tongs he is apparently carrying would trick thieves into thinking it is real silver – all *trompe-l'oeuil.*

**60. πρός ... κεῖνται:** tmesis; see 18n. Either 'lies on him' or 'is laid on him' by the painter.

**οἱ:** dative of third person pronoun.

**61. hot, hot, θερμὰ θερμά:** the second θερμά, which a later hand has placed above the papyrus' first, has been added here to the main text to restore the metre. This kind of repetition is quite common, and lends emphasis; cf. Kallimachos 2.5 GP Λυσανίη, σὺ δὲ καλὸς καλός, 'Lysanias, you are handsome, handsome.' We must assume that a word for 'springs' has been left out, as at Xenophon, *Hellênika* 4.5.3 κατὰ τὰ θερμὰ προσῄει, 'he advanced by way of the hot springs.' It cannot be an adverb as Headlam-Knox (1921) 201 take the neuter plural (so also LSJ[9] s.v. θερμός IV), for that ignores οἷα, which is indeed an adverbial neuter plural, 'like'.

**62. τὠργύρευν:** Ionic dialect for τὸ ἀργύρεον (Attic ἀργυροῦν); see 10n.

**tongs, πύραυστρον:** this word is formed from πῦρ, 'fire', + αὔειν, 'light a fire', and the ending –τρον, which denotes an implement (as in ἄροτρον, 'plough'). It therefore must refer to the tongs with which the boy stoked the sacrificial fire. The boy will therefore be the procession's πυρφόρος, 'fire-carrier', whose duty it was to carry the embers for the sacrifice. For the long υ in πυρ-, which is usually short in compounds with πῦρ, see Schmidt (1968) 103.

**63. Myellos:** we know from Hesychios λ 1410 Schmidt (1861) 3 56 of a Myllos, who 'was ridiculed for his stupidity', perhaps on the comic stage; the spelling Myellos comes from a correction on the papyrus restoring the metre. A Pataikiôn is known for his thievery (Bekker [1814] 298.5): the name with the -iskos ending is a diminutive variant.

**64. have their eyes standing out on stalks:** reminding us of Kynnô's description of Kydilla's crab-like gaze at 44, as she stares in awe at all the statues in the plaza.

**τὰς κούρας:** 'pupils of the eye': LSJ[9] s.v. κόρη III. So also at 71.

**67. the man with his hair sticking up:** Pollux 4.137 Bethe (1900) 1 242, 6 uses the word ἀνάσιλλος in reference to a type of servant in comedy with bristling hair.

**68. have the look of life and day:** ζωήν and χἠμέρην are internal accusatives.

**69. too showy for a woman:** respectable Greek women do not draw attention to themselves. For the Ionic contraction in -ευ- in ἐδόκευν see *Mim.* 1.88n.

**71. sideways glare:** the ox is therefore painted in three-quarter profile. The effect of being followed by a portrait's eyes is of course a commonplace these days, but the *trompe-l'oeuil* seems to have been something new and strikingly realistic in Herodas' time.

**Κυννί:** this is the third form of the vocative of Kynnô's name, Κυννοῖ occurring at 20, 30, 35, 52, 56, and Κύννα at 60; similarly, in *Mim.* 6 both Κοριττοῖ and Κοριττί are used, for metrical convenience.

**72–8.** Kynnô offers a spirited defence of Apelles against the charge that he avoided ordinary subjects like the sacrifice scene for painting.

**72. true:** ἀληθινός, *alêthinos*, 'true to life', was a technical term in art and art criticism; see Gelzer (1985) 99, 101, 103–4, 113, 116.

**of Ephesos:** Apelles' birth-place was Kolophon, but he was Ephesian by adoption through residence.

**73. lines:** Apelles was famous for his drawn lines (here γράμματα = Latin *lineae*; on this and related terms see Pollitt [1974] 375–6, 392–7, 442–4), as is attested by the anecdote about his leaving the artist Protogenes a single line (*linea*) as a visiting card, which Protogenes immediately recognized as Apelles': Pliny, *Natural History* 35.81–2. Apelles wrote treatises on painting (Pliny, *Natural History* 35.79), and is likely to have written about his forte; see Gelzer (1985) 103–4, 111.

**75. ᾧ: ὅ οἱ,** by crasis (in addition to the parallels adduced by Headlam [1922] and Cunningham [1971] ad loc., see Knox's note on 6.102), literally 'whatever [came] to him into his mind'. For the idiom, see e.g. Theognis 633 ὅ τοί κ' ἐπὶ τὸν νόον ἔλθῃ, 'whatever comes into your mind.'

**ψαύειν:** this infinitive, meaning 'to touch', is governed by ἠπείγετο, the imperfect passive of ἐπείγω, 'urge on', meaning 'hurry oneself' (LSJ[9] s.v. ἐπείγω III.3), hence my 'strove'.

**to touch / [the perfection of] even the gods:** this is the majority interpretation of the difficult expression. It is argued for most recently by Di Gregorio (1997) 297–8. Adducing convincing parallels (e.g. Plutarch, *Demosthenes* 22.6, where the phrase 'touching heaven' is put in the mouth precisely of Apelles as a supreme accolade), he takes the phrase as meaning 'to reach even the perfection which is special to the gods'. This makes unforced sense of 'even'/'also' (which critics like Cunningham [1971] 143–4, [2002] 233, who read θέων, 'at a run', 'eager' are forced to ignore), and gives excellent sense to the whole statement: Apelles could render any subject with consummate art. This does not exclude the possibility that Herodas is defending Apelles against negative assessments of his realistic material (like the sacrifice-scene described in the painting), which Massa Positano (1974) 92–5 claims is at issue. On the question whether Herodas is defending his own realism, see the Discussion.

**77. ὀρώρηκεν:** this form of the perfect of ὁράω is an example of what was called by the ancient grammarians 'Attic reduplication', whereby some verbs beginning with α, ε, or ο prefixed their first two letters and lengthened the following vowel as in the temporal augment. The process is not peculiar to Attic, occurring in Homer and, as in Herodas, Ionic. It occurs with ὁράω in Herodas also at *Mim.* 5.4, 6.19, 6.44; note ἀκήκουκας at *Mim.* 5.49.

**78. hung up by the foot:** ποδός is the genitive of a thing touched or grasped, as at e.g. *Il.* 4.463 τὸν δὲ πεσόντα ποδῶν ἔλαβε, 'he caught him, when he had fallen, by the feet'; see Schwyzer (1950) 2 129–30. This form of punishment is attested in New Comedy, e.g. by Menandros, *Fr.* 79 Kassel-Austin (1998) 6.2 83. The significance of the laundry is probably that Apelles' detractor will receive the same treatment as dirty clothing, and will be ignominiously hung up and beaten. A striking parallel for punishment in a laundry is found at Plautus, *Pseudolus* 782, where the slave says that if he can't find a birthday present for Ballio today '*cras mihi potandus fructus est fullionis*', 'tomorrow I'll have to drink the fruit of the launderer': this refers directly to the human urine used to treat cloth before dyeing (see Willcock [1987] ad loc.), and indirectly to the beating in store.

**79–85:** The temple-attendant appears, and pronounces the acceptability of the women's sacrifice. His blessing is characterized by liturgical language and phraseology. **Your sacrifice is ... favourable** (καλ' ὗμιν ... τὰ ἱρά, 79) has a close parallel at Aristophanes, *Birds* 1118, τὰ μὲν ἱέρ' ἡμῖν ἐστιν … καλά. Cunningham (1971) ad loc. compares **perfectly** (ἐντελέως, 79) with the 'perfect sacrificial bulls' at Sophokles, *Women of Trachis* 760, and takes the adverb to mean 'perfectly in accordance with ritual'. **Looking on the auspicious side** (ἐς λῷιον ἐμβλέποντα, 80) employs λῷιον as commonly in oracular utterances (Wilamowitz-Moellendorff [1909] 262–3); for ἐμβλέπω meaning simply 'look', see LSJ[9] s.v. 2. **Has pleased** (ἠρέσατο, 81) is conventional (see e.g. Xenophon, *Memoirs of Sokrates* 4.3.16, … νόμος … πανταχοῦ ἐστι … ἱεροῖς τοὺς θεοὺς ἀρέσκεσθαι, 'it is the custom everywhere for men to please the gods with sacrifices'). **Glory, glory to you, Paiêôn** (ἰὴ ἰὴ Παίηον, 82, 85) was originally a shout of joy or, rarely, grief, and cannot be unconnected with the common παιάν-cry found in the *Paians* of Pindar (on which see Rutherford [2001] 18–19). **ἔασ'** ('are', 84) is a Homeric form, probably to give solemnity to the blessing. **May this be so** (ὧδε ταῦτ' εἴη, 85) is a standard type of concluding prayer (cf. Sophokles, *Oidipous the King* 1096: ἰήιε Φοῖβε, σοὶ δὲ ταῦτ' ἀρέστ' εἴη, with Fraenkel [1950] on Aischylos, *Agamemnon* 217).

**81. ἧπερ οὖν:** 'than in fact.' Cunningham (1971) ad loc. cites Denniston (1954) 421: 'οὖν, following περ, is sometimes used after relative adjectives and adverbs (in particular, ὥσπερ) … to stress the correspondence between idea and fact.'

**84. related…. by marriage, ὀπυιηταί:** the noun is found only here, but ὀπυίω is common in epic for 'marry'.

**86–8a.** The temple-attendant having finished his blessing, one of the women responds with an 'amen to that' (εἴη γάρ). These lines should be given to Kokkalê, who is addressed at 88. There the paragraphos indicates a change of speaker, who must now be Kynnô; the speech at 88–95 fits in with her greater experience of the ritual worship of Asklêpios.

**89. τεμεῦσα:** a hyperionicism, as also at *Mim.* 5.54 δραμεῦσα and *Mim.* 6.90 πιεῦσα, formed by the false analogy with ποιεῖν and the Ionic present feminine participle, ποιεῦσα; the Ionic form of the aorist feminine participle was, like the Attic, τεμοῦσα, δραμοῦσα and πιοῦσα.

**the little leg:** the Greek word σκελύδριον is a diminutive (from σκέλος), and further indicates Kynnô's embarrassment at the smallness of the offering. It was standard practice to offer a portion of the sacrifice to the priest or his representative (at Euripides, *Iôn* 323 the attendant says βωμοί μ' ἔφερβον, 'altars fed me'), and the leg was a common perk.

**90–2. cake-coin:** Herzog (1907) has demonstrated that originally a meal-cake of barley, oil and wine (πελανός) was offered to Asklêpios' holy serpent (see above, 27–9n.) through a hole in its lair (τρώγλη), but by the Hellenistic period the cake had

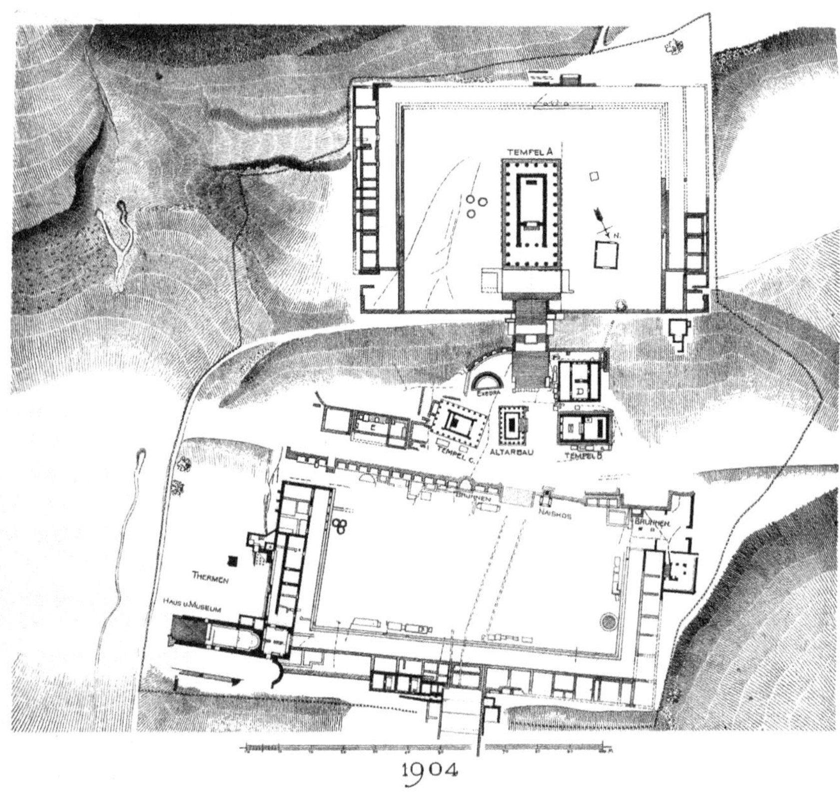


*Fig. 1. plan of Koan Asklêpieion. Herzog and Schazman (1932) illustration 37.*

been replaced by a coin, which was dropped through a hole (still called the τρώγλη) in a collection-box with an effigy of a snake on its top. As noted above (p. 106), Herzog discovered a collection-box in the naos of the Asklêpieion on Kos, which strengthens the case for the identification of the Asklêpieion of the poem with the Koan.

**92. moisten the barley-cakes:** with honey or wine. These cakes were standardly placed on the altar for Asklêpios: cf. Aristophanes, *Wealth* 660–1, 676–8.

**92. at home, οἰκίης ἕδρηι:** 'site of the house', a mildly grandiose periphrasis for 'at home'; see, similarly, the expansive phraseology describing Kynnô's home at line 12.

**93. ἐπί:** to be taken with λάθηι (tmesis: see 18n.).

**αὕτη:** this must refer to Kydilla the slave. Kynnô addresses her in exactly the same way at 42 and 55; see 42n.

*Fig. 2. plan of temple B: Herzog and Schazman (1932) illustration 16.*

**94. ὑγιίης:** = ὑγιείης; depending on the interpretation of the next two lines, this has been taken to mean either 'holy bread' or 'health' (as also at 95). For the meaning 'holy bread' see Athenaios, *Scholars at Dinner* 115a ὑγίεια δὲ καλεῖται ἡ διδομένη ἐν ταῖς θυσίαις μᾶζα ἵνα ἀπογεύσωνται, 'The barley-cake which everyone is given to taste at sacrifices is called a "health".' It seems likely that ὑγιίης is a partitive genitive after φέρειν.

**94–5.** Text and meaning disputed. **λωι** has never been convincingly explained. A general reconstruction of the lines may run thus: '[Do x, y and z with the rest of the sacrificial offerings], and don't forget to bring some of the holy bread, you there, Kydilla; hand out <…>, for at sacrifices the holy bread outweighs the loss of the portion [given to the gods].' This is in fact close to the text conjectured by Massa Positano, which would mean 'For certainly at sacrifices the holy bread has greater weight than the meagre portion of the flesh of the sacrificed victim which falls to the gods.' But line 95 is unmetrical (ὑγίη, with long ι). Cunningham's hypothetical suggestion, which would mean 'For certainly at sacrifices after which it [health] follows (ἁμαρτεῖ taken as ὁμαρτεῖ) there is pleasure (ἧσις) at one's lot', would get rid of the problem of unmetricality, but his diffident suggestion that ὑγίη is a gloss on the rare word ἧσις seems far-fetched. His obelization of the line is preferred by Di Gregorio (1997) 309.

## DISCUSSION

### *1. Constructing the scene*

As we realise in the course of reading this poem, Herodas feeds us broad hints that the scene is the Koan Asklêpieion, and he allows us to construct quite a precise picture of the women's movements within the precincts of the early-third century temple on the second terrace of the beautiful site.[1] So we can 'supplement' the poem's 'stage-directions' in our mind's eye. This kind of supplementation is quite characteristic of Hellenistic poetry and art, as I argue in detail elsewhere.[2] Locating his poem in a known Asklêpieion may also have been a means by which Herodas could help his contemporary Hellenistic audiences 'fill in the gaps' in their mental images of the works of art that the women see and react to in the precincts; their knowledge of the art-holdings of the temple would have helped them visualise the works of art to which the women refer without actually giving a description.

We ourselves have been able to envisage the first 26 lines as locating the women facing the altar of Asklêpios and Hygieia, lines 27 to 38 as indicating their change of attention to the human statues displayed between the altar and the temple. We can also without forcing the text at all picture the women at lines 39–56a still outside the naos or inner temple when Kynno, referring to the treat in store there, says 'My dear, come with me'. Lines 56b to 58 will be delivered in the pronaos, the temple's front hall, where Kokkalê greets the statue of Athene, and lines 59–95 will take place in the naos itself while the women admire Apelles' paintings, receive the attendant's blessing and make their offering of the *pelanos*, 'the cake-coin' offering, in the *thêsauros*, or 'offertory chest'. In terms of the real temple's layout on the Koan Asklêpieion (see Fig. 2, above, p. 121), the distances are quite small, 9.4 metres between the altar and the entrance to the pronaos, 7.2 metres from the door to the naos (the pronaos itself is only 5.3 metres in depth), and 6.8 metres for the depth of the naos; the *thêsauros* (1.6 × 2.15 metres) is directly to your left as you enter the naos. This makes the brevity of the women's changes of position even more understandable, at least for those who had seen the temple. The text, together with a first-hand knowledge of the site, is perfectly sufficient to allow listeners and readers to supplement the poem's 'staging' and 'stage-directions' in their minds. There is no necessity whatsoever for actual stage-performance complete with stage-props, which would in fact have inevitably been both unconvincing and disproportionately extensive for the few minutes it would have taken to perform the *Mimiamb*.[3]

There can be no real doubt that many in the original audiences of the poem would have first-hand knowledge of its location, especially if the *Mimiambs* were originally for Alexandrian consumption.[4] I have already noted that the complex built on the second terrace of the Koan site in the first quarter of the third century (see Fig. 1, above, p. 120) was immediately popular, and indeed that the opening of the temple there might have been the actual occasion for the composition of *Mimiamb* 4. Moreover, the island was intimately connected with Alexandria under Soter and Philadelphos, and appears especially to have enjoyed the latter's personal favour and interest. It was, after all, the base for Soter's navy against Antigonos in 309, and was an important scene of Ptolemaic naval activity at least down to the defeat by Gonatas during the Chremonidean War, perhaps in 262.[5] Then we have Philadelphos' apparently deeply felt personal connections with the island where he was born in 309, an event so strikingly celebrated in Kallimachos' *Hymn to Delos* (160–90) and Theokritos' *Enkômion to Ptolemy* (56–72), and from which his tutor, Philetas, hailed.[6] Philetas' significance for the Alexandrian poets is hardly in dispute, if only as demonstrated by the praise accorded him in Theokritos' seventh *Idyll* (39–41) and now by Poseidippos' epigram in the new Milan papyrus describing the statue erected in his honour by Philadelphos.[7] He will have added significantly to interest in the island among the Alexandrian intelligentsia. At the very least, we may say that Kos was, in particular as a favoured ally cultivated by Philadelphos, *en vogue* at the time of Herodas' composition of the poem.

But what then of the audiences or readers of the poem who had no direct experience of the island and its Asklêpieion? A helpful parallel is provided by the walk taken by Simichidas and Lykidas to the harvest festival of Theokritos' *Idyll* 7; the walk can be located with precision in the region south-west of Kos-city, and the poem moreover refers to places of specifically Koan topography as the walk proceeds.[8] Clearly, for the reasons just stated, many of Theokritos' original readers will have known the topography of the walk; interestingly, it leads one past the Asklêpieion itself. For such readers, it will have come as an added bonus that they could picture the walk, and relate landmarks like Mount Ôromedôn (on Simichidas and Lykidas' left) to Simichidas' profession of his poetic preferences (45–48); the literary pronouncements will have been vivid indeed. But other readers, who had no first-hand experience of Kos, would still have enjoyed the *Idyll* as a poem set in a place of known locality, or as one valid enough universally.

The same strategy seems to be at work in *Mimiamb* 4. Herodas describes a visit to a famous temple on a significant island in a way which would have been picked up by many members of his original audiences, and this will have helped them picture the women's progress from the altar, across the plaza before the pronaos, and through the temple itself. Familiarity with the *mise en scène* will have added to their enjoyment of the piece. But Herodas has catered quite sufficiently for audiences of the poem who had no direct experience of the locale. These people will, like us, have had pleasure in knowing that the *Mimiamb* is played out in a known, real and popular setting, which is moreover sufficiently generalised to be appreciated on its own terms. For these readers, the game of supplementation will have been even more exciting, for they will have found something new to add to their mental picture with each step. It is, finally, interesting that, if the identifications discussed here are correct, at least two poems show such an intimate knowledge of the south-west of Kos-city in the area around the Asklêpieion.

## *2. Constructing the works of art in the scene*

A similar process of supplementation operates in the case of the works of art in the temple-complex. They are not described directly, and so the women's reactions to them cannot be called true *ekphraseis agalmatôn* or 'descriptions of works of art' in the ancient sense of the term,[9] but we can form a surprisingly accurate mental image of them from the women's comments.

The original audiences of the mimiamb will have been in a far better position than we are to fill in details for their mental images of the works of art. An illustration of this fact is present in the poem's opening evocation of the statue group of Asklêpios and Hygieia, the god touching his wife with his right hand (1–5). We have seen that we have actual groups of the two deities in the pose indirectly described by Herodas,[10] and they would have been part of any Hellenistic audience's experience; the supplementation of the image would have come very naturally indeed. But even we find ourselves drawn into the act of filling in the absent details.

Immediately after the greeting to Asklêpios, his parents, Korônis and Apollo, are addressed (3–4; χαίροιεν, 'hail'). We may perhaps place them on Asklêpios' left. Next come his children, Panakê, Êpiô and Îêsô, 'to whom these altars belong' (5–6). Their altars can be envisaged as separate from that of Asklêpios and Hygieia, though they are not located spatially in relation to the main group. The same is true of Podaleirios and Machaon (7–9), and 'all the other deities who inhabit your hearth, Paiêôn' (10–11). Though the last is a standard precautionary all-inclusive formula, the effigies are present, as is made clear by the fact that the gods are said to inhabit Asklêpios' hearth. The panorama thus opens out from

Asklêpios' family to include other deities associated with his cult on Kos.

These economical indications would have been perfectly sufficient to help a Hellenistic audience to visualise the poem's altar-scene with a mental image. Such a picture, including that of the spatial arrangement of the cult-images, would have been confirmed through their knowledge that the Asklêpieion in question was the famous, recently constructed sanctuary on Kos, and that the sculptors involved were the distinguished sons of the Praxiteles who had made for the Koans their draped version of the Knidia.[11]

The mental image that we are given of the votive statues which the women proceed to view in the plaza between the altar and the pronaos is more precise, at least in part because votive statues were individualised to a greater degree than the more formally traditional cult-statues, and thus required additional visual description. With the first word of the dialogue in the plaza, ὅρη, 'look!' (27), we have the first instance of an invitation to look, which means for the addressee, Kokkalê, a command to look at the votive statues, and for the audience of the poem an invitation to visualise the statues in the mind's eye. The demonstratives 'that girl' (27), 'that old man' (30), 'this statue' (35–6), 'this likeness' (38) perform a similar dual function. First, they give the dialogue an impression of spatial location within the scene (as do 'this marble' [21], 'that writing' [23–4]; cf. 32, 48, 59, 67, 71). The demonstratives and similar expressions no more point to actual – and necessarily crude – stage-replicas of the works of art than Battos' reference to 'that calf' in Theokritos, *Idyll* 4.15.[12] They are like the deictics of the Farmhand in *Idyll* 25, who gives directions to Herakles on how to find Augeas, but in the process subtly and indirectly evokes in the reader a precise and detailed mental picture of Augeas' huge estate and the task awaiting Herakles in the stables.[13] But, secondly, within the mime-form of *Mimiamb* 4 they have the effect of giving the audience the sense that they are included as actual onlookers. As in a play, the audience also feels included in the exchange of responses, or at least a direct witness of them: we are invited to call up an image of what is being commented on and thus do some of the work, and so feel involved.[14] This heightened form of audience-inclusion, which is a pronounced feature of Hellenistic poetry, is similar to what we find in the mimetic hymns of Herodas' contemporary, Kallimachos, where it is left open whether the master of ceremonies is addressing the dramatic audience of worshippers or the actual readers of the poem. It is also similar to the many epigrams of the period with the 'Do you see?' formula, which invites the poem's reader to assume the rôle of a fellow onlooker at the works of art under review.[15] The technique is analogous to the viewing-process prompted by much Hellenistic art, most particularly in the context of *Mimiamb* 4, by the Boy with Goose in the Vatican, with the little child's gesture of appeal directly to the spectator.

The pose of the first statue, the girl gazing at the apple, is described comparatively directly: she is looking longingly upwards at the fruit. The speaker's question, 'Don't you think she'll faint ...?' (23–4) helps us mentally fill in the girl's facial expression. There are extant parallels – they need be no more than that – for the subject in a funerary relief[16] and in a statue[17] so the theme will have been a familiar one in Herodas' time, and the ancient audience's experience of it may have given them a quite nuanced image and context.

'That old man' (30) next claims the women's attention, but this is abruptly caught up with the low-base statue of the boy with an Egyptian goose (30–4). The statue is in marble (λίθος, 33), and is in front of the women's feet; the boy is squashing the goose, and 'will speak' – λαλήσει (33). There can be no real doubt that here we are dealing with the Boy with a Goose.[18] There is a temptation to regard λαλήσει as a simple commonplace, given the frequency with which Greek poetry of the Hellenistic period in particular celebrates the effect of a statue looking as if it were in the act of speaking,[19] but here it refers to an actual effect intended and executed by the sculptor, for the boy's mouth is open, and, given his right-arm gesture to the onlooker to pick him up, he is 'voicing' a command. This leads naturally to the more general notion that one day sculptors will be able to put life into stone (33–4).

Truth to life is of course the focus of attention in the case of the statue of Batalê. We have noted that the statue is called an *andrias* as is appropriate for a statue of a human, unlike Timarchos and Kêphisodôtos' cult-statue group. To judge by the name of Batalê's mother, Myttês, and her own name, she is likely to have been all *too* human and, in Greek society, not respectable.[20] All we are directly told about her pose is that she is standing (βέβηκεν, 36), but perhaps we are invited to fill out the picture of her stance from what her name suggests about her character.[21] We have seen that, when the speaker says 'Any man who hasn't seen Batalê herself, if he looks on this likeness he wouldn't need the real thing' (37–38), there may be mild censure: any male onlooker should be content with the woman's representation, and not be tempted to approach the real item.[22] If so, this would lend added and ironic colour to the ethos of the sculpture.

In this section of the poem, the spatial relationship of the four statues to one another is left completely open, and gives a feeling of haphazardness. That suits the realities of display in front of a Greek temple, and also contributes to the impression that the women are responding adventitiously and impulsively to the sculptures as they catch their eye, though, again, an audience with first-hand acquaintance with the Koan Asklêpieion might have been able to call to mind the details even of the sculptures' arrangement. However, in the next scene, the naos, the spatial disposition becomes more definite.

When the curtain is removed, the women first look into the naos from the pronaos. This is clear from the way Kynnô is asked 'can't you see / what wonderful works of art?' (56–7).[23] The comment 'you'd say that Athene over there chiselled (γλύψαι, 58) these beautiful things' allows us to infer that the women first look at statues. Kokkalê immediately greets the goddess, which probably allows us to infer that one of the statues is of Athene. The women then appear at line 59 to move further into the naos, for they can evidently observe at close quarters the figures on the painting (62) by Apelles depicting a sacrificial procession. Moreover, as is natural in a composite scene like that in the painting, the spatial disposition of the figures in the painting can be imagined more precisely than was the case with the statues in front of the temple.

The first figure to catch the women's attention is 'this naked boy' (59), whose flesh seems so pulsatingly alive (59–62). The silver of his sacrificial tongs would make a dimwit's or a thief's eyes stand out on stalks (62–5). We have a wonderful counterpart for the subject in Hellenistic sculpture, the Girl from Antium, who carries sacrificial implements on a tray.[24] Of additional interest is the fact that she was designed as a single, isolated figure from whom the onlooker was meant to create the whole context of the sacrificial procession in which she must have stood if she were real. She therefore provides a perfect analogue not only for the subject-matter but also for the way Herodas makes us fill in the gaps in his description of the temple's art-treasures. After the naked boy, the centre of attention turns to the bull and his attendants (66–71). From the way the bull's eye glares sideways and terrifies Kokkalê we can tell that the animal's head was painted in three-quarter profile.

As with the statues decorating the altar and those displayed in the open air of the temple-precinct, therefore, a surprisingly clear and comprehensive mental image can be constructed through the 'chance' clues in the women's excited reactions. The mode of the image-creation is dramatic rather than directly descriptive. Herodas' procedure is perfectly analogous with the visual art of his time, like the Girl from Antium, in that he invites his audience to fill in material which he avoids actually describing.

In his evocation of a mental image of the art-objects that catch the women's eye, Herodas therefore proceeds in a manner strikingly similar to techniques developed in contemporary art itself. He uses the supplementation-technique analogous to the one developed by the art of his times. He allows us to create from the hints in the women's comments a fuller picture than is conveyed by the words alone, both of the free-standing pieces and of the Asklêpios and sacrifice groups. Moreover, he employs the strategy of viewer-inclusion explored in art. The reader of *Mimiamb* 4 gets 'included in the conversation' and involved in the process of judging the art on display.[25] The women themselves are presented as being included in the works of art that they look at, as when Kokkalê is scared by the sideways glare of the sacrificial bull (69–71), who she thinks is looking specifically at her, or when Kokkalê and Kynnô look at the boy with the goose and expect him to speak, just as the actual statue in the Vatican seems to be doing. By using this analogous procedure, Herodas may possibly be advertising his appreciation of contemporary Hellenistic art's techniques of viewer-inclusion, which would in turn signal that his characters' artistic criteria are essentially valid and to be taken seriously.

### *3.* **Mimiamb** *4 and Hellenistic art criticism*

And indeed, for all the humour that we associate with Kynnô and Kokkalê's reactions,[26] we can also observe strands of serious Hellenistic art criticism in them. Behind their informal and popular phrasing Thomas Gelzer has identified formalised criteria of τὸ καλόν, beauty,[27] truth to life or ἀλήθεια[28] (observable in the Girl with the Apple, the Boy with the Goose, Batalê, and the sacrifice-scene, with its *trompe-l'oeuil* effects), excellence of γράμματα, lines,[29] and evocation of ἦθος, character[30] (here the Girl with the Apple is a particular case in point). Gelzer has also contrasted the discernible anti-idealism with the emphasis on 'positive' subject-matter as upheld by Xenophon's Sokrates,[31] and has seen connections with the known judgments of Xenokrates of Athens (who admired Apelles) and Duris of Samos, who was the collector of Pliny's anecdotes, especially concerning Apelles and the one about his thinking 'the masses a more diligent critic than himself' – *uulgum diligentiorem iudicem quam se.*[32]

We should take special note, finally, of Kynnô's defence of Apelles and the charge that he avoided certain subject-matter (72–8). Here it is important to bear in mind that the art which is made to excite the women's real interest is, apart from Timarchos and Kêphisodôtos' Asklêpios group, exclusively concerned with ordinary, even ugly, life; the divine is, apart from the Asklêpios group, perhaps relegated to Kynnô's statement that Apelles was able 'even to touch the gods'; in this context, it would incidentally be understandable why the Aphrodite Anadyomene isn't mentioned, if in fact she was housed in this part of the Asklêpieion. There can therefore be no real doubt that Herodas saw Apelles not only as an artist worth admiration in his own right but also as an analogue to his own stance in literature. In particular, Apelles' interest in low subject-matter is a corroboration of Herodas' own choice of material, though he too can present the divine, in the religious sections of *Mimiamb* 4, which stands out in this respect from his other poems.[33]

But we can go one important step further. All this can in fact be put in Aristotelian terms.[34] At *Poetics* 48a1–6 Aristotle seems to be saying that the 'tragic' painter Polygnôtos depicted people of higher than ordinary social status, while the caricaturist Pausôn depicted people inferior on the social scale (χείρους), and did so without idealization.[35] Herodas would clearly have put the Apelles that he commends in the same category as Pausôn, whose subject-matter Aristotle regarded as identical to that of the literary genre of comedy; and he would have regarded his *Mimiambs* as a subset of comedy. This confirms the view that in the Hellenistic period there was a real sense that poetry and visual art were analogous in that they could be classified in terms of the grandeur or 'lowness' of their subject-matter.[36] Knowledge of this fact is a significant advance on our understanding of how Hellenistic onlookers 'placed' art's different tonal effects. For our present purposes, it is particularly significant that Herodas exhibits deeply ingrained late Classical and contemporary habits of thought about classifying art on the basis of subject-matter. It is a further and important instance of his use of the technical criteria of the art-criticism of his day.

In *Mimiamb* 4, therefore, Herodas' engagement with contemporary Hellenistic art and art-taxonomy is more intimate, complementary and complimentary than has been noted so far. Not only does Herodas share with it some of its most innovatory features, especially reader/viewer-supplementation and inclusion, but he comments on it in a serious way and uses it to convey his own literary stance on, notably, the subject-matter and tonal placement of his own *Mimiambs*.

## *Notes*

1. See esp. p. 106 and the notes on lines 1–18, 5, 20–6, 27–38, 30, 39–56, 56b–78.
2. Zanker (2004) 72–102.
3. See Cunningham's comments on Mastromarco's reconstruction of the performance of the *Mimiambs* at Cunningham (1981) 161–2. Moreover, Mastromarco (1984) 62–3 is forced to postulate that Herodas distorted archaeological reality with his scenery: 'he imagines that the

statues are visible in the vestibule of the temple by moving the altar towards it: in this way the statues put in the vestibule could be looked at, while watching the door carefully.' And what then of the paintings in the naos? Puchner (1993) 21–4 criticizes Mastromarco's view that *Mim.* 4 is meant for stage-performance on the grounds that the poem exhibits 'no fixed spatial conception'. The present discussion may serve as a corrective to Puchner's conclusion, but that need not at all affect his overall position (that the poems were most likely performed as a 'recitation from a text together with differentiating gestures and changes of voice', p. 32), which so often emphasizes the need for 'work on the part of the audience's imagination to supplement the scene', p. 34. The case for the actual performance of the *Mimiambs* as any Menandrean comedy or any sub-literary mime might have been performed is put by Hunter (1993). At pp. 38–9 Hunter argues that sub-literary mime 'appealed to a much more elaborate stage-setting than the audience actually saw', and that arguments that *Mim.* 4's staging-requirements preclude performance 'carry very little weight'. But, by the same token, if audiences were meant to supplement a great deal of the stage-setting of performed sub-literary mime, why could they not have been expected to do so for a recitation? On the performance of the *Mimiambs* see above, pp. 4–6.

4. See Introduction to this poem above, pp. 106–7.
5. See Sherwin-White (1978) 108–9, Will (1979) 224–7.
6. For the history of the favoured position of Kos in its alliance with the first three Ptolemies see Sherwin-White (1978) 82–118; Habicht (2007).
7. Pap. Mil. Vogl. VIII 309 X 16–25. The statue was probably displayed in the royal court at Alexandria, as Spanoudakis (2002) 27 remarks; see also Bastianini-Gallazzi (2001) 189 on line 24.
8. Zanker (1980); see also Arnott (1979). For acceptance of my findings see most recently e.g. Spanoudakis (2002: 145).
9. *Ekphrasis agalmatôn*, ἔκφρασις ἀγαλμάτων, 'description of works of art', is merely a subset of *ekphrasis*, ἔκφρασις, or 'vividly visual description', and its introduction as a category of *ekphrasis* in fact comes comparatively late in the Greek rhetors themselves, first appearing in the fourth-century A.D. *Progymnasmata* of Nikolaos the Sophist: Zanker (2003) with lit., (2004) 82–3 with n. 26 at pp. 184–5.
10. See above, 5n.
11. Pliny, *Natural History* 36.20.
12. Contrast the general proposition of Mastromarco (1984) 22–3, that the demonstratives oblige us to accept that the *Mimiambs* were staged.
13. Zanker (1996).
14. Cf. Goldhill (1994) and Preisshofen (1978) 264 (followed by Gelzer [1985] 101 n. 14) on 'naive' terminology.
15. Zanker (2004) 109–23.
16. Webster (1964) 159 with Pl. VIIIa.
17. See 27–9n.
18. See 30–4n.
19. E.g. Apollonios of Rhodes 1.763–7, Antipater of Sidon 40 GP, and the passages from later writers collected by Headlam-Knox (1922) on 33; Aischylos, *Agamemnon* 241–2 gives evidence that the effect was an aim of painting in the Classical period.
20. See 35–6n.

21. See 36n.
22. See 37–8n.
23. Kynnô has known all along where these objects were: when as early as lines 39–40 she encourages her friend to follow her and see art more lovely than she's ever seen in her life, she must be referring to Apelles' painting in the naos; so e.g. Massa Positano (1973) on 39–40.
24. For illustrations see Stewart (1990) Plates 721 and 722, and Zanker (2004) 74.
25. Cf. Goldhill (1994), who discusses a similar feature of Hellenistic epigram and Theokritos' fifteenth *Idyll*. See further Männlein-Robert (2006). This is not the only effect of Herodas' dramatic mode of description: another important effect is to make the lifelike quality of the *objets d'art* more plausible by describing the reactions of viewers which 'prove' the claim.
26. The extreme case in *Mim.* 4 is perhaps the possible response to the works of art by the slave, Kydilla, whom Kynnô abuses for 'gawping this way and that' (42), most likely at one work of art to the next; admiration from a Kydilla is an endorsement which comes from a lowly source indeed, especially when it is part of the most indecorous comic business of the whole poem. See further Männlein-Robert (2006) 212–4.
27. Gelzer (1985) 100, 115–16.
28. Gelzer (1985) 99, 101, 103–4, 113, 116.
29. Gelzer (1985) 103–5.
30. Gelzer (1985) 111, 115–16.
31. Gelzer (1985) 111–12.
32. Gelzer (1985) 112–16. Simon (1991) 58–67 (followed by Puchner [1993] 21 n. 56) attempts to disprove that *Mim.* 4 has any serious art-criticism or bearing on Herodas' poetic aims, basing his argument on the assumption that we can hardly expect anything serious from women who are such 'Banausen' and who are so prone to intemperate outbursts. That assumption requires more defence than Simon offers: cf. the studies cited above, n. 14 and below, n. 33. And, in denying to Herodas the scale of subjects that Kynnô ascribes to Apelles, Simon does not consider the opening hymn of the fourth *Mimiamb* itself. Di Gregorio (1997) 244 follows Simon in arguing that Kynnô and Kokkalê's reactions are aesthetically naive and limited, and in the exclusive service of characterization and humour. At pp. 296–7 he admits that Kynnô avails herself of technical terms like 'truth to life', *alêtheia*, and 'line' or 'design', *grammata* (though, significantly, he sidesteps *to kalon*, 'beauty'), and at p. 299 he is prepared to admit that Kynnô's defence of Apelles echoes the anti-realist response to his work, but sees behind its intemperate invective 'il sorriso ironico del poeta'. This approach also fails to see that Herodas' aim as a comic poet is indeed to arouse laughter, but that behind comic irony the poet is still at liberty to say 'serious' things. Moreover, we remain justified in seeing, with Gelzer, an interest in the technical terminology of art-criticism that goes beyond what is required just to characterize Kynnô as a bluestocking *manquée*.
33. As Gelzer (1985) 109–10 notes, the Dream shows that Herodas was prepared to present his literary programme in low contexts. See especially Preisshofen (1978) on the early evolution of technical terminology from the artists' workshops, which put the beginnings of art-criticism on a more banausic level than those of literature. For a vigorous statement of the view that Herodas is also using art criticism as a reflection of his own poetic stance see Männlein-Robert (2006).
34. Zanker (2000).
35. See Zanker (2000) on *Politics* 1340a 35–9 where the matter of idealization is mentioned.
36. Zanker (2004) 134–9, 161–7.

## 5. ΖΗΛΟΤΥΠΟΣ

*(ΒΙΤΙΝΝΑ)* λέγε μοι σύ, Γάστρων, ἦδ' ὑπερκορὴς οὕτω
ὥστ' οὐκέτ' ἀρκεῖ τἀμά σοι σκέλεα κινεῖν
ἀλλ' Ἀμφυταίῃ τῇ Μένωνος ἔγκεισαι;
*(ΓΑΣΤΡΩΝ)* ἐγὼ Ἀμφυταίῃ; τὴν λέγεις ὁρώρηκα
γυναῖκα; προφάσις πᾶσαν ἡμέρην ἕλκεις.
Βίτιννα, δοῦλός εἰμι· χρῶ ὅτι βούλῃ μοι
καὶ μὴ τό μευ αἷμα νύκτα χἠμέρην πῖνε.
*(ΒΙ.)* ὅσην δὲ καὶ τὴν γλάσσαν, οὗτος, ἔσχηκας.
Κύδιλλα, κοῦ 'στι Πυρρίης, κάλει μ' αὐτόν.
*(ΠΥΡΡΙΗΣ)* τί ἐστι;
*⟨ΒΙ.⟩* τοῦτον δῆσον - ἀλλ' ἔθ' ἕστηκας; –
τὴν ἱμανήθρην τοῦ κάδου ταχέως λύσας.
ἢν μὴ καταισκίσασα τῇ σ' ὅλῃ χώρῃ
παράδειγμα θῶ, μᾶ, μή με θῇς γυναῖκ' εἶναι.
ἦρ' οὐχὶ μᾶλλον Φρύξ; ἐγὼ αἰτίη τούτων,
ἐγῷμι, Γάστρων, ἥ σε θεῖσ' ἐν ἀνθρώποις.
ἀλλ' εἰ τότ' ἐξήμαρτον, οὐ τὰ νῦν εὖσαν
μώρην Βίτινναν, ὡς δοκεῖς, ἔθ' εὑρήσεις.
φέρ', εἷς σύ, δῆσον, τὴν ἀπληγίδ' ἐκδύσας.
*(ΓΑ.)* μὴ μή, Βίτιννα, τῶν σε γουνάτων δεῦμαι.
*(ΒΙ.)* ἔκδυθι, φημί. δεῖ σ' ὀτεύνεκ' εἰς δοῦλος
καὶ τρεῖς ὑπέρ σευ μνᾶς ἔθηκα γινώσκειν.
ὡς μὴ καλῶς γένοιτο θἠμέρῃ κείνῃ
ἥτις σ' ἐσήγαγ' ὧδε. Πυρρίη, κλαύσῃ·
ὁρῶ σε δήκου πάντα μᾶλλον ἢ δεῦντα·
σύσσφιγγε τοὺς ἀγκῶνας, ἔκπρισον δήσας.
*(ΓΑ.)* Βίτινν', ἄφες μοι τὴν ἁμαρτίην ταύτην.

## 5. THE JEALOUS WOMAN

*(Bitinna)* Tell me, Gastrôn, is *this* [*indicating his penis*] so sated
that it's not enough for you to move my legs any more,
but you're devoted to Menôn's Amphytaiê?
*(Gastrôn)* Me to Amphytaiê? Have I seen the woman you're talking about?
You drag out pretexts the whole day long.
Bitinna, I'm a slave. Use me as you want,
and don't suck my blood night and day.
*(Bi.)* What a big tongue you've grown, too, you rascal!
Kydilla, where's Pyrrhiês? Call him to me.
*(Pyrrhiês)* What is it?
*⟨Bi.⟩* Tie this man up – are you still standing around? –
once you've hurried up and untied the rope from the bucket.
[*to Gastrôn*] If I don't shame you and make an example of you to the whole place,
for heaven's sake don't call me a woman.
Aren't you really a [proverbial] Phrygian slave? I'm at fault,
I think, Gastrôn, the one who placed you[, a mere slave,] among [free] men.
If I made that big mistake in the past, you're not going to find
Bitinna so stupid any more now, as you think.
[*to Pyrrhiês*] Come on, you, get that cloak off him by yourself and tie him up.
*(Ga.)* No, no, Bitinna, I beg you by your knees.
*(Bi.)* Strip him, I say! You've got to realise you're a slave
and that I paid three minas for you.
Damn that day
that brought you here. –Pyrrhiês, you'll be sorry.
I can see you doing everything, I do believe, except tying him up.
Tie his elbows together, tightly, and make the rope saw them off!
*(Ga.)* Bitinna, forgive me this mistake.

ἄνθρωπός εἰμ', ἥμαρτον· ἀλλ' ἐπὴν αὖτις
ἕλῃς τι δρῶντα τῶν σὺ μὴ θέλῃς, στίξον.
*(ΒΙ.)* πρὸς Ἀμφυταίην ταῦτα, μὴ 'με πληκτίζευ,
μεθ' ἧς ἀλινδῇ καὶ ἐμὲ [χ]ρὴ ποδόψηστρον –
*⟨ΠΥ.⟩* δέδεται καλῶς σοι.
*⟨ΒΙ.⟩* μὴ λάθῃ λυθεὶς σκέψαι.
ἄγ' αὐτὸν εἰς τὸ ζήτρειον πρὸς Ἕρμωνα
καὶ χιλίας μὲν ἐς τὸ νῶτον ἐγκόψαι
αὐτῷ κέλευσον, χιλίας δὲ τῇ γαστρί.
*(ΓΑ.)* ἀποκτενεῖς, Βίτιννα, μ' οὐδ' ἐλέγξασα
εἴτ' ἔστ' ἀληθέα πρῶτον εἴτε καὶ ψευδέα;
*(ΒΙ.)* ἃ δ' αὐτὸς εἶπας ἄρτι τῇ ἰδίῃ γλάσσῃ,
'Βίτινν', ἄφες μοι τὴν ἁμαρτίην ταύτην';
*(ΓΑ.)* τήν σευ χολὴν γὰρ ἤθελον κατασβῶσαι.
*(ΒΙ.)* ἕστηκας ἐμβλέπων σύ, κοὐκ ἄγεις αὐτόν
ὅκου λέγω σοι; θλῆ, Κύδιλλα, τὸ ῥύγχος
τοῦ παντοέρκτεω τοῦδε. καὶ σύ μοι, Δρήχων,
ἤδη 'φαμάρτει τῇ σοι ἂν ἡγῆται.
δώσεις τι, δούλη, τῷ κατηρήτῳ τούτῳ
ῥάκος καλύψαι τὴν ἀνώνυμον κέρκον,
ὡς μὴ δι' ἀγορῆς γυμνὸς ὢν θεωρῆται.
τὸ δεύτερόν σοι, Πυρρίη, πάλιν φωνέω,
ὅκως ἐρεῖς Ἕρμωνι χιλίας ὧδε
καὶ χιλίας ὧδ' ἐμβαλεῖν· ἀκήκουκας;
ὡς ἤν τι τούτων ὧν λέγω παραστείξῃς,
αὐτὸς σὺ καὶ τἀρχαῖα καὶ τόκους τείσεις.
βάδιζε καὶ μὴ παρὰ τὰ Μικκάλης αὐτόν
ἄγ', ἀλλὰ τὴν ἰθεῖαν. εὖ δ' ἐπεμνήσθην –
κάλει, κάλει δραμεῦσα, πρὶν μακρήν, δούλη,
αὐτοὺς γενέσθαι.
*(ΚΥΔΙΛΛΑ)* Πυρρίης, τάλας, κωφέ,
καλεῖ σε. μᾶ, δόξει τις οὐχὶ σύνδουλον
αὐτὸν σπαράσσειν ἀλλὰ σημάτων φῶρα.
ὁρῇς ὅκως νῦν τοῦτον ἐκ βίης ἕλκεις

30 ἐμὲ [χ]ρὴ leg. Milne ap. Knox (1925)[2] 15

I'm a human being, I made a mistake. But if ever you
catch me doing anything you don't like again, disgrace me with a tattoo.
*(Bi.)* Don't make up to me like this. Make up to Amphytaiê
with whom you have your tumble, while I must like a toe-rag –
<*Py.*> He's nicely tied up for you.
<*Bi.*> Make sure he doesn't get loose without your noticing!
Take him to Hermon in the jail
and order him to give him a thousand blows on the back
and a thousand on his belly.
*(Ga.)* Are you going to kill me, Bitinna, without even first examining
whether it's true or lies?
*(Bi.)* What about what you yourself just said with your own tongue,
'Bitinna, forgive me this mistake'?
*(Ga.)* That was because I wanted to calm down your anger.
*(Bi.)* [*to Pyrrhiês*] – Are you standing there spectating, and not taking him
where I tell you? – Kydilla, give this villain's snout a bruising.
And I want you, Drêchôn,
to go with this man at once wherever he leads you.
Girl, give the cursed man
a rag to cover his disgusting cock
so he won't be seen naked [as he passes] through the market-place.
Pyrrhiês, I'm telling you again for a second time
to tell Hermôn to give him a thousand *here*
and a thousand *here* – have you heard me?
Since if you wander one step from my orders
you will pay both the principal and interest yourself.
Go, and don't take him past Mikkalê's,
take the straight route. [*has second thoughts*] – Just as well I remembered:
girl, run and call them, call them, before
they get too far.
*(Kydilla)* Pyrrhiês, you deaf wretch,
*she*'s calling you. For heaven's sake, you wouldn't think it was a fellow slave
he was ripping into but a grave-robber.
Do you see how violently you're dragging this fellow

ἐς τὰς ἀνάγκας, Πυρρίη; σέ, μᾶ, τούτοις
τοῖς δύο Κύδιλλ' ἐπόψεθ' ἡμερέων πέντε
παρ' Ἀντιδώρῳ τὰς Ἀχαικὰς κείνας,
ἃς πρῶν ἔθηκας, τοῖς σφυροῖσι τρίβοντα.
*(ΒΙ.)* οὗτος σύ, τοῦτον αὖτις ὧδ' ἔχων ἧκε
δεδεμένον οὕτως ὥσπερ ἐξάγεις αὐτόν,
Κόσιν τέ μοι κέλευσον ἐλθεῖν τὸν στίκτην
ἔχοντα ῥαφίδας καὶ μέλαν. μιῇ δεῖ σε
ὁδῷ γενέσθαι ποικίλον. κατηρτήσθω
οὕτω κατάμυος ὥσπερ ἡ Δάου τιμή.
*(ΚΥ.)* μή, τατί, ἀλλὰ νῦν μὲν αὐτόν – οὕτω σοι
ζῴη Βατυλλὶς κἠπίδοις μιν ἐλθοῦσαν
ἐς ἀνδρὸς οἶκον καὶ τέκν' ἀγκάλῃς ἄραις –
ἄφες, παραιτεῦμαί σε. τὴν μίαν ταύτην
ἁμαρτίην …
*(ΒΙ.)* Κύδιλλα, μή με λύπει τι
ἢ φεύξομ' ἐκ τῆς οἰκίης. ἀφέω τοῦτον
τὸν ἑπτάδουλον; καὶ τίς οὐκ ἀπαντῶσα
ἔς μευ δικαίως τὸ πρόσωπον ἐμπτύοι;
οὐ τὴν Τύραννον, ἀλλ' ἐπείπερ οὐκ οἶδεν,
ἄνθρωπος ὤν, ἑωυτόν, αὐτίκ' εἰδήσει
ἐν τῷ μετώπῳ τὸ ἐπίγραμμ' ἔχων τοῦτο.
*(ΚΥ.)* ἀλλ' ἔστιν εἰκὰς καὶ Γερήνι' ἐς πέμπτην.
*(ΒΙ.)* νῦν μὲν σ' ἀφήσω, καὶ ἔχε τὴν χάριν ταύτῃ,
ἣν οὐδὲν ἧσσον ἢ Βατυλλίδα στέργω,
ἐν τῇσι χερσὶ τῇς ἐμῇσι θρέψασα.
ἐπεὰν δὲ τοῖς καμοῦσιν ἐγχυτλώσωμεν
ἄξεις τότ' ἀμελι[τῖ]τιν ἑορτὴν ἐξ ἑορτῆς.

85 αμ̣λιτ ̣ ̣ P: ἀμελι⟨τῖ⟩τιν Headlam (1899) 154

to torture, Pyrrhiês? For heaven's sake, Kydilla will see you
with these two eyes within a week
in Antidôros' wearing out those [achy] Achaian chains
on your ankles, which you only got rid of the day before yesterday.

*(Bi.)* [*to Pyrrhiês*] You there, come back here again with him
tied up in just the way you're leading him off,
and order Kosis the tattooist to come to me
with his needles and ink. [*to Gastrôn*] You have to get different colours
all at one go. [*to Pyrrhiês*] Let him be hung up
gagged like his honour Daos the slave.

*(Ky.)* Don't, mummy dearest, but just this once – as you hope
your Batyllis will live and you'll see her gone
to the house of a husband and you'll carry her children in your arms –
forgive him, I beg you. Just this one
mistake ...

*(Bi.)* Kydilla, don't give me any grief
or I'll run out of the house. Me, forgive this
seven-times-over slave? What woman meeting me
wouldn't rightly spit in my face?
No, by the Mistress, since he doesn't know
himself though he's a human being, he's soon going to know [himself],
because he'll have that inscribed on his forehead.

*(Ky.)* But it's the twentieth, and the Gerênia are in four days.

*(Bi.)* [*to Gastrôn*] I'll pardon you for now, so be grateful to this woman
whom I love no less than Batyllis,
having brought her up in my own arms.
But when we've poured our libations to the dead
you'll then celebrate festival after festival with no honey.

## COMMENTARY

SYNOPSIS Bitinna owns a slave, Gastrôn, who provides her with sex. She claims that Gastrôn has slept with another woman (1–3), a charge which Gastrôn alternately denies (4–5) and tacitly admits to by asking for pardon and promising never to repeat the performance (26–7), finally complaining that Bitinna has not ascertained the truth of the matter (35–6). Bitinna proves alert to the inconsistencies (37–8). She asks a favourite slavegirl, Kydilla, to fetch another slave, Pyrrhiês, to tie Gastrôn's arms up, strip him and take him in the company of yet another slave, Drêchôn, by the most direct route to the jailer of a local slave-prison for a savage beating (9–53). She orders Kydilla to find a covering for Gastrôn's genitals, so that they won't be seen by all and sundry in the agora (44–6). She has second thoughts about the sufficiency of the punishment, and sends Kydilla to bring the party back so that she can inform them of her new demand (53–5a). Kydilla remonstrates with Pyrrhiês over the cruelty with which he is carrying out his orders (55b–62). Bitinna announces that she has decided that Gastrôn should also be tattooed (63–8). Kydilla urges Bitinna to exercise forgiveness, in return for which she wishes Bitinna may see her daughter, Batyllis, reach maturity, get married, and provide Bitinna with grandchildren (69–73). Bitinna makes a show of her intention to have her wish carried out, claiming that she would lose the respect of all other women if she didn't (73–9), but relents immediately when Kydilla tactfully provides her with a credible and face-saving pretext: it's a day on which for religious reasons executions must be postponed. Bitinna tells Gastrôn that her leniency is motivated by her affection for Kydilla, which is no less than that for her own daughter, and issues him with a parting threat (80–5).

The mimiamb therefore divides into two sections. In lines 1 to 53a we have a dialogue between Bitinna and Gastrôn, together with Bitinna's commands to Kydilla, Pyrrhiês and Drêchôn for Gastrôn's punishment (9, 18, 20–5, 31b–4, 40–53a) and a brief interjection by Pyrrhiês (31); Bitinna lashes herself into increasing fury, which culminates in the wish to have Gastrôn stigmatized. Lines 54–85 foreground Kydilla and her tactful intervention, which calms her mistress' violent emotional state.

SOURCES Liaisons of free women with slaves are well attested for Greek and Roman life. Herodotos 6.68.2 tells how the deposed Spartan king Demaratos asked his mother whether the rumour was true that she bore him from intercourse with a muleteer, 'for, if you have done what people say, you're not the only one to have done so, but are one among many' (see also 1.173.5, on women and slaves in Lykia). The code of Gortyn in Crete (probably from the mid-fifth century) allowed slaves to marry free women: columns 6.55–7.10, printed by Willetts (1967) 44–5 with commentary at p. 69 (Willetts argues that in this context the term 'slave' means something more like 'serf'; but cf. Guarducci [1950] 162). Claudius the emperor put a motion to the Senate concerning the punishment of women who had relations with slaves; this became law in 52 A.D. Trimalchio boasts how as a slave he satisfied his mistress' needs; Petronius, *Satyricon* 75.11. Herodas was therefore presenting a familiar situation, but his depiction is informed by literature: comedy and, in particular, mime.

*Mimiamb* 5 has several debts to comedy. The motif of women committing adultery with slaves can be found for example at Aristophanes, *Women at the Thesmophoria* 491–2; see also Aristophanes, *Fr.* 715 Kassel-Austin (1984) 7.2 365, 'you who press against your mistress in the sweet-smelling sheets.' Plautus' *Haunted House* 1114–81 is evidence for the motif of a third party successfully intervening on behalf of a slave threatened with punishment by his master, and at *The Captives* 657–750 the third party tries to stop the master from sending the slave to prison, though unsuccessfully. Plautus' *Casina* 144–278, 937–1011 furnishes us with the theme of an imperious mistress being jealous of her husband's gallivanting with younger women and slaves, and Di Gregorio (2004) 57 suggests that Herodas presents us with an inversion of the situation. Bitinna's apparently sudden change of mind is paralleled at the end of Menander's *Bad-Tempered Man*, when Knêmôn unexpectedly yields to Getas and Sikôn's attempts to get him to join the revel (lines 955–60). Again, at line 74 Bitinna has a dilemma in that her favourite Kydilla is pleading on behalf of the cause of all her anger; she attempts to solve the impasse simply by fleeing the house. As Di Gregorio (2004) 55, 120 demonstrates in detail, the motif of this kind of evasion is found in comedy when a character threatens to travel to outlandish places when the going gets tough. So, for example, the disappointed Moschiôn in Menandros, *The Woman of Samos* (616–29) announces his intention of leaving Athens for Baktria or Karia; in another literary mime, Theokritos, *Idyll* 14.55–6, the jilted Aischinas tells Thyonikos that he will sail overseas and become a soldier. Gastrôn's cry 'Bitinna, forgive me this mistake. I'm a human being, I made a mistake. But if ever you catch me doing anything you don't like again, disgrace me with a tattoo' (26–7) has a striking echo at, for example, Terence, *The Eunuch* 852–3, *unam hanc noxiam/ amitte: si aliam admisero unquam, occidito*, 'Forgive me this one offence; if I ever commit another, kill me', and an even more remarkable affinity with the

Menandros-fragment ἄνθρωπος ὢν ἥμαρτον, 'being human I have erred' (*Fr.* 389 Kassel-Austin [1998] 6.2 239). There is much to be said for the conclusion of Hunter (1995) 160, 163 that the *Mimiambs* in general put comic material at a lower level of society than was the province of comedy, in the 'lower' milieu of mime and iambos.

However, no comedy known to us takes for its main subject a free woman's sexual relations with a slave, probably precisely because the subjects of comedy were traditionally expected to be less low than those of mime (see Zanker [1987] 144–5 on the apparently Theophrastan definitions which illustrate the ancient thinking here), and Herodas' principal source is to be located in the latter genre. We can say this with confidence firstly because the second-century B.C. writer Aristokles (in Athenaios, *Scholars at Dinner* 612c, discussed above, p. 21) informs us that the branch of mime called *magôidia* dealt with 'adulterous women' or 'women as adulteresses' (if the text is correct; otherwise 'women and adulterers'). More importantly, we have the second-century A.D. mime, preserved on papyrus (*POxy* 413 verso, most recently printed by Cunningham [2004] 47–51), and known nowadays as *The Adultress*. In the first scene, the anonymous adultress is angry with her slave Aisôpos for his liaison with Apollonia, another slave, and orders him to be whipped for not 'fucking' her, rebuking him for finding her 'cunt' harder than hard agrarian labour, and finally demanding that the other slaves take the couple away for execution. The rest of the mime is taken up with further nasty business as the adultress plots to poison her husband. The similarities to Herodas' mime are clear (they will be examined further in the Discussion, together with significant points of difference, including the softening of Bitinna's persona through her affection for Kydilla and Batyllis, 81–3), and though we need not conclude that the writer of the later piece knew Herodas' it is undeniable that Herodas' material derives from the mime tradition. It is interesting that his obscenity seems quite moderate in comparison.

Setting There is no evidence in this poem for its geographical setting, and no attempt at identifying it is worth mentioning here; see Cunningham (1966) 115–6 n. 6, and Di Gregorio (2004) 44–7. All that can be said with any certainty about the dramatic scene is that it must be a town, for Bitinna wants to make an example of Gastrôn 'to the whole place' (12), and is concerned for other women's reactions if she bumps into them (75–6), and the locality has its own agora (46), jail for punishing slaves (32), and its own festivals (80). The action is played out in a room or, more likely, the courtyard of Bitinna's house; see further the Discussion.

DATE The poem yields no evidence.

PURPOSE The characterization of an imperious woman's infuriation at finding that her slave and sex-object has been sharing his sexual favours.

**1–7.** Bitinna makes her accusation; Gastrôn fudges the issue.
**1. Gastrôn, Γάστρων:** 'Fatty', from γαστήρ, 'stomach', and hence with associations of greed, including sexual lust: see Headlam (1922) 228, Cunningham (1971) 148, Konstan (1989) 270–1, Simon (1991) 26 n. 15.
**ἥδ':** '*this*' probably refers to Gastrôn's penis, the κέρκος (a feminine noun) of line 45 (on which see n.); if the *Mimiambs* were recited, the reciter could have made a gesture, e.g. pointing to the level of the genitals of the imaginary interlocutor. The fact that Gastrôn is still dressed (18, 20) is no obstacle to this reconstruction. Cf. Mastromarco (1984) 48, who regards the reference as explicable only if the scene were staged with more than one actor; but we know from the vocative that a male is present, even if only in our mind's eye. Some have suggested that the noun to be supplied is γαστήρ, which is suggested by the immediately preceding Γάστρων; see e.g. Gerber (1978), persuasively refuted by Di Gregorio (2004) 71–2.
**so sated, ὑπερκορής:** not elsewhere attested of sexual appetite, but κόρος, 'surfeit', is; see e.g. *Il.* 13.636.
**move my legs, σκέλεα κινεῖν:** the idea of 'moving a woman's legs' is also present in the expression ἄραντες … τὼ σκέλει used by Aristophanes at *Peace* 889. Herodas' phraseology explains how κινεῖν, meaning basically 'move', came to mean the same as βινεῖν, 'fuck' (possibly related etymologically to βία, 'rape'), as we see in the expressions like κινεῖν τινα, κινεῖσθαι, exemplified by Aristophanes, *Frogs* 148, *Clouds* 1103, 1371; see further Henderson (1975) 151–2. The -εα ending of σκέλεα must be scanned as a long syllable (as at *Mim.* 3.40), since Herodas does not permit a tribrach in the first half of the third metron: see Bo (1962) 14.
**3. Menôn's Amphytaiê, Ἀμφυταίῃ τῇ Μένωνος**: in accordance with Herodas' use of such names (*Mim.* 1.50, 76, 4. 36, 6.87) Amphytaiê might be either Menôn's wife or daughter. Her name has grand associations, since it is elsewhere most closely approximated by the name of one of the charioteers of the Dioskouroi, Amphytos; see e.g. Pliny, *Natural History* 6.5.16. This seems to be another example in Herodas of resonating diction, here a name, in a low context.
**ἔγκεισαι:** the verb ἔγκειμαι in the sense of 'to be devoted to' occurs also at Theokritos, *Id.* 3.32–3; see LSJ[9] s.v. II, and the Supplement s.v. II.3.b.
**4. τὴν λέγεις:** this is the corrected reading of the papyrus. The scribe has crossed out the Μένων in his original τηνμενων-. His correction is easily explained: his eye had wandered back to the previous line's similar word-cluster Ἀμφυταίῃ τῇ, and he had started copying the Μένωνος immediately following it: Cunningham (1971) 149, Di Gregorio (2004) 73–4. **τὴν** is a relative pronoun, as standardly in Herodas; cf. e.g. 3.21, 4.17. For the 'synekphônêsis', or 'synizêsis' in ἐγὼ Ἀμφυταιῃ, where the loss of the -ω- is not reflected in the spelling, see above, p. 9.

**ὀρώρηκα:** for the 'Attic reduplication' see above, *Mim*. 4.77n.

**5. You drag out pretexts, προφάσις ... ἕλκεις:** the reason why Gastrôn says that Bitinna keeps dragging out pretexts is clear from what he goes on to say: he is her slave, so she is free to treat him just as she wishes – without continually raking up excuses like the story about Amphytaiê and tormenting him all the time; so Di Gregorio (2004) 75 against Cunningham (1971) 149. **προφάσις**, with long ι, is accusative plural, Attic προφάσεις; it is the papyrus' reading.

**7. don't suck my blood:** a common image, which can have an erotic connotation, as when Simaitha in Theokritos, *Id*. 2.55–6 says to Love 'Why have you drunk all my dark blood from my body clinging like a lake-dwelling leech?'

**my blood, τό μευ αἶμα:** Herodas places the genitive of a personal pronoun between the article an the noun elsewhere at line 39 and 6.41, as against the general use of the usual word-order; Cunningham (1971) 150 regards it as 'a sporadic survival of original freedom, which has been generally restricted'.

**8–18:** Bitinna orders the slave Pyrrhiês to tie Gastrôn up, to make an example of him and to teach him a lesson.

**8:** the line is found also at *Mim*. 3.84, though there the papyrus gives us ὅσσην. Perhaps it involves a colloquial formula: in both cases, the sarcastic comment about the miscreant's 'big mouth' is followed up by the threat of punishment. **καί** here probably conveys the sarcastic implication that Gastrôn has a big penis (1) *as well as* a big tongue.

**you rascal, οὗτος:** nominative exclamation instead of vocative, as at line 63 below: Bo (1962) 48.

**9. Kydilla:** a slave also in *Mim*. 4. The name may involve a pun on κῦδος, 'Honoured One', or κύδος (= λοιδορία: cf. e.g. the scholium on Apollonios, *Argonautika* 1.1337 Wendel [1935] 120.24 – 121.1), 'Rebuked One'. The scansion of -υ- can be either long or short here.

**κοῦ:** this is the corrected Ionic form of the papyrus' ποῦ, which some prefer on the grounds that Herodas may have used the Attic form in order to create alliteration with Πυρρίης, but why not with Κύδιλλα? The Ionic κοῦ is the papyrus' majority spelling: 3.8, 60 (twice), 68, 6.19, though at 3.59 the original Attic has been corrected to Ionic. At *Mim*. 2.28, however, I accept the papyrus' Attic form ποίου because of the alliteration with πηλοῦ; see n. there.

**μ':** elision from μοι, as commonly in Homer, and cf. Hippônax, *Fr*. 47.2 Degani (1991) 68.

**10:** on the setting and Pyrrhiês' immediate appearance see below, p. 156.

**ἀλλά:** the particle here and at lines 16 and 27 (as elsewhere in Herodas) denotes a new step within an argument.

**are you... standing around, ἕστηκας:** the perfect is often used to convey the idea of laziness; see also line 40 in this poem, *Mim*. 4.44, Aristophanes, *Lysistrata* 424, *Birds* 206, 1308, Menandros, *The Woman of Samos* 105 ἕστηκας ἐμβλέπων ἐμοί;, 'Are you standing around looking at me?' Bitinna is so impatient that she expects her order to have been carried out before she has finished issuing it.

**11. rope, ἱμανήθρην:** an otherwise unattested form of ἱμάς and ἱμονία, the usual words for a well-rope; the latter is the Attic usage.
**bucket, κάδου:** genitive of separation after λύσας.
**12. σ':** the pronoun is interposed between an article and its noun quite frequently in Herodas (cf. line 19 below, *Mim*. 3.71, 73 and 7.53, 126) and elsewhere in Greek to give prominence to the person denoted by the pronoun; here Bitinna is emphasizing Gastrôn as the person worthy of her exemplary punishment. **τῇ ... ὅλῃ χώρῃ, to the whole place**, is in the sense of 'to everybody'.
**12–13:** for the whole sentence Herodas may have had in mind the words of Knêmôn in Menandros, *The Bad-Tempered Man* 483–5 ἂν μὴ πᾶσι τοῖς ἐν τῷ τόπῳ / παράδειγμα ποιήσω, νομίζεθ' ἕνα τινὰ / ὁρᾶν με τῶν πολλῶν, 'If I don't make an example [of him] to the whole neighbourhood, think that in me you're looking on any Tom, Dick or Harry.' The sentiment in 'don't call me a woman' is in perhaps conscious contrast with Kreôn's remark at Sophokles, *Antigone* 484–5 ἦ νῦν μὲν ἐγὼ μὲν οὐκ ἀνήρ, αὕτη δ' ἀνήρ, / εἰ ταῦτ' ἀνατὶ τῇδε κείσεται κράτη, 'I am not the man now, but she is the man, if this authority will be flouted by her unpunished.'
**14. Aren't you really a [proverbial] Phrygian slave?:** this question is based on the proverb Φρὺξ ἀνὴρ πληγεὶς ἀμείνων καὶ διακονέστερος, 'Once given a beating, a Phrygian is better and more manageable', used also by Battaros at *Mim*. 2.100 (where see n.). I supply εἶς, Ionic 'you are,' adopted in my translation. The elliptical expression is generally taken to mean literally 'Isn't [this] more [a case of a] Phrygian?', which is difficult. μᾶλλον, 'more' or 'rather', is perhaps best taken with what immediately follows, when Bitinna blames herself for raising Gastrôn above his station: his status is 'rather' that of a Phrygian slave.
**15. who placed you[, a mere slave,] among [free] men, ἥ σε θεῖσ' ἐν ἀνθρώποις:** slaves were considered as objects in antiquity, not persons, and could only come to be regarded as human beings after manumission; in Petronius' *Satyricon* 74. 13 Trimalchio tells how *de machina substuli, hominem inter homines feci*, 'I raised her from the slaves' auction-floor, and made her a human among humans', by buying and marrying her. Bitinna has not freed Gastrôn; he is clearly still a slave (cf. δοῦλος at line 6). However, she has elevated him above his lowly servile condition by allowing him to be in the society of free people like herself. This is special pleading indeed.
**17. μώρην:** the papyrus has μωραν, with a line over the second half of ω and the first part of ρ. The copier has apparently atticized the termination, which some editors replace with the Ionic; so e.g. Cunningham (1971) 151, who regards the macron as a miswritten acute accent. I Ionicize with hesitation.
**18. just you, εἷς σύ:** from passages like Aristophanes, *Frogs* 605–6 it is evident that it was customary for two men to act as torturers; Pyrrhiês therefore probably hesitates because he is waiting for a fellow-slave to help him (perhaps also being afraid to harm Bitinna's favourite: Headlam-Knox [1922] 238), and Bitinna has to spell out her unusual demand.
**cloak:** the ἀπληγίς seems to have been a mantle worn on top of the chiton over both shoulders; see e.g. Pollux 7.47 Bethe (1931) 2 65, 1–3. It seems to have been a

garment for free men, slaves standardly wearing the ἑτερομάσχαλος, which left the right arm bare. It is therefore probably a perquisite of Gastrôn's elevated position in Bitinna's household; see above, 15n.

**19–25:** Bitinna intends to put Gastrôn firmly in his place.

**19. no, no, μὴ μή:** sc. τοῦτο ποιήσῃς. The repetition of the negative gives a plaintive tone.

**by your knees, τῶν ... γουνάτων:** the genitive after verbs of supplication can denote the part of the body by which a person is supplicated; cf. e.g. *Il.* 9.451 ἐμὲ λίσσέσκετο γούνων. The form γουνάτων is archaic and frequent in Homer; see e.g. *Il.* 5.176. It may be intended as an attempt by Gastrôn to confer solemnity on his appeal. **δεῦμαι** is another archaism, though it is also attested in Sophrôn (*Fr.* 35 Kassel-Austin [2001] 1 210), and might therefore be meant to bring Gastrôn back to his proper register. For δέομαι taking the accusative instead of its normal genitive see Thoukydides 5.36.2; here the object of the verb is probably put in the accusative by analogy with other verbs of entreating like ἱκετεύω.

**σε:** for the emphatic position of the pronoun between the article and the noun see above, 12n.

**20. ἔκδυθι:** for the ending -θι in the second singular person imperative of athematic verbs and verb-tenses (here second aorist, like γνῶθι) see Schwyzer (1939) 1 800.

**σ':** with γινώσκειν at the end of the next line.

**ὁτεύνεκα:** the use of the word after verbs of saying and perceiving is found in tragedy in its Attic form ὁθούνεκα, as e.g. at Euripides, *Alkêstis* 796 and more commonly in Sophokles (e.g. *Oidipous the King* 1016, *Women of Trachis* 277, *Aias* 123); now it is Bitinna's turn to assume the grand tone.

**21. three minas:** a reasonable price for a slave, to judge by Xenophon, *Memoirs of Sokrates* 2.5.2, where the cheapest slave is said to be bought for half a mina, and one on the most costly end of the normal scale might 'even' be bought for ten minas.

**ἔθηκα:** 'pay', 'pay down': see LSJ[9] s.v. A.II.8. Bitinna is asserting her owner's rights.

**22. ὡς μή ... γένοιτο:** exclamatory ὡς, 'would that', with the optative for present wishes occurs in intense moments in epic (see. e.g. *Il.* 18.107).

**23. that day that, ἥτις:** personifications like this in Greek literature are very natural, and are found in comic (Aristophanes, *Ploutos* 1097–9), tragic (Sophokles, *Philoktetes* 236–7), epic ([Theokritos], *Id.* 25.44) contexts, as well as in ironically high-flown prose (Loukianos 29 [*Twice Accused*] 10, Τίς δὲ ὑμᾶς, ὦ Ἑρμῆ, χρεία δεῦρο ἤγαγεν;, 'What business has brought you here, Hermes?'). Though it may have had some grand associations about it, such personification does not seem to have had the intense feel in Greek literature that it had in Latin, as can be seen by contrasting the present passage with Plautus, *The Captives* 464–8.

**you'll be sorry, κλαύσῃ:** in the sense of 'to weep as a result of a beating', this verb is particularly common in comedy: Aristophanes, *Peace* 255, *Clouds* 58 etc.

**24. δήκου:** this is also found in *Mim.* 3.90 and, in the form δήκουθεν, at *Mim.* 2.2; it means here 'I believe', as Denniston (1954) 267 defines δήπου. Why does Bitinna say that Pyrrhiês is not fulfilling her commands? Her impatience may be a factor, but so also is the stereotypical laziness of slaves, at least to her way of thinking. It is unlikely to be any loyalty to his class on Pyrrhiês' part, given the zest with which he lays into Gastrôn later (55–62).

**everything, πάντα:** supply ποιεῦντα, as at e.g. Theophrastos, *Characters* 25.5 καὶ πᾶν μᾶλλον [ποιεῖν] ἢ μάχεσθαι τοῖς πολεμίοις, 'do everything other than fight the enemy', and in the regular phrase οὐδὲν ἄλλο ἤ [ποιεῖν], '[do] nothing other than', as at Aischylos, *Persians* 209 ὁ δ' οὐδὲν ἄλλο γ' ἢ πτήξας δέμας / παρεῖχε, '[doing] nothing other than cower, it left its body exposed'.

**25. make the rope saw them off!:** the association with sawing is vivid.

**26–30:** Gastrôn asks for forgiveness, a change from his earlier protestations of innocence which does not escape Bitinna (36–7), and suggests that she tattoo him if he misbehaves again, an idea which she takes up later (65).

**26:** cf. Chaerea at Terence, *The Eunuch* 852–3, cited above, p. 139. By changing his plea to one of guilty Gastrôn demonstrates his craven opportunism.

**27. I'm a human being, I made a mistake:** it seems likely that Herodas has in mind Menandros, *Fr.* 389 Kassel-Austin [1998] 6.2 239, quoted above, p. 139. Konstan (1989) 274 perceptively argues that Gastrôn is following up Bitinna's statement that she has put him in the company of free people at line 15, is now stating that he and Bitinna share the status of being humans (as opposed to the gods, who make no mistakes), and is trying to appeal to their common humanity; he is thus 'switching implicitly from the contrast between a human being and a slave to that between a human being and a god'. Bitinna is of course not persuaded, and throws his admission back in his face when he pleads with her not to kill him before determining his guilt or innocence (35–8).

**ἐπῆν:** here the uncontracted Ionic ἐπεάν is contracted into the Attic form to give the long that falls at position 10 (the second syllable of the last metron); at line 84 ἐπεάν is not contracted since it preserves Herodas' predominant Ionic and gives the admissible anapaest of positions 1 and 2 (the first half of the first metron).

**28. ἕλῃς τι δρῶντα:** supply με.

**θέλῃς:** in all other cases (1.31, 3.80, 5.43, 6.25) Herodas uses ἄν with the subjunctive in relative clauses; see Kühner-Gerth (1955) 2 424–7.

**disgrace me with a tattoo:** tattooing, on the neck, legs, arms or, in the case of slaves, on the forehead, was a means of punishment for slaves (Menandros, *The Woman of Samos* 323), including runaway slaves (Aristophanes, *Birds* 760), and a mark of disgrace for wrong-doers (Aristophanes, *Frogs* 1511) and temple-robbers (Plato, *Laws* 854d).

**29. πρός:** governing 'με as well.

**make up to me, πληκτίζευ:** 'flirt', 'make up to', with erotic overtones, with πρός plus accusative as here or the dative. **ταῦτα** is an adverbial accusative. Bitinna's sarcasm is her immediate reply to Gastrôn's plea. For the Ionic contraction in -ευ- see *Mim.* 1.88n.

**30. you have your tumble, ἀλινδῇ:** this verb is also used in an erotic sense by Hippônax in Kallimachos, *Fr.* 191.42 Pfeiffer (1949) 166, and Herodas may be citing the obscenity from the older poet.

**I must like a toe-rag, ἐμὲ [χ]ρὴ ποδόψηστρον:** with this supplement we must assume that Bitinna was going to say ὑμέων γενέσθαι or the like, but is interrupted by Pyrrhiês. ἐμὲ [χ]ρὴ gives an anapaest at positions 7 and 8 (the second half of the second metron), which is rare in Herodas; it occurs elsewhere only at *Mim.* 6.55 in the first three syllables of μακαρῖτις, 'bless her memory'.
**31–9:** Pyrrhiês has tied Gastrôn up, Bitinna commands that he take Gastrôn to the local slaves' jail for a beating, Gastrôn protests that Bitinna hasn't even examined whether he is guilty or not, and Bitinna hurls his confession of his 'mistake' back in his face.
**31. σοι:** ethic dative: cf. 42 below and *Mim.* 6.10. The tone of καλῶς is sarcastic.
**32. jail, ζήτρειον:** a place for the punishment of slaves: see e.g. Hesychios ζ 149 Schmidt (1860) 2 257 τὸ τῶν δούλων κολαστήριον, where the ζητρός ('executioner', 'torturer') performed his duties; see Frisk (1960) I 613–4 s.v. ζητήρ. (ει is scanned short.) The word elsewhere occurs in comic contexts: Eupolis, *Fr.* 387 Kassel-Austin (1986) 5 512 and Theopompos, *Fr.* 64.3 Kassel-Austin (1989) 7 738; the *Etymologicum Magnum* 411.33 Gaisford (1848) quotes the usage in Herodas, though he misattributes it to Herodotus. The motif of a slave being sent to a *carnifex*, 'executioner', is common in the *palliatae* (the Roman comedies which Greek characters were introduced in Greek dress): see e.g. Plautus, *The Little Carthaginian* 369, *The Captives* 1019 (*ob furtum ad carnificem dabo*, 'because of your theft I'll take you to the executioner'), *The Two Bacchises* 687. Herodas therefore seems to be drawing on comedy for diction and theme here. Ἕρμων is an amply attested name in papyri and epigraphs.
**33–4. ἐς τὸ νῶτον … τῇ γαστρί:** the change in construction from the preposition to the dative is for the sake of stylistic variation.
**a thousand, χιλίας**: supply πληγάς, 'blows'. Two thousand blows would of course be fatal; the exaggeration is the product of Bitinna's hysterical anger.
**36. first, πρῶτον:** meaning the same as πρότερον, 'before': LSJ[9] s.v. πρότερος B III 3 c. It goes with ἐλέγξασα in the previous line.
**37. ἃ δ':** Cunningham (1971) 153 convincingly takes the sentence as a 'quizzical interrogation': 'and the things you've just said …?'; Bitinna's quotation of Gastrôn's words (from line 26) will then be in apposition. Her response is as often sarcastic, and in this case unanswerable.
**your own, ἰδίῃ:** the adjective is unusual in referring to parts of one's own body.
**γλάσσῃ:** the Ionic form; cf. *Mim.* 3.84n.
**39. γάρ:** '[I said this] because …'
**to calm down your anger, κατασβῶσαι:** possibly an Ionic contraction for the active aorist infinitive κατασβοάσαι (from σβοάω, a postulated form of σβέννυμι; cf. βώσῃ for Attic βοήσῃ at *Mim.* 3.23), but the form has not yet been fully explained; see Di Gregorio (2004) 97 for a summary of the debate. The phrase reminds us of Diomedes' remark about Achilles at *Il.* 9.678 κεῖνός γ' οὐκ ἐθέλει σβέσσαι χόλον; there is ironical humour in putting Gastrôn's intention to douse his mistress' anger on the same level as the idea of the heroic Achilles' extinguishing *his* anger: Di Gregorio (2004) 65, 97.
**40–53a.** Bitinna urges Pyrrhiês to get on with it, and commands another slave, Drêchôn,

to accompany him. She orders Kydilla to fetch a rag to cover Gastrôn's genitals for his appearance in the market, and repeats to Pyrrhiês her demand that Gastrôn be punished, insisting that he lead the party by the shortest route to the jail.

**40. ἕστηκας:** for ἑστάναι meaning 'to stand around lazily' see above, 10n.

**41. give ... a bruising, θλῆ:** cf. Theokritos, *Id.* 22.45 τεθλασμένος οὔατα, of the boxer Amykos' cauliflower ears.

**snout, ῥύγχος:** properly the snout of an animal, especially a pig, but also of a human in comedy: Athenaios, *Scholars at Dinner* 3.95a–e.

**42. villain, παντοέρκτεω:** found here only, but cf. πανοῦργος, 'a person who is up to all tricks', hence 'villain', and similar words. Pyrrhiês must be meant after Bitinna's complaints at his tardiness. The changes of addressee in lines 40–7 come thick and fast, though the vocatives give clear enough indication of who is referred to.

**43. to go with this man:** i.e. Pyrrhiês.

**'φαμάρτει:** present imperative singular of ἐφαμαρτέω, the papyrus' spelling of ἐφομαρτέω.

**44. δώσεις:** the future indicative can on its own act as an imperative, as at Plato, *Protagoras* 338a ὧς οὖν ποιήσετε καὶ πείθεσθέ μοι, 'so act in this way and obey me'; see Schwyzer (1950) 2 291. Alternatively, δώσεις might be a question, still giving an imperative sense, as at Aristophanes, *Women at the Assembly* 1083 βαδιεῖ δεῦρο, 'come here!'; see Headlam-Knox (1922) 249.

**cursed, κατηρήτῳ:** the Ionic form is κατάρατος with the second α long, though in Attic it is short. It seems most likely that the hyperionicism resulting from the replacement of the second long α by η is Herodas'; so Cunningham (1971) 154 and Di Gregorio (2004) 102; cf. Schmidt (1968) 39–40.

**45. to cover, καλύψαι:** infinitive of purpose, frequent in Homer: *Il.* 1.347. See Goodwin (1965) 329 para. 1532. Why does Bitinna want to hide Gastrôn's penis? She is apparently still attached enough to him not to want to let other women see his assets, an intimacy she jealously guards; see further below, p. 155.

**disgusting, ἀνώνυμον:** literally in the sense of 'unmentionable', which it means at *Mim.* 6.14. However, Bitinna implies Gastrôn's penis in line 1, and explicitly mentions it here.

**cock, κέρκον:** at *Mim.* 3.68 the word is used in its proper sense of 'tail'; here it is used in the sense of 'penis', as at Aristophanes, *Women at the Thesmophoria* 239.

**48–9. *here* / and ... *here*:** on the mode of performance suggested above, pp. 4–6, a solo reciter could have indicated where Gastrôn is to be beaten either by pointing to the relevant parts on his own body or by gesturing at the imaginary Gastrôn's. In a group recitation the actor playing Bitinna could have pointed to the actor reciting Gastrôn's rôle.

**48. ὅκως ἐρεῖς:** for this common colloquial imperative, before which a verb like ὅρα or σκόπει must be supplied, see also Aristophanes, *Frogs* 627–8: Kühner-Gerth (1955) 2 376, Goodwin (1965) 288 para. 1352.

**here, ὧδε:** a reciter could indicate with a gesture the parts of Gastrôn's body to be beaten.

**49. ἀκήκουκας:** an otherwise unattested form of the perfect of ἀκούω with 'Attic reduplication' (see *Mim*. 4.77n.); analogously, ὀρώρηκα at line 4, *Mim*. 4.77, 6.19, 44.
**50. ὧν**: the relative has been attracted into the case of its antecedent τούτων.
**wander ... from, παραστείξῃς**: Herodas chooses a verb and a form which is unique instead of the more common παραβαίνειν; the more normal (second) aorist of στείχω is ἔστιχον, the first aorist is found only at *Od*. 4.277, and στείχειν here is an archaism. The use of rare or obsolete vocabulary is typical of Herodas' manner, and has a distancing effect from the vulgarity of the context and subject-matter. For further examples of Herodas' procedure see e.g. below, 53n. and Bo (1962) 124.
**51. the principal and the interest, τἀρχαῖα ... τόκους:** the interest, τόκος, literally 'offspring', is metaphorically the 'child' of the capital, and the phrase 'to pay the capital and interest' is colloquial; see e.g. Aristophanes, *Clouds* 1156.
**52. Mikkalê:** a rarely attested name, probably deployed merely to give local colour; the neuter plural article plus the genitive is an idiom; cf. e.g. Theokritos, *Id*. 2.76 ᾆ τὰ Λύκωνος, 'where Lykôn's is', with Gow's note at Gow (1952) 2 50–1. The point is clearly that the route to Hermôn's jail past Mikkalê's is longer than the 'straight' one.
**53. τὴν ἰθεῖαν:** supply ὁδόν, 'road', though by this period the adjective was commonly thought meaningful by itself, especially when it qualified a word semi-cognate with the main verb.
**ἐπεμνήσθην:** at *Mim*. 6.42 the aorist of ἐπιμιμνήσκομαι is used in its usual post-Homeric meaning of 'mention', while here 'remember' is demanded as in Homeric usage: see e.g. *Od*. 1.31. The turn of phrase with the pronoun in apposition with a full sentence (here an order) is colloquial; see e.g. Theophrastos, *Characters* 7.2 ὃ παρέλιπον, 'as I omitted to mention', with *Mim*. 6.15, 42.
**54. run and, δραμεῦσα:** see *Mim*. 4.89n.
**μακρήν:** the feminine accusative singular from μακρός takes on a common adverbial sense LSJ[9] s.v. μακράν, with ὁδόν understood as at line 53 above.
**55. γενέσθαι:** of being at a distance, as commonly: cf. Xenophon, *The Education of Kyros* 4.3.16.
**Πυρρίης:** a nominative used as a vocative, probably because the ending has been assimilated into the form of the following adjective (of which the vocative is properly ταλάν); so Schmidt (1968) 90–2. Elsewhere (23, 47 and 59) the regular vocative is used.
**56. calling, καλεῖ:** with the omission of the colloquial αὐτός or αὐτή, 'the master' or 'the mistress'; cf. Aristophanes, *Clouds* 218, Theokritos, *Id*. 24.50. Not even 'herself' is necessary to indicate who is issuing the orders in this household, as Cunningham (1971) 156 remarks.
**For heaven's sake, μᾶ:** see *Mim*. 4.43n.
**δόξει τις:** Herodas frequently uses the future where the optative plus ἄν is the more common expression (*Mim*. 4.28, 33, 57, 6.65), but the future is more vivid. See also e.g. Theokritos, *Id*. 15.79.
**fellow slave, σύνδουλον:** properly 'a slave of the same master': Mastromarco

(1984) 88, n. 38, citing e.g. Aristophanes, *Peace* 745. Kydilla expresses surprise that Pyrrhiês is agreeable to treating a fellow-slave so violently.
**57. ripping into, σπαράσσειν:** used particularly of dogs tearing their prey to pieces: Plato, *Republic* 539b, Aristophanes, *Peace* 641.
**grave-robber, σωμάτων φῶρα:** = τυμβωρύχον, 'a grave-robber', who was placed on a par with murderers and temple-robbers for criminality: Loukianos 28 (*The Fisherman*) 14 ἦ που τυμβωρύχος (τυμβωρύχος ms β : λυποδύτης ms γ) τις ἢ ἀνδροφόνος ἢ ἱερόσυλός ἐστιν;, 'He's some kind of grave-robber, murderer or temple-robber, I suppose?' Lines 56–7 show Kydilla as a woman with firm moral principles in the midst of a household without moral reference-points.
**58. violently, ἐκ βίης:** = Attic πρὸς βίαν: cf. *Mim.* 4.77 ἐκ δίκης, 'justly'.
**59. to torture, ἐς τὰς ἀνάγκας:** used in the sense of 'torture' also by e.g. Herodotos 1.116, Thoukydides 1.99.1.
**with these two eyes, τούτοις / τοῖς δύο:** the ellipse of the word for 'eyes' is found also at *Mim.* 6.23; so too e.g. Theokritos, *Id.* 6.22 where the Kyklops swears τὸν ἕνα γλυκύν, ᾧ ποθορῷμι, 'by my one sweet [eye], with which may I see…'. Given the apparent colloquiality of the expression, it does not necessarily follow that Kydilla explains the ellipse by recourse to a gesture, *pace* Cunningham (1971) 156 and others.
**60. ἡμερέων πέντε:** genitive of time within which: Kühner-Gerth (1955) 1 385–7, Goodwin (1965) 241 para. 1136.
**61. in Antidôros':** a reference to the workshop in which Gastrôn had been working in chains; the name gives local colour.
**τὰς … κείνας:** supply πέδας.
**Achaian chains:** why the fetters are specified as coming from Achaia is not clear. As Cunningham (1971) 156 and Di Gregorio (2004) 110 suggest, perhaps Herodas is connecting the adjective with ἄχος, 'pain' (hence my 'achy'), because Ἀχαία was an epithet of Dêmêtêr, 'grieving' for Persephone; see e.g. Herodotos 5.61.2, Hesychios α 8809 Schmidt (1858) 1 341. An ironic reference (proposed by Bücheler [1892] 35) to the ἐυκνήμιδες Ἀχαιοί, the 'well-greaved (no pun intended) Achaians' of Homer (*Il.* 1.17 etc.), cannot be ruled out.
**62. πρῶν:** a contraction from the normal πρώην.
**you got rid of, ἔθηκας:** 'take off', of clothing; Headlam-Knox (1922) 255 quote Herodotos 1.10.1, where Gyges watches Kandaules' wife τιθεῖσαν τὰ εἵματα.
**wearing out, τρίβοντα:** with σε at line 59 above; cf. e.g. *compedium tritor*, 'chain-chafer', at Plautus, *The Persian* 420.
**63. You there, οὗτος σύ:** nominative exclamation instead of vocative; cf. n. on line 8 above. Pyrrhiês has reappeared with Gastrôn at the door leading from the street to the courtyard; see below, p. 156.
**ὧδε**, 'to this place', goes with ἧκε, οὕτως with δεδομένον.
**65. Kosis:** the name is especially associated with Thrace: Headlam-Knox (1922) 256, who also point out that tattooing was common practice there; see e.g. Herodotos, 5.6.2. Kosis would therefore be a credible person to administer a tattooing.
**tatooist, στίκτην:** one of Herodas' many *hapax legomena*: Bo (1962) 118–9.

Bitinna's second thoughts take up Gastrôn's earlier offer to have himself tattooed (28). Tattooing was a punishment for slaves; see 28n. Di Gregorio (2004) 113 argues that the punishment has a special significance for Bitinna, who is so keen to establish her ownership over Gastrôn; see below, p. 155.

**66. needles:** it is unclear why more than one needle should be used. Similarly, a character in Eupolis, *Fr.* 277 Kassel-Austin (1986) 5 463 says to a slave ἐγὼ δέ γε στίξω σε βελόναισιν τρισίν, 'I shall tattoo you with three needles'. Perhaps it is merely a matter of Bitinna exaggerating in her anger.

**all at one go, μιῇ ... / ὁδῷ:** found also in this sense at Euripides, *Helen* 765; perhaps it is a colloquialism; see Dale (1967) 119.

**67. different colours, ποικίλον:** the reason why Gastrôn's body will have different colours is not only because of the tattoo (which will be only black, since the ink will be black), but because Gastrôn will undergo the additional punishment described at lines 67–8; cf. *Mim.* 3.89.

**68. gagged, κατάμυος:** Cunningham (1971) 157 derives this from μῦς, which at *Mim.* 3.85 denotes a gag, and explains the compound adjective on the analogy of e.g. κατάπτερος, 'winged'.

**his honour Daos the slave, ἡ Δάου τιμή:** Daos is a common name for slaves in comedy (see Headlam-Knox [1922] 258–9 for documentation), and Bitinna may be alluding to the comic stage; thus τιμή suggests a sarcastically high-flown phrase based on tragic diction like ὦ μητρὸς ἐμῆς σέβας, 'my holy mother' at [Aischylos], *Prometheus Bound* 1091. Headlam-Knox (1922) 259 suppose that slaves in comedy were commonly hung up and gagged. It is just possible that we are to imagine that there was a slave named Daos in Bitinna's household who had suffered such a fate on some occasion.

**69–85:** Kydilla now intercedes on Gastrôn's behalf, playing on Bitinna's maternal desire to see her daughter Batyllis married, and on Bitinna's affection for Kydilla as a foster-child; after a further show of displeasure with Gastrôn, Bitinna capitulates at Kydilla's appeal to her religious scruples – a welcome face-saver and pretext.

**69–73a:** syntactic structure complex, though the lines read quite naturally. On the text given here, Kydilla begins with a prohibition, moves to what will be a request at first giving the object of the request (αὐτόν) with μέν qualifying νῦν, inserts a long parenthesis (οὕτω σοι ... ἄραις), finally provides the imperative (ἄφες), caps her request with another parenthesis (παραιτεῦμαί σε), attempts to start a new sentence (τὴν μίαν ταύτην / ἁμαρτίην), presumably intending to say something like 'forgive him', but is interrupted by the impatient Bitinna.

**69. mummy dearest, τατί:** a pet name, not otherwise attested, but cf. *Mim.* 1.60n. and 6.77 (ταταλίζειν).

**μέν:** we expect e.g. 'but later', though Kydilla does not follow up the μέν with a δέ – a case of μέν solitarium; see Denniston (1954) 380, 382.

**αὐτόν:** dependent on ἄφες in line 72.

**σοι:** ethic dative, as at *Mim.* 3.79 εἴ τί σοι ζῴην.

**ζῴη:** see *Mim.* 3.79 (with n.), quoted in the previous n.

**Batyllis:** a diminutive, not known elsewhere, though names beginning in Βατ- or Βαττ- are amply attested.
**70. you'll see, κὴπίδοις:** ἐφοράω is regularly used in funerary inscriptions where the deceased express joy over having seen their offspring and having cuddled their grandchildren, or sorrow at not having done so: Groeneboom (1922) 171–2, quoting e.g. Herodotos 6.52.2. He also compares Kydilla's phraseology with Herodas' contemporary, Phoinix of Kolophon, *Korônistai*, *Fr.* 2 10–13 Powell (1925) 233, 'Gods, may my daughter be blameless in every way, find a rich and notable husband, place a son in her old father's arms and a daughter on her mother's knees.'
**71b–72a. just this one mistake:** the phrase functions as a kind of *Leitmotif*, Gastrôn pleading for forgiveness for 'this mistake' (26), Bitinna quoting his words back at him (38), and now Kydilla using it on Gastrôn's behalf. Nor does it necessarily confirm that Gastrôn is guilty as charged: he uses it to calm Bitinna down, Bitinna's jealousy might be the reason she is so sensitive to any admission of guilt, and Kydilla might also be mollifying Bitinna (note μίαν). On Bitinna's interruption see above, on 69–73a.
**74. I'll run:** on Bitinna's attempt to evade the issue see above, p. 139.
**ἀφέω:** deliberative second aorist subjunctive from ἀφίημι, ἕω being the Ionic form for Attic ὧ; on deliberatives see Goodwin (1965) 289 para. 1358.
**75. seven-times-over slave:** comic exaggeration of the colloquial τρίδουλος, possibly even parodying Homerisms like ἑπταβόειος, 'made of seven ox-hides' (*Il.* 4.406 etc.). It may be borrowed from Hippônax, *Fr.* 190.2 Degani (1991) 165: Suetonius, *On Insults* 261–3 (Taillardat [1967] 63) states that the word was used by the iambographer; so also Eustathios, *Commentary on the* Iliad *of Homer* 725.39 (van der Valk [1976] 2 623). The fact that Eustathios, *Commentary on the* Odyssey *of Homer* 1542.49–50 quotes ἀφέω τοῦτον τὸν ἑπτάδουλον and ascribes it to Hippônax has been explained on the theory that Eustathios saw the expression quoted anonymously, remembered what Suetonius had said, and reached the wrong conclusion; so Cunningham (1971) 158, Di Gregorio (2004) 121–2.
**καὶ τίς:** καί before an interrogative can commonly 'convey an emotional effect of surprise, contempt, and so forth': Denniston (1954) 309–10.
**76. ἔς μευ δικαίως τὸ πρόσωπον:** for the placement of a genitive personal pronoun outside the normal position after the definite article and its noun see also above, on line 7, *Mim.* 1.58, 2.81, 3.42, 6.82–3; the position of an adverb (or adverbial phrase) like δικαίως between the genitive personal pronoun and the article is paralleled in the same passages. The word-order is therefore no index of Bitinna's agitation, unlike the καί of the preceding line.
**spit, ἐμπτύοι:** spitting in a person's face is as much a gesture of contempt in ancient Greek society as it is in ours: Sophokles, *Antigone* 1232. For the potential optative without ἄν see Kühner-Gerth (1955) 1 230.
**77. No, by the Mistress, οὐ τὴν Τύραννον:** oaths introduced by οὐ or ναί without μά are a feature of Doric, as at Aristophanes, *Lysistrata* 986, 990, where the Spartan herald says οὐ τὸν Δί', or Theokritos, *Id.*4.29 οὐ Νύμφας; Cunningham (1971) 158–9, citing Sophokles, *Antigone* 758 οὐ τόνδε Ὄλυμπον in a passage of dialogue, suggests that

the usage may have been extended to poetry in other dialects by the mediation of tragic lyric. Candidates for the identity of the 'Mistress' include Aphrodite, Hera, Persephone and an unknown oriental deity. Most recently, Fountoulakis (2007) has made a strong case for Aphrodite, on the evidence that Bitinna is a hetaira or ex-hetaira or a woman of similar moral standards and standing, and because Aphrodite is naturally and frequently invoked by women of her status; see further the Discussion, p. 154.

**78. though he's a human being:** at 27 Gastrôn has said he is a human being, and Bitinna here picks up the declaration. Now, however, she reverts to the distinction between a human being and a slave (Gastrôn having tried to shift the reference to the distinction between a human and a god), and asserts her ownership of him by threatening a tattoo, since tattooing was a punishment especially reserved for slaves. Since Bitinna says that Gastrôn 'doesn't know himself', his inscription is likely to have been the Delphic 'Know yourself.' This is made even clearer by τὸ ἐπίγραμμα τοῦτο, where 'this' must refer backwards to 'he doesn't know himself'; Cunningham (1971) 159. If so, the reference to the famous maxim is sarcastic: indeed the slave will know himself as such, but he will actually do so as a result of the physical intrusion on his person in a manner fit for a slave. See further Konstan (1989) 277–9, followed by Di Gregorio (2004) 125–6.

**80. the twentieth, εἰκάς:** the twentieth day of the month was thought to be the birthday of Apollo, as an alternative to the more usual seventh; cf. *Mim.* 3.53n.

**the Gerênia are in four days, Γερήνια ἐς πέμπτην:** a verb like ἔσται must be understood, though English requires the present 'are'. For εἰς plus the accusative of an ordinal with or without ἡμέραν in the sense of 'in x minus 1 days' (the reckoning being inclusive as always in Greek) see LSJ[9] II.2. The Gerênia is otherwise unknown, except that it was a festival in honour of the dead (84). Perhaps it is connected with Homer's Nestor, whose frequent epithet in epic is 'Gerenian' (e.g. *Il.* 2.336, *Od.* 3.68), and there was a medical guild on Kos named the Νεστορίδαι: see Paton-Hicks (1891) 37.53. Otherwise, we may guess from ἐγχυτλώσωμεν at line 84 that the festival was like the Attic Χύτροι, which involved libations; χύτλα, 'libations', were a Hellenistic equivalent of a χοή: Pfeiffer (1949) 388 on Kallimachos, *Fr.* 540. For a complete doxography of the problem see Di Gregorio (2004) 44–7. Kydilla's point is that during such festivals punishment of criminals was forbidden, in order to keep the state free from pollution. The most familiar example of a postponement of an execution until after religious dues had been performed is that of Sokrates till after the sacred ship had returned from its mission to Delphi: Plato, *Phaidôn* 58b. We may assume that Kydilla's strategy is to gain a reprieve for Gastrôn during which Bitinna will have time to cool down. We may further assume that her strategy will be effective: she has offered Bitinna the perfect method by which to save face, and Bitinna can claim generously that it is her affection for Kydilla that has helped move her.

**81. νῦν μέν:** corresponding with ἐπεὰν δέ in 84.

**84. ἐπεάν:** for the uncontracted form see above, 27n.

**to the dead:** οἱ κάμοντες, 'those whose work is done', are the dead, as in Homer (e.g. *Od.* 11.470).

**85. with no honey, ἀμελι⟨τῖ⟩τιν:** 'unhoneyed', that is 'bitter'; the word, conjectured by Headlam-Knox (1922) 271–2, is not found elsewhere, but the conjecture is superior to the ἀμέλει τήν, 'have no fear', which can be extracted from the papyrus, but which Headlam-Knox show is ungrammatical. Honey played a major part in libations to the dead among the Greeks (and presumably therefore at festivals to the dead like the Gerênia): Usener (1902) 182–5, 192–3. **ἑορτὴν ἐξ ἑορτῆς** conveys 'the notion of succession, continuity' (Headlam-Knox [1922] 268), and ἑορτή is used here metaphorically in the sense of 'good times', as at Theokritos, *Id.* 15. 26 ἀεργοῖς αἰὲν ἑορτά, 'It's always a party for people who don't work.' Bitinna is therefore claiming the final word, and promising Gastrôn a lastingly unhappy time of it after the festival that has meant his reprieve.

## DISCUSSION

### *1. Characters and characterization*

W. Geoffrey Arnott rightly regards *Mimiamb* 5 as an instructive example of what he calls the 'mosaic' technique, whereby 'The author takes a character who begins by representing a general type or basic emotion (here jealousy), and he goes on to individualize this type figure by encrusting on to it a mosaic of little details, individual details of behaviour that have been observed from real life.'[1] Since his article, however, scholars have been at variance over what precisely the basic type of emotion is in the poem.

Cunningham essentially agrees with Arnott, as can be seen from his description of the poem's purpose, 'The portrayal of neurotic fury and its pacification'.[2] On the other hand, David Konstan has placed the emphasis on Bitinna's despotism: she echoes the social independence that women were beginning to enjoy in the early Hellenistic period, but through her lack of self-control subverts and parodies the ideal of her male counterpart from the Classical age.[3] His approach has influenced Di Gregorio, who presses the idea of Bitinna's despotism further, stripping her of any vestige of love for Gastrôn other than sexual lust.[4]

Her position in her household is a key, though contentious, matter. Given that she has a daughter whose age is such that Kydilla can talk of her marriage (69–71), Bitinna must be in her mid-to-late thirties or her forties. And, given that there is no mention of her husband, it is possible that she is a widow, and therefore not an adultress. However, it would be a surprise if any woman (or her household slaves) would mention her husband in circumstances like Bitinna's; surely any thought of her husband would be the last thing on her mind? Similarly, in poem 6 the women act in secret, and only mention men when their erections are unfavourably compared with the dildoes under consideration (*Mim.* 6.69–70), while in poem 7 Kerdôn only mentions Mêtrô's husband or regular lover to say how lucky he is – and to make a pass at her (*Mim.* 7.111–2). Silence over whether Bitinna has a husband is therefore no argument for the non-existence of one. In any case, even when we know that Herodas' women have living husbands, as in *Mimiamb* 3, they can act as independently as Mêtrotimê. If that is so, Bitinna is an adultress, and she is indeed acting with despotic autonomy. On the other hand, Fountoulakis has cogently argued from Bitinna's willingness to let her attachment to Gastrôn be public knowledge that she is 'a hetaira or an ex-hetaira or … an independent woman with similar moral standards who would be considered part of this social group'.[5] On either reading of her circumstances, however, we can at the very least say with Konstan and Di Gregorio that she is projecting the image of the despotic householder.

The trouble for this householder is that her accustomed sense of absolute possession over her household has been challenged by a crisis of ownership of the most intimate nature. Using Arnott's general analysis, Herodas has grafted on to Bitinna's essential despoticism the individualising detail of her extreme emotional reaction to betrayal by one of her special chattels.

The challenge to her pride in ownership and the sense of sexual betrayal help explain Bitinna's state of emotions. As Konstan stresses, Bitinna has raised Gastrôn to her social level by admitting him to her bed, but the fact of the matter remains that she is his owner and social superior.[6] Hence her obsession with having placed Gastrôn among ordinary society (15), while insisting on the fact that he is her slave (20–3) and calling him a 'seven-times-over slave' (75). Her thinking on the matter has become confused. She claims that she must make a public example of Gastrôn, or 'for heaven's sake don't call me a woman' (12–13),[7] but in fact she immediately turns the blame on herself, for raising him in status. Later, she says she cannot let Gastrôn off his punishment for 'What woman meeting me wouldn't rightly spit in my face?' (75–6). It seems she doesn't want to be seen as over-tolerant of a disobedient slave.[8]

The sense of betrayal in both these ways heightens Bitinna's vindictive cruelty particularly in her command that Pyrrhiês cut into Gastrôn's arms with the ropes (25), in her demand that Hermôn give him such an excessive beating (32–4, 47–9), and in the way she picks up Gastrôn's own suggestion that she have him tattooed (27–8, 65–7). It also motivates her hysterical proneness to flare up when she feels her orders are not being carried out with due haste (10, 23–4, 40–2, 50–1), her sarcasm (1–3, 29–30), and her aliveness to Gastrôn's inconsistencies as he first denies knowing her rival (4–5), admits his 'mistake' (26), and pleads that Bitinna find out the truth of the matter (35–6), at which she throws his words about the 'mistake' back in his face (37–9). It is only to be expected that in the circumstances she resorts to her natural vulgarity (1–3, 28–9, 45), though it is interesting that the mistress in the second-century A.D. *Adultress* mime is, as we have seen,[9] even grosser in this respect.

Yet Bitinna is not the totally immoral figure of the *Adultress* mime, who orders the death of Aisôpos and his beloved Apollonia and plots to kill her husband by poisoning. Though her interest in Gastrôn is purely sexual, it is significant that she asks Kydilla to cover his genitals as he passes through the market-place (44–7): evidently, she is still emotionally vulnerable enough in her physical attraction to Gastrôn to be unwilling to share even the sight of his penis, for all that she blusters about his being 'cursed' and his penis 'disgusting'. She is also touched by her relationship with her foster-daughter, Kydilla (she admits she can be hurt by Kydilla at lines 73–4), and registers her fondness for her real daughter, Batyllis (81–3), so much so as to let Gastrôn off his punishment for the moment. It is true that at this stage she only needs a face-saving excuse, which she finds in her affection for Kydilla and the reminder about the Gerênia (80), but her apparent volte-face is too sudden (coming directly after her savage wish that Gastrôn's forehead be tattooed) to allow us not to believe that she has already been softening.[10] Herodas' 'mosaic' technique does indeed allow for elegantly complex characterization.

Of the minor characters, Gastrôn[11] remains the type of pure opportunism, as we have seen from his changing positions on his culpability. Even his ostensibly humanistic appeal for forgiveness on the grounds that he is a man, and therefore able to make mistakes, is merely a last straw to grasp at: the contrast traditionally conjured up by the statement is one between human beings and gods, though Bitinna can pick up his phraseology and make the contrast between free men and slaves, a boundary which he has only transcended thanks to her.[12] Gastrôn therefore is hardly on the same level as Aisôpos, who defies his mistress' designs by remaining faithful to Apollonia unto death. Kydilla is universally and rightly considered to be an attractive personality. The rebuke she delivers the horrid Pyrrhiês for his rough treatment of his fellow-slave, her suggestion that he looks as if he is man-handling a grave-robber, and her reminder that his purchase into slavery was just 'the day before yesterday' (55–62) all show that she has a sense of decency and humanity, to say nothing of her compassion for Gastrôn in trying to secure his release, her tact in working her connection with Bitinna and her psychological insight in bringing up the Gerênia (69–83).[13]

## 2. Setting

In contrast with what we have found in the other *Mimiambs*, in the case of the fifth poem we have considerable difficulty in envisaging the actual staging, including precisely where in Bitinna's residence the scene is set. It could, for example, be either in a room or the courtyard. The courtyard is perhaps the more likely: it would explain why Bitinna can ask Pyrrhiês to be so quick in untying the rope from the well-bucket (11), which is naturally to be found near the well in the courtyard, and why she can ask Kydilla to recall Pyrrhiês, Drêchôn and Gastrôn so quickly after their departure, for we can imagine Kydilla running across the courtyard to the street-door and shouting after the party to come back, and the party walking back into the courtyard as Kydilla chides Pyrrhiês for his roughness (56–62). This seems a reasonable reconstruction, even if there is no mention of the door leading on to the street: it could have been inferred by the original Greek audiences if they had concluded that the main action is played out in the courtyard. Pyrrhiês' apparently immediate appearance after Kydilla has fetched him (10) is easily enough explained by his having been in a room giving on to the courtyard, though again there is no explicit evidence for this in the text.

The movements of the slaves, Kydilla and Drêchôn, are also left quite vague. Where is Kydilla between lines 9 and 41, and how long has Drêchôn, who is only mentioned once (42), been present? It is not difficult to envisage them being on stage all the time, though some have argued that line 18 suggests that Pyrrhiês does not have anyone to help him strip and tie up Gastrôn at that point (literally 'you alone'). Nor is it made clear whether we are to envisage Kosis the tattooist as appearing with his needles and ink (65–85), though Kydilla remains present till the end and therefore has not gone to fetch him, in which case it seems logical to conclude that Kosis does not make an appearance.

Mastromarco,[14] Puchner,[15] and Di Gregorio[16] offer further discussion of the staging-difficulties in *Mimiamb* 5. Mastromarco sees the unclarities as needing the clarification that a staged presentation would have provided, while Puchner argues that the unclarities are further proof that the *Mimiambs* as a whole are not dramatic texts in the usual sense, and that the mode of presentation must have been similar to that of a modern radio play. However, when we consider the precision with which Herodas locates the scene and movements of *Mimiamb* 4, it is reasonable to conclude that he is precise about such matters when the situation calls for it (the fourth poem is very focused on the sights in the Asklêpieion), but is content to supply less spatial detail for his audience's visual reconstruction of staging when his main interest lies in other things, here obviously in his characterization of Bitinna. *Mimiamb* 5 perhaps illustrates the minimal degree of visual supplementation which the audience was expected to bring to their hearing or reading of the poems. All of this is in complete harmony with the thesis that *Mimiamb* 5 was performed by a single reciter, who supplies sufficient detail for creating a mental image of stage-setting and movements.[17]

## Notes

1. Arnott (1971) 125.
2. Cunningham (1971) 148.
3. Konstan (1989).
4. Di Gregorio (2004) 60–6; see also Simon (1991) 26.
5. Fountoulakis (2007).
6. Konstan (1989) esp. 273; so already Arnott (1971) 126.
7. The formula is ironically typical of a self-determining free man; it is used, for example, by Knêmôn at Menandros, *The Bad-Tempered Man* 483–5.
8. Konstan (1989) esp. 279. Konstan also argues that her subsequent oath in the name of the Tyrant Goddess is an appeal to the arbitrary despoticism she idealizes, but this is unlikely if the goddess is identified with Aphrodite; see 77n.
9. Above, p. 140.
10. The conclusion of Simon (1991) 115–16 that Bitinna is entirely unmoved by Kydilla's intervention thus seems superficial; cf. Di Gregorio (2004) 69. Di Gregorio (2004) 63 thinks that even the business with Kosis is only a means of saving her lover from the beating, even if momentarily.
11. For the paronomasia see 1n.
12. Konstan (1989) 274.
13. It is however questionable whether we should think of her as representing Herodas' 'voice'; cf. Simon (1991) 114–16, Di Gregorio (2004) 67–70. On the question of Herodas' engagement with social issues, see below, pp. 184–6.
14. (1984) 47–50.
15. (1993) 24–9.
16. (2004) 47–51.
17. On the performance of the *Iambs* see above, pp. 4–6. The use of deictics by the characters of *Mim.* 5 is also perfectly consonant with the theory. When Bitinna repeats her command about where Hermôn is to beat Gastrôn (48–9), namely 'a thousand *here* and a thousand *here*,' the reciter could have pointed to his back and stomach, as dictated by 33–4. At 60, when Kydilla says she'll see Pyrrhiês' come-uppance 'with these two eyes', he could have gestured to his own eyes (though not necessarily; see 59n.). The only contentious case is Bitinna's '*this*' in line 1, referring most likely to Gastrôn's penis (as explicitly at 45), which Mastromarco (1984) 47 sees as needing more than one actor to make clear, on the grounds that a solo reciter would be using a female voice at this point and no mere gesture could have made sense. However, Puchner (1993) 25 persuasively warns against underestimating the performance capabilities of ancient reciters, and reminds us of comedy's rich repertoire of phallic gestures that accompanied such deictics: see Henderson (1975) 117, cited by Mastromarco himself at p. 48.

## 6. ΦΙΛΙΑΖΟΥΣΑΙ Η ΙΔΙΑΖΟΥΣΑΙ

*(ΚΟΡΙΤΤΩ)* κάθησο, Μητροῖ. τῇ γυναικὶ θὲς δίφρον
ἀνασταθεῖσα· πάντα δεῖ με προστάσσειν
αὐτήν· σὺ δ' οὐδὲν ἄν, τάλαινα, ποιήσαις
αὐτὴ ἀπὸ σαυτῆς· μᾶ, λίθος τις, οὐ δούλη
ἐν τῇ οἰκίῃ κεῖσ'· ἀλλὰ τἄλφιτ' ἢν μετρέω
τὰ κρίμν' ἀμιθρεῖς, κἢν τοσοῦτ' ἀσποστάξῃ
τὴν ἡμέρην ὅλην σε τονθορύζουσαν
καὶ πρημονῶσαν οὐ φέρουσιν οἱ τοῖχοι.
νῦν αὐτὸν ἐκμάσσεις τε καὶ ποεῖς λαμπρόν
ὅτ' ἐστὶ χρείη, ληστρί; θῦέ μοι ταύτῃ
ἐπεί σ' ἔγευσ' ἂν τῶν ἐμῶν ἐγὼ χειρέων.
*(ΜΗΤΡΩ)* φίλη Κοριττοῖ, ταὔτ' ἐμοὶ ζυγὸν τρίβεις·
κἠγὼ ἐπιβρύχουσ' ἡμέρην τε καὶ νύκτα
κύων ὑλακτέω τῇς ἀνωνύμοις ταύτῃς.
ἀλλ' οὕνεκεν πρός σ' ἦλθον – ἐκποδὼν ἧμιν·
φθείρεσθε, νώβυστρ', ὦτα μοῦνον καὶ γλάσσαι,
τὰ δ' ἄλλ' ἑορτή – λίσσομαί σε, μὴ ψεύσῃ,
φίλη Κοριττοῖ, τίς κοτ' ἦν ὅ σοι ῥάψας
τὸν κόκκινον βαυβῶνα;
*(ΚΟ.)* κοῦ δ' ὁρώρηκας,
Μητροῖ, σὺ κεῖνον;
*(ΜΗ.)* Νοσσὶς εἶχεν ἡρίννης
τριτημέρῃ νιν· μᾶ, καλόν τι δώρημα.
*(ΚΟ.)* Νοσσίς; κόθεν λαβοῦσα;
*(ΜΗ.)* διαβαλεῖς ἤν σοι
εἴπω;
*(ΚΟ.)* μὰ τούτους τοὺς γλυκέας, φίλη Μητροῖ,
ἐκ τοῦ Κοριττοῦς στόματος οὐδεὶς μὴ ἀκούσῃ
ὅσ' ἂν σὺ λέξῃς.
*(ΜΗ.)* ἡ Βιτᾶδος Εὐβούλη
ἔδωκεν αὐτῇ καὶ εἶπε μηδέν' αἰσθέσθαι.

25 βιτᾶτος P, Βιτᾶδος Schulze (1893) 251–2

## 6. WOMEN VISITING
*or*
## WOMEN HAVING A PRIVATE CHAT

(*Korittô*) Sit down, Mêtrô. – [*to a slave*] Get up and give the lady a chair.
I have to order you to do everything myself.
You wretch, you wouldn't do anything
on your own. Good grief, you're a stone, not a slave,
lying like a dead weight in the house. But if I measure out your meal
you count the crumbs, and if I drop the smallest amount
the walls cave in with your muttering
and huffing and puffing the whole day.
Is it only now when we need the chair
that you wipe it and clean it, you robber? Be grateful to this woman,
since I might have given you a taste of my fists otherwise.
(*Mêtrô*) Korittô dear, you're chafing under the same yoke as me.
I'm also shouting day and night at these unmentionable women
and turning into a barking dog.
But the reason I'm visiting you is – [*to her slaves*] get out of our way;
get the hell out of it, you dimwits, all ears and tongues,
on holiday for everything else! – I beg you, don't lie to me,
Korittô darling, who was it who stitched
the scarlet dildo for you? (*Ko.*) Where did you see
it, Metrô? (*Mê.*) Nossis, Erinna's daughter,
had it the day before yesterday. My, what a lovely present!
(*Ko.*) Nossis? Where'd she get it from? (*Mê.*) Will you bad-mouth me
if I tell you? (*Ko.*) By these sweet eyes of mine, Mêtrô dear,
no one is going to hear from Korittô's mouth
a word of whatever you say.
(*Mê.*) Bitas' wife, Euboulê,
gave it to her and said to let no one know.

*(KO.)* γυναῖκες. αὕτη μ' ἡ γυνή κοτ' ἐκτρίψει.
ἐγὼ μὲν αὐτὴν λιπαρεῦσαν ᾐδέσθην
κἤδωκα, Μητροῖ, πρόσθεν ἢ αὐτὴ χρήσασθαι·
ἣ δ' ὥσπερ εὕρημ' ἁρπάσασα δωρεῖται
καὶ τῇσι μὴ δεῖ. χαιρέτω φίλη πολλά
ἐοῦσα τοίη, χἠτέρην τιν' ἀνθ' ἡμέων
φίλην ἀθρείτω. τἀμὰ Νοσσίδι χρῆσαι
τῇ μὴ δοκέω, – μέζον μὲν ἢ γυνὴ γρύξω,
λάθοιμι δ', Ἀδρήστεια – χιλίων εὔντων
ἕν' οὐκ ἂν ὅστις λεπρός ἐστι προσδώσω.
*(MH.)* μὴ δή, Κοριττοῖ, τὴν χολὴν ἐπὶ ῥινός
ἔχ' εὐθύς, ἤν τι ῥῆμα μὴ σοφὸν πεύθῃ.
γυναικός ἐστι κρηγύης φέρειν πάντα.
ἐγὼ δὲ τούτων αἰτίη λαλεῦσ' εἰμι
πόλλ', ἀλλὰ τήν μευ γλάσσαν ἐκτεμεῖν δεῖται.
ἐκεῖνο δ' οὗ σοι καὶ μάλιστ' ἐπεμνήσθην,
τίς ἔσθ' ὁ ῥάψας αὐτόν; εἰ φιλεῖς μ', εἶπον.
τί μ' ἐμβλέπεις γελῶσα; νῦν ὁρώρηκας
Μητροῦν τὸ πρῶτον; ἢ τί θἄβρά σοι ταῦτα;
ἐνεύχομαι, Κοριττί, μή μ' ἐπιψεύσῃ,
ἀλλ' εἰπὲ τὸν ῥάψαντα.
*(KO.)* μᾶ, τί μοι ἐνεύχῃ;
Κέρδων ἔραψε.
*⟨MH.⟩* κοῖος, εἰπέ μοι, Κέρδων;
δύ' εἰσὶ γὰρ Κέρδωνες· εἷς μὲν ὁ γλαυκός
ὁ Μυρταλίνης τῆς Κυλαιθίδος γείτων,
ἀλλ' οὗτος οὐδ' ἂν πλῆκτρον ἐς λύρην ῥάψαι·
ὁ δ' ἕτερος ἐγγὺς τῆς συνοικίης οἰκέων
τῆς Ἑρμοδώρου τὴν πλατεῖαν ἐκβάντι
ἦν μέν κοτ' ἦν τις, ἀλλὰ νῦν γεγήρακε·
τούτῳ Κυλαιθὶς ἡ μακαρῖτις ἐχρῆτο –
μνησθεῖεν αὐτῆς οἵτινες προσήκουσι.
*(KO.)* οὐδέτερος αὐτῶν ἐστιν, ὡς λέγεις, Μητροῖ·
ἀλλ' οὗτος οὐκ οἶδ' ἢ Χίου τις ἢ 'ρυθρέων

34 ηγυνηγρυξω P, sscr. ηδικηγρυζω m. alt.
36 λεπρος P, σα sup. λε m.alt.
38 σοφον P, sscr. καλ m. alt. σοφὸν Stobaeus 4.23.14 Wachsmuth-Hense (1909) 4.575
41 γλωσσαν P, γλάσσαν Meister (1893) 698–9

*(Ko.)* Women! That one's going to be the death of me some day.
I took pity on her when she was pleading with me
and I gave it to her before I'd used it myself.
She snatched her bit of luck and is giving it away
even to women she shouldn't. Good riddance
to a friend like that, and she can look for some other girlfriend
than me. To think that she lent my things to Nossis
to whom I don't think...– I'm going to grumble more than a woman should,
Adrêsteia, but may you not hear me – though I had a thousand
I wouldn't give even one which is rough.
*(Mê.)* Korittô, don't let it get up your nose immediately
if you hear anything stupid.
A good woman puts up with everything.
I'm guilty of this with my blabbing so much,
and I ought to have my tongue cut out.
But back to the thing I specially mentioned to you:
who is the man who stitched it for you? Tell me, if you love me.
Why are you looking at me with that smile? Is this the first time
you've seen Mêtrô? Why so coy about all this?
I implore you, Korittô sweety, don't lie to me any more;
tell me who did the stitching? *(Ko.)* Heavens, why are you imploring me?
Kerdôn stitched it. ⟨*Mê.*⟩ Tell me, which Kerdôn?
There are two Kerdôns, one the grey-eyed neighbour
of Myrtalinê, Kylaithis' daughter,
but that one wouldn't even stitch a plectrum for a lyre,
and the other's the one living near the tenement
of Hermodôros as you come off the main street
who used to be, used to be, a somebody once, but now he's grown old;
Kylaithis, bless her memory, had a relationship with this one –
may all her relatives remember her.
*(Ko.)* As you say, it's neither of them, Mêtrô.
The one I mean comes either from Chios or Erythrai, I don't know which,

ἥκει, φαλακρός, μικκός· αὐτὸ ἐρεῖς εἶναι
Πρηξῖνον, οὐδ' ἂν σῦκον εἰκάσαι σύκῳ
ἔχοις ἂν οὕτω· πλὴν ἐπὴν λαλῇ, γνώσῃ
Κέρδων ὁτεύνεκ' ἐστὶ καὶ οὐχὶ Πρηξῖνος.
κατ' οἰκίην δ' ἐργάζετ' ἐμπολέων λάθρη,
τοὺς γὰρ τελώνας πᾶσα νῦν θύρη φρίσσει.
ἀλλ' ἔργ', ὁκοῖ' ἐστ' ἔργα· τῆς Ἀθηναίης
αὐτῆς ὁρῆν τὰς χεῖρας, οὐχὶ Κέρδωνος,
δόξεις. ἐγὼ μέν – δύο γὰρ ἦλθ' ἔχων, Μητροῖ –
ἰδοῦσ' ἁμίλλῃ τὤμματ' ἐξεκύμηνα·
τὰ βαλλί' οὕτως ἄνδρες οὐχὶ ποιεῦσι
– αὐταὶ γάρ εἰμεν – ὀρθά· κοὐ μόνον τοῦτο,
ἀλλ' ἡ μαλακότης ὕπνος, οἱ δ' ἱμαντίσκοι
ἔρι', οὐχ ἱμάντες. εὐνοέστερον σκυτέα
γυναικὶ διφῶσ' ἄλλον οὐκ ἀνευρήσεις.
*(ΜΗ.)* κῶς οὖν ἀφῆκας τὸν ἕτερον;
*⟨ΚΟ.⟩* τί δ' οὐ, Μητροῖ,
ἔπρηξα; κοίην δ' οὐ προσήγαγον πειθοῦν
αὐτῷ; φιλεῦσα, τὸ φαλακρὸν καταψῶσα,
γλυκὺν πιεῖν ἐγχεῦσα, ταταλίζουσα,
τὸ σῶμα μοῦνον οὐχὶ δοῦσα χρήσασθαι.
*(ΜΗ.)* ἀλλ' εἴ σε καὶ τοῦτο ἠξίωσ', ἔδει δοῦναι.
*(ΚΟ.)* ἔδει γάρ· ἀλλ' ἄκαιρον οὐ πρέποντ' εἶναι·
ἤληθεν ἡ Βιτᾶδος ἐν μέσῳ δούλη·
αὕτη γὰρ ἡμέων ἡμέρην τε καὶ νύκτα
τρίβουσα τὸν ὄνον σκωρίην πεποίηκεν,
ὅκως τὸν ωὐτῆς μὴ τετρωβόλου κόψῃ.
*(ΜΗ.)* κῶς δ' οὗτος εὗρε πρός σε τὴν ὁδὸν ταύτην,
φίλη Κοριττοῖ; μηδὲ τοῦτό με ψεύσῃ.
*(ΚΟ.)* ἔπεμψεν αὐτὸν Ἀρτεμεὶς ἡ Κανδᾶδος
τοῦ βυρσοδέψεω τὴν στέγην σημήνασα.
*(ΜΗ.)* αἰεὶ μὲν Ἀρτεμείς τι καινὸν εὑρίσκει,
πρόσω πιεῦσα τὴν προκυκλίην θάμνην.
ἀλλ' οὖν γ' ὅτ' οὐχὶ τοὺς δύ' εἶχες ἐκλῦσαι

68 ἁμι..η P, ἁμίλλῃ Blass (1892)[1] 234, ἅμ' ἰδμῇ Meister (1892) 1332

81 βιτατοσ P, Βιτᾶδος Schulze (1893) 251–2; δουλη P, <Εὐ>βούλη Jevons (1891) 384, Kaibel (1891) 586

87 κανδατος P, Κανδᾶδος Schulze (1893) 251–2

90 θα…ν P, θάμνην Blass (1892)[2] 864 94 in mg. sup. sscr. m. alt.

he's bald and short; you'd think he's the exact image of Prêxînos,
and you wouldn't be able to find two figs so alike,
except that when he talks you'd know
that it's Kerdôn and not Prêxînos.
He works at home, doing his sales in secret,
for every door fears the tax-collectors these days.
But his workmanship, what workmanship it is!
You'd think you're looking at the handiwork of Athênê herself, not Kerdôn's.
But I – he came with two, Mêtrô –
when I saw them my eyes nearly popped out of my head with eagerness.
Men can't make their pricks stand as straight –
it's all right, we're on our own. And not only that,
their smoothness is sleep itself, and their dear little straps are
wool, not leather. You wouldn't find a shoemaker more considerate
of a woman's needs if you searched high and low.
*(Mê.)* So how come you let the other one go? *(Ko.)* I did everything, Mêtrô.
What means of persuasion didn't I use on him?
I kissed him, stroked his baldness,
poured him a drink of sweet wine, caressed him,
and did everything but give him my body to use.
*(Mê.)* But if he wanted that as well, you should have given it to him.
*(Ko.)* Yes, I should have, but it's not decent not to choose the right moment:
that slave of Bitas' was grinding corn near us,
for she has been wearing our millstone away day and night
and has ground it to dust,
just so that she needn't have her own repaired for four obols.
*(Mê.)* How did this man find his way to you here,
Korittô dear? Don't lie to me about this, either.
*(Ko.)* Artemeis, the wife of Kandâs the tanner,
pointed out our house and sent him here.
*(Mê.)* Artemeis is always on to some new deal,
for she's still drinking from the go-between's cup.
But since you weren't able to relieve Kerdôn of the two items

ἔδει πυθέσθαι τὸν ἕτερον τίς ἡ ἐκδοῦσα.
*(ΚΟ.)* ἐλιπάρεον, ὁ δ' ὤμνυ' οὐκ ἂν εἰπεῖν μοι·
† ταύτῃ γὰρ καὶ ἠγάπησεν, Μητροῖ. †
*⟨ΜΗ.⟩* λέγεις ὁδόν μοι νῦν πρὸς Ἀρτεμεῖν εἶναι,
ὅκως ὁ Κέρδων ὅστις ἐστὶν εἰδήσω.
ὑγίαινέ μοι, Κοριττί. λαιμάττει χὤρη
ἡμῖν ἀφ[έρπειν] ἐστί.
*(ΚΟ.)* τὴν θύρην κλεῖσον,
αὕτη σύ, [νεοσσ]οπῶλι, κἀξαμίθρησαι
αἱ ἀλεκτορῖδες εἰ σόαι εἰσί, τῶν τ' αἰρέων
αὐτῇσι ῥῖψον· οὐ γὰρ ἀλλὰ πορθεῦσι
ὡρνιθοκλέπται, κἢν τρέφῃ τις ἐν κόλπῳ.

98 αφ[……] P, ἀφ[έρπειν] Crusius (1892)$^{2}$ 126
99 ν[..]σσοπωλι P, ν[εο]σσοπῶλι Diels ap. Crusius (1892)$^{1}$ VIII

at least you should have found out from him who had ordered the other.
*(Ko.)* I begged and begged him, but he swore he wouldn't tell me.
† ...with her and he loved her, Mêtrô. †
*<Mê.>* You mean that I must now make a trip to Artemeis,
so that I can find out who Kerdôn is.
Farewell, Korittô sweety. Something's hungry, and it's time
for us to [leave]. (*Ko.*) Close the door,
you there, [birdseller], and count the hens to see
whether they're safe, and throw them some darnel,
for it's a sure thing that chicken-robbers will filch them
even if you rear them on your lap.

## COMMENTARY

This poem forms the first half of a diptych with *Mimiamb* 7. In *Mimiamb* 6, Mêtrô learns how she can get in contact with the maker of Koritto's dildo, Kerdôn, and in *Mimiamb* 7 we see her and other women in Kerdôn's shop, presumably after a lapse of some time. See further the Discussion of *Mimiamb* 7.

Location The location of *Mimiamb* 6 will therefore be the same as that of *Mimiamb* 7. The mention of the month Taureôn at *Mimiamb* 7.86 (where see n.) suggests Ionia, where the name is attested on inscriptions. The conjectured origins of Kerdôn, Chios and Erythrai (6.58), together with the association of dildoes and Miletos (see e.g. Aristophanes, *Lysistrata* 108–110), possibly confirm an Ionian setting, but further precision is unfounded.

Synopsis Mêtrô has come to visit her friend Korittô. After she has been seated and we have heard Korittô delivering the usual abuse of the servant for laziness (1–14), Mêtrô comes to the point, asking where Korittô acquired her red dildo, but Korittô initially only wants to know where Mêtrô learned of its existence (19–25). The lending-circle turns out to be extensive. Mêtrô tells her that Euboulê, Bitas' wife, to whom Korittô had originally given it, had lent it under condition of strict secrecy to Nossis, the daughter of Erinna, and Nossis was Mêtrô's source (25–6). This makes Korittô curse Euboulê (27–36). Mêtrô tries to calm her down with platitudes, and soothingly accepts the blame for upsetting Korittô by her gossip (37–41); she then steers Korittô back to the main topic (42–7). On learning that the craftman's name is Kerdôn, Mêtrô mentions two Kerdôns of her acquaintance, only to discount them (48–56). Korittô expatiates on the Kerdôn in question – his possible origins, physical appearance, his use of his home as a workplace, and sublimely satisfying artistry (57–73). Learning that Kerdôn visited Korittô with two dildoes, Mêtrô asks why her friend didn't secure the second one as well, and Korittô makes it clear that she used every trick in the book, though she couldn't let Kerdôn have sex with her because Euboulê was in the way while borrowing Korittô's grindstone (74–84). Mêtrô inquires how Kerdôn found his way to Korittô's house, and is told that the wife of Kandâs, Artemeis, who may be an active go-between, pointed the house out to him (85–90). Mêtrô says Korittô should have pressed Kerdôn for the identity of the woman who ordered the other dildo, but Korittô claims that Kerdôn was obdurate, possibly because he was keen on the woman (91–4). Mêtrô takes her cue to visit Artemeis straight away in order to find out about Kerdôn, and farewells Korittô, apparently in a state of urgent arousal (95–8). Korittô gives orders for the door to be closed and the chickens to be counted and fed, for bird-thieves are about (98–102).

Setting The scene is the living-room in the house of Korittô; this is joined to other rooms (into which the slaves can withdraw: 15); and the house has a chicken-yard (99–102), although it is situated in a town, to judge by the proximity of neighbours like Euboulê, who can borrow Korittô's grindstone with ease (81–4), and the speed with which Mêtrô seems to assume she'll be able to visit Artemeis (95).

Date The poem yields no evidence.

Structure The poem falls into three parts: the seating of Mêtrô and the abuse of the slave (1–14); the conversation about the dildoes (15–98a); and Korittô's arrangements for her chickens (98b–102). The second section falls into four parts, each headed by a question or plea from Mêtrô: the identity of the manufacturer of Korittô's dildo (15–41; 17); the first subject repeated more insistently (42–73; 46); the reason why Korittô could not extract the whereabouts of the second dildo from Kerdôn (74–84; 74); the identity of the person who put Kerdôn in touch with Korittô, and Mêtrô's determination to pay a call on Artemeis (85–98; 86). The actual conversation, with its tone of semi-guilty sexual excitement, is therefore flanked by moments from more ordinary everyday life, with their humdrum, domestic tone.

Sources The theme of wives seeking sexual gratification apart from their husbands is common in Old Comedy, as is evidenced in Aristophanes' *Women at the Thesmophoria* 478–89, 493–6, 499–501 and *Peace* 978–86. Lysistrata's complaint at *Lysistrata* 108–10 that the revolt of Miletos has dried up the supply of dildoes shows that recourse to the *olisbos* (as it is more commonly known) was also part of the comic repertoire (see also Epicharmos, *Fr.* 226 Kassel-Austin [2001] 1 132 and Kratinos, *Fr.* 354 Kassel-Austin [1983] 6 294), but the dildo figured in mime as well, as we can see from Sophrôn, *Fr.* 23 Kassel-Austin (2001) 1 205. There someone asks a female friend about 'the widows' delight', so we may have quite a close precursor to Herodas in that Sophrôn seems to have presented a steamy conversation among women about dildoes.

The motif of visiting goes back to Homer (*Il.* 3.419–25, 6.354, 18.379–90 and the *Homeric Hymn to Demeter* 184–191), but it is attested in comedy (see e.g. Apollodôros, *Fr.* 15 Kassel-Austin [1991] 2 514), and more pertinently in mime, for we have someone ordering someone else to bring a chair in Sophrôn, *Fr.* **10 Kassel-Austin (2001) 1 200, which seems to be a model for Theokritos, *Idyll* 15.2. In fact, the opening scene of the fifteenth *Idyll* (lines 1–43) also shares with Herodas's poem the motifs of abusing one's slaves for laziness or negligence, and of settling the domestic animals, in Theokritos' case the cat (28–9), in Herodas' the chickens (99–102).

Herodas' poem also shares with Theokritos certain striking turns of phrase. Mêtrô's advice not to 'let it get up your nose', τὴν χολὴν ἐπὶ ῥινός (37), reminds us of Thyrsis' warning not to play the pipes at noon because Pan is tetchy, and οἱ ἀεὶ δριμεῖα χολὰ ποτὶ ῥινὶ κάθηται, 'bitter wrath always sits on his nostril' (*Id.* 1.18). Mêtrô also calls the dead Kylaithis ἡ μακαρῖτις, 'bless her memory' (55), while Simaitha in *Idyll* 2.70 uses the same designation of a Thracian nurse. Korittô's description of the dildo's smoothness as ὕπνος, 'sleep' (71; see n. for the figure), has an affinity with Theokritos' formulae ὕπνου μαλακώτερα, 'softer than sleep', and μαλακώτεροι ὕπνου, 'softer than sleep' (*Idylls* 5.51 and 15.125), used to describe, respectively, lambskins and wool (note that at *Mimiamb* 6.72, moreover, the laces of the dildo are said to be wool), and the bedcovers of the Adonis tableau. Gorgô's 'Time to go', ἕρπειν ὥρα κ' εἴη, at *Idyll* 15.25 provides an easy supplement at *Mimiamb* 6.97–8, χὤρη / ἡμῖν ἀφ[έρπειν] ἐστί, 'and it's time / for us to leave', and her complaints about her husband's need for lunch has been seen as comparable with Mêtrô's λαιμάττει, 'something's hungry', at line 97 (though see n.). Simon (1991) 136–9, 143–4 argues for Herodas' overall dependence on Theokritos in *Mimiamb* 6 (with the possible exception of the use of the word μακαρῖτις at *Mimiamb* 6.55, but see my n.). I would add that it is an appealing thought that Herodas may have recycled a phrase used to describe the covers of Adonis and Aphrodite's bed in order to describe the laces of a dildo.

Purpose The humorous characterization of two suburban housewives who will (almost) stop at nothing for sexual gratification, though Herodas gives no reason or context for their obsession. As the companion-piece to *Mimiamb* 7, the poem also presents a preliminary, indirect picture of Kerdôn, the shoemaker who appears in person there.

**1–14:** Korittô welcomes Mêtrô by asking her to be seated, but abuses her slave for her laziness in not having a chair ready for immediate use; Mêtrô commiserates with Korittô over slaves and how one must constantly shout at them. The similarity of these lines to Plautus' *Stichus* 58–64 led Headlam-Knox (1922) 282 to suggest a common source in Menandros.

**1. κάθησο:** κάθημαι, here in its second-person singular imperative middle form, is used in the middle sense of 'to seat oneself, sit', as is demonstrated by Homer, *Il.* 2.191 αὐτός τε κάθησο καὶ ἄλλους ἵδρυε λαούς, 'sit down yourself and get the rest of the men seated'; see also e.g. Euripides, *Iphigeneia at Aulis* 627. Korittô first orders her friend to be seated, and only discovers that no chair is available when she asks the slave to give one to Mêtrô; her embarrassment perhaps adds to the vehemence of her tirade.

**4. μᾶ:** see *Mim.* 1.82–5n.

**λίθος τις, οὐ δούλη:** λίθος, 'a stone', is commonly used for stupid persons; see e.g. Aristophanes, *Clouds* 1202 ὄντες λίθοι, 'being stones'. The asyndeton is a regular feature of such expressions; see e.g. Theokritos, *Id.* 15.8–9 ἰλεόν, οὐκ οἴκησιν, 'a hovel, not a house'.

**τις:** here with the meaning 'some kind of', implying that the word to which it is joined is not to be taken strictly, as at Plato, *Republic* 334a κλεπτής … τις … ἀναπέφανται, 'he has been revealed as some kind of thief'; see Schwyzer (1950) 2 215.

**5. κεῖσ(αι):** almost proverbially of being dead: cf. Theognis 568–9 κείσομαι ὥστε λίθος ἄφθογγος, 'I shall lie like a voiceless stone.'

**ἢν μετρέω:** there is a hint here that Korittô is stingy, as there is elsewhere (at lines 10, 27–36, 81–4, 99–102) that she is frightened of being robbed. Cunningham (1971) 162 refers to the disgraceful profiteer of Theophrastos' *Characters* 30.11, who measures out the rations for the household in person from a measure which has an obsolete and ungenerous standard and is dented at the bottom, and carefully levels off the top.

**5–8:** for the motif of the servant who is anything but lacking in initiative when it comes to food see also lines 60–1 of the passage from Plautus' *Stichus* cited above at 1–14 n.: *uos meministis quotcalendis petere demensum cibum: / qui minu' meministis quod opus sit facto facere in aedibus?*, 'You remember to claim your rations every first day of the month; why don't you remember to do what's needed in the house?'

**6. τὰ κρῖμνα:** properly of the coarser particles of meal: Headlam-Knox (1922) 284.

**ἀμιθρεῖς:** for the metathesis for ἀριθμεῖς see e.g. Kallimachos, *Fr.* 314 Pfeiffer (1949) 383 and the *Hymn to Demeter* 86, and this poem at line 99. Cunningham (1971) 162 considers it 'a feature of Ion. popular speech'. It is not, however, equivalent to an English malapropism.

**8. πρημονῶσαν:** a *hapax*, equivalent to πρημαίνω at *Mim.* 7.98, properly meaning 'puffing'; cf. πρήθω, 'blow out', 'make to swell', e.g. of wind filling a sail. It derives from the postulated stem πρη- and its postulated noun πρημονή, which appears as πρησμονή, 'swelling', at *Greek Treatises on Veterinary Surgery* 77.23 Oder-Hoppe

(1924) 1 299,13 (the σ being the regular sibilation of a dental like the θ in πρήθω); hence the -μον- element. The slave will blow the house down!

**10. you robber:** an address to a slave which Korittô shares with Gorgô at Theokritos, *Id.* 15.30.

**be grateful to, θῦε:** cf. 2.72 with 2.71n.

**11.** there is an ellipse of a clause like 'if it weren't for Mêtrô', as commonly in such contexts; see 2.72n., 4.15.

**given you a taste of, ἔγευσα:** at *Od.* 20.181 Melanthios says to Odysseus that they won't part from one another πρὶν χειρῶν γεύσασθαι, 'before we taste one another's fists', and there may be an epic tone to the expression here in Herodas.

**χειρέων:** a false Ionic form; cf. 2.80 (with n.), 7.3.

**12. you're chafing under the same yoke as me, ταὔτ' ἐμοὶ ζυγὸν τρίβεις:** i.e. we are yoked like cattle to the same burden, a proverbial expression; see also e.g. Theokritos, *Id.* 12.15 ἀλλήλους δ' ἐφίλησαν ἴσῳ ζυγῷ. τρίβειν, 'to wear out', emphasizes the strain; cf. Theokritos, *Id.* 13.31, of cattle τρίβοντες ἄροτρα, 'wearing out the ploughs'. Zenobios 3.43 Leutsch-Schneidewin (1839) 1 68, 7–8 shows that the usual verb was the more neutral ἕλκειν, 'drag'.

**13. shouting, ἐπιβρύχουσ':** governing τῇς ἀνωνύμοις ταύτῃς in the next line, the dative being semi-objective with ἐπι-.

**14. dog, κύων:** by an expression usual in Greek, the person doing an action (here barking) becomes identified with the thing which naturally does the action (here a dog). The turn of phrase is more direct than a simile, effectively being a metaphor, and is common in comedy; see e.g. Aristophanes, *Lysistrata* 231 οὐ στήσομαι λέαιν' ἐπὶ τυροκνήστιδος, 'I shall not adopt the position of lioness on the cheesegrater.'

**ἀνωνύμοις: unmentionable**, as at *Mim.* 5.45; cf. Di Gregorio (2004) 102, 154, who defends the meaning 'maledetto', 'cursed', in both passages.

**15–19a:** Mêtrô shifts the conversation to the reason for her visit, interrupting herself to command the slaves to leave the room.

**15a. οὕνεκεν:** see *Mim.* 5.53n.

**15b–17a:** despite the lack of paragraphoi (not a convincing criterion in itself), some editors give these lines to Korittô as the mistress of the house and as the more imperious of the two friends; so e.g. Di Gregorio (2004) 155–6. But, as Cunningham (1971) 163 notes, Mêtrô might be demonstrating the barking that she has just talked about. Moreover, women standardly had slaves to accompany them when walking in public (as we see happening in Theokritos' fifteenth *Idyll*), so Mêtrô is most probably addressing Korittô's slave *and* a slave or slaves of her own.

**16. get the hell out of it, φθείρεσθε:** φθείρομαι in the sense 'go to hell' is colloquial and found in comedy (e.g. at Aristophanes, *Wealth* 598, 610), but also in Euripides (at e.g. *Elektra* 234). The plural is probably used because she is giving orders to the slave of Korittô who eventually got her a chair and to the slave we must assume came with her.

**you dimwits, νώβυστρα:** a *hapax*, composed of νόος, βύω ('block', 'plug') and the suffix –τρον, most likely means literally 'of blocked mind'; hence the translation.

**all ears and tongues, ὦτα μοῦνον καὶ γλάσσαι:** the use of a name of a thing or an abstract to characterize a person is common in Greek from Hesiod, *Theogony* 26, where the Muses berate shepherds for being γαστέρες οἶον, 'mere stomachs'; see Kühner-Gerth (1955) 1 10–13. Slaves were proverbial for eavesdropping and passing on gossip; see e.g. Aristophanes, *Frogs* 750–3.

**17. holiday, ἑορτή:** another instance of the stylistic procedure described in the previous note. The phrase was proverbial; see the *Appendix Proverbiorum* 2.76 Leutsch-Schneidewin (1839) 1 409, 17–21, which gives the proverb in the form of ἑορτὴ πόδας ἔχουσα – 'a party on legs'! Theokritos has ἀεργοῖς αἰὲν ἑορτά, 'it's always a party for people who don't work', at *Id.* 15.26, and Herodas may have had the passage before him. See also *Mim.* 5.85n.

**I beg you, λίσσομαί σε, μή:** the same expression occurs in Hippônax, *Fr.* 49.3 Degani (1991) 71–2, where a slave begs Athene to save him from a beating by his master; it is another instance of Herodas' debt to the older poet; so Degani (1984) 54.

**19. scarlet, κόκκινον:** red was the colour of the phalloi worn by comic actors; see Aristophanes, *Clouds* 538–9, from which it appears that the colour was meant to be realistic.

**dildo, βαῦβωνα:** probably related to the verb βαυβάω, 'sleep, or 'lull to sleep', or, more to the point, 'sleep with', as at Euripides, *Syleus*, *Fr.* 694 Kannicht (2004) 2 678, *Adespota*, *Fr.* 165 Kannicht-Snell (1981) 2 61. βαυβών, which will consequently mean 'bonker', is used here for the usual word, *olisbos*, which is found in Sappho or Alkaios (Sappho, *Fr.* 99.1.5 Lobel-Page [1968] 82–3 = Alkaios, *Fr.* 303 Voigt [1971] 281) and comedy (e.g. Aristophanes, *Lysistrata* 109); its use is also referred to by Sophrôn (*Fr.* 23 Kassel-Austin [2001] 1 205–6); see above, p. 167, for further references.

**19b–26:** Korittô does not answer Mêtrô's question, but asks where Mêtrô saw the dildo, and is told that Nossis had it, and had been given it by Euboulê.

**19b: ὀρώρηκας:** 'Attic reduplication'; see above, *Mim.* 4.77n.

**20. Nossis, Erinna's daughter:** Nossis, the epigrammatist, datable to the first two decades of the third century (Gow-Page [1965] 2 435), and Erinna, the authoress of the *Distaff* in hexameters and some epigrams, probably wrote in the first half of the third century (Gow-Page [1965] 2 281–2), and were two of the most important women-poets of Herodas' age. His learned audience must have thought that he was referring directly to his two famous female contemporaries. In her epigrams Nossis aligns herself with Sappho (Nossis 11 Gow-Page [1965] 1 154), and Erinna's *Distaff* was a dirge for the death of her friend, Baukis. It seems that Herodas is making misogynistic fun of the women poets through Mêtrô, probably also partly along the divide between realistic and erotic poetry.

**22. will you bad-mouth, διαβαλεῖς:** literally, 'will you disparage (me to Nossis' source for telling you)?', Cunningham (1971) 165, rightly: Mêtrô does not want to be put in a bad light with Euboulê, along with Nossis.

**23. by these sweet eyes of mine, μὰ τούτους τοὺς γλυκέας:** supply ὀφθαλμούς, as at *Mim.* 5.59–60. A gesture may be involved.

**24. οὐδεὶς μὴ ἀκούσῃ:** οὐ plus μή and their compounds used with the aorist subjunctive denote an emphatic future negative; see e.g. Xenophon, *Anabasis* 4.8.13 οὐδεὶς μηκέτι μείνῃ τῶν πολεμίων, 'not one of the enemy shall stand any longer', with Schwyzer (1950) 2 317.

**26. εἶπε μηδέν' αἰσθέσθαι:** her actual words were μηδεὶς αἰσθέσθω (for μηδείς + aorist imperative see e.g. Plato, *Apology* 17c μηδεὶς ὑμῶν προσδοκησάτω ἄλλως, 'let no one among you expect [that it will be] otherwise'); Mêtrô is just as gossipy as the slaves she has told to leave the room (16).

**27–36:** Korittô vents her spleen about Euboulê's passing the dildo on to others before Korittô had even used it, and expresses her disdain for Euboulê's beneficiary, Nossis, claiming that, even if she had a thousand such instruments of pleasure, she wouldn't even give her one uncomfortable one.

**27. Women!, γυναῖκες:** nominative, expressing an exclamation. That women were untrustworthy keepers of secrets was proverbial; see e.g. Menandros, *One-Line Sayings* 486 Jäkel (1964) 61 μήποτε λαβῇς γυναῖκας εἰς συμβουλίαν, 'Never take on women for consultation.' It is of course ironical that Korittô as a woman sould say this, especially when she must have shown the dildo to Euboulê.

**That one, αὕτη ἡ γυνή:** this formula commonly expresses impatience.

**28. ἠδέσθην:** in the circumstances, an incongruously solemn traditional phrase for accepting a supplication: see e.g. *Il.* 1.23. Korittô emphasizes the charity she showed Euboulê.

**29. πρόσθεν ἤ:** on the analogy with πρίν or πρότερον ἤ plus infinitive, as also at e.g. Sophokles, *Oidipous the King* 832. Korittô is again parading her generosity.

**30. bit of luck, εὕρημα:** synomymous with the more common ἕρμαιον, 'a piece of luck'.

**33. she can look for, ἀθρείτω:** again a word in the grand style, normally denoting 'to look', but here used in a recherché meaning, 'to look for'.

**34b–6:** text and punctuation hotly disputed. With the text printed here τἀμὰ Νοσσίδι χρῆσαι ('to lend') will be an exclamation; τῇ a relative pronoun, going with Nossis; μή will depend on an unfinished construction with δοκέω, after which, because of the interposed address to Adrêsteia, Korittô changes the construction of her sentence; the future (προσδώσω, 'I shall give in response to a plea') with ἄν and with or without οὐκ is a construction found in Homer, but also occurs later in Attic (if rarely and controversially), as at e.g. Plato, *Phaidôn* 61c σχεδὸν οὖν…οὐδ' ὁπωστιοῦν ἄν σοι ἑκὼν εἶναι πείσεται, 'he will not in the least obey you if he can help it', and in Hellenistic poetry, as at Kallimachos, *Hymn to Zeus* 93, τίς κεν Διὸς ἔργματ' ἀείσει;, 'Who would sing the accomplishments of Zeus?' (Schwyzer [1950] 2 351–2 has further instances and discussion).

**34. I'm going to grumble more than a woman should, μέζον μὲν ἢ γυνὴ γρύξω:** at *Mim.* 4.69 we have μέζον ἢ γυνή with the same sense of inappropriate fuss, and the corrector's δίκη γρύζω seems unnecessary. γρύζω is used by Hippônax (*Fr.* 69.6 Degani [1991] 84; cf. Degani [1984] 49, 53) and may well be another instance of Herodas' alignment with his poetry.

**35. Adrêsteia, Ἀδρήστεια:** Adrêsteia, who came to be identified with Nemesis, was the goddess who punished excess, and her anger had to be averted by a prayer like this; cf. Plato, *Republic* 451a προσκυνῶ δὲ Ἀδράστειαν … χάριν οὗ μέλλω λέγειν, 'I pay homage to Adrêsteia … for what I am about to say.' Like many of Herodas' women, Korittô wants to avoid making a fuss.
**χιλίων εὔντων:** genitive absolute with concessive or conditional meaning (Cunningham [1971] 166 opts for the latter).
**36.** for P's **λεπρός**, 'rough', the corrector has σαπρός, 'rotten', which Cunningham (1971) 166 accepts, but this seems more likely to be a simplification of a more difficult reading.
**προσδώσω:** see 34b–6n.
**37–48a:** Mêtrô tries to calm Korittô down by saying she mustn't get angry whenever she hears something silly, and takes the blame for Korittô's anger by saying it is all due to her gossiping. This is a preparation for her return to the burning question about the identity of the dildo's manufacturer. Pretending that Korittô's silence and smile are mere coyness when she must know that Korittô is simply unwilling to part with the information, she begs her friend once more, and Korittô replies that it was Kerdôn.
**37. let it get up your nose, τὴν χολὴν ἐπὶ ῥινός:** the Goatherd of Theokritos, *Id.* 1.18 says of Pan that he is tetchy at noontide, καί οἱ ἀεὶ δριμεῖα χολὰ ποτὶ ῥινὶ κάθηται, 'bitter wrath always sits at his nostril', where the expression also denotes anger. Simon (1991) 137–8 argues that Theokritos adopted it from a motif (otherwise unknown to us) in the traditional iconography of Pan, and Herodas applied Theokritos' phrase to another context.
**38.** P.'s reading **μὴ σοφόν**, 'stupid', seems secured by its quotation in Stobaios, though μὴ καλόν, 'not nice', would perhaps better decribe what Korittô has just heard.
**39. A good woman, γυναικός ἐστι κρηγύης:** this is an adaptation of a proverb used elsewhere of men: see e.g. Theognis 658 χαῖρ', ἐπεὶ ἔστ' ἀνδρὸς πάντα φέρειν ἀγαθοῦ, 'Farewell, since a good man puts up with everything.' κρήγυος appears in reference to a woman also at *Mim.* 4.46, where see n.
**40. blabbing, λαλεῦσ':** elsewhere in Herodas (4.33, 6.61) λαλεῖν means simply 'to speak', so πολλά (next line) is required to convey the meaning of loquacity.
**41. ἀλλά:** this is an instance of what Denniston (1954) 21–2 calls the 'progressive' use of the particle, whereby the speaker, when adding something important to what has been said, wishes to give it an emphasis for which e.g. δέ is not strong enough.
**γλάσσαν:** the papyrus has the Attic form, γλῶσσαν, while the Ionic is used elsewhere in Herodas, as at line 16 above; if we accept the Attic form, the anomaly could be put down to variation in dialect; see above, p. 3.
**to have my tongue cut out, ἐκτεμεῖν:** cutting out the tongue of a gossip is a comic motif; see e.g. Plautus, *The Braggart Soldier* 318 *non tu tibi istam praetruncari linguam largiloquam iubes?*, 'Aren't you asking me to cut out that gossiping tongue of yours for you?' Mêtrô is feigning subservience out of opportunism.
**δεῖται:** the impersonal middle with the infinitive has the same sense as the active δεῖ also at e.g. Sophokles, *Oidipous at Kolonos* 570.

**42. back to the thing I specially mentioned to you, ἐκεῖνο δ' οὗ ... ἐπεμνήσθην**: ἐκεῖνο refers to what Mêtrô has asked at lines 17–18; being in apposition with Mêtrô's question in the next line, it is in the accusative case, as also at e.g. Plato, *Republic* 462d καὶ τοῦτο ὃ ἐρωτᾷς, ..., 'and as to the thing which you asked, ...'; see Schwyzer (1950) 2 86–7. The use of the pronoun here is colloquial, occurring also at *Mim*. 5.53, where see n. ἐπεμνήσθην at *Mim*. 5.53 means 'I remembered', but here the verb has its usual post-Homeric meaning, 'mention'.
**43. if you love me:** for φιλέω in requests, here emphatic, see LSJ[9] s.v. I.7.
**44. Why are you looking at me?:** Korittô's smile and look are most likely 'knowing' and betoken superiority.
**ὀρώρηκας:** for the 'Attic reduplication', see above, *Mim*. 4.77n.
**45. Why so coy about all this?, ἢ τὶ θάβρά σοι ταῦτα;:** literally, 'why are these things a matter of coyness for you?'; = ἢ τὶ ταῦτα ἁβρύνῃ, 'why do you act coyly as to these things?' Mêtrô knows that Korittô has the information she wants, but she puts her reticence down to shyness. Similarly, the Choros at Aischylos, *Agamemnon* 1205, faced with Kassandra's silence up till now over how she received her gift of prophecy from Apollo, says ἁβρύνεται γὰρ πᾶς τις εὖ πράσσων πλέον, 'Everyone is coy when things go well.'
**46. Κοριττί:** the diminutive form of Κοριττώ, Κοριττίς, is used also at 97. Mêtrô has so far exclusively used the non-diminutive form (12,18, 37; cf. 86); she is desperate.
**don't lie to me any more:** the prefix of the verb **ἐπιψεύσῃ** means 'further' as Headlam-Knox (1922) 301 explain, and Mêtrô is referring back to line 17, when she said μὴ ψεύσῃ. It is true, as Cunningham (1971) 168 says, that Korittô has not exactly 'lied', but she is holding out in devious ways.
**48b–56:** Mêtrô asks which Kerdôn she means; she knows two men of that name herself, but for various reasons they are unlikely candidates.
**48. κοῖος:** Mêtrô says 'Which (of several options)?' because, though she mentions only two Kerdôns, she is sure that the real one must be yet another.
**49. grey-eyed, γλαυκός:** despite Athene's ancient cult name, grey eyes were not admired in humans in later Greek society; see e.g. Loukianos 80 (*Dialogues of the Courtesans*) 2.1.
**50. neighbour of Myrtalinê, Kylaithis' daughter:** as at *Mim*. 1.50, women talking among themselves naturally use the matronymics to identify other women. The Kylaithis mentioned here must be the same person as the Kylaithis of line 55, who is deceased (see n.). Her daughter's name has sexual connotations, and probably means she is a hetaira; see *Mim*. 1.89n.
**51. wouldn't even stitch a plectrum for a lyre, οὐδ' ἂν πλῆκτρον ἐς λύρην ῥάψαι:** a lyre-plectrum cannot have been made by stitching, because plectrums were made of ivory, horn, bone or wood (leather was used only for the soundbox); see Maas-Snyder (1989) 4–9, 180–1, who discuss *The Homeric Hymn to Hermes*, 47–51 and Sophokles' satyr-play, *The Trackers*, *Fr*. 314.298–328, 374–6 Radt (1977) 4 295–7, 299. A musical plectrum resembled a dildo because of its shape and the straps holding it to the lyre like the straps holding a dildo to a partner's body (71),

and πλῆκτρον was a double-entendre for 'penis'; see e.g. Achilles Tatios, *Leukippê and Kleitophôn* 8.9.4. The expression therefore probably has the connotation of 'having an erection to penetrate a woman's vagina'; the word for stitching, ῥάψαι, is used because stitching dildoes is what is foremost in Mêtrô's mind, as Cunningham (1971) 168 suggests.
**52. tenement:** the Greek word also occurs at *Mim*. 3.47.
**53. Hermodôros:** this personal name seems designed purely to give imaginary local colour, though in Greece well known landmarks belonging to private individuals were essential for street-directions, because streets were not named and houses were not numbered.
**as you come off, ἔκβαντι:** literally 'to [the person] having come out [on to]'; the dative participle is frequently used on its own in expressions identifying the direction in which one moves (see Kühner-Gerth [1955] 1 423–4, and Schwyzer [1950] 2 152), and governs the accusative, here τὴν πλατεῖαν (supply ὁδόν), 'the broad street', hence the main street.
**54. used to be, used to be a somebody once, ἦν μέν κοτ' ἦν τις:** the repetition of ἦν, 'used to be', suggests Mêtrô's sadness over this Kerdôn's fallen capabilities, which, to judge from the following line, may again be sexual. See LSJ[9] A.II.5.a for τις meaning 'a someone', as at Theokritos, *Id*. 11.79 δῆλον ὅτ' ἐν τᾷ γᾷ κἠγών τις φαίνομαι ἦμεν, 'it is plain that on land I too am somebody'.
**γεγήρακε:** for the short α see Schmidt (1968) 15–8.
**55. Kylaithis, bless her memory, Κυλαιθὶς ἡ μακαρῖτις:** the scholiast on Aischylos' *Persians* 633 informs us that *makaritis* was used of the dead, and *makarios* of the living. The whole phrase can be compared with Theokritos, *Id*. 2.70 καί μ' ἁ Θευμαρίδα Θρᾷσσα τροφὸς ἁ μακαρῖτις, 'Theumaridas' Thracian nurse, bless her memory'. Arguments for priority of authorship are futile: cf. e.g. Simon (1991) 136, who gives the priority to Herodas precisely because the epithet makes sense in Herodas while its intention is unclear in the context of Theokritos' usage.
**ἐχρῆτο:** 'had sexual relations with'; cf. line 78.
**56. may all her relatives remember her, μνησθεῖεν αὐτῆς:** the pious prayer is typical of Herodas' women's observance of outward form when engaging in prurient detail.
**57–67a:** Korittô confirms that neither of the men mentioned by Mêtrô is the Kerdôn in question, whom she proceeds to describe, comparing him in appearance and contrasting him in voice with another artisan named Prêxinos. She claims that her Kerdôn has to work in his private home, and has to sell his wares in secret, because, she alleges, he fears the tax-collectors. She praises his workmanship in superlative terms.
**57. As you say, ὡς λέγεις:** though Mêtrô has not 'said' explicitly that she has ruled out her two Kerdôns, lines 51 and 54 show that she has done so in fact.
**58. ἠ ... ἤ:** the disjunctive interrogative in this form is often found in epic; see e.g. *Il*. 10.342–3 [Theokritos], *Id*. 25.170–1. Herodas' use of it in the context may involve some ironical deflation of Korittô.
**Chios or Erythrai, Χίου ... ['E]ρυθρέων:** the genitive of provenance is attested at e.g. Hesiod, *Fr*. 257.3 and, in the Hellenistic period, at Theokritos, *Id*. 24.129.

Hippônax, *Frr.* 20.1, 41.2 Degani (1991) 39, 58 also refers to the two cities in morally dubious contexts; Degani (1984) 54 regards Herodas' mention of them as a deliberate recollection.

**59. bald and short, φαλακρός, μικκός:** baldness and shortness of stature were regarded as signs of moral and physical inferiority; see e.g. Ploutarchos, *On Exile* 607a. Herodas may be thinking of the 'little bald tinker' of Plato's *Republic* 495e, who is given the same adjectives and is decidedly vile.

**the exact image, αὐτό:** Prêxinos 'in person'. αὐτός defines an object more closely, and comes to denote abstract concepts, and in Plato the neuter form of the pronoun is used to refer to the concept to be defined, as at *Theaitêtos* 146e γνῶναι ἐπιστήμην, αὐτὸ ὅτι ποτ' ἐστίν, 'to understand precisely what knowledge is'; see Kühner-Gerth (1955) 1 653–4. From there it is an easy step for the neuter form to refer to persons when close identification needs to be conveyed; so for instance we have the coinage by the epigrammatist Nossis (Nossis 8 GP) of the name Αὐτομέλιννα, 'Melinna to the life', referring to an accurate portrait of the woman.

**αὐτὸ ἐρεῖς:** the anceps at the beginning of the third metron has been resolved into two shorts, -ὸ ἐ-, giving a 'fifth-foot' anapaest, with hiatus (in which both vowels retain their face values) between the words.

**ἐρεῖς:** like δόξεις at line 67 (see also *Mim.* 4.28 [with n.], 33, 57, 73) the future is used instead of the optative with ἄν.

**60. Prêxinos:** apparently another artisan of the two women's acquaintance.

**σῦκον:** Herodas is adapting the proverb ὁμοιότερος σύκου, 'more alike than a fig', in English 'like two peas in a pod'.

**62. ὁτεύνεκα:** = ὅτι also at *Mim.* 5.20 (with n.), 7.45.

**63. at home, κατ' οἰκίην:** as opposed to κατ' ἀγοράν.

**ἐμπολέων:** the verb is ἐμπολάω, the α in -άω verbs becoming ε before ο, ου and ω in Ionic: see Cunningham (1971) 216 and above, p. 11.

**64. tax-collectors, τελώνας:** scholars like Smotrytsch (1962) 134 and Luria (1963) 413 (quoting Meister [1893] 759) take this line as Herodas' stand against oppressive taxation under Ptolemy II Philadelphos. But the fact that Herodas has put such criticism in the mouth of a reprobate like Korittô, in defence of a scoundrel like Kerdôn, hardly supports the idea; see Mastromarco (1984) 91–2. Herodas' purpose seems more likely to be the ironic presentation of Korittô: she is imputing to Kerdôn a motive which every reasonable person will understand, while suppressing the less palatable fact that he is plying a trade which was clandestine and at least disreputable. She is therefore trying to put the most reputable public complexion possible on unseemly matters of private interest to her, which is standard practice among Herodas' women. See further Di Gregorio (2004) 183–4.

**66. handicraft, τὰς χεῖρας:** 'workmanship', as at *Mim.* 4.72 and 7.24. Comparison of Kerdôn's work with that of the maiden-goddess is a masterstroke of grotesque humour.

**67–73:** Korittô reveals that Kerdôn had two dildoes with him, and in voluptuous detail extols their superiority to the real thing.

**68. eagerness, ἁμίλλῃ:** Gorgias, *In Praise of Helen* 19 says that that Helen's face gave Paris' soul a προθυμίαν καὶ ἅμιλλαν ἔρωτος, 'a will and a longing for [her] love', or, as a hendiadys, 'an eagerness to compete for her love' with Menelaos when he had seen her at Sparta, which shows that ἅμιλλα on its own means not 'sexual desire' but a 'competition' to possess something. The rival conjecture is ἅμ' ἰδμῇ, 'along with the seeing' (so Cunningham [1971] 170), but this seems redundant after ἰδοῦσ' just before it.
**69. pricks, βαλλία:** the meaning is self-evident, but the etymology is uncertain; some connect it with φάλλος, which would perhaps mean that it was a Macedonian dialect-word, since Macedonian uses unaspirated voiced labial plosives in the place of aspirated voiceless labial plosives; so Βερενίκη for Φερενίκη. Others connect it with an equivalent of φάλλος in a Balkan language such as Thracian and Phrygian, or with βάμβαλον, a Phrygian word for the genitals; see Chantraine (1968) s.v.
**70. εἰμεν:** Ionic for Attic ἐσμεν, though the papyrus is too damaged here to indicate which form we should adopt.
**71. their smoothness is like sleep itself, ἡ μαλακότης ὕπνος:** identification of the smoothness with sleep is perhaps more emphatic than a comparison such as we find in Theokritos, *Idylls* 5.51 and 15.125 ὕπνω μαλακώτερος, 'smoother than sleep'.
**straps:** ἱμαντίσκος is a colloquial diminutive indicating not smallness but affectionate familiarity.
**72–3:** a common expression; see Herodotos 5.24.1 ἐγὼ φροντίζων εὑρίσκω ἐμοί τε καὶ τοῖσι ἐμοῖσι πρήγμασι εἶναι οὐδένα σεῦ ἄνδρα εὐνοέστερον, 'on reflection, I find there to be no one more kindly disposed to me and my affairs than you', Aristophanes, *Frogs* 73–4, *Wealth* 104–5.
**διφῶσ(α):** a rare verb, and probably Ionic; Degani (1984) 54 thinks Herodas has borrowed the word from the compound form in Hippônax, *Fr.* 87.8.(c) Degani (1991) 100, ἐξεδίφησ[.
**74–84:** Mêtrô asks why Korittô let the other dildo get away, and Korittô replies that she did everything to persuade Kerdôn except offering to let him sleep with her. Mêtrô says she should have done that as well, if Kerdôn had demanded it. Korittô agrees, but claims that Euboulê was in the way, borrowing her grindstone when she should have spent a little money to fix her own.
**75. didn't I use, προσήγαγον:** a military metaphor, προσάγω with accusative and dative meaning 'to lead an army against'; see e.g. Thoukydides 1.64.2. Korittô gave it her best shot.
**means of persuasion:** πειθοῦν is an Ionic form of the accusative singular of words ending in –ω; cf. Μητροῦν at line 45 and Λητοῦν at *Mim.* 2.98. Herodas may have had in mind that Sappho called persuasion 'the daughter of Aphrodite' (*Fr.* 200 Lobel-Page [1955] 105).
**76. stroked his baldness, τὸ φαλακρὸν καταψῶσα:** at Sophokles, *The Trackers*, *Fr.* 314.368 Radt (1977) 4 299 the Chorus is mocked for τὸ λεῖον φαλακρὸν ἡδονῇ πιτνάς, 'exciting [your] smooth bald knob in pleasure', a clear reference to masturbation; for τὸ φαλακρόν meaning the 'knob' of the penis, see also Aischylos,

*Diktyoulkoi*, Fr. 47a.24 Radt (1985) 3 170, Sophokles, *Dionisiskos*, *Fr*. 171.3 Radt (1977) 4 176. Herodas' phraseology therefore seems to make a *double entendre* inevitable: on the surface level, Korittô is stating that she stroked Kerdôn's bald head (n.b. line 59; on this interpretation, the article with the neuter denotes the abstract, here literally 'baldness'), while on the other she will be claiming that she masturbated him, which makes an extra point of her insistence that she didn't let him have her body. Other editors like Cunningham (1971) 171 argue that stroking someone's hair (or, as here, the lack of it) was merely an expression of affection rather than erotic involvement, pointing to e.g. Plato, *Phaidôn* 89b and Xenophon, *The Apology of Sokrates* 28. But, if no sexual meaning is to be assigned to the phrase, what of 'I kissed him'?

**77. sweet:** with γλυκύν supply οἶνον as at Theokritos, *Id.* 18.11.

**caressed, ταταλίζουσα:** 'to call someone τάταλε' which is connected with τατί, a pet-name, at *Mim*. 5.69; see also *Mim*. 1.60 (with n.).

**78. χρῆσασθαι:** 'to have sexual relations with', as at line 55.

**80. it's not decent not to choose the right moment, ἄκαιρον οὐ πρέποντ' εἶναι:** the text is much disputed. With the text provided here (defended by e.g. Cunningham [1971] 171 and Di Gregorio [2004] 194–5), πρέποντ(α) is a plural standing instead of the singular (common in Ionic: Kühner-Gerth [1955] 1 66–7), and requires us to supply ἐστί, 'it is not appropriate, fitting …'; an ἄκαιρος is a person who does things at the wrong time, and the accusative and infinitive (εἶναι) construction depends on 'it is not fitting'.

**81. ἤληθεν:** the asyndeton is explanatory.

**that slave of Bitas', δούλη:** this is the reading of the papyrus. The word must refer to the wife of Bitas, who is Euboulê (line 25), because a slave cannot have owned a grindstone (cf. ωὗτης at line 84). There is, however, no need to emend δούλη into [Εὐ]βουλή, as is done e.g. by Cunningham (1971) 171 following Headlam-Knox (1921) 309 after Jevons (1891) 384, because, as Di Gregorio (2004) 197–8 suggests, Korittô is maliciously implying that Euboulê is continually grinding meal as if she were Bitas' slave; for the identification compare κύων ὑλακτέω, 'I'm turning into a barking dog', at line 14.

**83. millstone, τὸν ὄνον:** literally 'donkey'; the Greco-Roman grindstone consisted of a solid cone of stone on which revolved a stone hollowed to fit; the grain was poured into a hole in the upper stone and was ground between the two stones; the upper stone was called 'the donkey', presumably because a donkey was often used to turn it; see further Moritz (1958) 10–17.

**for four obols, τετρωβόλου:** it is logical to infer that Korittô regards this as a paltry sum; see also e.g. Menandros, *The Girl with her Hair Cut Short* 380, 393, where Daos insultingly calls Sosias and Polemon τετρώβολοι, which was apparently the lowest daily payment for a mercenary at that time.

**84. repaired:** literally 'strike' (κόψῃ), i.e. with a stone chisel, the technical word for re-boring the grindstone; see e.g. Aristophanes, *Wasps* 648 νεόκοπτος, 'recently ground'.

**85–98:** Mêtrô asks how Kerdôn found Korittô's address, and Korittô tells her that the source was Artemeis. Mêtrô tells Korittô that she should have found out who ordered the second dildo, but is told that Kerdôn was obdurate, and announces her intention to visit Artemeis to find out more about Kerdôn. She bids Korittô farewell, and leaves.
**85.** As Cunningham (1971) 172 notes, Mêtrô's question implies another: how did Kerdôn know that Korittô would be interested in his products?
**86. μηδὲ τοῦτο:** 'don't lie to me about this either', picking up lines 17 and 46.
**90:** text and interpretation difficult. The damaged last word is almost certainly θάμνην, 'a cup'. **προκυκλίην** is clearly an adjective from προκυκλίς, 'go-between', the first title of *Mim.* 1. **πρόσω** can mean 'further', 'still' (see Aischylos, *Eumenides* 747). The aorist participle, **πιεῦσα**, could be a true 'aorist' in aspect, i.e. denoting time of any duration, so, linked with πρόσω, it could mean 'continuing to drink'; for its hyperionic form see *Mim.* 4.89n. The resultant sense would therefore be '[Artemeis is always coming up with something new] because she continues to drink the go-between's cup.' In other words, Artemeis is still plying her trade as a go-between, a figure typically presented as bibulous (see the Discussion of *Mim.* 1, p. 32), so is on the lookout for possible connections.
**91. ἀλλ' οὖν γε:** best explained by Cunningham (1971) 172–3: ἀλλ' οὖν answers μέν in line 89, and signifies 'an elimination of the secondary or irrelevant' (Denniston [1954] 443–4) as Mêtrô turns away from her remark about Artemeis and on to the main issue at hand; γέ goes logically with ἔδει πυθέσθαι in the next line ('at least you should have inquired…').
**relieve of, ἐκλῦσαι:** i.e. 'to set them free from imprisonment with Kerdôn' (Cunningham [1971] 173).
**92. ordered, ἐκδοῦσα:** 'commissioning', 'ordering'; of ordering a statue at Demosthenes, *On the Crown* 122. There is a punning contrast with this word and ἐκλῦσαι in the same final position of the previous line.
**93. ὤμνυ' οὐκ:** the more usual form of the negative with potential ἄν + infinitive is μή; see e.g. Xenophon, *Anabasis* 7.7.40 ὄμνυμι δέ σοι μηδὲ ἀποδιδόντος δέξασθαι ἄν, 'I swear to you that even if you were to pay what was due I would not have accepted it.' οὐ not μή is used because Korittô is quoting the actual content of Kerdôn's oath, οὐκ ἂν εἴποιμι, 'I will not tell.'
**94:** this line was not printed in the original text of the papyrus, but was written in the margin at the top of the column by another hand. It should be included despite its metrical deficiency and defective syntax as it stands, because it offers an explanation for Kerdôn's oath. The general sense seems to be that he was emotionally involved with the woman in question.
**95. λέγεις:** with the papyrus' εἶναι at the end of the line, this must be literally translated as 'You mean that the journey [μοί, 'for me' = 'my'] now leads to Artemeis.' The meaning 'your words signify' and the use of an infinitive are paralleled in Menandros, *The Arbitrators* 1091 λέγεις γὰρ ἐπίπονόν τιν' αὐτοὺς ζῆν βίον, 'your words mean that they live a hard life.' The article is omitted from ὁδόν as commonly with the object after verbs of saying, as at e.g. Aristophanes, *Wealth*

637 λέγεις μοι χαράν, λέγεις μοι βοάν, 'what you say to me means shouts of joy.'
**97. ὑγίαινε:** literally 'keep well', i.e. 'goodbye', as at e.g. Aristophanes, *Frogs* 165.
**λαιμάττει:** 'devours voraciously', 'is incontrollably hungry' (cf. *Mim.* 4.46), best taken as an obscene reference to Mêtrô's vagina, to which the actor or, more likely, the reciter, may have gestured (which would go some way to explaining the subjectless verb); so Di Gregorio (2004) 205–7. The alternative, that the verb refers to Mêtrô's hungry husband at home (along the lines of Theokritos, *Id.* 15.147), is open to the objection that Mêtrô is hardly in the mood at present to go home and feed her husband.
**98. to leave, ἀφ[έρπειν]:** the supplement is suggested in particular by Theokritos, *Id.* 15.26 ἕρπειν ὥρα κ' εἴη.
**98b–102:** Korittô orders the slave who looks after and sells her chickens to close the door after Mêtrô and count the hens and feed them some darnel: bird-thieves can steal them, no matter how closely you guard them.
**99. you there, αὕτη σύ:** the nominative functions as a vocative is such expressions; see also *Mim.* 4.55, 7.122, and, in the masculine, 5.63 and 7.66. To construct the 'stage-directions' of this *envoi*, all that is required is that we imagine that Korittô shouts her orders to the slave, who need not have made an entrance and may even be in another part of the house.
**birdseller, [νεοσσ]οπῶλι:** the supplement gives a hapax, but there are manifold composites ending in –πωλις or –πωλης. The slave will have had the particular duty of looking after and selling the hens.
**κἠξαμίθρησαι:** second person of the middle aorist imperative, with the same metathesis as at line 6.
**100. εἰ:** the meaning 'to see if' is also found at *Mim.* 7.1.
**αἰρέων:** partitive genitive.
**101. οὐ γὰρ ἀλλά, for it's a sure thing:** see Denniston (1954) 31–2. The particles in this connection seem to be within the tradition of the iambographers, and Degani (1984) 47, 241–3 argues that Herodas is once again citing Hippônax.
**102. chicken-robbers, ὡρνιθοκλέπται:** = οἱ ὀρνιθοκλέπται. Korittô's fear seems on a par with Theokritos' Praxinoa at *Id.*15. 28, where she orders her slave, Eunoa, to put away the spinning, because 'cats like sleeping on soft things'. However, Korittô's concern about thieves has an added point: after all, she has just lost her dildo to Euboulê and Nossis.
**on your lap, ἐν κόλπῳ:** Korittô's idea of nursing hens is metaphorical; they were not household pets.

So far, this tailpiece looks like other Hellenistic poems which close on a humdrum domestic note, as happens with Theokritos' fifteenth *Idyll.* With a Hellenistic poet like Herodas, however, we must be alert to secondary levels of reference. As Henderson (1975) 128–9, 140 and 147 demonstrates, in Greek slang birds could denote penises and a woman's lap could mean a cunt. Given these popular usages, Korittô appears not only to be referring to her humble circumstances, but also still to be thinking of sexual satisfaction and to be punning on the idea that penises should be carefully guarded and nourished since people steal them just as much as Euboulê and Nossis have stolen Korittô's leather dildo – even if a woman guards them in her cunt. The coda therefore indeed operates on two levels.

## DISCUSSION

### *1. Characters and characterization*

Herodas' technique of creating an interplay between Korittô and Mêtrô is almost as important as his characterization of the two women by themselves, but treating their characterization at first singly will put their interaction with one another into a helpful relief. Korittô, who is the more expansive (she has 61 lines to Mêtrô's 41), is characterized first and foremost as obsessed with sexual gratification, and the object with which she intends to get it. In fact, most of her lines are devoted to her narrative of her admiration for the dildo, which she dwells on in loving detail, admiring, with her eyes out on stalks, its stiffness and smoothness, and the softness of its straps (65–73); to the report of her circumspectly come-hitherish handling of Kerdôn, whom she kisses, strokes (in one way or another), offers wine to and calls pet-names (57–64, 74–8); and, within the poem's action, to the dramatization of her concern over the dildo's present whereabouts (19–20, 22, 23–5, 27–36). The fact that she says she would have allowed Kerdôn to make love to her to get the second dildo if Euboulê weren't present (78–81) only means that she was perfectly willing to do so in the normal run of things, and that shows how far she was prepared to go. Her outrageous comparison of Kerdôn's workmanship with that of Athene (65–7) is perhaps the crowning hyperbole in her enthusiasm for the dildo.

Alongside her obsession with sex, she is presented as being almost paranoid in her concern with what people think of her. She supplies a socially reasonable if not acceptable explanation why Kerdôn manufactures his illicit wares at home when she claims that he's avoiding the tax-collectors like everyone these days (63–4). When she asserts that Kerdôn's dildoes are straighter and smoother than men's penises, she guiltily excuses herself by saying that she and Mêtrô are 'on our own' (70). She shows a similar concern with respectability in her insistence that she did not let Kerdôn sleep with her (78), as if that were her spontaneous choice, but, when Mêtrô challenges her, she reveals that in fact she was shamed into abstinence by Euboulê's presence. Related to the concern with the image she projects in society is her constant paranoia over the possibility that people might be putting one over her. We can see this trait in her abuse of her slave, whom she says is lazy in everything but claiming her food-rations (2–11), in her ringing condemnation of Euboulê and Nossis for betraying her trust (27–36), and in her warnings about chicken-thieves to the slave in charge of the hens (99–102).

Otherwise, though she doesn't indulge in gossip as much as Mêtrô, it is quite clear from her expressed intention to end her friendship with Euboulê that she will betray her promise to Mêtrô not to tell who gave the dildo to Nossis by naming Mêtrô (19–36), so that the gossiping over the dildo will form a chain among five women, Korittô to Euboulê, Euboulê to Nossis, Nossis to Mêtrô, and Mêtrô to Korittô, with Artemeis acting as the contact between Kerdôn and Korittô.[1] And she was the one who brought the dildo out into the public arena in the first place. She is every bit as much a gossip as Mêtrô, if less naïve over it.

Moreover, she very much thinks that she is mistress in her household and of her property. Her abuse of and orders to her slaves are certainly a case in point, but she also adopts a superior tone over the dildo. She makes Mêtrô wait thirty-one lines before revealing the identity of the dildo-stitcher, while she pursues her own inquiry into how Mêtrô learnt about the dildo itself (18–48), and when she finally gives Kerdôn's name, she does so expressing surprise that Mêtrô feels she needs to beg her for the information. Just before the revelation, she has smiled at Mêtrô (44), and this must entail at least a measure of condescension and delight at seeing her friend having to work so hard. And the manner in which she occupies the high moral ground over Euboulê's faithlessness is ostentatious, and even patronising when she says she showed ritual respect to Euboulê's supplication (28).[2] Of course, her superiority is in the circumstances a farce.

Mêtrô, for her part, is manically tenacious in her quest to get a dildo, so she shares with Korittô an obsession with sex. Her technique in obtaining the information is both dogged and devious. Three times she steers the conversation to the matter at hand, first after her show of how she can abuse slaves just as well as Korittô (18–19), secondly after Korittô has spent so much time on Euboulê and Nossis (42–3, 46–7a), and thirdly when she inquires who pointed Korittô's house out to Kerdôn (85–6), each time with a plea to Korittô not to lie. Moreover, she has shown a lively interest in the second dildo since the moment she heard of its existence, making her suggestion that Korittô should have let Kerdôn sleep with her to get it (74,

79). She demonstrates true tactical skill in her questioning about the second dildo. She establishes that Korittô doesn't have it. Her question about how Kerdôn found the way to Korittô (85) is a subterfuge for another question: 'Who put Kerdôn on to you?', which will reveal the intermediary. She then finds out that it was indeed a go-between, Artemeis (87–90). Her further question, why Korittô didn't find out who commissioned the second dildo (92), confirms that Korittô doesn't know. Her course is now clear: she must visit Artemeis forthwith. We are left to guess that when she meets Kerdôn she will do exactly what she had suggested Korittô should have done.[3]

A good deal of her naïveté is in fact a means of achieving her goal. When she tells Korittô that they are both 'chafing under the same yoke' in their experience of the servants' indolence, she is already trying to secure Korittô's sympathy and good will (12–14). If the ascription of lines 15b–17a to Mêtrô is correct,[4] she is showing her ability to 'bark' (14) at slaves as well as Korittô has just done, and, again, she is encouraging a positive response. Her platitudes to Korittô about not letting things get at her and to put up with everything, and her disarming self-accusation for her loose tongue are once more the perfect preparation for shepherding Korittô back to the real topic (37–41). She ostensibly takes Korittô's knowing smile as fastidiousness when really they've been friends for such a long time (44–5), which again is merely a pretence of inferiority designed to flatter Korittô into parting with the information. She is indeed tenacious in the pursuit of her goal, and claims that Korittô is the superior partner must be viewed with some reservation.[5]

She is of course the real gossip of the pair. She tells Korittô from whom Nossis got the dildo, when Euboulê had sworn Nossis to secrecy, and Nossis has obviously broken her oath, now broken in turn by Mêtrô's indiscretion (25–6). Her gossip-driven life is made clearest when she tries to guess whether Korittô's Kerdôn is one of the two in her acquaintance: we get the address and a virtual history of the sex-life of the second candidate, who used to be 'someone' once, but has now grown old (which is likely to be a sexual reference), and had a thing with the now-deceased Kylaithis (48–55). Her pious wish that Kylaithis' relatives still remember her is perhaps the only evidence she shows that she is concerned with being thought of as socially acceptable (56).

One of the chief sources of the humour of *Mimiamb* 6 is, we may conclude, the collision of three of its major elements, the private intimacy of the discussion, the concern with appearances and public respectability, and the potency of gossip. Korittô and Mêtrô's world is evidently rife with gossips, Mêtrô being a prime culprit in this respect, though even Korittô has let the real cat out of the bag, and the guilty secret already has quite an audience. To see Mêtrô so insouciant over public opinion because of her dark obsession makes Korittô's dilemma over hers all the more delicious.

## *2. The objectivity of Herodas*

The subject-matter of the collection in our papyrus fits in perfectly with what Theophrastos regarded as the proper material of mime, 'things permissible and not permissible',[6] but *Mimiamb* 6, along with poem 5, perhaps represents an extreme case of what is not 'permissible' in polite society. Scholars have questioned what attitude Herodas may have had towards his material, and this is a good place to discuss the problem.

Can we trace any moral stance on Herodas' part? Opinions have varied enormously since the publication of the papyrus. More recently, Mastromarco[7] points out in connection with *Mimiamb* 6 that Korittô finds Kerdôn's dildoes more satisfying than men's penises (70–1), and usefully contrasts this preference with the women of the *Lysistrata*, who have recourse to dildoes for sexual satisfaction only because the war has kept their husbands from home (107–10). He comes to the conclusion that the objects of pleasure in the poem are a threat to social stability, and that Herodas condemns the women for their depravity. Finnegan[8] argues that the negative picture that Herodas presents of the female sex is designed as a comic expedient purely in order to raise a laugh among the male audience or readership of the mime. Simon[9] suggests that Herodas presents the women of *Mimiamb* 6 satirically, but without the indignation of Juvenal's sixth *Satire*. Di Gregorio[10] feels that Herodas is critical of the corruption of women in his time, but that he has no interest in taking the matter seriously, his mind being set on comic effect.

In each of these positions there is much truth: Mastromarco puts his finger on the extremity of the two women's desire for sexual gratification; Finnegan is probably right to suggest that a good deal of the humour in Herodas' presentation of women is aimed at a male audience or readership; Simon's identification of caricature and a satirical element in his presentation is certainly well-placed; and Di Gregorio's insistence that Herodas' aim is ultimately non-serious is, as I shall argue, compelling. We might also point out that there is, *pace* Simon, a degree of irony in the characterization of the women. For instance, after the condemnation of slaves, in our text by Mêtrô, for being 'just ears and tongues' (16), we have Mêtrô passing on

Euboulê's secret about her lending Korittô's dildo to Nossis (25–6), and Korittô complaining about Euboulê for not keeping its existence a secret.

What has perhaps gone unremarked, however, is that Herodas' use of immoral and outrageous material for comic effect presupposes a firm apprehension of the moral and 'normal'. Bitinna, possibly a widow, may seek sexual satisfaction in a relationship with a slave, but Mêtrichê in *Mimiamb* 1 proves impervious to Gyllis' proposal of a candidate to put an end to her celibacy with Mandris in Alexandria. Again, Bitinna's threats to punish Gastrôn for his suspected infidelity are excessively violent, but Kydilla's intervention acts as a reminder of more humane standards. Without these moral yardsticks, Herodas' more outrageous comic humour would have lost its full effect; to a certain extent, therefore, Herodas actually depends on them. True, he speaks to us as a good observer of human behaviour, but he shows no interest in any in-depth psychological probing, quite apart from moral criticism: this would have been fatal for his poems' type of humour. But there is no case here for any moral reformism, merely for morality in the service of humorous effect.[11]

Nor is there any evidence of social or political engagement. The key passage for those who have tried to detect such commitment in Herodas is *Mimiamb* 6.64, 'for every door fears the tax-collectors these days'. Korittô's statement no doubt reflects popular (and universal) sentiment over taxation, but we saw in the note discussing the line that its validity as evidence for a socio-political stance is weakened because it is Korittô's attempt to whitewash the disreputablility of Kerdôn's trade. In any case, coming from Korittô, the comment is automatically undermined. Nor, for instance, can we see any evidence of Herodas' sympathy for slaves: abuse of slaves was a stylized motif taken from comedy, as we have seen, and our sympathy for the unfortunate Gastrôn is relativised by his opportunistic amorality.

When the papyrus first appeared early in the 1890s, the Realist movement was in full swing, and the early commentators were naturally predisposed to see Herodas as an ancient realist.[12] More recently, W. Geoffrey Arnott[13] has warned us about the 'verismo trap', and scholars have given up regarding Herodas as an antique Zola. As I have argued,[14] realism is a perennial mode, and is shaped in any age by convention; nineteenth-century Realism took the lot of the middle and lower classes and tried to reveal the psychological, social and political pressures on them. Herodas' realism consists of his selection of the middle and lower classes for depiction, in the exclusive pursuit of humour. Moreover, as we saw in the Introduction,[15] his realistic subject-matter is depicted in a metre which was obsolete, in a dialect which was erudite and artificial, and in a form which was an amalgam of two originally separate forms, choliambic poetry like that of Hippônax and mime like that of Sophrôn; and the amalgam was one example of a sophisticated literary strategy of the poets of the age. In the *Mimiambs*, therefore, we can see realism of content, from which we are distanced by artificiality of form.[16] And the dramatic form is something which enables Herodas to conceal any opinions he might have had of social and political justice, though we only need to recall the example of Old Comedy to remind us that poets can use the voices of others to express truths about such matters.

However, there is one area of human life in which Herodas shows total personal commitment. This is his poetry, and visual art in so far as it complements his poetic tastes. We shall see in our discussion of *Mimiamb* 8, *The Dream,* that Herodas is indeed vigorous in the defence of his poetry.[17] In particular, it is striking that he modifies the dramatic form by placing himself in it so that he can express his defence directly, and by reporting a dream which is at once confirmatory and (he hopes) prophetic. But his personal position on poetry is also discernible in the poems in which he is not presented as an actor. We have seen that Kynnô's defence of Apelles the painter in *Mimiamb* 4 is unlikely to be the parody of common and popular taste that it is sometimes thought to be, but rather that it is coherent, informed and supportive, and in all likelihood represents the poet's own opinion. Moreover, we have considered the probability that his comments on Apelles' art are also a gloss on his own chosen medium.[18] We have, finally, concluded that the unflattering reference in *Mimiamb* 6 to the contemporary or near-contemporary poetesses, Nossis and Erinna, is misogynistic, and yet this animosity is at least partly because Herodas viewed the depiction of their personal emotions, especially of love and longing, as antithetical to his own preferences in subject-matter, and therefore turns out to be a further instance of his engagement with poetry.[19] Such seriousness is noticeably lacking in his portrayal of his characters' psychological, social and political circumstances.

## *Notes*

1. Simon (1991) 41.
2. See n.
3. Simon (1991) 43.
4. See 15b–17a n.
5. Arnott (1971).
6. Diomedes 24.3.16–7 Koster (1975) 122; on the attribution of the definition to Theophrastos see above, p. 40 n. 2.
7. (1984) 93–4.
8. (1992) 34.
9. (1991) 41–4.
10. (2004) 143–4.
11. Simon (1991) 113–6 similarly doubts that Mêtrichê and Kydilla can be seen as representatives of Herodas' opinions.
12. Mastromarco (1984) 65–80, 87–94 has a convenient summary of the phenomenon and the challenges to which it had to succumb.
13. (1971) 125 n. 1.
14. (1987) 3–8, 27–8; on Herodas see pp. 158–60.
15. Above, pp. 2–4.
16. Simon (1991) 117–26 helpfully uses this distinction in his differentiation between the 'ironical realism' of Theokritos' second and fifteenth *Idylls*, in which the contrast of form and content is stronger, and the 'sardonic realism' of Herodas, who takes negative material to an extreme and lessens the tension between form and content, while avoiding the constituent seriousness of satire.
17. Below, pp. 233–5.
18. Above, pp. 128–9.
19. Above, 20n. For *Mim.* 1.71, 'I'd have taught her to sing her lame songs with a limp', see the note and p. 35.

## 7. ΣΚΥΤΕΥΣ

*(ΜΗΤΡΩ)* Κέρδων, ἄγω σοι τάσδε τὰς [γυνὰς εἴ] τι
τῶν σῶν ἔχεις αὐτῇσιν ἄξιον δεῖξαι
χειρέων νοῆρες ἔργον.
*(ΚΕΡΔΩΝ)* οὐ μάτην, Μητροῖ,
ἐγὼ φιλέω σε. τῇς γυναιξὶν οὐ θήσεις
τὴν μέζον' ἔξω σανίδα; Δριμύλῳ φωνέω·
πάλιν καθεύδεις; κόπτε, Πίστε, τὸ ῥύγχος
αὐτοῦ, μέχρις τὸν ὕπνον ἐκχέῃ πάντα·
μᾶλλον δὲ τὴν ἄκανθαν ὡς ἔχ[ει ἐν] καλῇ
ἐκ τοῦ τραχήλου δῆσο[ν. εἶ]α δή, [Κέρκ]ωψ,
κίνει ταχέως τὰ γοῦνα· μέζον [ἴχηνας]
τρίβειν ξοφεῦντα νουθ[ετημάτων] τῶνδε;
νῦν ἔκ μιν αὐτὴν, λε[….., λαμπρ]ύνεις
καὶ ψ[ῇ]ς; [ἐγώ] σευ τὴν [……….]ψήσω.
ἕζεσθε, Μητροῖ. Πίστ[ε, τὴν διπλῆν ο]ἴξας
πυργῖδα, μὴ τὴν ὧδ[ε, τὴν δ' ἄνω κείνη]ν,
τὰ χρήσιμ' ἔργα τοῦ τρ[ίβωνος Κέρδων]ος
ταχέως ἔνεγκ' ἄνωθ[εν. ὦ μάκαρ Μη]τροῖ,
οἶ' ἔργ' ἐπόψεσθ'. ἡσυχῆ [σύ, λαίμαστρ]ον,

1 [γυνὰς] Diels (1892) 388 εἴ] τι Blass (1891) 730, Ellis (1891) 362
8 ἔχ[ει ἐν] Cunningham (1971) 177
9 δῆσο[ν. εἶ]α Diels (1892) 388, [Κέρκ]ωψ Headlam (1891) 538
10 [ἴχηνας] Knox (1922) 331, 336
11 νουθ[ετημάτων] Headlam (1922) 319
12 λαμπρ]ύνεις Headlam (1892) 89
13 καὶ ψ[ῇ]ς; [ἐγὼ] Knox (1922) 319
14 Πίστ[ε Headlam (1892) 89, τὴν διπλῆν Herzog (1926) 206, ο]ἴξας Diels (1892) 389
15 ὧδ[ε, τὴν δ' ἄνω κείνη]ν Headlam (1922) 319
16 τρ[ίβωνος Κέρδων]ος Sitzler (1896) 164
17 ἄνωθ[εν Blass (1892)[1] 235, ὦ μάκαρ Headlam (1922) 332, Μη]τροῖ Blass (1892)[1] 235
18 [σύ, λαίμαστρ]ον Knox (1922) 333

## 7. THE SHOEMAKER

(*Mêtrô*) Kerdôn, I'm bringing you these [ladies] here to see if
you have some skilled handiwork
worth showing them. (*Kerdôn*) I have every reason, Metrô,
for loving you. – Aren't you going to put
the larger bench out for the ladies? I'm talking to Drimylos;
are you asleep again? Pistos, hit him on his snout
till he's got rid of all his sleepiness.
No, instead tie the thorny brush just as [it is in] a good knot
from his neck. Come on, [Kerkôps],
move your knees quickly. [Did you want]
to feel the chafing of things that make a louder noise than these warnings?
Are you only now, you [….], [polishing]
and [wiping] it? I'll wipe your [….].
Sit down, Mêtrô. Pistos, [... ] open
the double display-cabinet, not the one here, [but that one up there]
and quickly bring down from there
the useful handiwork of [the master-shoemaker, Kerdôn]. [Ah, lucky Mêtrô],
what products you're going to see. Quietly, [you greedy thing],

τὴν σαμβαλούχην οἶγ[ε. τοῦθ' ὅρη] πρῶτον
Μητροῖ· τελέων ἄρη[ρεν ἐκ μερ]έων ἴχνος.
θηεῖσθε χὐμεῖς, ὦ γυ[ναῖκες· ἡ πτ]έρνη
ὁρῆθ' ὅπως πέπηγε, χ[ὤτι σ]φην[ίσκ]οις
ἐξηρτίωται πᾶσα, κο[ὐ τ]ὰ μὲν κ[αλ]ῶς
τὰ δ' οὐχὶ καλῶς, ἀλλὰ πάντ' ἴσαι χ[εῖρε]ς.
τὸ χρῶμα δ' οὕτως ὗμιν ἡ Πά[φου] δοίη
μ[εδέουσ' ὅσωνπ]ερ ἰχανᾶσθ' ἐπαυρέσθαι
ἄλ]λο τῷ̣δε ἴσον χρῶμα
] κοὐδὲ κηρὸς ἀνθήσει.
χ[ρυσοῦ στατῆρας] τρεῖς ἔδωκε Κανδᾶτ[ος
]τοῦτο χἤτερον χρῶμα
ὄμνυ]μι πάνθ' ὅσ' ἐσθ' ἱρά
]τὴν ἀληθείην βάζειν
]οὐδ' ὅσον ῥοπὴν ψεῦδος
] Κέρδωνι μὴ βίου ὄνησις
μ[ηδ' ]γίνοιτο καὶ χάριν πρός με
οὐ γ]ὰρ ἀλλὰ μεζόνων ἤδη
] κερδέων ὀριγνῶνται.
]τὰ ἔργα τῆς τέχνης ἡμέων
πί]συγγος δὲ δειλαίην οἰζύν
]νύκτα χἠμέρην θάλπω.
ἐπεὶ τί]ς ἡμέων ἄχρις ἑσπέρης κάπτει

19 οἶγ[ε. τοῦθ' ὅρη] Blass (1892)[1] 235
20 ἄρη[ρεν Blass (1892)[1] 235, ἐκ μερ]έων Knox (1922) 318
21 γυ[ναῖκες, ἡ πτ]έρνη Rutherford (1891) 31
22 χ[ὤτι σ]φην[ίσκ]οις Kenyon (1901) 384
23 κο[ὐ τ]ὰ μὲν κ[αλ]ῶς Blass (1891) 730
24 χ[εῖρε]ς Headlam (1922) 334–5
25 Πά[φου] Knox (1925) 15
26 μ[εδέουσ' Knox (1925) 15, ὅσωνπ]ερ Knox (1925) 15
27 ἄλ]λο Crusius (1892)[1] 61
29 χ[ρυσοῦ στατῆρας] Knox (1925) 15, Κανδᾶτ[ος Diels (1892) 389
31 ὄμνυ]μι Blass (1892)[1] 235
35 μ[ηδ' Sitzler (1896) 165
36 οὐ γ]ὰρ Bücheler (1892) 50
39 πί]συγγος Blass (1892)[1] 235
41 ἐπεὶ τί]ς Knox (1926)[2] 77

open the shoe-box. [Look at this] first,
Mêtrô: the sole is put together from perfect [materials].
You have a look, too, ladies: see how the heel
is fixed, and that it's all fitted out with [little wedges],
and not that some parts are well made
while others aren't, but the handiwork is equal all over.
But the colour – as I hope the [Paphian], [who rules over]
[whatever] you crave, may grant that you enjoy it
…………...] any other colour equal to this one
………………....] nor will the beeswax shine.
………………....] Kandas' [wife] gave three [gold staters]
…………..….] this and another colour.
................I swear] by all that's holy
……………I'm] telling the truth
…………….....] nor as much as a lie [weighs down] the balance
……………] may Kerdôn have no enjoyment of life
[nor ...........] may it be, and thanks to me
…………] for it's certain that now they are grasping for greater
……………] profits.
……………...] the results of my skill.
But [I, a cobbler], ... wretched misery
……………....] I warm night and day.
Since who] of us gulps down any food till evening

ἢ πίετ]αι πρὸς ὄρθρον; οὐ δοκέω τόσσον
τὰ Μικίωνος κηρί'[
κοὔπω λέγω τρισκαίδε[χ' οὓς ἐγὼ β]όσκω,
ὀτεύνεκ', ὦ γυναῖκες, ἀργ[ίη πάντε]ς,
οἵ, κἢν ὕῃ Ζεύς, τοῦτο μοῦ[νον ἴσασιν,
φέρ' εἰ φέρεις τι, τἆλλα δ' ἀ[σ]φ[αλεῖς ἧν]ται
ὄκως νεοσσοὶ τὰς κοχώνας θάλποντες.
ἀλλ' οὐ λόγων γάρ, φασίν, ἡ ἀγορὴ δεῖται
χαλκῶν δέ, τοῦτ' ἢν μὴ ὗμιν ἀνδάνῃ, Μητρ[οῖ,
τὸ ζεῦγος, ἕτερον χἄτερον μάλ' ἐξοίσει,
ἔστ' ἂν νόῳ πεισθῆτε μὴ λέγειν ψευδέα
Κέρδωνα. τάς μοι σα[μβα]λουχίδας πάσας
ἔνεγκε, Πίστε,[
ὑμέας ἀπελθεῖν, ὦ γυναῖκες, εἰς οἶκον.
θήσεσθε δ' ὑμεῖς· γένεα ταῦτα παντοῖα·
Σικυώνι', Ἀμβρακίδια, Νοσσίδες, λεῖαι,
ψιττάκια, κανναβίσκα, Βαυκίδες, βλαῦται,
Ἰωνίκ' ἀμφίσφαιρα, νυκτιπήδηκες,
ἀκροσφύρια, καρκίνια, σάμβαλ' Ἀργεῖα,
κοκκίδες, ἔφηβοι, διάβαθρ'· ὧν ἐρᾷ θυμός
ὑμέων ἑκάστης εἴπατ', ὡς ἂν αἴσθοισθε
σκύτεα γυναῖκες καὶ κύνες τί βρώζουσιν.
*(ΜΗ.)* κόσου χρεΐζεις κεῖν' ὃ πρόσθεν ἤειρας
ἀπεμπολῆσαι ζεῦγος; ἀλλὰ μὴ βροντέων
οὗτος σὺ τρέψῃς μέζον εἰς φυγὴν ἡμέας.
*(ΚΕ.)* αὐτὴ σὺ καὶ τίμησον, εἰ θέλεις, αὐτό
καὶ στῆσον ἧς κότ' ἐστιν ἄξιον τιμῆς.
ὁ τοῦτ' ἐῶν γὰρ οὔ σε ῥηιδίως ῥινᾷ.
ζευγέων, γύναι, τὠληθὲς ἢν θέλῃς ἔργον,
ἐρεῖς τι – ναὶ μὰ τήνδε τὴν τεφρὴν κόρσην,
ἐφ' ἧς ἀλώπηξ νοσσιὴν πεποίηται –
τάχ' ἀλφιτηρὸν ἐργαλεῖα κινεῦσι.

42 ἢ πίετ]αι Knox (1926)² 77
44 οὓς ἐγὼ Edmonds (1925) 135, β]όσκω Bücheler (1892) 50
45 ἀργ[ίη πάντε]ς Headlam (1922) 321
46 μοῦ[νον ἴσασιν Crusius (1892)² 136–7
47 ἀ[σ]φ[αλεῖς Herzog (1926) 206, ἧν]ται Headlam (1892) 89
53 σα[μβα]λουχίδας Bücheler (1892) 51

or drinks] till dawn? I don't think to that extent
Mikiôn's honey [....................................].
What's more, there are thirteen [whom I] feed,
because, ladies, they are [all laziness],
who, even if skies are grey, only [know] this:
'Bring it to us, if you've got anything to bring', but otherwise they [sit tight]
warming their bottoms like chicks.
– But, as they say, the marketplace doesn't need words
but copper coins. So if this pair doesn't give you satisfaction, Mêtrô,
he'll bring out another and another
until you're convinced that Kerdôn isn't telling lies.
Bring all the shoe-boxes for me,
Pistos. [..................................................]
you [must] go back home [.....], ladies.
You'll see for yourselves, there are all kinds here:
Sikyonians, little Ambrakians, Nossises, smooths,
parrot-greens, hemps, Baukises, slippers,
Ionic shoes with buttons on the sides, night-slippers,
ankle-boots, red crabshoes, Argive sandals,
scarlets, ephebes, flat-heels – name the ones
the hearts of each of you desire, so you can find out
why women and dogs eat leather.
(*Mê.*) How much do you want to sell the pair
you picked up earlier for? But, you, don't you any more
make us run away by bellowing.
(*Ke.*) You value it yourself, you, if you please,
and decide whatever price it's worth.
Anybody who lets you do that isn't going to lead you by the nose easily.
If it's true workmanship in pairs of shoes you want, lady,
you'll say something which – yes, by this ash-grey head of mine,
on which the alopecian fox has made his lair –
will soon bring bread and butter to men who work with tools.

Ἑρμῆ τε Κερδέων καὶ σὺ Κερδείη Πειθοῖ,<br>
ὡς, ἤν τι μὴ νῦν ἧμιν ἐς βόλον κύρσῃ,<br>
οὐκ οἶδ᾽ ὅκως ἄμεινον ἡ χύτρη πρήξει.<br>
*(ΜΗ.)* τί τονθορύζεις κοὐκ ἐλευθέρῃ γλάσσῃ<br>
τὸν τῖμον ὅστις ἐστὶ ἐξεδίφησας;<br>
*(ΚΕ.)* γύναι, μιῆς μνῆς ἐστιν ἄξιον τοῦτο<br>
τὸ ζεῦγος· ἢ ἄνω ᾽στ᾽ ἢ κάτω βλέπειν· χαλκοῦ<br>
ῥίνημ᾽ ὃ δήκοτ᾽ ἐστὶ τῆς Ἀθηναίης<br>
ὠνευμένης αὐτῆς ἂν οὐκ ἀποστάξαι.<br>
*(ΜΗ.)* μάλ᾽ εἰκότως σευ τὸ στεγύλλιον, Κέρδων,<br>
πέπληθε δαψιλέων τε καὶ καλῶν ἔργων.<br>
φύλασσε κάρτα σ᾽ αὐτά· τῇ γὰρ εἰκοστῇ<br>
τοῦ Ταυρεῶνος ἡ ᾽κατῆ γάμον ποιεῖ<br>
τῆς Ἀρτακηνῆς, χὐποδημάτων χρείη·<br>
τάχ᾽ οὖν, τάλης, ἄιξουσι σὺν τύχῃ πρός σε,<br>
μᾶλλον δὲ πάντως. ἀλλὰ θύλακον ῥάψαι<br>
τὰς μνέας ὅκως σοι μὴ αἱ γαλαῖ διοίσουσι.<br>
*(ΚΕ.)* ἤν θ᾽ ἡ ᾽κατῆ ἔλθῃ, μνῆς ἔλασσον οὐκ οἴσει,<br>
ἤν θ᾽ ἡ Ἀρτακηνή. πρὸς τάδ᾽, εἰ θέλεις, σκέπτευ.<br>
*(ΜΗ.)* οὔ σοι δίδωσιν ἡ ἀγαθὴ τύχη, Κέρδων,<br>
ψαῦσαι ποδίσκων ὧν Πόθοι τε κἤρωτες<br>
ψαύουσιν; ἀλλ᾽ εἶς κνῦσα καὶ κακὴ λώβη<br>
ὥστ᾽ ἐκ μὲν ἡμέων † λιολεοσεω † πρήξεις.<br>
ταύτῃ δὲ δώσεις κεῖνο τὸ ἕτερον ζεῦγος<br>
κόσου; πάλιν πρήμηνον ἀξίην φωνήν<br>
σεωυτοῦ.<br>
*(ΚΕ.)* στατῆρας πέντε, ναὶ μὰ θεούς, φοιτᾷ<br>
ἡ ψάλτρι᾽ Εὐετηρὶς ἡμέρην πᾶσαν<br>
λαβεῖν ἀνώγουσ᾽, ἀλλ᾽ ἐγώ μιν ἐχθαίρω,<br>
κἢν τέσσαράς μοι Δαρικοὺς ὑπόσχηται,<br>
ὁτεύνεκέν μευ τὴν γυναῖκα τωθάζει<br>
κακοῖσι δέννοις· εἰ δ[έ σοί γ᾽ ἔσ]τι χρείη<br>
φέρ᾽ – εὐλαβοῦ σὺ τῶν τριῶν [μιᾷ] δοῦναι,

96 λιολεοσεω P Αἰολέος Beare (1904), Αἰολέως Cunningham (2004) 29, tum e.g. [δῶρον]<br>
104 δ[έ σοί γ᾽ ἔσ]τι Blass (1892)[1] 236<br>
105 φερευλαβου⟨ ⟩ P φέρ᾽ – εὐλαβοῦ σὺ Headlam (1891) 314, [μιᾷ] Headlam (1893) 404

Hermes of Profit Kerdonian, and Kerdonian Persuasion of Profit,
[I call on you] because, if something doesn't land in my net now,
I don't know how the cooking-pot is going to fare any better.
(*Mê.*) Why do you keep muttering while you haven't freely
disclosed what its price is?
(*Ke.*) Lady, the value of this pair is one mina.
You can look happy or downcast; the slightest shaving of copper whatsoever
wouldn't come off the price
if Athene herself were the customer.
(*Mê.*) Kerdôn, no wonder your little establishment
is full to brimming with plenty of lovely things.
Look after them very carefully: on the twentieth
of the month of Taureôn Hekatê is is putting on the marriage
of Artakênê, and shoes will be needed.
So, you scoundrel, maybe with a bit of luck they'll make a rush on your wares,
or rather, they absolutely will. Have your money-sack stitched up
so that the pet-weasels don't make off with all your minas.
(*Ke.*) If Hekatê comes, she won't take the pair away for less than a mina,
nor if Artakênê comes. Please bear that in mind and decide.
(*Mê.*) My, Kerdôn, isn't it your good luck that's granting that you touch
the delicate little feet that the Desires and Loves touch?
–You're irritating, and a disgrace,
so you'll get [...] out of us.
How much will you give that other pair to this lady for?
Again, talk at a volume worthy of yourself.
(*Ke.*) Euetêris the harpist keeps asking me to take five staters for them,
by the gods, visiting me every day,
but I hate her,
even if she promises me four Darics,
because she scoffs at my wife
with horrible insults. [*to the woman mentioned at line 97*] But if [you're in] need,
come, make sure you don't give them [to one] of the three women,

καὶ ταῦτα καὶ ταῦτ' ἦ ὗμιν ἑπτὰ Δαρεικῶν
ἕκητι Μητροῦς τῆσδε· μηδὲν ἀντείπῃς.
δύναιτό μ' ἐλάσαι σὴ ἂν [ἰὴ] τὸν πίσ[υγγον
ἐόντα λίθινον ἐς θεοὺς ἀναπτῆναι·
ἔχεις γὰρ οὐχὶ γλάσσαν, ἡδονῆς δ' ἠθμόν.
ἆ, θεῶν ἐκεῖνος οὐ μακρὴν ἄπεσ[θ' ὡν]ήρ
ὅτεῳ σὺ χείλεα νύκτα χἠμέρην οἴγεις.
φέρ' ὧδε τὸν ποδίσκον· εἰς ἴχνος θῶμεν.
πάξ· μήτε προσθῇς μήτ' ἀπ' οὖν ἕλῃς μηδέν·
τὰ καλὰ πάντα τῇς καλῇσιν ἁρμόζει·
αὐτὴν ἐρεῖς τὸ πέλμα τὴν Ἀθηναίην
τεμεῖν. δὸς αὕτη καὶ σὺ τὸν πόδ'· ἆ, ψωρῇ
ἄρηρεν ὁπλῇ βοῦς ὁ λακτίσας ὑμέας.
εἴ τις πρὸς ἴχνος ἠκόνησε τὴν σμίλην,
οὐκ ἄν, μὰ τὴν Κέρδωνος ἑστίην, οὕτω
τοὔργον σαφέως ἔκειτ' ἂν ὡς σαφέως κεῖται.
αὕτη σύ, δώσεις ἑπτὰ Δαρικοὺς τοῦδε,
ἡ μέζον ἵππου πρὸς θύρην κιχλίζουσα;
γυναῖκες, ἢν ἔχητε χἠτέρων χρείην
ἢ σαμβαλίσκων ἢ ἃ κατ' οἰκίην ἕλκειν
εἴθισθε, τήν μοι δουλίδ' ὧδε δεῖ πέμπειν.
σὺ δ' ἧκε, Μητροῖ, πρός με τῇ ἐνάτῃ πάντως
ὅκως λάβῃς καρκίνια· τὴν γὰρ οὖν βαίτην
θάλπουσαν εὖ δεῖ 'νδον φρονεῦντα καὶ ῥάπτειν.

108 σὴ ἂν [ἰὴ] τὸν πίσ[υγγον Knox (1922) 362
111 ἄπεσ[τ' ὡν]ήρ Blass (1891) 730

and consider this pair and that yours for seven Darics
thanks to Mêtrô here. [*to Mêtrô, now chatting her up*] Don't contradict me:
your [voice] would be able to drive me, the cobbler,
even though I am stony-hearted, to fly to the gods.
For it's not a tongue you have, but a filter of pleasure to refine it.
Ah, that [man is] not far from the gods
to whom you open your lips night and day.
Bring your precious little foot here. Let's place it on the sole.
Perfect! Don't add or still less take away a thing.
All beautiful things fit beautiful women.
You'd think Athene herself had cut the sole.
[*to another woman*] Let me have *your* foot, too. Oh dear! The ox
that trampled you *did* have a scabby hoof!
[*removes the old shoes and puts on the new*] If someone sharpened his knife on the sole,
the product, I swear by Kerdôn's hearth,
wouldn't have fitted as perfectly as it does fit perfectly.
[*to another woman*] – You over there, the lady giggling by the door louder than a horse,
Will you give me seven Darics for this pair?
[*to the group*] – Ladies, if you need anything else besides,
little sandals or whatever you're used to wearing at home,
you just have to send your slave here to me.
But you, Mêtrô, be sure to visit me on the ninth
to pick up your red crabshoes. Anybody with brains in his head
should rightly also stitch the coat that keeps him warm.

## COMMENTARY

At the close of *Mimiamb* 6 we saw Mêtrô leaving Korittô's house to find Artemeis, the person who brokered the negotiation over the dildo between Korittô and Kerdôn; she hoped to make contact with Kerdôn through Artemeis. In the present poem, the longest in the preserved collection, Mêtrô and Kerdôn appear, the latter this time in the flesh. Mêtrô has brought some female friends with her, who are looking for the products of Kerdôn's primary work, shoes. It is therefore evident that Mêtrô has made contact with Kerdôn some time earlier, that Mêtrô's immediate reason for making contact with him is now less acute, and that she has established a *modus operandi* with the shoemaker. She may be introducing new customers to Kerdôn in recognition of services already rendered. There is clear evidence, on the other hand, that Mêtrô and Kerdôn maintain their business connection on its original lines. On the continuities between the 6th and 7th poems see further the Discussion.

Synopsis The poem starts with Mêtrô and friends already inside Kerdôn's shop. Mêtrô tells Kerdôn that she has come with her friends to check out his wares (1–3a). Kerdôn thanks her, and makes an ostentatious show of his powers of slave-abuse as he orders them set up a bench for the ladies to sit on and bring in the shoe-boxes (3b–17a). He produces a pair of shoes, and proceeds to praise their workmanship and colour, swearing that another customer is prepared to pay handsomely for them (17b–35). He then expatiates on the cut-throat prices he must pay his suppliers for the materials, the long hours he must work, and the obligation he has to feed his large number of dependants (36–50a). He then promises to show as many pairs as it takes to prove his knowledge of women's needs (50b–63). Mêtrô (on the part-attributions offered here) asks him to lower his voice and tell them the price of the first pair, which prompts Kerdôn to get her to name her own price, while emphasizing his need of a good one (64–76). Mêtrô repeats her question, and Kerdôn declares them worth a mina (77–82). She then sarcastically comments that it's no wonder that Kerdôn's establishment is so full of fine products, and tells Kerdôn of a forthcoming marriage for which shoes will be in great demand (83–99a). Asked the price of another pair, Kerdôn obliges, claiming that a local harpist has been pestering him for them, but he dislikes her for slandering his wife; nonetheless, he can offer a cut price for Mêtrô's sake, on whose 'lips' he lavishes praise in rather dubious taste (99b–112). He makes Mêtrô try the pair on, pronouncing a perfect fit, and gets another lady to try on another pair, disparaging the maker of her old pair, and claiming that his own creations might have been made by Athene (113–21). After abusing a woman standing at the door for giggling, he tells the women that they only have to send their maidservant if they have any footwear needs, and asks Mêtrô to return soon to pick up her 'crab-shoes': one should, he reasons, spend a bit of extra care on such a valued customer (122–8).

Structure The poem divides naturally and without emphatic demarcation into three parts: 1–14a, in which the women are seated; 14b–63, in which Kerdôn shows his wares; and 64–129, the bargaining, bartering and farewell-scene.

Text *Mimiamb* 7 is, after 8 and 9, the most fragmentary of the preserved collection. Column 35 of the papyrus (lines 8–25) is heavily damaged on the right side, column 36 (lines 26–42) on the left, and column 37 (lines 43–61) on the top right. I have admitted into the text as many of the supplements as I consider to be either convincing or giving the likely sense, in order to provide a text with as much connected Greek as possible within the bounds of editorial responsibility.

Line-allocation is again difficult. The attribution to Mêtrô of all the lines not spoken by Kerdôn is the procedure of Cunningham in his various editions, and is adopted here. However, Di Gregorio (2004) 215–20 is one of the modern critics who assign only lines 1–3a to Mêtrô, and all the others, not spoken by Kerdôn, to an unnamed woman in Mêtrô's party, i.e. lines 64–6, 77–8, 83–90, and 93–99a. There is some good sense in this: for example, the female speaker's tone might strike us as too imperious for an established client of a craftsman. But relegating Mêtrô's contribution to three lines and giving the rest to an unnamed member of Mêtrô's party seems a strange procedure in a diptych, and the at times sharp and sarcastic tone might just as easily be put down precisely to Mêtrô's fear that her secret familiarity with Kerdôn will be made public.

Setting See the Introduction to *Mimiamb* 6, whose location is the same. The stage-setting, imagined or real, is different, though sparsely indicated. Kerdôn's shop looks out on to the street, as we can tell from his complaints about the woman heckling him 'by the door' (123). Kerdôn orders Drimylos to bring out the larger bench from the inner workshop (5), and from lines 14–19 it looks as if there are shelves against the walls of the front shop for the shoe-boxes to be stored on.

Casting On the text offered here, there are two main speakers, Mêtrô and Kerdôn, but Mêtrô's retinue must contain three or more mute figures (the dual is not used when referring to them), Kerdôn has two non-speaking slaves, Pistos and Drimylos, and then there is the non-speaking part of the woman at the door. That is, at least eight actors would have been needed to stage the piece. Combine this with the observation of Puchner (1993) 29 that fetching the bench and the shoe-box would have been boring to watch if the poem were presented on a stage, and part of the fun for the audience as they imagined the comic business from a recitation-performance, and we begin to have considerable sympathy for his view that the mode of performance was recitation by one actor. The fact that most of the speaking in the poem belongs to Kerdôn is another strong argument for Puchner's performance-scenario.

Date No evidence.

Sources Shoemakers were of course a fact of every-day reality in ancient Greece, but they hardly enjoyed the standing of Wagner's Hans Sachs. Aristophanes' *Women at the Assembly* 385–7, where the characteristic paleness of shoemakers (a result of their indoor drudgery) is part of the joke, is evidence of the disdain in which the trade was held; see Ussher (1973) 129–30. As usual, however, Herodas' shoemaker is seen through the filter of literature, in particular comedy. Euboulos wrote a play called the Σκυτεύς, *The Shoemaker* (*Fr.* 96 Kassel-Austin [1986] 5 246), and many have assumed Herodas' debt to it. There is also Nikochares' *Kretans*, which refers to one of a shoemaker's tools (*Fr.* 12 Kassel-Austin [1989)] 7 45). And we have already seen the comic deployment of dildoes, traditionally made by shoemakers, in connection with *Mimiamb* 6 (p. 167).

There are several verbal recollections of Hippônax: the word κοχώνη (48) may have occurred in *Fr.* 202 Degani (1991) 177; on οὐ γ]ὰρ ἀλλά (36, and 6.101) see Degani (1984) 47, 241–3; for κηρία (43) in the rare sense of 'honey' see *Fr.* 37.3 Degani (1991) 53 and (1984) 54; for the diminutives in e.g. Kerdôn's list of shoes see Degani (1984) 53–4; for ἐξεδίφησας at line 78 see *Fr.* 87c.8 Degani (1991) 100. Herodas might also have known of Rhinthôn of Syracuse's Phlyax-play *Iphigeneia in Aulis*, *Fr.* 5 Kassel-Austin (2001) 1 264, where there appears to have been a list of shoes. This is interesting, because the early Hellenistic poet Alexandros the Aitolian praises the elegiac poet Boiôtos of Syracuse for his parodies of Homer, in which he included characters like πίσυγγοι, the word used for shoemakers at lines 39 and 108. There also seems to be a list of shoes in the comedian Lysippos' *Bakchai*, *Fr.* 2 Kassel-Austin (1986) 5 619. Finally, *Mim.* 7 has elements of epic parody, for example at line 7, where Kerdôn's order to Pistos to punch Drimylos' nose so that he will 'pour out all his sleepiness' is an inversion of the Homeric motif of a deity pouring sleep on the eyebrows of a person, as at *Il.* 14.164–5 and *Od.* 2.395.

PURPOSE The shoemaker is by far the major figure in this long poem, and amply fills out the picture that we have received of him indirectly in *Mim.* 6. It seems likely that the direct mode of his representation here is meant to complement the preceding poem's indirect approach. Kerdôn's characterization in *Mimiamb* 7, in particular the portrayal of his sales-pitch, more than lives up to expectations, and is a second main aim of the poem, even if, as is argued below, pp. 214–15, we should not accept the view of Cunningham (1971) 174 that the objects over which the shoemaker and the women are negotiating are not shoes at all, and that the shoe-names are aliases for dildoes throughout.

**1–13:** The poem opens with Mêtrô introducing potential new clients to Kerdôn, with whom she has been doing business for some time since she left Korittô's house at the end of *Mim.* 6. Kerdôn expresses his appreciation of Mêtrô's gesture, and bullies his slave, Drimylos, into bringing out a bench for the women to sit on.
**1. γυνάς:** this form (= γυναῖκας) occurs in comedy: see e.g. Menandros, *Fr.* 457 Kassel-Austin (1998) 6.2 267, Pherekrates, *Fr.* 203 Kassel-Austin (1989) 7 203.
**εἰ:** 'to see if', as at *Mim.* 6.100.
**τι:** I accept Blass and Ellis' τι, 'some'.
**2–3a. you have some skilled handiwork worth showing them:** in this translation, which is favoured by e.g. Headlam-Knox (1922) 319 and Nairn-Laloy (1991) 93, τῶν σῶν... χειρέων is a possessive, and δεῖξαι is dependent on ἄξιον. This seems simpler and more natural than to translate, with e.g. Cunningham (2002) 259, 'to see if you can show them skilled handiwork that's worthy of your craft'; in this version, ἄξιον, the object of δεῖξαι, goes with τι νοῆρες ἔργον, and governs τῶν σῶν... χειρέων; ἔχεις could either mean 'to be able to', or 'to have', with δεῖξαι being an explanatory infinitive.
**3b. οὐ μάτην...:** cf. the Latin *merito te amo*, 'it's right that I love you', as at Terence,

*The Eunuch* 186, based on Menandros' play of the same name; it is possible that Herodas and Terence owe the phrase to Menandros. But Cunningham (1971) 176 is surely right to regard it as the first suggestion that Mêtrô and Kerdôn have more than a purely business relationship; so also Di Gregorio (2004) 229 and Kutzko (2006) 176.

**4. οὐ θήσεις;:** a negative future question, conveying a threatening tone.

**5. Δριμύλῳ:** considering that the name is based on the adjective δριμύς, 'sharp', it seems likely that Herodas had an ironical intention in giving it to such a sleepy-head.

**6. Πίστε:** the name means 'Faithful'; he is the 'loyal' slave to whom Kerdôn turns when action is needed.

**τὸ ῥύγχος:** a punch on the nose by another slave is also administered at *Mim.* 5.41 to galvanise an inert servant.

**7. till he's got rid of all his sleepiness:** for the epic parody see above, p. 201. This is a case of 'opposition by imitation', *oppositio in imitando*: we are meant to pick up the echo, and contrast the material common to the original and the citing passage, here for comic purposes.

**8. thorny brush:** Cunningham (1971) 177, following Headlam (1922) 330, takes 'the thorn' to refer to 'a brush used to treat the leather'. When it is hung from Drimylos' neck, he will prick himself on the spiky brush if he nods off.

**καλῇ, good:** supply e.g. δέσει, 'knot'; on the brachyology, whereby a noun can be supplemented from a verb (here δῆσον), see Kühner-Gerth (1955) 2 564–5.

**9. Kerkôps, [Κέρκ]ωψ:** the mythological Kerkôpes tried to cheat Zeus, and were punished by Herakles, who hung them upside down from a yoke across his shoulders; their name came to mean 'rogue'; see Headlam-Knox (1922) 331 and Di Gregorio (2004) 234. All this makes Headlam's conjecture attractively appropriate.

**10–11. μέζον:** qualifying ξοφεῦντα, 'things that make a louder noise', i.e. chains.

**Did you want**: if Knox's supplement is correct, the tense of the verb is strange; but the only support for the supplement is the verb's appearance at line 26.

**τρίβειν:** as at *Mim.* 5.62, where see n. The syntax of the line is ['did you want'] + nominative and infinitive, τρίβειν ('to feel the chafing of'), governing the neuter accusative plural participle ξοφεῦντα ('things making a noise') as direct object, and with a genitive of comparison, 'than these warnings', after the comparative adverb μέζον, 'more loudly'.

**12. ἐκ:** in tmesis with λαμπρ]ύνεις if Headlam's supplement is correct (though its only support is *Mim.* 6.9 νῦν ... ποεῖς λαμπρόν;, 'only now … you clean [the chair]?'). It is likely that the word before the supplement was a vocative, probably abusive.

**14–19a:** with promises of the treat in store, Kerdôn invites the women to sit down, and orders Pistos to bring down his masterpieces from a shelf and open the shoe-box.

**14. ο]ἴξας:** we have to wait two lines till the main verb, ἔνεγκ', because of Kerdôn's fussy directions.

**16. τρ[ίβωνος:** for the sense 'master at a craft', see LSJ[9] s.v. B.1; however, LSJ[9] s.v.

B.2 gives 'old hand', 'rogue', and Herodas might be making a punning joke at Kerdôn's expense; but again it must be emphasized that we are dealing with a supplement.
**18. οἶ' ἔργ' ἐπόψεσθ':** we recall Sophokles, *Oidipous the King* 1224, οἶ' ἔργ' ἀκούσεσθ', οἷα δ' εἰσόψεσθ', 'What deeds you will hear of, what deeds you will see', though it prefaces an announcement of ghastly things while Kerdôn goes on to list objects that will give delight. The elevated tone and inversion of context are perfectly within Herodas' style of humour, and suit Kerdôn's build-up.
**[greedy thing], λαίμαστρ]ον:** used also at *Mim.* 4.46.
**19b–35:** Kerdôn shows Mêtrô the first pair of shoes, praising their materials, then invites the other women to inspect the construction and decoration of their heels, and the all-over excellence of the shoes' workmanship. He singles out the colour for special praise, claiming that the wife of Kandas, probably the Artemeis of *Mim.* 6.87, has been offering a large sum for them because of it. He emphatically swears he is telling the truth.
**19. σαμβαλούχην**: σάμβαλον was a form of the word for a sandal, σάνδαλον, in Aeolic, Doric and Ionic Greek; see also below, lines 60 and 125.
**20. ἄρηρεν**: the Ionic intransitive perfect from ἀραρίσκω; see LSJ[9] s.v. B.III, 'to be fitted, furnished with', with dative; the verb is also found below, line 118.
**ἴχνος:** this usually means 'track', or 'footstep', but in this context, it denotes the sole of a shoe, as also at lines 113 and 119.
**22. χὤτι:** = καὶ ὅτι (crasis); there is a change from an indirect question (ὅπως) to an indirect statement.
**23. ἐξηρτίωται:** from ἐξαρτιόω, a *hapax legomenon*.
**23–4:** for this construction ('[it is] not [the case that] some things are done well, others not well, but…') cf. e.g. Herodotos 1.139, οὐ τὰ μέν, τὰ δ' οὔ, ἀλλὰ πάντα ὁμοίως, [You will find that Persian names end in sigma,] and not that some do, while others do not, but all similarly [end in sigma].'
**24. χεῖρες:** the word ironically and bathetically puts Kerdôn's skill on a par with Apelles' 'true hands' in the art of painting at *Mim.* 4.72; the same bathos is found at line 70.
**25–6. οὕτως ὗμιν … δοίη/… ἐπαυρέσθαι:** the expression 'as I hope that the gods may grant you enjoyment of x, so may y happen' is present at *Mim.* 3.1–2, and presumably this sentence ended in a parallel manner. Presumably, too, χρῶμα, 'colour', is intentionally repeated at line 27 after Kerdôn's expostulation. **ἐπαυρέσθαι** is another case of an infinitive functioning as an accusative noun; see *Mim.* 2.54 with n. and 3.2.
**25. ἡ Πά[φου:** i.e. Aphrodite, who had a famous precinct and cult in Paphos on Kypros, though even if we accept this supplement, Kerdôn need only be wishing the women happiness in their love-lives as a means of ingratiating himself with them; cf. Cunningham (1971) 178, who thinks Kerdôn is alluding to dildoes, 'the real subject'; see however below, pp. 214–15.
**26–42:** these lines constitute column 36 of the papyrus. A strip on the left-hand side, containing the initial letters of each line, had become detached from the papyrus,

but was relocated by Sitzler (1896). I have only printed the initial letters where something significant can be made of them.

**26. ἰχανᾶσθ':** this Ionic verb occurs only here in the middle voice.

**28. nor will the beeswax shine:** Headlam-Knox (1922) 336–7 explain the point of the reference to beeswax by showing that it was used in encaustic painting to give a translucent patina to the surface: Kerdôn will then be saying that not even the brilliance of encaustic painting will outshine that of the colour of his shoes.

**29. Κανδᾶτ[ος:** it is probable that a word for 'wife' has been lost, in which case it seems certain that Kandas will be the tanner of *Mim.* 6.87, and his wife the Artemeis who showed Kerdôn where to find Korittô.

**31. πάνθ':** the accusative by which Kerdôn swears his oath; see Kühner-Gerth (1955) 1 296–7.

**32. βάζειν:** originally an epic verb; compare its use at *Mim.* 2.102, where see n.

**33. balance:** the ῥοπή is the point at which a balance begins to tilt; 'turn of the scale', LSJ[9] s.v. I.1, 2a and 2b. It seems probable that a verb like 'to weigh down' has been lost, and that Kerdôn is saying that there is so little untruth in what he says that it would not tilt a balance, i.e. it does not exist at all.

**35. πρός:** this is more likely to be a preposition governing με rather than an adverb, for με is otherwise stranded; cf. πρός σε at the end of line 88.

**36–48:** In what amounts to a sob-story, Kerdôn explains the difficult circumstances under which he works: his suppliers are after greater and greater profits, the shoemaker's hours are long and allow no leisure, and, what's more, he has thirteen dependants to support who do nothing but take.

**36. οὐ γ]ὰρ ἀλλά:** for the particle-combination see *Mim.* 6.101n.

**39. a cobbler, πί]συγγος:** see above, p. 201 for the use of this apparently colloquial word in epic parody.

**41–2:** in the text offered here, Kerdôn is rhetorically asking whether any of his fellow-shoemakers can enjoy the luxury of eating till evening or drinking till (πρός) dawn.

**43. τὰ Μικίωνος κηρί':** κηρία must mean 'honey' here, as it does in Hippônax: see above, p. 200. Mikiôn must be an otherwise unknown, but high-quality local beekeeper. Kerdôn may therefore be saying that Mikiôn's labours in producing his exceptional honey cannot equal the hours Kerdôn has to put into making his shoes.

**44. What's more:** κοὔπω λέγω is a common parenthetical formula; see e.g. Plato, *Gorgias* 463e οὐ γάρ πω σαφὲς λέγω, 'I haven't made myself clear yet.'

**τρισκαίδε[χ' οὕς]:** supply εἰσί, literally 'they are thirteen whom I feed.'

**β]όσκω:** 'feed', but, used of human beings, it often conveys a sense of contempt: the scholiast to Aristophanes, *Knights* 256 (Jones [1969] 63.9) says that the word is used of irrational animals, and cf. e.g. *Lysistrata* 260, γυναῖκας, ἃς βόσκομεν κατ' οἰκίαν ἐμφανὲς κακόν, 'women, whom we feed at home as an evil for all to see'. By contrast, γηροβοσκέω, 'to care for parents', has no negative value, and cf. *Mim.* 8.15 with n.

**45. all laziness, ἀργ[ίη]:** for the use of an abstract to characterize people, see nn. on *Mim.* 6.16, 17.

**46. κἢν ὕῃ Ζεύς:** literally 'even when Zeus rains', i.e., 'even when times are bad [for us]': compare Theokritos, *Id.* 4.41–3, where Korydôn consoles Battos by saying χὠ Ζεὺς ἄλλοκα μὲν πέλει αἴθριος, ἄλλοκα δ' ὕει, 'Zeus sometimes has clear skies, and sometimes he rains.'

**47. Bring it to us, if you've got anything to bring, φέρ' εἰ φέρεις τι:** a proverbial expression; cf. the *Swallow Song* 17, *Fr.* 848 Page (1962) 450, ἂν δή φέρῃς τι, μέγα δή τι φέροις, 'If you bring anything, may you bring something big.' The expression itself is in apposition with τοῦτο μοῦ[νον in the previous line.

**ἀ[σ]φ[αλεῖς]:** normally, all they do is 'sit tight'; otherwise, they are only active when food is concerned.

**48. ὄκως:** = ὡς, 'as'.

**chicks, κοχώνας:** for the possible echo of Hippônax see above, p. 200. The word also occurs in Euboulos' comedy, *The Shoemaker*, *Fr.* 96 Kassel-Austin (1986) 5 246, though it is not necessarily the case that Herodas is borrowing the word specifically from Euboulos.

**49–63:** Kerdôn brings his hard-luck story to an abrupt close, probably because he notes that his clients are becoming impatient, and orders all the shoe-boxes to be brought out: if one pair doesn't satisfy the ladies, another will. He gives a staccato catalogue of the types of shoes he has for sale, and promises satisfaction.

**49. ἀλλ':** goes with ἦν in the next line: Kerdôn interposes his piece of folk wisdom, which could be printed with dashes before οὐ and after δέ, as Cunningham (1971) 181 suggests. ***ἀλλὰ ... γάρ*** marks Kerdôn's return to the real point at issue after his digression; see Denniston (1954) 103.

**But, as they say, the marketplace doesn't need words / but copper coins, οὐ λόγων γάρ ... ἡ ἀγορὴ δεῖται / χαλκῶν δέ:** Kerdôn advertises the fact that he is quoting a proverb by his use of φασίν, 'as they say'. The actual form of the proverb was οὐ λόγων ἀγορὰ δεῖται Ἑλλάδος, ἀλλ' ἔργων, 'The marketplace of Hellas doesn't need words but action' (Suidas O 906 Adler [1933] 3 587, 1–2). Kerdôn banalises the stirring sentiment by changing 'action' into 'money', the thing that he most associates the agora with. χαλκός means generally 'money' at this period: Schmidt (1968) 43–6, but cf. line 80 below.

**51. ἕτερον χἄτερον μάλ':** the adverb μάλα reinforces the pronoun and means 'yet'.

**ἐξοίσει:** the subject is probably Pistos, who is addressed in line 54 and asked to perform the same task.

**52. ψευδέα:** this accentuation presupposes that the adjective ψευδής is being used, but it could also be ψεύδεα, from the noun ψεῦδος.

**53. σα[μβα]λουχίδας:** the same meaning as σαμβαλούχη at line 19; cf. Theokritos, *Id.* 5.145 κερουχίδες, 'having horns', of goats.

**54–5:** restorations of the remnants of line 54b are unconvincing; the translation of line 55 has taken its contents as an accusative and infinitive, possibly dependent on the word δεῖ traceable in line 54b: 'You must go back home well shod', or the like.

**56–61:** for lists of shoes in comedy see above, p. 201; the motif in Herodas' poem may therefore be one from comedy. However, the aim of Kerdôn's list is to demonstrate his salesmanship: his unfaltering cascade of words suggests a seasoned practitioner, offers

the performer many opportunities to show off his comic skill, and displays Herodas' detailed knowledge of shoe-types. Cunningham (1971) 181 points out that Kerdôn's excitement as he opens the boxes 'is increased by the frequent resolutions (two in 57, 60, 61, one in 58...)'. We know of many of the shoes only from the lexicographers like Pollux and Hesychios; otherwise, names are attested mainly from comedy.
**57. Sikyonians, little Ambrakians:** shoes named after their place of origin, Sikyôn on the southern coast of the Korinthian Gulf and Ambrakia in Thesprotia. 'Sikyonians' occur also in the *Chreiai* of Herodas' contemporary Machon, line 158 Gow (1965) 42.
**Nossises:** Pollux 7.89 Bethe (1931) 2 77, 2–8 mentions shoes named after notable people who had worn them, and it seems likely that this particular type is named after the early third-century epigrammatist, Nossis of Lokroi. Given that the poetess is maliciously alluded to in *Mim.* 6.20 (where see n.), there may be an ulterior intention here, too; see below, 58n.
**λεῖαι, smooths:** though this word does not appear elsewhere referring directly to a shoe-type, it is just the feminine nominative plural of the common adjective, with its noun supplied from the context, and the feminine Νοσσίδες precedes it.
**58. parrot-greens:** a green shoe; the word is derived either from ψιττακός, 'parrot' *qua* green parrot, or from the green fruit and nut of the πιστάκη, 'pistacchio tree'.
**hemps:** only elsewhere in the lexicographers, e.g. Pollux 7.94 Bethe (1931) 2 78, 20–1, where it is attested in the form of καννάβια.
**Baukises:** at *Mim.* 6.20 Nossis is said to be the daughter of Erinna, and it is likely that the two poetesses are being made fun of: see the note. Erinna composed her dirge in hexameters, the *Distaff*, on the death of her friend, Baukis. There is, therefore, a triad of roughly contemporary poetesses on whom Herodas seems to be venting his spleen. However, 'Baukises' are attested as a type of woman's shoe as early as Aristophanes; see *Fr.* 355 Kassel-Austin (1984) 3.2 200, so Herodas cannot be inventing a new shoe to poke fun at Erinna's friend with. These facts seem to point to the conclusion that Kerdôn is speaking on two levels. For Mêtrô's friends, he is talking on the most obvious level, namely about shoes, but for Mêtrô's consumption, he is hinting at dildoes, which lesbians were traditionally thought to use. See further 60n., 61n. and the Discussion, pp. 214–15.
**59. shoes with buttons on the sides:** found in this form also at Hesychios α 4121 Latte (1953) 144 (though Latte wrongly emends Hesychios' text to ἀμφίσφυρα); the compound is precisely paralleled in adjectives like ἀμφιθάλασσος, '[a place with] sea on both sides', as at Pindar, *Olympian* 7.33 (used of Rhodes); see Schwyzer (1939) 1 435.
**νυκτιπήδηκες:** elsewhere only found at Pollux 7.94 Bethe (1931) 2 78, 21; it is formed from the words for 'night', νύξ, and 'leap', πηδάω, giving a literal meaning of 'night-leapers', or 'night-hoppers'.
**60. ankle-boots, ἀκροσφύρια:** in this diminutive form found elsewhere only in Pollux 7.94 Bethe (1931) 2 78, 22; it means 'shoes reaching the top of the ankles', as e.g. Di Gregorio (2004) 278–9 argues.

**red crabshoes:** this was the name of a real shoe, as we know from Pherekrates, *Fr.* 192 Kassel-Austin (1989) 7 197. However, if we accept the thesis based on the facts that crabs are red and that dildoes are too (*Mim.* 6.19), and if we accept that when Kerdôn reminds Mêtrô to pick up her 'crabshoes' at line 128 he is referring to dildoes, not shoes, the situation seems best accommodated by the explanation offered above, 58n.: Kerdôn is using a word which will mean one thing to Mêtrô's friends and another to Mêtrô herself. Cf. 63n. and the Discussion, p. 215.
**σάμβαλ':** for the form see above, 19n.
**61. scarlets, κοκκίδες:** a *hapax legomenon*; however, since we have the κόκκινος βαυβών, 'scarlet dildo', of *Mim.* 6.19, and since κόκκος, 'pomegranate seed', in the singular was used to mean 'cunt' while its plural referred to a young woman's firm breasts (Henderson [1975] 134, 149), 'scarlets' must have a sexual charge; see next n.
**ephebes, ἔφηβοι:** another *hapax legomenon*; but the word, which denotes a sexually mature young man, seems undeniably to be sexually suggestive, and, like 'scarlets' preceding it, operates on two levels, the innocent for Mêtrô's friends and the sexual for Mêtrô herself.
**flat-heels, διάβαθρ':** a real shoe-name: see e.g. Alexis, *Fr.* 103.8 Kassel-Austin (1991) 2 76 with note on line 7f.; it comes from the same word meaning 'a ship's gangway' or 'a drawbridge' (LSJ[9] s.v. διάβαθρον I and II), and the flat heels were preferrred by tall women who wanted to look shorter.
**ὧν:** = ἐκεῖνα ὧν, the latent ἐκεῖνα being absorbed into the form and the case of the relative pronoun; 'relative attraction'.
**62. ὡς ἂν αἴσθοισθε:** a purpose and relative clause, a construction predominantly found in Ionic (though it is used by Xenophon, its use is otherwise rare in Attic); see Kühner-Gerth (1955) 2 386.
**63. why women and dogs eat leather:** Kerdôn is building on the proverb which means that people find it difficult to unlearn a habit that they have become accustomed to, οὐδὲ γὰρ κύων παύσαιτ' ἂν ἅπαξ σκυτοτραγεῖν μαθοῦσα, 'a bitch does not stop when once she has learned to eat leather', as it is formulated in Loukianos 31 (*The Uneducated Book-Buyer*) 25. Cunningham (1971) 183 argues that Kerdôn is thinking of the 'lips' at line 112, i.e. a woman's labia (see note), and that therefore Herodas is saying that, like dogs with leather, women 'eat' leather dildoes, either with their labia or with their lips, i.e. orally (a practice attested in art; see e.g. Keuls [1985] 86 fig. 80). If there is a sexual reference, it is for Mêtrô's sake alone; for the other women, the surface meaning is most likely to be that women have an irrepressible shopping urge when it comes to fashion-accessories like shoes; similarly Lawall (1976) 167, who however denies the sexual reference *in toto*. See further above, 58n., 60n., 61n. and the Discussion, pp. 214–15.
**64–76:** Mêtrô asks what price Kerdôn wants for the first pair that he displayed; she asks him to moderate his voice (which he appears to have raised during the recital of his shoe-list) so that he doesn't intimidate her and her friends. Kerdôn asks her to name her price, provided that it will be adequate to his age and efforts. He makes a great show of apostrophizing the gods Hermes and Persuasion, because he needs a

good catch in order to improve his circumstances. For the assignment of the female speaking-part to Mêtrô from this point on see above, p. 199.

**64. κόσου:** genitive of price.

**the pair you picked up earlier:** this must be the pair that Kerdôn exhibited at line 19. κεῖν' goes with ζεῦγος.

**65. by bellowing, βροντέων:** used in Attic comedy of persons who act like an Olympian god; so of Perikles at Aristophanes, *Acharnians* 530–1. Kallimachos, *Aitia*, *Fr.* 1.20 Pfeiffer (1949) 4 famously remarks that thunder and the grand poetic tone belong to Zeus. Mêtrô is therefore asking Kerdôn to adopt a less bombastic tone and act like a normal human being. Her comment is a kind of actor's stage-direction indicating that Kerdôn's voice should rise in volume as he does his routine with the shoe-list; readers of the poem, too, will be enabled to imagine that Kerdôn has worked up a head of steam. Raising one's voice was a sign of vulgarity; see e.g. Demosthenes, *Against Stephanos* 1 77.

**66. But you, don't you, οὗτος σύ:** for this insulting form of address see *Mim*. 3.84n.

**make us run away, τρέψῃς ... εἰς φυγήν:** this was a military term: see e.g. Herodotos 8.89.2, Thoukydides 7.43.7. There is humour in comparing Kerdôn with an army routing its enemy.

**μέζον:** most editors take this adverb with βροντέων, but Di Gregorio (2004) 285 suggests that it go with τρέψῃς, which gives a more natural word-order; I have adopted the suggestion in the translation.

**67. αὐτὴ σὺ καὶ τίμησον:** καί intensifies αὐτή.

**εἰ θέλεις:** this formula, 'if you please' or 'please', found also at line 92 and *Mim*. 8.6, 14, occurs in Hippônax, and Degani (1984) 54 regards it as possible that Herodas may have derived it from him, but it is a quite common expression.

**68. decide, στῆσον:** causal aorist second-person imperative of ἵστημι; see LSJ[9] s.v. A.III.6 'fix by agreement'.

**69. lead you by the nose, ῥινᾷ:** this verb is also used by the comedians; see e.g. Menandros, *Sikyonios*, *Fr.* 10.

**70. τὠληθές:** with ἔργον; for the bathos contained in the reference to Kerdôn's 'true workmanship' in shoes see above, line 24n.

**71. by this ash-grey head of mine:** at *Mim*. 6.59 Kokkalê has already called Kerdôn 'bald', but he may be allowed some at least vestigial grey hair.

**72. ἀλώπηξ:** our word 'alopecia' comes from the ancient Greek medical term ἀλωπεκία (see e.g. Galênos, *Medical Definitions* 312 Kühn [1830] 19 431). Though ἀλώπηξ, *alôpêx*, 'fox', may not have anything to do with the derivation of the term, it was naturally associated with it, and led to personifications, like Kerdôn's here and Kallimachos' at the *Hymn to Artemis* 78–9, where the bald patch left on Brontes' hairy chest when the little goddess pulls out her handful is compared with the time when κόρσῃ / φωτὸς ἐνιδρυθεῖσα κόμην ἐπενείματ' ἀλώπηξ, 'the fox has settled on a man's head and has grazed upon his hair.' Perhaps the phrase was proverbial, and Herodas and Kallimachos are independently drawing on it.

**73. bread and butter, ἀλφιτηρόν:** that which will provide ἄλφιτα, literally 'barley-groats' but in comedy (e.g. Aristophanes, *Clouds* 106) metaphorical for 'bread and butter'; the formation of the adjective is just the same as with μοχθηρός etc., 'bringing x'.

**to men who work with tools, ἐργαλεῖα κινεῦσι:** the verb κινέω is common of any movement begun and continued; cf. Euripides, *Andromachê* 607 κινεῖν δόρυ, 'to move a spear', i.e. 'to start and carry on a war'.

**74. Ἑρμῆ τε Κερδέων ... Κερδείη Πειθοῖ:** Kerdôn prays to patron deities closest to his heart, Hermes as the god of merchants, and Persuasion as goddess of orators, both supplied with epithets related to Kerdôn's own name, **Profit Kerdonian** and **Kerdonian Persuasion of Profit**; Peithô was also thought to be Hermes' wife; see e.g. Nonnos, *Dionysiaka* 5.474–5, 8.220–1. The ending of the nominative epithet Κερδέων is an ancient Ionic formation; see Schwyzer (1939) 1 488, 521; Hermes is commonly called 'cunning as a fox', and note the nexus between the (feminine) noun for 'fox', κερδώ ('wily one'), and κερδαλέος, 'cunning'. Kerdôn therefore carries on the image of the fox (in another guise) from two lines earlier, and emphasizes his association with Hermes and Peithô; the parallelism and chiasmus in the line add to the mock solemnity of his prayer, with which we may compare the prayer to Hermes and Athene of Odysseus at Sophokles, *Philoktetes* 133–4 Ἑρμῆς δ' ὁ πέμπων δόλιος ἡγήσαιτο νῷν Νίκη τ' Ἀθάνα Πολιάς, ἣ σῴζει μ' ἀεί, 'May Hermes the Escorter, the cunning, lead us, and Victory and Athena Polias, who always keeps me safe.'

**75. because, ὡς:** this gives the reason for his prayer, so we have an ellipse along the lines of '[I call on you] because'.

**76. the cooking-pot, χύτρη:** the basic household-appliance marks the bottom line of Kerdôn's fight for survival, which is probably exaggerated in order to win his clients' pity and consequent yes-response.

**77–96:** Mêtrô impatiently demands that Kerdôn name the price of the first pair of shoes, and Kerdôn insists on a mina, which prompts Mêtrô's sarcasm.

**77. you keep muttering, τονθορύζεις:** at *Mim.* 6.7 Korittô uses this verb to describe her slave's sulky muttering, and at Aristophanes, *Frogs* 747 it is used to refer to a slave who cannot dare to speak openly. This is the point behind ἐλευθέρῃ γλάσσῃ, literally 'with a free tongue'. On the form γλάσσῃ see *Mim.* 3. 84n.

**78. value, τῖμον:** a mainly poetic word, used here for τιμή; since Herodas uses τιμή in the sense of 'price' at *Mim.* 2.82, 89 and elsewhere, Herodas' variation is probably to suit the metre.

**you haven't ... disclosed, ἐξεδίφησας:** for the rare verb διφάω and Herodas' possible debt to Hippônax see above, *Mim.* 6.72–3n.; with the prefix ἐκ it means, as Headlam-Knox (1922) 353 say, 'Rummage out, ferret out from the recesses of your mind'.

**79. this pair ... one mina:** here and at line 91 Kerdôn asks for 1 mina for this pair, at line 90 he asks for 5 staters for the other pair, saying that he wouldn't give them to Euetêris even for 4 Darics, at line 106 he asks a mere 7 Darics for three pairs out of his fondness for Mêtrô, and at line 122 he asks the woman giggling at the door whether she will pay 7 Darics for one pair. All attempts so far at imposing a rational and historical context on to these sums have significant flaws; see Cunningham (1971) 175–6 and Di Gregorio (2004) 294–6. All that can be said for certain is that 4 Darics are worth more than 5 staters. If 1 mina here is, as usual, worth 100 drachmai, Kerdôn's prices are exorbitant, because Aristophanes' *Wealth* 983 puts a very expensive pair at 8 drachmai, and at least in the time of Loukianos 80 (*Dialogues of the Courtesans*) 7.2 the price of a pair of shoes was about 2 drachmai. The reason for the apparently outrageous prices is very probably the characterization of Kerdôn and his salesmanship: after his pleas of poverty, and his difficulty with overpriced supply-materials, he obviously feels the time is right to try to extract the highest payment from his clients; so Di Gregorio (2004) 296. Cunningham (1971) 176 considers that the prices are so high because Kerdôn is talking about dildoes, but even so they would bring back to earth any client even in direst sexual desperation; see further the Discussion, pp. 214–15.

**80. look happy or downcast, ἢ ἄνω 'στ' ἢ κάτω βλέπειν:** literally 'you can look up or down'; looking up meant happiness, downwards sadness; see e.g. Euripides, *Kyklops* 211 βλέπετ' ἄνω καὶ μὴ κάτω, 'look up, not down'. **'στ'**, for ἔξεστι, 'it is possible'.

**81. ὃ δήκοτ' ἐστί ... οὐκ:** = οὐδ' ὁτιοῦν, 'not even anything'. The usual expression is ὅτι δήποτε ἐστί, as at Plato, *Theaitêtos* 160e ὅτι δήποτε τυγχάνει ὄν, 'whatever it happens to be'. δή here makes the relative comprehensive; see Denniston (1954) 221–2.

**82. ὠνευμένης·** for the Ionic contraction in -ευ- here and at line 92 σκέπτευ below see *Mim*. 1.88n.

**83. little establishment, στεγύλλιον:** the diminutive is not found elsewhere, but heightens Mêtrô's patronising sarcasm.

**84. πέπληθε:** poetic perfect with present sense from πλήθω, an intransitive form of πίμπλημι, 'to be full' (LSJ[9] s.v. I).

**τε καί:** Ionic has the idiom πολλά τε καί x, as at e.g. Herodotos 1.31.1; after the adjective 'plentiful' τε καί is, by analogy, perfectly natural.

**85. σ':** = σοι (elision), 'for yourself'.

**85b-8:** Mêtrô is sarcastically saying that there will be a run on shoes for the forthcoming marriage, so Kerdôn might be able to extract his prices after all, but not from her!

**86. Taureôn:** Taureôn was the name of a month in Asia Minor; at Samos and Miletos, for example, Trümpy (1997) 78–93 places Taureôn at the same time of year as the Athenian Mounychiôn, which corresponds more or less with our April/May. (I am grateful to Professor Robert Hannah for this reference.) For the importance of the mention of the month to the location of *Mim*. 6 and *Mim*. 7 see above, p. 166.

**Hekatê:** this is not the goddess but a woman, as line 91 makes clear.

**89. rather, they absolutely will, μᾶλλον δὲ πάντως:** correcting the impression of doubt left by τάχα, 'maybe', in line 88.

**money-sack:** Mêtrô is twitting Kerdôn by saying that he needs a sack for all his money, not a purse.

**90. ὅκως:** for ὅκως etc. with the future indicative in a final cause see Kühner-Gerth (1955) 2 384 n.4.
**pet-weasels:** the domestic weasel had the same reputation for thievery as the modern cat or jackdaw; see e.g. Aristophanes, *Wasps* 363, *Peace* 1151, *Women at the Thesmophoria* 559.
**make off with, διοίσουσι:** διαφέρω is here perhaps a poetic alternative to the more common διαφορέω, 'to plunder'; see LSJ[9] s.v. διαφορέω I.3.
**92. bear that in mind, πρὸς τάδ':** 'in view of this'.
**Please:** see 67n.
**94. the Desires and Loves:** these personifications of desire and love confer desirability and loveliness on those whom they touch; cf. the Muses at Theokritos, *Id.* 10.25 ὧν γάρ χ' ἅψησθε, θεαί, καλὰ πάντα ποιεῖτε, 'For you make beautiful whatever you touch, goddesses.' Mêtrô is sneeringly reminding Kerdôn of his luck in being able to handle such beautiful feet – when he himself is so unlovely.
**95. irritating, κνῦσα:** a *hapax*; LSJ[9] s.v. translates the word as 'scab', but κνύω means 'to scratch', as at Aristophanes, *Women at the Thesmophoria* 481, and hence my 'irritating'.
**a disgrace, κακὴ λώβη:** the address occurs also in Kallimachos' fourth *Iamb*, *Fr.* 194.102 Pfeiffer (1949) 184.
**96:** there is no convincing emendation of the obelized letters, though the drift of the line is 'so you won't get anything from me'. I hesitantly record Beare and Cunningham's 'of Aioleus', or 'of the Aeolian', and (following a suggestion of Chris Collard's in private correspondence) supply δῶρον, 'gift', from the phrase Αἰόλου δῶρον, 'gift of Aiolos', at *Mim.* 8.37; this would give the meaning that Kerdôn will get as his reward for his importuning 'the gift of Aiolos', i.e. a disastrous one, just like the one Odysseus received from the god of the winds. For πρήξεις see LSJ[9] s.v. πράσσω VI 'exact payment from'.
**97–112:** Mêtrô asks the price of another pair for one of her friends, again telling Kerdôn to moderate his voice. Kerdôn alleges that a harp-player, Euetêris, has been pestering him to let her have them for 5 staters, but he wouldn't give them to her for 4 Darics because she bad-mouths his wife. He then offers another 2 pairs, presumably in addition to the pair after which Mêtrô has been asking, for the discounted price of 7 Darics because of his friendship with Mêtrô, on whose tongue and lips he lavishes intimate praise.
**97. to this lady, ταύτῃ:** the deictic implies a gesture towards Mêtrô's friend.
**98. κόσου:** coming last in the sentence and at the beginning of the next line in enjambment, the question about the price probably gains emphasis, as is consistent with Mêtrô's insistence at this point.
**talk, πρήμηνον:** literally 'blow' a sound; cf. *Mim.* 6.8n. πάλιν refers to lines 65b–6, and Kerdôn has evidently raised his voice again at 79–82 and 91–2.
**99. visiting, φοιτᾷ:** this verb is the usual word for regular daily attendance at school (see *Mim.* 3.65 with n.); with 'the whole day' it emphasizes Kerdôn's annoyance at Euetêris' persistence.

**102. even if:** there is an ellipse of a clause like '[and I shall not sell them to her] even if'; Kerdôn is fond of such abbreviation; see above, line 75n.
**103. ὀτεύνεκεν:** the papyrus here has τ, not θ; as a variant of ὁθούνεκα denoting cause, this word is quite common in the Hellenistic authors; see e.g. [Theokritos], *Id.* 25.76.
**104. insults, δέννοις:** δέννος is an Ionic word, found also in Archilochos, *Frr.* 126.2 and 148.2 West (1998) 50, 57; the verb δεννάζω, however, occurs at Sophokles, *Aias* 243 and *Antigone* 759.
**105. come, make sure, φέρ' – εὐλαβοῦ:** text uncertain, but Headlam's articulation of the papyrus is the most convincing. For εὐλαβέομαι governing the infinitive δοῦναι (without μή) as its direct object see Kühner-Gerth (1955) 2 214–5, 398. '[to one] of the three women' refers to Hekatê, Artakênê and Euetêris.
**106. ἦ:** the jussive subjunctive in the second or third person, here after φέρ', which I translate as 'consider this pair and that yours', is secured for the Hellenistic period; see Schwyzer (1950) 2 316.4.
**107. ἔκητι:** here = ἕνεκα; cf. *Mim.* 2.77 with n.
**Don't contradict me:** Mêtrô's resistance may be her attempt to play down the suggestion in Kerdôn's offer of 'mate's rates' that she and Kerdôn are on closer than shopkeeper-client relations: Di Gregorio (2004) 314–15.
**109. λίθινον:** 'stony' people are impervious to love; so at e.g. Theokritos, *Id.* 23. 20 λάϊνε παῖ καὶ ἔρωτος ἀνάξιε, 'stony boy, unworthy of love'. Though Kerdôn disclaims an interest in sex (a disclaimer soon to be put into doubt: lines 111–12), he says that Mêtrô's voice transports him to heaven, a sexual metaphor; see Anakreôn 83 Gentili (1958) 61 ἀναπέτομαι δὴ πρὸς Ὄλυμπον πτερύγεσσι κούφαις / διὰ τὸν ἔρωτα, 'indeed I fly to Olympos on light wings because of love.'
**110. filter, ἠθμόν:** Mêtrô's tongue 'sifts' pleasure and makes it purer and more concentrated. But Kerdôn is warming to the theme of his relationship with Mêtrô, and is very likely referring to tongue-kissing, known in Greek as καταγλωττισμός.
**111. that [man is] not far from the gods:** it seems undeniable that Herodas is recalling the font of this commonplace, Sappho, *Fr.* 31.1–2 Lobel-Page (1968) 32 φαίνεταί μοι κῆνος ἴσος θέοισιν / ἔμμεν' ὤνηρ, ὄττις ..., 'That man seems to me to be the equal of the gods, who ...' But the elevated tone is soon dropped.
**112. lips, χείλεα:** on the surface, these are the lips of the mouth; on a secondary level, χείλη was also used to denote a woman's labia (Aristotle, *History of Animals* 583a16–25), and there can be little doubt that Kerdôn has the meaning in mind as well. At this public assessment of her charms, Mêtrô must be squirming.
**113–121:** Kerdôn invites Mêtrô to try on a pair of shoes, and then invites one of her friends to do the same, in each case proclaiming an expert's eye for a fit.
**113. your precious little foot:** the diminutive is flattering and endearing.
**114. Perfect!, πάξ:** this adverb, derived from the παγ- root of πήγνυμι ('become solid', or 'become set'), carries the sense that something has been satisfactorily completed, so comes close to the Italian 'basta!' It is used frequently in comedy; see e.g. Menandros, *The Arbitrators* 987.

**Don't add or still less take away a thing, μήτε προσθῇς μήτ' ἀπ' οὖν ἕλῃς μηδέν:** the expression 'don't either add to a thing or take away from it' to denote perfection is attested earliest at Theognis 809–10 οὔτε τι γὰρ προσθεὶς οὐδὲν .../ οὔτ' ἀφελών, 'for neither adding anything ... nor taking it away', but is common in all periods. **ἀπ'... ἕλῃς** is another instance of tmesis. **οὖν** with the second alternative gives emphasis to it, hence 'still less'; see Kühner-Gerth (1955) 1 158.
**115. καλά ... καλῇσιν:** the first syllable of καλά is long, that of καλῇσιν is short. The variation within close proximity is common in Hellenistic poetry; see e.g. Theokritos, *Id.* 6.19 τὰ μὴ καλὰ καλὰ πέφανται. Kerdôn is perhaps using a proverbial expression; in any case, his praise of Mêtrô's feet entails equally as much praise of his own craftsmanship.
**116:** The line has echoes of the discussion of art: for ἐρεῖς, 'you'd think', compare *Mim.* 4.28 with n.; for Athene's participation in quality workmanship see *Mim.* 4.57 with n., 6.65, 7.81. Kerdôn is putting his skill on a very high level.
**πέλμα:** the sole of either a foot or a shoe in Ionic and *koinê* Greek.
**117b–8. Oh dear! The ox / that trampled you *did* have a scabby hoof, ἆ, ψωρῇ / ἄρηρεν ὁπλῇ βοῦς ὁ λακτίσας ὑμέας:** this is a difficult expression, but Kerdôn is clearly criticizing the woman's current shoemaker, whom he is comparing with an ox. Literally, the line runs: 'the ox, the one which trampled you, was equipped with a scabby hoof'; i.e., probably, the ox (metaphorically, the shoemaker) scuffed the shoes most unpleasantly when he 'trod' (a derogatory metaphor for manufacturing?) on them. For ἄρηρεν see above, line 20n. ὑμέας is plural because Kerdôn is generalising his remark to refer to the other women as well; so Di Gregorio (2004) 319.
**119:** we must assume a pause in the action before this line while Kerdôn takes off the old shoes and puts on the new ones.
**knife, σμίλην:** a shoemaker's knife in Plato, *Alkibiades* 1.129c. It is unclear why sharpening a knife on the sole of a shoe should perfect its fit; perhaps it might soften the leather to make it more comfortable, but it is more likely that a proverbial expression lies behind Kerdôn's words.
**121. σαφέως:** σαφής can mean 'accurate', especially of seers, prophets and scribes (LSJ[9] s.v. I.2); its use here seems to be an extension of that sense. Kerdôn's phraseology again emphasizes his excellent eye for size and his craftsmanship. For κεῖμαι meaning 'lie' in the sense of 'fit' see LSJ[9] s.v. II.3.
**122–3:** Kerdôn fends off the sarcastic giggles of a woman at the shop's entrance.
**ἡ μέζον ἵππου ... κιχλίζουσα:** Clement of Alexandria, *The Educator* 2.5.46.3 Stählin-Treu (1972) 186.3 shows that κιχλισμός was the word used to describe the immodest laughter of women, and calls it πορνικός, 'whoreish'. To say that a woman is laughing in this way 'louder than a horse' makes the insult even more severe.
**124–9:** The women make moves to leave, and Kerdôn gives a general suggestion that they send their maidservants if they need anything in the line of shoes. He advises Mêtrô in particular that she has a date with him to pick up his products – one good turn deserves another.
**125. little sandals, σαμβαλίσκων:** this diminutive also occurs in Hippônax, *Fr.*

42b.2 Degani (1991) 62, and Degani (1984) 53 considers Hippônax to have been Herodas' source for it. On the form σάμβαλον, 'sandal', see line 19n.

**128. crabshoes, καρκίνια:** At *Mim.* 6.19 Mêtrô wanted to know who stitched Korittô's κόκκινος βαυβῶν, 'scarlet dildo', and the red colour is a feature of 'crabshoes' as well; see line 60n. Here again, it seems likely that Kerdôn is using a perfectly good word for a shoe for the benefit of Mêtrô's friends, and using the word in its other connotation for Mêtrô.

**128–9. Anybody with brains in his head / should rightly also stitch the coat that keeps him warm, τὴν γὰρ οὖν βαίτην / θάλπουσαν εὖ δεῖ 'νδον φρονεῦντα καὶ ῥάπτειν:** a much-disputed passage. On the text printed here, I take ἔνδον with φρονεῦντα ('anyone with brains in his head'), εὖ with δεῖ ('should rightly'), and καί with ῥάπτειν, meaning 'stitch/repair as well'. I take the sentence as a whole as meaning that if a coat keeps you warm, you should keep it in good repair in turn: just as Mêtrô has done Kerdôn a good service in bringing her custom and new customers (and doing him whatever other favours), so he should look after her as well. A βαίτη was a rustic coat made of skins; see Schmidt (1968) 126 n. 40b.

## DISCUSSION

### *1. Mêtrô and Kerdôn*

At the close of *Mimiamb* 6 Mêtrô makes her exit from Korittô's house to search for Artemeis who she hopes will introduce her to Kerdôn. At the beginning of *Mimiamb* 7 Mêtrô has clearly made contact with Kerdôn, and is equally clearly on an intimate footing with him indeed, if only to judge by his greeting 'I have every reason, Metrô, / for loving you' (3–4). What has happened in between?

Any conjecture we make depends in part at least on what we think Kerdôn is selling in *Mimiamb* 7. Headlam[1] suggested that the wares are actually those at the centre of *Mimiamb* 6, and Cunningham has stated the position more forcefully.[2] He bases his argument on what he sees as the ambiguities and sexual connotations of, in particular, lines 62–3 with the proverb about dogs and women eating leather; 108–12, the fixation with Mêtrô's 'lips'; and 127–9, where he says the coat is another word for a dildo. In the note on line 63, however, we have seen that the proverb might simply refer to women's fatal attraction to new, fashionable shoes. Moreover, Kerdôn's reference to Mêtrô's intimate charms need not have anything to do with dildoes (certainly not if Kerdôn were to have his way). And we have seen that the idea behind Kerdôn's reference to stitching a warm coat (128–9) is more likely to be that good customers deserve extra care.[3] Lawall in fact concludes that the shoemaker is selling nothing other than shoes.[4]

There remains the middle position, recently developed by Di Gregorio,[5] which has been adumbrated in the notes.[6] That is to say, Kerdôn is selling shoes to Mêtrô's companions, but hinting at his more intimate products for Mêtrô's benefit. This approach would seem to account for the moments when dildoes appear to be alluded to, as with the possible reference to the practice of using dildoes orally, while on the surface level the reference is to nothing but shoes.

In that case, the developments between the two *Mimiambs* can be constructed quite naturally. Mêtrô has contacted Kerdôn through the agency of Artemeis, and has procured the objects she has had in mind. From Kerdôn's apparently first-hand experience of Mêtrô's 'filter of pleasure' (110), she may have done with Kerdôn what she had told Korittô *she* should have done if it was necessary to secure possession of the second dildo. Mêtrô is now returning favours by introducing new clients to Kerdôn for shoes, his more public profession, and he cements his business relationship with her at the end of the poem by promising to have her crabshoes ready. Kerdôn certainly comes close to revealing his more intimate relations with Mêtrô in the three occasions he seizes to lavish his praise on Mêtrô's person at lines 3–4, 107, and 108–12.

In fact, it is perhaps precisely because Mêtrô is concerned about having her cover blown by Kerdôn that she so ostentatiously tries to preserve outward respectability in front of her friends. She adopts a guise of imperiousness, which at times turns into irony and sarcasm, as when she takes Kerdôn to task over his overpriced shoes (83–96). And this is a significant difference between the Mêtrô of *Mimiambs* 6 and 7: in the earlier poem of the diptych, Korittô and Mêtrô are alone, which gives Mêtrô the freedom to express her sexual obsession, and to act as the subservient person; now that she is in public – this is the main role of the non-speaking parts, though the woman giggling near the door at lines 122–3 indirectly offers a witty commentary on Kerdôn's pricing-system – she has to act the masterful superior, however touchy we must imagine her to be when Kerdôn cuts too close to the bone.[7]

## *2. Kerdôn's salesmanship*

The other major point of contact between *Mimiambs* 6 and 7 is the figure of Kerdôn. In poem 6, Korittô gives a picture of Kerdôn (*Mimiamb* 6.58–67), and some details of the indirect picture are made a separate point in the companion-piece; the baldness mentioned by Korittô at *Mimiamb*. 6.59 is capitalised on by Kerdôn in person when he uses it as an emotional bargaining point with Mêtrô at *Mimiamb* 7.71–2. Poem 7 fills out the indirect image of Kerdôn especially in terms of the protean guises and opportunistic strategies he adopts in his unrelenting pursuit of gain (inherent, of course, in his very name).[8]

Kerdôn's ostentatious rudeness to his servants (4–14, 18) is a calculated touch, designed to impress upon the women the seriousness with which he treats their visit and interest, and hence to make them feel important. He mounts an impressive build-up to his display of the first pair of shoes (17–19), and then praises their workmanship in detail, making special point of Aphrodite's role in the women's lives, and the attractive colour of the shoes (19–28), and drawing attention to the interest in the articles by an alleged competitor, about which he claims with suspicious emphasis that he is being honest (29–35). He is willing to draw a tear-jerking picture of his adverse business conditions, the hours he works and the mouths he has to feed (36–48). He brazenly perverts the proverbial saying about the need for 'action' – which he replaces with 'money' – when he senses that the women are growing restless at his spiel, and brings out another pair for inspection (49–55). His list of shoes has the feeling of being well-rehearsed, and ends, at least for Mêtrô, on a vulgar note (56–63), which makes Mêtrô complain about his mountebank tone, and to ask him to come clean with the price (64–6). Kerdôn's request that the women name their price is kept in careful check by his imprecations to Mêtrô for generosity and to the deities of profit (67–76), and he still manages to stave off the moment when he will have to declare the price. When Mêtrô presses the issue again his price is clearly exorbitant (whatever the actual values of the sums he specifies; 77–82); he is in all likelihood testing out the depth of the women's pockets in good bargaining-mode, though he claims he won't budge (91–2). Mêtrô's request for the price of another pair again meets with an outrageous answer, and with another claim that there is serious competition, from the local harpist, Euetêris, with whom however he insists he won't do business for the heart-warming reason that she has been rude about his wife (99–104). From now on his tone becomes more conciliatory as he offers a cut price for two pairs, all because of his admiration for Mêtrô, whose praises he sings with eyebrow-raising intimacy (105–12). When Mêtrô tries on a pair he talks of the perfection of the fit, and manages cloying praise of his friend which spills back on to his own skill: 'All beautiful things fit beautiful women' (115). He scorns his opposition with a vulgar turn of phrase when he takes off another woman's shoes before putting on her a pair from his factory (117–21). The laugh of the woman near the door, whom he angrily and rudely abuses, demonstrates that he is not making any headway on this occasion, so he unobtrusively and face-savingly signals defeat by asking the women, who are obviously making moves to leave, to apply to him if he can help with their footwear-needs, and reminds Mêtrô she has a pair of crabshoes to collect (122–9).

It can hardly be said that Kerdôn has missed a trick, except in the crucial matter of controlling his greediness. In some ways, he is comparable with Battaros in *Mimiamb* 2, whose powers of bluffing are similarly indefatigable, or, in terms of his knowing when he has met with consumer-resistance, with Gyllis in *Mimiamb* 1. He is therefore one of a very successful type of Herodas' rogues, though he is the only one graced with an appearance in an engaging diptych.

## Notes

1. Headlam-Knox (1922) l–lii.
2. Cunningham (1964) 35, (1971) 174; so also Schmidt (1968) 125, on which see also Cunningham's review in *Classical Review* 21 (1971) 23–4.
3. See the note on lines 128–9.
4. Lawall (1976); so also Simon (1991) 105 n. 84.
5. Di Gregorio (2004) esp. 279–80.
6. Cf. 58, 60, 61, 63, 125nn.
7. Most recently, Kutzko (2006) has made the very attractive suggestion that Mêtrô is the woman to whom Kerdôn has given the second dildo of *Mim.* 6, and that there she has been trying to work out whether her identity was known to Koríttô, so that the two poems of the diptych are put into even closer contact. The interpretation unfortunately suffers from several instances of the text being pressed too hard. For example, Kutzko (2006) 175 finds it 'slightly suspicious' that '...Mêtrô knows that the second dildo was ordered by someone in the first place ... Koritto had only said that Kerdon would not give it to her: she did not specify Kerdon's reasons for doing so, let alone that he was reserving it for another woman'. Surely Mêtrô is simply making a perfectly natural assumption? This detracts in no way, however, from Kutzko's helpful comparison of Herodas' diptych with similar exercises in pairing by the Roman elegists, notably Ovid at *Amores* 2.7 and 8; and many of his insights are valid on the interpretation that I offer here.
8. Simon (1991) 102–11 has an excellent discussion of Herodas' presentation of Kerdôn's sales-pitch. On Kerdôn's name, see above, line 74n.

## 8. ΕΝΥΠΝΙΟΝ

ἄστηθι, δούλη Ψύλλα· μέχρι τέο κείσῃ
ῥέγχουσα; τὴν δὲ χοῖρον αὐονὴ δρύπτει·
ἢ προσμένεις σὺ μέχρις εὖ ἥλιος θάλψῃ
τὸν κῦσον ἐσδύς; κῶς δ', ἄτρυτε, κοὺ κάμνεις
τὰ πλεῦρὰ κνώσσουσ'; αἱ δὲ νύκτες ἐννέωροι.
ἄστηθι, φημί, καὶ ἅψον, εἰ θέλεις, λύχνον,
καί τὴν ἄναυλον χοῖρον ἐς νομὴν πέμψον.
τόνθρυζε καὶ κνῶ, μέχρις εὖ παραστάς σοι
τὸ βρέγμα τῷ σκίπωνι μαλθακὸν θῶμαι.
δειλὴ Μεγαλλί, καὶ σὺ Λάτμιον κνώσσεις;
οὐ τὰ ἔριά σε τρύχουσιν· ἀλλὰ μὴν στέμμα
ἐπ' ἰρὰ διζόμεσθα· βαιὸς οὐχ ἧμιν
ἐν τῇ οἰκίῃ ἔτι μαλλὸς εἰρίων. δειλή,
ἄστηθι. σύ τε μοι τοὖναρ, εἰ θέλεις, Ἀννᾶ,
ἄκουσον· οὐ γὰρ νηπίας φρένας βόσκεις.
τράγον τιν' ἕλκειν [ἐκ] φάραγγος ᾦήθην
μακρῆς, ὁ δ' εὐπώγων τε κεὔκερως [
ἐπεὶ δὲ δὴ [............] τῆς βήσσης
ἡ[οῦς] φα[ούσης...] γὰρ ἐσσῶμαι
]αἰπόλοι [
..........................................................
κἠγὼ οὐκ ἐσύλευν [
καὶ ἄλλης δρυὸς [
οἱ δ' ἀμφὶ κάρτα [
τὸν αἶγ' ἐποίευν [
καὶ πλήσιον [

16 ἐκ Crusius (1914) 71
19 ἡ[οῦς] φα[ούσης Knox (1922) 371
24 ἀμφὶ κάρτα Crusius (1894) 71 αμφικαρτα P

## 8. A DREAM

[*Herodas speaks*] Get up, Psylla, my slave. How long are you going to lie
snoring? The drought is tearing at the sow.
Or are you waiting for the sun to crawl up your fanny
and warm it up? You tireless worker, how come you aren't tiring
your ribs as well with your snoring? The nights are nine years long.
Get up, I say, and light the lamp, if you please,
and send the noisy sow to pasture.
Go on muttering and scratching yourself till I stand over you
and soften up your head with my stick.
Megallis, you wretch, are you in a Latmian sleep too?
It's not your wool-work that's wearing you out:
we're looking hard for yarn for the rites: we don't have
the tiniest fleece in the house any more. You wretch,
get up. You, Annas, please listen to my dream,
for the brain you're feeding isn't stupid.
I thought I was dragging a goat [out] of a long gully,
and the goat [was] well-bearded and horned.
When [............................] of the glen
dawn having appeared [...] for I am beaten
] goatherds [
*(whole line unintelligible)*
and I did not rob [them?
of another oak [
and those round about [
made the goat [
and nearby [

.........................................
σχ[ιστὸν] κροκωτ[ὸν
] λεπτῆς ἄντυγος [
σ[τικτῆ]ς δὲ νεβροῦ χλανιδίῳ κατέζωστο
] κύπασσιν ἀμφὶ τοῖς ὤμοις
κό[ρυμβα δ'] ἀμφὶ κρητὶ κίσσιν' ἔστεπτο
]κοθόρνου[..........]καταζώστρῃ
] φρίκη[
.........................................
]λῶπος[..........] πεποιῆσθαι
]'Οδυσσέως[.........] Αἰόλου δῶρον
]λακτίζειν
]λῷστον
ὥσπερ τελεῦμεν ἐν χοροῖς Διωνύσου.
χοἰ μὲν μετώποις ἐς κόνιν κολυμβῶντες
ἔκοπτον ἀρνευτῆτες ἐκ βίης οὖδας
οἱ δ' ὕπτι' ἐρριπτεῦντο· πάντα δ' ἦν, Ἀννᾶ,
εἰς ἓν γέλως τε κἀνίη ['ναμιχ]θέντα.
κἀγὼ δόκεον δὶς μοῦ[νο]ς ἐκ τόσης λείης
ἐπ' οὖν ἁλέσθαι, κἠλάλαξαν ὤνθρωποι
ὥς μ' εἶδον [.......] τὴν δορὴν πιεζεῦσαν
*(lines 48–57 irretrievably damaged)*
τὰ δεινὰ πνεῦσαι, λὰξ πατε[
'ἔρρ' ἐκ προσώπου μή σε καίπερ ὢν πρέσβυς
οὔλῃ κατ' ἰθὺ τῇ βατηρίῃ κόψω.'
κἠγὼ μεταῦτις· 'ὦ παρεόντες[
θανεῦμ' ὑπὲρ γῆς, εἰ ὁ γέρων [
μαρτύρομαι δὲ τὸν νεην[ίην'
ὁ δ' εἶπεν ἄμφω τὸν δορέα [
καὶ τοῦτ' ἰδὼν ἔληξα. τὸ ἔνδυτον
]δ[ὸς] ὧδε. τὤναρ ὧδ' [

27 σχ[ιστὸν] κροκωτ[ὸν Vogliano (1906) 28
30 σ[τικτῆ]ς Knox (1926)[1] 245 n. 6
32 κό[ρυμβα δ'] Knox (1922) 372
44 ['ναμιχ]θέντα Knox (1922) 372
66 δ[ὸς] Knox (1922) 372

*(whole line unintelligible)*
[he wore a] saffron-coloured [dress
.. ] of a slight [body-]curve [
he was girt with a cloak of dappled fawn-skin
] with a tunic around his shoulders
and his head was crowned with clusters of ivy fruit
] of a boot [.....................................] with lace.
] shivering (*or* bristling) [...
*(whole line unintelligible)*
] skin [...........................] to have been made
] of Odysseus [..................] the gift of Aiolos
to trample on
] best
as we perform in the choruses of Dionysos.
Some, plunging into the dust on their foreheads,
struck the ground violently – divers, they were –,
while others were thrown on to their backs. Annas, the whole scene
was a [mix] of laughter and pain.
It seemed that I alone among such a crowd twice
made the leap on to the skin-bag, and the men shouted
when they saw the skin buoying me up.
*(10 lines unintelligible)*
to blow terribly, trampling with feet [
'Get out of my sight in case, though I'm an old man, I strike you
down flat with the full length of my stick.'
And I replied, 'Onlookers, [
I shall die on behalf of the land, if the old man [
I call the young man to witness....'
He said the flayer [...] both <of us?> [
On seeing this I stopped <dreaming>. Give the cloak
] here. What went on in the dream in this way [

] αἶγα τῆς φάραγγος ἐξεῖλκον
] καλοῦ δῶρον ἐκ Διωνύσου
]αἰπόλοι μιν ἐκ βίης ἐδαιτρεῦντο
τὰ ἔνθεα τελεῦντες καὶ κρεῶν ἐδαίνυντο,
τὰ μέλεα πολλοὶ κάρτα, τοὺς ἐμοὺς μόχθους,
τιλεῦσιν ἐν Μούσῃσιν. [
τὸ μὴν ἄεθλον ὡς δόκευν ἔχειν μοῦ[νο]ς
πολλῶν τὸν ἄπνουν κώρυκον πατησάντων,
κὴ τῷ γέροντι ξύν' ἔπρηξ' ὀρινθέντι
..] κλέος, ναὶ Μοῦσαν, ἤ μ' ἔπεα [
μέγ' ἐξ ἰάμβων, ἤ με δευτέρῃ [
ἐ]μ[οῖ]ς μεθ' Ἱππώνακτα τὸν παλαι[
τὰ κύλλ' ἀείδειν Ξουθίδῃς † επιουσι †[

73 μοῦ[νο]ς Herzog (1924) 391
78 ἐ]μ[οῖ]ς Herzog (1924) 392, 420

] I dragged the goat from the gully
] a gift from handsome Dionysos.
] the goatherds violently carved up the goat
performing the rites, and feasted on the meat,
very many will pluck my corpus, my labours,
among the Muses. [
Yet as I seemed to be the only one to have the prize
among the many men who had trodden on the air-tight skin-bag,
even if I shared with the angry old man the same success
] fame, yes, by the Muse, who [...] me poems,
great fame from iambs, or as a second [taught me]
after Hippônax of old [
to sing limping songs to my own [future] Xouthid [Ionians].

## COMMENTARY

SYNOPSIS The state of the papyrus, despite heroic successes in reconstructing the fragments, makes any synopsis of this poem hazardous. The general outlines, however, are discernible. Herodas wakes up a female slave, Psylla, early one winter morning, and orders her to put the sow out for watering and to light the lantern (1–9). Another slave, Megallis, is also ordered to get up and attend to her wool-work: wool is necessary for the performance of rites (10–14a). He orders a third slave, Annas, who might be either male or female, to listen to a dream he has had (14b–15). Herodas tells how he thought he was leading a handsome goat out of a gully at dawn (16–19), but was overcome, possibly by goatherds (20). He seems to have protested that he himself had done nothing wrong (22–5). A male figure appeared, wearing clothing and attributes which show that he was Dionysos (26–34). Meantime, the goatherds had apparently skinned the goat, and turned the skin into an inflated ball, like Aiolos' bag of winds; they were trying to stand upright on it in a game associated with Dionysos, *askôliasmos* (36–44). Herodas thought that he was the only competitor to have stood successfully on the skin twice (45–7). Nothing can be made of lines 48–57. The text resumes with an old man berating Herodas (the reasons for which are lost in the gap), while Herodas called the young man, presumably the Dionysos who appeared earlier, to witness; and Dionysos seems to have resolved the dispute (58–65). Asking Annas for a cloak to keep him warm, Herodas proceeds to interpret the dream: the goat he was dragging along was a gift from Dionysos, and, just as the goatherds ritually dismembered it, so will Herodas' critics treat his poetry in the future; he alone, however, won the contest, and, although he fared the same as the angry old man (apparently despite their earlier disagreement, whatever it may have been), he will win great fame for his choliambic poetry, after Hippônax, as he sings it to the Ionians (65–79).

Structurally, therefore, the poem is tripartite, two sections framing the narration of the dream. It is typical of an Alexandrian poet's procedure that the framing sections are of precisely equal length, fifteen lines.

In term of its subject-matter, the autobiographical eighth *Mimiamb* comes as a surprise after the first seven poems of the collection, and there is no hint in the fragments after it of any personal appearance by the poet. However, it was a tradition among the Greek poets from Hesiod on to present themselves when they defended their poetry or stated its mission, and the procedure is very common in Hellenistic poetry; see below, *Sources*, and the Discussion, with further details of the complex cast-list.

TEXT When the papyrus was first published, the only continuous lines were 1 to 3. The rest of the poem, together with *Mimiamb* 9, was subsequently reconstructed from fragments. For details of this fascinating detective-work see Cunningham (1971) 195.

SETTING There is no direct evidence for the geographical location of this poem. The dramatic setting is a farmhouse owned by the poet, who has at least three slaves (all mute roles), a sow and some pasture land; 'stage-props' include a lantern (6), possibly woolworking implements (11–13) and a cloak (65).

DATE There is no evidence for absolute dating, though it seems reasonable to suppose that the poem, as a reaction to the reception of Herodas' work, must have been written after at least some of his poems had been published. The poem is set in winter: the nights are 'nine years long' (5, where see n.). It is before dawn: Herodas demands that Psylla light a lantern (6). The narrated dream will also have a winter-setting, because Dionysiac rites like the Rural Dionysia (with which, among other festivals, the *askôliasmos*-contests were associated: see Pickard-Cambridge [1968] 45) took place in (roughly) our December.

SOURCES Dreams in classical literature normally involve interpretation by another person, or by a figure in the dream. Penelopê's dream of the geese at *Odyssey* 19.535–58 needs to be interpreted to her by Odysseus in disguise. While not itself a dream, Hesiod's meeting with the Muses at *Theogony*, 22–34 is the ancestor of many dreams experienced by poets as a kind of poetic investiture; the Muses give their instructions directly. In Kallimachos' *Dream*, *Fr.* 2 Pfeiffer (1949) 9–11 (with the Florentine scholia), the Muses likewise address the poet. Ennius' famous dream from the first book of the *Annales*, *Frr.* ii–x Skutsch (1985) 70–1, involves Homer's telling Ennius that after his own death his soul transmigrated into a peacock and thence into Ennius. Herodas is unique in that he makes his persona interpret his own dream. And while Kallimachos makes Hippônax return from the grave in his first *Iamb*, *Fr.* 191 Pfeiffer (1949) 161–71, and impart his opinions directly, in Herodas the same poet, if the interpretation of lines 59–60 offered below is correct, is merely one of the dream's characters, and apparently becomes, despite initial differences, the model for Herodas' *Mimiambs*.

It is possible that *The Dream* is a reaction to Theokritos' seventh *Idyll*, *The Thalysia*, which may in that case be considered a source. Both poems involve the poet's arrival at a festival, and a poetic competition, even if in Herodas' case a competition symbolizing a poetic contest; Lykidas' gift to Simichidas is ironically replaced by the old man in Herodas threatening Herodas with his stick. The sharpening of the irony in Herodas' poem supports the thesis that Herodas has Theokritos in mind. See further the Discussion, below, pp. 233–5.

The theme of the *askôliasmos* is represented in figurative art. There is, for example, the mosaic from Ostia now in Berlin in which Dionysos and Ariadne are judges at the game in which satyrs are competing; see Crusius-Herzog (1926) Plate XVI, Webster (1964) 97 n.1 and 174.

PURPOSE Herodas defends his poetry against his critics, states the tradition in which he works and foretells his own fame. Despite various attempts at identifying the 'goatherds' among the contemporaries of Herodas (like Theokritos or Kallimachos), no consensus has been reached. It is just as possible that Herodas has nobody specifically in mind, however generally he might be engaging with Theokritos' *Thalysia*.

**1–15:** the poet wakens his household before dawn and orders a slave to listen to a dream he has just had.
**1. ἄστηθι:** in this intransitive aorist imperative of ἀνίστημι (repeated at lines 6 and 14), equivalent to the Attic ἀνάστηθι, the second α has been lost by apocope, and the ν, brought into contiguity with the σ, is also lost through assimilation; the process is attested in different dialects, and is not specific to Ionic. Esposito (2001) 141–2 considers that the command, '**Get up**', is based on similar Homeric commands, like ὄρσεο, Πηλεΐδη …, 'Rise up, son of Peleus…' at *Il.* 18.170, and that it is placed in humorous juxtaposition with such a lowly address as 'Psylla, my slave'.
**Ψύλλα:** either an ethnic name, the Psylloi being an African tribe (Herodotos 4.173, though actually he reports how they became extinct), or a nickname meaning 'Flea'.
**τέο:** Ionic for τοῦ/τίνος.
**2. ῥέγχουσα:** Ionic for Attic ῥέγκω, as at Aristophanes, *Clouds* 5 οἱ δὲ οἰκέται ῥέγκουσιν, 'the servants are snoring'. Herodas may have had *Clouds* 1–5 in mind: note especially the motifs of the length of the night and of an order to a slave to light the lantern, common to both passages.
**αὐονή:** Archilochos, *Fr.* 230 West (1998) 86 uses this word of a drought sent by Zeus, and Aischylos, *Eumenides* 333, 345 uses it of the 'withering' that the Eumenides

bring to mortals; the word is incongruously grand in the present context.
**is tearing at, δρύπτει:** another elevated expression, drawn from the ritual laceration of a woman's cheeks in lamentation; so Euripides, *Elektra* 150. Again, we have humorous incongruity.
**3. μέχρις εὖ ... θάλψῃ:** the expected ἄν with the subjunctive is also missing from *Mim.* 2.43.
**4. fanny, κῦσον:** a colloquial vulgarism, here used of a woman's sex-organ, while at *Mim.* 2.44 Herodas uses it of the male anus; for the word's dual function see Henderson (1955) 131.
**You tireless worker, ἄτρυτε:** ironically used of an alleged lazybones. The passage seems otherwise to be a reminiscence of Kallimachos, *Iamb* 4, *Fr.* 194.81–2 Pfeiffer (1949) 182 φεῦ τῶν ἀτρύτων, οἷα κωτιλίζουσι· / λαιδρὴ κορώνη, κῶς τὸ χεῖλος οὐκ ἀλγεῖς;, 'Oh, these tireless creatures, how they chatter on! Shameless crow, how come your lip is not hurting?'
**5. with your snoring, κνώσσουσ':** this verb normally means simply 'to sleep soundly', as at line 10; but it must mean 'snore' here, if sense is to be made of a reference to damaging ribs while sleeping.
**nine years long:** this means 'very long', so Psylla should have had enough time for sleep. The adjective appears in Homer with the meaning 'nine years old' of an ointment at *Il.* 18.351, and of an ox at *Od.* 10.19.
**6. if you please, εἰ θέλεις:** for this colloquial expression, possibly a recall of Hippônax, see *Mim.* 7.67n.
**7. noisy, ἄναυλον:** perhaps best explained as a compound of ἄνευ + αὐλός, 'flute', i.e., 'un-melodic', hence 'noisy'; compare Sophokles, *Fr.* 699 Radt (1977) 483 μέλη βοῶν ἄναυλα καὶ ῥακτήρια, 'the unmelodic and discordant songs of cattle', where 'discordant' is decisive for the first adjective's meaning. On this analysis the sow will be squealing noisily to be let out.
**8. τόνθρυζε:** cf. τονθυρίζω at *Mim.* 7.77, of which this is perhaps the original form.
**κνῶ:** present middle imperative of κνάομαι; cf. Theokritos, *Id.* 7.110 κνάσαιο.
**9. head, τὸ βρέγμα:** the forehead, strictly speaking; see *Mim.* 4.51.
**with my stick, τῷ σκίπωνι:** a σκίπων, *skipôn*, is often used of an old man's stick, as at Kallimachos, *Iamb* 1, *Fr.* 191.69 Pfeiffer (1949) 169. The poet-figure of the narrator's dream must, however, be an athletic type, and probably therefore young. Perhaps the older narrator-Herodas has dreamt of a crucial juncture in his youth; compare Kallimachos, *Fr.* 1.6, 21–2, 33–8 Pfeiffer (1949) 2–8, who recalls when Apollo initiated him as a young man. These will be references to Herodas' dramatic age, and need have nothing to do with his actual age.
**10. Latmian:** with a suppressed ὕπνον, this is an internal accusative. The phrase was proverbial; see e.g. Zenobios 3.76 Leutsch-Schneidewin (1839) 1 75, 6–11. Mount Latmos in Karia was where Endymiôn, who slept everlastingly, either spent time or was buried. The adjective is therefore indirect and learned.

**11. τρύχουσιν:** even in Attic prose a neuter plural may govern a plural verb, for example if there is emphasis on the plurality of the subject, but the use with the plural verb becomes increasingly common from the Hellenistic period on: Schwyzer (1950) 2 607–8, citing e.g. Thoukydides 5.75.2.

**12. ἐπ' ἰρά:** after a dream a sacrifice was commonly offered to avert any threatened misfortune, and wool was presumably used in such rituals to wreathe the altar with; see Headlam-Knox (1922) 380–2. The papyrus has π, not φ', but ἱερός has an Ionic form in ἰρός; see García-Ramón (1992) 194.

**14. Ἀννᾶ:** the accent is given in the papyrus, which probably entails a man's name, Ἀννᾶς, though the female Ἀννᾶ cannot be ruled out absolutely; see Schmidt (1968) 47 n. 1. Simon (1991) 70 n. 139 argues that a female servant would fit in better with the other slavewomen, Psylla and Megallis.

**15. βόσκεις:** for 'nourishing' a mind compare Pindar, *Pythian* 5.109–10 κρέσσονα μὲν ἁλικίας νόον φέρβεται, 'He nourishes a mind beyond his age.'

**16–65:** the poet narrates the dream.

**(a) 16–35:** the poet drags a goat out of the glen; he is apparently set upon by goatherds, who, to judge from the interpretational τιλεῦσιν of the dream at line 72, kill the goat; Dionysos appears on the scene.

**16. a goat [out] of a long gully:** seeing goats and gullies in a dream portended all manner of bad things in store according to the ancient students of dreams; see Artemidôros 2.12 and 2.28 Pack (1963) 119, 20–1 and 150, 10–12. The goat symbolizes Herodas' poetry (see line 71), and is probably the gift of Dionysos mentioned at line 68. That ἐκ should be the supplemented preposition before φάραγγος seems secured by ἐξεῖλκον at line 67.

**17. εὔκερως:** for the accent in compound adjectives ending in -ως see Goodwin (1965) 27, para. 114 and Kühner-Gerth-Blass (1890) 1.1 321; cf. also e.g. ὑψίκερως, 'high-horned', of a deer at *Od.* 10.158.

**18. of the glen:** apparently the same defile as at line 16.

**19. ἑσσῶμαι:** this present contracted form of the verb, accepted by most editors, is a mixture of the Ionic ἑσσόομαι and the Attic ἡσσάομαι; for such mixtures in Herodas compare λείης at line 45. Cunningham (1971) 198, following LSJ[9] s.v. ἡσσάομαι and Schmidt (1968) 75, Ionicizes and prints ἕσσωμαι, the perfect passive of ἑσσόομαι.

**20. goatherds:** the identity of these figures will be examined in the Discussion, pp. 233–4.

**22. and I did not rob [them:** Herodas seems to be denying that he has given the goatherds any reason for their treatment of him, most likely by denying that he has stolen the goat. For the Ionic contraction in -ευ- in ἔσύλευν here and below at lines 25 (ἐποίευν) and 73 (δόκευν) see *Mim.* 1.88n.

**23. of another oak:** it is possible that the goat has chewed the bark of at least two oaks. Oaks were associated with Dionysos' rites: Headlam-Knox (1922) 383 quote Nonnos, *Dionysiaka* 46.145. Perhaps this is a motive for the goatherds' slaughter and flaying of the goat.

**25. made the goat:** lines 69–70 supply the general sense of the second half of this line, 'carved up the goat'.
**28. saffron-coloured [dress], σχ[ιστὸν] κροκωτ[όν:** Hesychios σ 3034 Schmidt (1862) 4 120 and Pollux 7.54 Bethe (1931) 2 67, 7–9 tell us that a σχιστός (literally 'divided', 'split') was a kind of woman's *chitôn* which was fastened with a brooch on the chest; Pollux 4.116 Bethe (1900) 1 235, 12–3 says that a κροκωτός was a *himation* worn by Dionysos. It seems that Dionysos is feminised.
**29. λεπτῆς ἄντυγος:** 'a slight curve', presumably of the body; Headlam-Knox (1922) 385–6 collect attestations from later Greek writers.
**30–1:** the syntax of these lines is hard to reconstitute. κατέζωστο goes with the instrumental dative χλανιδίῳ, but a verb governing κύπασσιν seems to have been lost in the lacuna.
**30. νεβροῦ:** this is a clear reference to the νεβρίς, the cloak which was worn by Dionysos and Bakchai; see Dodds (1960) on *Bakchai* 111.
**31. tunic, κύπασσιν:** this rare word appears in the once-off diminutive form κυπασσίσκος in Hippônax, *Fr.* 42b.1 Degani (1991) 61, and may be another example of Herodas' conscious alignment with the older iambographer. It also possibly occurs in Iôn of Chios' *Omphalê*, *Fr.* 59 Snell (1986) 113, where, interestingly, the wearer's sex is a problem: is it Herakles, made by Omphalê to dress as a woman? See Krumeich-Pechstein-Seidensticker (1999) 480–90. The idea of the garment's use in cross-dressing would suit Herodas' evocation of Dionysos, the god being associated with effeminacy; see e.g. Euripides, *Bakchai* 453–9.
**32. ἔστεπτο:** στέφω, probably middle perfect.
**33. boot:** the characteristic footwear of Dionysos, as is amply attested on vases depicting him.
**καταζώστρῃ:** not found elsewhere; it comes from ζώννυμι, 'gird', and we have ζώστρα of head-bands at Theokritos, *Id.* 2.122; hence 'lace', or possibly 'strap'.
**34. φρίκη:** this could refer to the cold of dawn or to the shivering or to the hair standing on end caused when one is confronted by a god (as at e.g. Xenophon, *Education of Kyros* 4.2.15). The identity of the figure described in these lines is certainly Dionysos, typical attributes of whom are the colour of saffron, the *nebris*, the *kothornos*, and the grapes and ivy around the head.
**36–65a:** the game of *askôliasmos* in which Herodas emerges as the victor; an old man demurs; Herodas settles the matter by calling Dionysos to witness.
In the *askôliasmos*-contest competitors tried to stand in balance on a wineskin which was filled with air; see e.g. Pollux 9.121 Bethe (1931) 2 180, 22–7, Suetonius, *On Games* 12 Taillardat (1967) 71, and, in general Latte (1957) 700–7. It was associated in popular thought with the Rural Dionysia at Athens, but Pickard-Cambridge (1968) 45 emphasizes that that was unlikely to have been the only venue. Fountoulakis (2002) 316–7 points to the widespread popularity of the cult of Dionysos in the Hellenistic period, and to the fact that it had a significant following on Kos, where Herodas might have seen the competition performed.

**36. λῶπος:** this word can mean 'cloak' (Photios λ 505 Theodoridis (1998) 2 528 λῶπος· ἱμάτιον), and is taken to mean that by Cunningham (2002) 273, but it also means 'skin' (*Etymologicum Genuinum* AB s.v. Colonna [1967] 30), which certainly fits the present context better, given the reference to Aiolos' bag of the winds in the next line. It was used by Hippônax, *Fr.* 4a Degani (1991) 27, though it is uncertain in what sense; it is consequently uncertain whether Herodas has taken it from his predecessor.

**37. the gift of Aiolos:** the wineskin is compared with the bag in which Aiolos tied the winds as a gift to Odysseus at *Od.* 10.19–20, 36; similarly, too, Herodas' goat is a gift to him from Dionysos (line 68).

**40. in the choruses of Dionysos:** festivals in honour of Dionysos were accompanied by dancing; see e.g. Euripides, *Bakchai* 220. Though the papyrus gives us Διονύσου, the long ω is required by the metre; this less usual spelling is found also in e.g. Hesiod, *Theogony* 941, 947.

**42. divers, ἀρνευτῆτες:** identification instead of comparison; see *Mim.* 6.14n. In Homer, the word is found in comparison, as at *Il.*12.385. The meaning is more likely to be 'divers' than the alternative, 'acrobats'. The picture is of men who jump on to the inflated skin with their feet (lines 38 and 46), try to balance on it, and, when they lose their balance, fall on the ground on their heads as if diving.

**43. ὕπτι':** this is an elided form of the adverb ὕπτια rather than ὕπτιοι; the final vowel -α is elided frequently in Herodas, but -οι is elided only at *Mim.* 5.9.

**44. γέλως τε κἀνίη:** the 'laughter' and 'pain' have been thought to possess a programmatic reference to the mixing of the genres, comic and serious, of the *Mimiambs*; see the Discussion, pp. 234–5.

**45. crowd, λείης:** apart from 'booty', this word comes to mean 'flock' or 'herd' in Herodas' period (see LSJ[9] s.v. 4); it seems here to be applied to human beings. In form the word is neither Attic (λεία) nor Ionic (ληΐη), which illustrates the artificiality of Herodas' dialect; cf. above, line 19n.

**46. ἐπ' οὖν ἀλέσθαι:** earlier authors like Herodotos use οὖν in tmesis when habitual action is involved; see Denniston (1954) 429.

**shouted, ἠλάλαξαν:** if ἀλαλάζω refers here to the Bacchic cry (as at Euripides, *Bakchai* 593, 1133), it would mean that Herodas' enemies (if they are 'the men' of line 46) are to be thought of as now applauding him or giving him encouragement, which seems strange. It is possible that we are to imagine that an audience was present. However, ἀλαλαγμός can carry a hostile meaning, as the word for a war-cry, which would seem to suit the context; see Herodotos 8.37.3.

**47. buoying up, πιεζεῦσαν:** literally 'squeezing'; with this reading, which is offered by the papyrus, 'The pressure is that of the half-inflated skin round the foot': Headlam-Knox (1922) 392; in this way, the skin supports the person standing on it. The verb is πιεζέω, a secondary form of πιέζω. As we saw above, p. 8, the combination of ε with ου gives ευ in Ionic, whence the spelling πιεζεῦσαν.

**58. τὰ δεινὰ πνεῦσαι:** given the preceding loss of text, we cannot be sure whether this expression means simply 'to blow terribly', or whether there is a connotation of boasting or threatening. The subject and the function of the definite article are also unknowable. **πατε[:** the word for trampling recurs at line 74, πατησάντων, so perhaps the reference here is, as there, to treading on the inflated skin.

**59. old man:** the majority of critics agree that Hippônax of Ephesos is the old man: the poet was frequently characterized as old in the Hellenistic period, as e.g. by Alkaios of Messene, *Epigram* 13 GP; he was regarded as bad-tempered (*Testimonia* 8, 9b, 12a, 15–17a, 25, 57 Degani [1991] 3–8, 12, 20); Herodas' old man is made to use Hipponaktean diction; see further Esposito (2001) 141–50, who points to the way in which the historical Hippônax uses the figure of Odysseus in the presentation of his *persona*, and to the reminiscences in the present passage of the encounter between Odysseus and Iros in *Od.* 18.20–3.

**60. strike you ... with ... my stick, τῇ βατηρίῃ κόψω:** this half-line is borrowed directly from Hippônax, *Fr.* 8 Degani (1991) 32 τῇ βακτηρίῃ κόψαι, the spelling βατηρίῃ without the κ probably being a learned rationalisation of the short α in Hippônax' βακτηρίῃ. **οὔλῃ** is the Ionic form of the Attic ὅλος, 'whole', 'entire', though the Attic form is found at *Mim.* 3.18, 5.12, 6.7.

**62. I shall die on behalf of the land:** without the context the meaning of the expression is unclear; Di Gregorio (2004) 376 suggests alternatively that Herodas replies to the old man that he'd prefer to die (ὑπὲρ γῆς meaning 'above the ground') than to let the old man administer his beating.

**63. I call to witness:** Fountoulakis (2000) points to the ancient Greek and Roman custom of calling bystanders to witness if one is being harmed, both for immediate help and in the hope of witnesses if the case goes to law; see e.g. Menandros, *The Woman of Samos* 474–5.

**the young man:** i.e. Dionysos, described at lines 28–33.

**64. the flayer, τὸν δορέα:** nouns ending in –εύς denote agents, in which case the flayer will be the subject of some lost infinitive ('tie up'?) with the object 'both'; however, it is just possible that δορέα is a secondary formation from δορά, in which case the meaning might be that Dionysos orders that 'both' (Hippônax and Herodas?) share the skin (cf. δορήν at line 47).

**65b–74:** Herodas interprets the dream, which presages a hostile reception of his choliambic poetry, though he will ultimately win great fame.

**65. the cloak:** Herodas asks Annas for his cloak because he is cold (it is winter, as we have seen above, p. 225) and because he is experiencing the fear usually sensed by the Greeks and Romans after a dream; see e.g. Ovid, *Amores* 3.5.45–6 *gelido mihi sanguis ab ore / fugit*, 'The blood rushed from my frozen face.'

**66. τὦναρ:** this is the Ionic form in crasis of τὰ ὄναρ (τὸ ὄναρ would result in τοὖναρ; see above, p. 8); if the scribe has not made a simple error, the meaning must be literally 'the matters concerning the dream' (Cunningham [1971] 201).

**68. gift:** most likely the goat in the previous line: the goat and the thing it symbolizes in the dream, Herodas' poetry, are a gift from Dionysos.

**69. carved up, ἐδαιτρεῦντο:** if the reading is correct, the word is a *hapax*.
**70.** the genitive **κρεῶν** is partitive.
**71. my corpus, τὰ μέλεα:** the word can mean both 'limbs' and 'sung lyric poetry', and the precise ambiguity is untranslatable in English; my translation plays on the Latin word for 'body' and the English application to a collection or body of writings; it is possibly also found at Aristophanes, *Frogs* 862, where Euripides speaks of the μέλη and the νεῦρα, 'sinews' / 'what affects us', of tragedy. The ambiguity does not seem totally successful, for Herodas has had to use a term appropriate to lyric poetry when he is talking about his *oeuvre* in general.
**τοὺς ἐμοὺς μόχθους:** the idea of poetry as hard work is common among Herodas' contemporaries; see e.g. Kallimachos, *Epigram* 56 GP on Aratos' going without sleep (ἀγρυπνίη), and Theokritos, *Id.* 7.51, where Simichidas advertises the ditty he is going to sing as something that he 'produced with toil' (ἐξεπόνασα).
**72. among the Muses:** this could be an allusion to the Museum at Alexandria, an idea initiated by Crusius (1905) 75–6, in which case Herodas' enemies are the poets associated with the Museum, like Kallimachos and Theokritos; alternatively, it could mean 'in poetry, in their poems' (Hunter [1993] 35–6), in which case the enemies are less closely defined. The reference to large numbers of critics in the preceding line interestingly recalls Timôn of Phlious' comment, 'In the populous land of Egypt many are they who get fed, cloistered bookworms, endlessly arguing in the bird-cage of the Muses', *Fr.* 786 *SH*; it perhaps lends slight support to Crusius' interpretation.
**73. Yet, μήν:** an adversative particle; see Denniston (1954) 334.
**δόκευν:** the augment is omitted from the imperfect verb (as also at line 45), probably in imitation of the manner of messenger-speeches; see Di Gregorio (1967) 12, 14.
**74. air-tight, ἄπνουν:** the best explanation for this much debated adjective is that of Crane (1986) 89–90, who points out that, since πνοή means 'a breath', Herodas' adjective does not mean 'without air' or 'empty', but that the air inside does not 'breathe out'.
**75. I shared … the same success, ξύν' ἔπρηξ':** ξυνά = κοινά with πράσσω can be either transitive, 'I did things in common with', 'had the same result as', or intransitive, 'I fared the same as'. If the old man is Hippônax, Herodas will be saying that he shared the honours with the older poet as his worthy successor; he is claiming not superiority, but equality, as Dionysos seems to have ruled at line 64. Why then did Hippônax object to Herodas' victory at lines 59–60? See the Discussion, below, pp. 233–4.
**κἠ:** καὶ εἰ
**ὀρινθέντι:** this verb more usually denotes fear rather than anger, but Cunningham (1971) 203 adduces *Od.* 17.216 ὄρινε δὲ κῆρ Ὀδυσῆος, '[Melantheus] angered the heart of Odysseus.'
**76. poems, ἔπεα:** normally of epic, but here of iambic poetry, as in the third-century comic prologue in Page (1941) 324 (No. 72 [2]) τῶν ἐπῶν γὰρ ὧν μέλλομεν ἐρεῖν, 'Each iamb that we shall say...'.

**79. limping songs, τὰ κύλλα:** of choliambic poetry, with the same sense as Kallimachos, *Fr*. 203.14 Pfeiffer (1949) 206 τὰ χωλά. With 'or', ἤ, at line 77, there is apparently an opposition between purely iambic verse and choliambs; for the metrical differences see above, p. 6. See further the Discussion, below, p. 234.
**Xouthid:** Hesychios ξ 89 Latte (1966) 2 727 explains 'Xouthidai', 'sons of Xouthos', as meaning the Ionians, since Iôn was the son of Xouthos, and his descendants colonised Asia Minor from Athens. This is the general view in antiquity, attested e.g. in Herodotos 7.94, 8.44, though in his *Iôn* Euripides deliberately makes Apollo the real father, and Xouthos the unwitting stepfather; see especially lines 1571–605.
**[future], επιουσι:** the first iota is long, and the verb has been thought to be from ἔπειμι, 'come after', but the only places in which the iota is long in ἔπειμι are the singular of the indicative and the subjunctive. It is therefore likely that we are dealing with a corruption; so Cunningham (1971) 203–4. If the participle is indeed from ἔπειμι, its meaning will be 'to come in the future'.

## DISCUSSION

### Mimiamb *8 as a statement of Herodas' literary programme*

The self-conscious Hellenistic poets were, as no Greek poets before them, concerned to set their own seal, or *sphragis*, on their poetry, and to defend it against its detractors. Most famous perhaps, are Kallimachos' *Against the Telchines*, *Fr.*1 Pfeiffer (1949) 1–8; *The Dream*, *Fr.* 2 Pfeiffer (1949) 9–10; the thirteenth *Iamb*, *Fr.* 203 Pfeiffer (1949) 205–9; and the coda to the *Hymn to Apollo*, *Hymn* 2.105–13; Theokritos has the exchange on contemporary poetic taste between Simichidas and Lykidas in *Idyll* 7. 35–48. With his eighth *Mimiamb*, Herodas proves to be no exception to Hellenistic practice.

Key in the understanding of Herodas' dream and its importance for his poetry are the dream's personnel. It is generally agreed that the narrator is Herodas: his statement of his calling as a iambographer at the close of the poem, in however fragmentary a form, assures us of this. The Young Man must be Dionysos.[1] The Old Man is nowadays almost unanimously[2] regarded as Hippônax, Herodas' sixth-century model and guarantor.[3] The Goat must stand for Herodas' poetry, if only because Herodas the narrator describes it as the 'gift of Dionysos'.[4] Precisely whom the Goatherds represent is less easily defined, and Herodas may have purposely left their identity vague. The general impression is that they suggest the people of Theokritos' pastoral mimes, and, given Herodas' apparent debt to *Idylls* 2, 14 and 15,[5] he may not have wanted to make his opposition to Theokritos too sharply defined.

Certainly, there are several points of contact between *Mimiamb* 8 and *Idyll* 7: both poems have a festival as their setting; both poems involve a rustic contest, ultimately over poetry; Lykidas' gift of the shepherd's staff has a counterpart in both the stick with which Hippônax threatens Herodas and the prize of the goatskin awarded to Herodas by Dionysos; and both poems have elements of the motif of a poetic initiation.[6]

If this casting is correct, why in particular is Hippônax as the old man so vehemently opposed to Herodas, who professes to be Hippônax' successor (78)? It is impossible to hope for a totally comprehensive and convincing answer to this vital question, because we lack the lines which must have described the meeting of Herodas and the old man (48–57) and because the crucial lines 71–9 are so fragmentary and difficult to construe. However, Ralph Rosen has offered an interpretation which both accounts for what is known and explains Hippônax' resistance on the admittedly scant evidence available.[7] He argues that the key is the poem's setting, a festival to Dionysos, the god of drama, and this should alert us to the dramatic element in Herodas' *Mimiambs*. When Herodas refers to iambic poetry at line 77, it is natural within the setting that he is referring to the 'straight' iambs of drama, here specifically those of comedy. When he refers in the last line to 'limping songs', he is referring to the choliambs of Hippônax and his own poetry.[8] Dionysos at line 64 may have ruled that 'both' Hippônax and Herodas should have the prize, and at line 75 Herodas explicitly says that he shared with Hippônax the success. This implies that the god of dramatic poetry authorizes the use of choliambic poetry in a dramatic mode. In that case, Hippônax' objection, overruled by Dionysos, will have been to Herodas' adulteration of choliambic poetry by the introduction of the dramatic element.[9]

Herodas therefore presents Hippônax as criticising Herodas' poetry for crossing the form of the genre of comic drama and the metre of the genre of iambic invective. He pleads guilty as charged, but none the less defends and maintains his procedure. This he does by invoking the sanction of the god of poetry, but we should also note that there are signs of humility present in his closing comment that he will sing choliambic poetry 'after' Hippônax, that is 'after' both in time and ranking.

This 'crossing of genres' is now a well known and understood characteristic of Hellenistic poetry.[10] I have elsewhere[11] explored the ways in which the Hellenistic poets cross the form of the 'grand' genres, especially the hexameter of epic, with the subject-matter and people of 'low' genres like comedy and mime, with widely divergent creative effects. These range from the humorous clash of content and form in Theokritos' fourth and fifth *Idylls*, where country folk pass the time of day or obscenely abuse one another in grand hexameters, to the sympathetic portrayal of a lowly figure like Hekale in Kallimachos' epic.[12] Herodas fits in as perfectly with this scenario as he does with so much else that is typical of his contemporary poets.[13]

## *Notes*

1. See notes to 23, 28, 30, 33, 34.
2. Cf. Rist (1998), who opts for Archilochos, though we have no evidence that Herodas wrote 'pure', invective iambic poetry.
3. See notes to 59 and 60.
4. See notes to 68, 71.
5. See Simon (1991) 127–44 on Theokritos' priority.
6. See further Simon (1991) 74–82, who represents the view that Herodas is drastically capping Theokritos' irony in his depiction of Lykidas.
7. Rosen (1992).
8. Rosen (1991) 214–5 regards the η's of lines 76 and 77 as disjunctive, 'either…or' (ἤ … ἤ), but taking the first η as a relative pronoun (ἥ) going with 'the Muse' as in the text that I offer does not significantly affect Rosen's point.
9. Fountoulakis (2002) makes the attractive suggestion that Herodas is in fact referring specifically to the 'disreputable' genre of mime, not merely drama, but we need more evidence of a connection between mime and Dionysos in the early third century B.C. than the late witnesses he cites at 311–3.
10. See most recently Fantuzzi in Fantuzzi-Hunter (2004) 1–41 for a magisterial general survey.
11. Zanker (1987) 155–227.
12. See further Zanker (1998) 225–7, with nn. 2 and 3.
13. Moreover, as we have seen (1, 59nn.), Elena Esposito has pointed to the humour that Herodas achieves when he cites Homer. This is also genre-crossing: grand Homeric diction and motifs are embedded in the low form of mime, and the two components of the genres are set on a humorous collision-course.

## *THE FRAGMENTS*

### 9. ΑΠΟΝΗΣΤΙΖΟΜΕΝΑΙ

ἕ]ζεσθε πᾶσαι. κοῦ τὸ παιδίον; δεξ[
...........]Ευέτειραν καὶ Γλύκην .[
3 τὴν ἕτοιμον 4 μή σε [κν]ισμάτων
8 δειλαίοις 13 σ' ἤειρα

### 10. ΜΟΛΠΙΝΟΣ

ἐπὴν τὸν ἑξηκοστὸν ἥλιον κάμψῃς
ὦ Γρύλλε, Γρύλλε, θνῆσκε καὶ τέφρη γίνευ·
ὡς τυφλὸς ὁ ὑπὲρ κεῖνο τοῦ βίου καμπτήρ·
ἤδη γὰρ αὐγὴ τῆς ζοῆς ἀπήμβλυνται.

Cited by Stobaios 4.50.56 Wachsmuth-Hense (1912) 5 1042

# THE FRAGMENTS

## 9. WOMEN AT BREAKFAST

Sit down, everyone. Where's the child? Take (show?)...
..............Eueteira and Glykê ..............
3 the one that's ready 4 lest you ... of scratches 8 with wretched
13 I have reared you

The title and pitiful textual remains are preserved at the end of the papyrus. The poem started with a welcome of female friends by a mother with her children to breakfast. It appears that from line 3 on there was abuse of a slave or slaves. The domestic scene has some affinity with a mime of Sophrôn, *Frr.* 14–*17 Kassel-Austin (2001) 1 202–3, and may also owe something to Menandros, *Women having Breakfast* (Συναριστῶσαι), *Fr.* 334 Kassel-Austin (1998) 6.2 214.

## 10. MOLPINOS

When you have rounded the turn of your sixtieth sun,
Gryllos, Gryllos, die, and become ash,
since the lap of life beyond that is blind,
because the ray of life has already been dulled.

Death or suicide in one's sixtieth year in order to avoid old age or being a burden to others is entertained at e.g. Strabo 10.5.6: 'Among these people (the people of Keios) a law seems to have been passed which Menandros also mentions: "Phanias, the law of the Keians is a fair one, that the man who cannot live well should not die in misery" (*Fr.* 879 Kassel-Austin [1998] 6.2 416). It seems that the law commanded those who have lived beyond sixty years take hemlock so that there might be sufficient food for the others.'

## 11. ΣΥΝΕΡΓΑΖΟΜΕΝΑΙ

προσφὺς ὅκως τις χοιράδων ἀνηρίτης

Cited by Athenaios, *Scholars at Dinner* 86b

## 12. FROM A *MIMIAMBOS* OF UNKNOWN TITLE

ἢ χαλκέην μοι μυῖαν ἢ κύθρην παίζει
ἢ ταῖσι μηλάνθαισιν ἅμματ' ἐξάπτων
τοῦ κεσκίου μοι τὸν γέροντα λωβῆται.

Cited by Stobaios 4.24.51 Wachsmuth-Hense (1909) 4 617

## 13. FROM A *MIMIAMBOS* OF UNKNOWN TITLE

ὡς οἰκίην οὐκ ἔστιν εὐμαρέως εὑρεῖν
ἄνευ κακῶν ζώουσαν· ὃς δ' ἔχει μεῖον,
τοῦτόν τι μεῖζον τοῦ ἑτέρου δόκει πρήσσειν.

Cited by Stobaios 4.34.27 Wachsmuth-Hense (1912) 5 834

## 11. WOMEN AT WORK TOGETHER

Clinging like a sea-snail on the rocks.

The subject may be male or female, and the image may be erotic.

## 12. FROM A *MIMIAMBOS* OF UNKNOWN TITLE

He plays either brazen fly or pot
or, by attaching threads made of flax to cockchafers,
he robs my distaff.

1. 'Brazen fly' was a children's games similar to our blind man's buff, the name 'fly', μυῖα, deriving from a pun on καταμύω, 'close one's eyes', 'brazen' presumably being used metaphorically for 'brave'; 'pot' involved a child sitting in a ring of other children, the child in the middle trying to catch the others who hit him. 2. Tying flaxen strings to cockchafers was a child's sport, mentioned also e.g. at Aristophanes, *Clouds* 763. 3. A distaff was called an 'old man' because it was decorated with an old man's face. The fragment looks as if it presents a mother complaining about the results of her son's playing; if so, its situation resembles that of *Mim.* 3.

## 13. FROM A *MIMIAMBOS* OF UNKNOWN TITLE

Since it is not possible to find easily a house
which lives without troubles. Whoever has less trouble,
consider this man to be doing better than the other.

For a close parallel to this sentiment see Menandros, *Fr.* 846.1–2 Kassel-Austin (1998) 6.2 402 ἄνευ κακῶν γὰρ οἰκίαν οἰκουμένην / οὐκ ἔστιν εὑρεῖν, 'It is not possible to find a house inhabited without troubles.'

# BIBLIOGRAPHY


Adler, A. 1928, 1931, 1933, 1935, 1938. *Suidae Lexicon, Lexicographi Graeci* 1, 5 vols. (repr. 1971 Stuttgart)

Arnott, W.G. 1971. 'Herodas and the Kitchen Sink', *Greece and Rome* 18, 121–32

Arnott, W.G. 1979. 'The Mound of Brasilas in Theocritus' Seventh *Idyll*', *Quaderni urbinati di cultura classica* 30, 99–106

Arnott, W.G. 1984. 'The Women in Herodas, *Mimiamb* 4', *Corolla Londiniensis* 4, 10–12

Arnott, W.G. 1996. *Alexis: The Fragments, Cambridge Classical Texts and Commentaries* 31 (Cambridge)

Bastianini, G. and Gallazzi, C., with the collaboration of Austin, C. 2001. *Posidippo di Pella: Epigrammi (P. Mil. Vogl. VIII 309), Papiri dell' Università degli Studi di Milano* 8 (Milan)

Baumeister, A. 1885, 1887, 1888. *Denkmäler des klassischen Altertums*, 3 vols. (Munich and Leipzig)

Beare, J.I. 1904. 'Herondas, VII. 96', *Classical Review* 18, 287–8

Bekker, I. 1814. *Anecdota Graeca*, vol. 1 (Berlin)

Bethe, E. 1900, 1931, 1937. *Pollucis Onomasticon*, 3 vols., *Lexicographi Graeci* 9 (Leipzig)

Bieber, M. 1923–24. 'Die Söhne des Praxiteles', *Jahrbuch des Deutschen Archäologischen Instituts* 38–39, 242–275.

Blass, F. 1891. Review of Kenyon, F.G., *Classical Texts from Papyri in the British Museum, including the newly discovered poems of Herodas* (London 1891), in *Göttingsche gelehrte Anzeigen*, 728–32

Blass, F. 1892[1]. Review of Bücheler, F., *Herondae Mimiambi* (Bonn 1892), in *Göttingsche gelehrte Anzeigen* (1892) 230–37

Blass, F. 1892[2]. Review of Crusius, O., *Untersuchungen zu den Mimiamben des Herondas* (Leipzig 1892) and Crusius, O., *Herondae Mimiambi* (Leipzig 1892), in *Göttingsche gelehrte Anzeigen* (1892) 857–67

Bo, D. 1962. *La Lingua di Eroda* (Turin)

Boter, G.J. 1990. 'A Note on Herondas III 40', *Mnemosyne* 43, 155–6

Bücheler, F. 1892. *Herondae Mimiambi* (Bonn)

Cameron, A. 1995. *Callimachus and his Critics* (Princeton)

Chantraine, P. 1942–53. *Grammaire Homérique* (Paris)

Chantraine, P. 1968. *Dictionnaire étymologique de la langue grecque* (Paris)

Collard, C. 1975. *Euripides: Supplices*, 2 vols. (Groningen)

Colonna, A. 1967. *Etymologicum Genuinum: Littera Λ* (Rome)

Crane, G. 1986. 'Three Notes on Herodas 8', *Harvard Studies in Classical Philology* 90, 85–90

Crusius, O. 1892[1]. *Herondae Mimiambi* (Leipzig)
Crusius, O. 1892[2]. *Untersuchungen zu den Mimiamben des Herondas* (Leipzig)
Crusius, O. 1894. *Herondae Mimiambi*[2] (Leipzig)
Crusius, O. 1905. *Herondae Mimiambi*[4] (Leipzig)
Crusius, O. 1914. *Herondae Mimiambi*[5] (Leipzig)
Crusius, O. and Herzog, R. 1926. *Die Mimiamben des Herondas: Deutsch mit Einleitung und Anmerkungen* (Leipzig)
Cunningham, I.C. 1964. 'Herodas 6 and 7', *Classical Quarterly* 14, 33
Cunningham, I.C. 1966. 'Herodas 4', *Classical Quarterly* 16, 113–125
Cunningham, I.C. 1971. *Herodas: Mimiambi* (Oxford)
Cunningham, I.C. 1971. Review of Schmidt, V. 1968. *Sprachliche Untersuchungen zu Herondas* (Berlin) in *Classical Review* 21, 22–4
Cunningham, I.C. 1981. Review of Italian original of Mastromarco (1984), *Journal of Hellenic Studies* 101, 161–162.
Cunningham, I.C. and Rusten, J.C. 2002. *Theophrastus, Characters; Herodas, Mimes; Sophron and Other Mime Fragments* (Cambridge, Mass. and London)
Cunningham, I.C. 2004. *Herodas: Mimiambi* (Munich and Leipzig)
D., F. 1891. *The Academy* 40, 409
D., F. 1892. 'Notes on Herodas', *The Academy* 42, 72
Dale, A.M. 1967. *Euripides: Helen* (Oxford)
Danielsson, A.O. 1891. 'Zu Herondas' Mimiamben I' and 'Zu Herondas' Mimiamben II', *Wochenschrift für klassische Philologie* 7, 1323–7, 1353–7
Degani, E. 1984. *Studi su Ipponatte* (Bari)
Degani, H. 1991. *Hipponactis Testimonia et Fragmenta*[2] (Leipzig)
Denniston, J.D. 1939. *Euripides: Electra* (Oxford)
Denniston, J.D. 1954. *The Greek Particles*[2], revised by K.J. Dover (Oxford)
Di Gregorio, L. 1967. *Le Scene d'annuncio nella tragedia greca* (Milan)
Di Gregorio, L. 1995. 'La figura di Metriche nel primo mimiambo di Eronda', in Belloni, L., Milanese, G. and Porro, A. (eds), *Studi classici Iohanni Tarditi oblata, Biblioteca di Aevum Antiquum* 7 (Milan), 675–94
Di Gregorio, L. 1997. *Eronda: Mimiambi (I–IV), Biblioteca di Aevum Antiquum* 9 (Milan)
Di Gregorio, L. 2004. *Eronda: Mimiambi (V–XII), Biblioteca di Aevum Antiquum* 16 (Milan)
Diels, H. 1892. 'Zum 6. und 7. Gedichte des Herodas', *Sitzungsberichte der königlich Preussischen Akademie der Wissenschaften zu Berlin* (25) 387–92
Dodds, E.R. 1960. *Euripides: Bacchae* (Oxford)
Dunbar, N. 1995. *Aristophanes: Birds* (Oxford)
Edmonds, J.M. 1925. 'Some Notes on the Herodas Papyrus', *Classical Quarterly* 19, 129–46
Ehlers, W.-W. 2001. 'Auribus escam oder Der intendierte Rezitator – Produktions-

und rezeptionsästhetische Aspekte der Mündlichkeit antiker Texte,' in Benz, L. (ed.), *ScriptOralia Romana: Die römische Literatur zwischen Mündlichkeit und Schriftlichkeit*, *ScriptOralia* 118 (Tübingen)

Ellis, R. 1891. 'Emendations of Herodas', *Classical Review* 5, 360–3.

Esposito, E. 2001. 'Allusività epica e ispirazione giambica in Herond. 1 e 8', *Eikasmos* 12, 141–59

Fantuzzi, M. and Hunter, R.L. 2002. *Muse e modelli: La poesia ellenistica da Alessandro Magno ad Augusto* (Roma-Bari)

Fantuzzi, M. and Hunter, R.L. 2004. *Tradition and Innovation in Hellenistic Poetry* (Cambridge)

Finnegan, R.J. 1992. 'Women in Herodian Mime', *Hermathena* 152, 21–37

Fountoulakis, A. 2000. '*Ω ΠΑΡΕΟΝ[ΤΕΣ* in Herondas 8.61', *Zeitschrift für Papyrologie und Epigraphik* 131, 27–8

Fountoulakis, A. 2002. 'Herondas 8.66–79: Generic Self-Consciousness and Artistic Claims in Herondas' *Mimiambs*', *Mnemosyne* 55, 301–19

Fountoulakis, A. 2007. 'Bitinna and the Tyrant: Some Remarks on Herondas 5.74–77', *Philologus* 151, 230–43

Fraenkel, E. 1950. *Aeschylus: Agamemnon*, 3 vols. (Oxford)

Fraser, P.M. and Matthews, E. 1987. *A Lexicon of Greek Personal Names*, vol. 1: *The Aegean Islands, Cyprus, Cyrenaica* (Oxford)

Frisk, H. 1960, 1970, 1972. *Griechisches etymologisches Wörterbuch*, 3 vols. (Heidelberg)

Gaisford, T. 1848. *Etymologicon Magnum* (Oxford)

García-Ramón, J.L. 1992. 'Griechisch *ἱερός* und seine Varianten, vedisch *isirá-*', in Beekes, R. *et al.* (eds) *Rekonstruktion und relative Chronologie: Akten der VIII. Fachtagung der Indogermanischen Gesellschaft Leiden, 31. August–4. September 1987* (Innsbruck) 183–205

Gelzer, Th. 1985. 'Mimus und Kunsttheorie bei Herondas, Mimiambus 4', in Schäublin, Ch. (ed.), *Catalepton: Festschrift für Bernhard Wyss zum 80. Geburtstag* (Basel) 96–116

Gerber, D.E. 1978. 'Herodas 5.1', *Harvard Studies in Classical Philology* 82, 161–5

Gentili, B. 1958. *Anacreonte* (Rome)

Goldhill, S. 1994. 'The naive and knowing eye: ecphrasis and the culture of viewing in the Hellenistic world', in Goldhill, S. and Osborne, R. (eds), *Art and text in ancient Greek culture* (Cambridge) 197–223

Goodwin, W.W. 1965. *A Greek Grammar* (London, New York)

Gow, A.S.F. 1952. *Theocritus*, 2 vols. (Cambridge)

Gow, A.S.F. 1965. *Machon* (Cambridge)

Gow, A.S.F. and Page, D.L. 1968. *Hellenistic Epigrams* (Cambridge)

Groeneboom, P. 1922. *Les Mimiambes d'Herodas I–VI* (Groningen)

Guarducci, M. 1950. *Inscriptiones Creticae IV: Tituli Gortynii* (Rome)

Gutzwiller, K.J. 1991. *Pastoral Analogies: The Formation of a Genre* (Madison, Wisconsin)

Habicht, C. 2007. 'Neues zur hellenistischen Geschichte von Kos', *Chiron* 37, 123–52

Headlam, W. 1891. *The Academy* 40, n. 1014 p. 314; n. 1016 p. 362; n. 1023 p. 538

Headlam, W. 1892. *The Academy* 41, 88–9

Headlam, W. 1893. 'Herodas', *Classical Review* 7, 404

Headlam, W. 1899. 'On Herodas', *Classical Review* 13, 151–6

Headlam, W. and Knox, A.D. 1922. *Herodas: the Mimes and Fragments* (Cambridge)

Henderson, J. 1975. *The Maculate Muse* (New Haven and London)

Herzog, R. 1903. 'Das Kind mit der Fuchsgans', *Österreichische Jahreshefte* 6, 215–36

Herzog, R. 1924. 'Der Traum des Herondas', *Philologus* 79, 387–433

Herzog, R. 1926. Reviews of Terzaghi, N., *Eroda: I Mimiambi* (Turin 1925), Headlam, W. and Knox, A.D., *Herodas: the Mimes and Fragments* (Cambridge 1922), and Groeneboom, P., *Les Mimiambes d'Herodas I–VI* (Groningen 1922), in *Philologische Wochenschrift* 46, 193–211

Herzog, R. 1927. 'Herondea', *Philologus* 36, 27–66

Herzog, R. and Schazman, P. 1932. *Asklepieion: Baubeschreibung und Baugeschichte*, in Herzog, R. (ed.), *Kos: Ergebnisse der deutschen Ausgrabungen und Forschungen*, vol. I (Berlin)

Hopkinson, N. 1988. *A Hellenistic Anthology* (Cambridge)

Hunter, R.L. 1993. 'The Presentation of Herodas' *Mimiamboi*', *Antichthon* 27, 31–44

Hunter, R.L. 1995. 'Plautus and Herodas', in *Plautus und die Tradition des Stegreifspiels: Festgabe für E. Lefèvre zum 60. Geburtstag* (Tübingen) 155–69

Jäkel, S. 1964. *Menandri Sententiae* (Leipzig)

Jevons, F.B. 1891. 'Notes on Hero[n]das', *The Academy* 40, n. 1015, pp. 336–7; n. 1017, p. 384

Jones, D.M. 1969. *Prolegomena de Comoedia; Scholia in Acharnenses, Equites, Nubes* Pars 1 Fasc. 2: *Scholia vetera in Aristophanis Equites* (Groningen)

Kaibel, G. 1891. 'Zu Herodas', *Hermes* 26, 580–92

Kannicht, R. and Snell, B. 1981. *Tragicorum Graecorum Fragmenta*, vol. 2 (Göttingen)

Kannicht, R. 2004. *Tragicorum Graecorum Fragmenta*, vol. 5, 2 parts (Göttingen)

Kassel, R. and Austin, C. (eds). 1983–2001. *Poetae Comici Graeci*, 8 vols. (Berlin and New York)

Kenyon, F.G. 1891. *Classical Texts from Papyri in the British Museum* (London)

Kenyon, F.G. 1901. 'Some New Fragments of Herodas', *Archiv für Papyrusforschung* 1, 379–87

Kerkhecker, A. 1999. *Callimachus' Book of* Iambi (Oxford)

Keuls, E.C. 1985. *The Reign of the Phallus: Sexual Politics in Ancient Athens* (New York)

Knox, A.D. 1925. 'The Dream of Herodas', *Classical Review* 39, 13–5

Knox, A.D. 1926[1]. 'Herodes and Callimachus', *Philologus* 81, 241–55

Knox, A.D. 1926[2]. 'Herodas', *Philologische Wochenschrift* 46, 77–8

Konstan, D. 1989. 'The Tyrant Goddess: Herodas' Fifth Mime', *Classical Antiquity* 8, 267–82

Koster, W.J.W. 1975. *Prolegomena de Comoedia, Scholia in Aristophanem* part 1 fasc. IA (Groningen)

Krumeich, R., Pechstein, N. and Seidensticker, B. 1999. *Das griechische Satyrspiel, Texte zur Forschung* 72 (Darmstadt)

Kühn, C.G. 1827. *Claudii Galeni Opera Omnia* vol. 14 (Leipzig)

Kühn, C.G. 1830. *Claudii Galeni Opera Omnia* vol. 19 (Leipzig)

Kühner, R., Gerth, B. and Blass, F. 1890, 1892, 1898, 1904. *Ausführliche Grammatik der griechischen Sprache*[3], 4 vols. in 2 parts (Hannover and Leipzig)

Kühner, R. and Gerth, B. 1955. *Ausführliche Grammatik der griechischen Sprache*[4], vol. 2: Satzlehre, 2 parts (Hannover)

Kutzko, D. 2006. 'The Major Importance of a Minor poet: Herodas 6 and 7 as a Quasi-Dramatic Diptych', in Harder, M.A., Regtuit, R.F. and Wakker, G.C. (eds), *Beyond the Canon, Hellenistica Groningana* 11 (Leuven) 167–83

Latte, K. 1953, 1966. *Hesychii Alexandrini Lexicon*, 2 vols. (Copenhagen)

Latte, K. 1957. 'ΑΣΚΩΛΙΑΣΜΟΣ', *Hermes* 85, 385–91 (= Gigon, O. *et al.* [eds]. 1968. *Kurt Latte: Kleine Schriften* [Munich])

Lawall, G. 1976. 'Herodas 6 and 7 Reconsidered', *Classical Philology* 75, 165–9

Lehman, K. 1945. 'The Girl beneath the Apple Tree', *American Journal of Archaeology* 49, 430–33

Leutsch, E.L. von and Schneidewin, F.G. 1839. *Corpus Paroemiographorum Graecorum*, vol. 1 (Göttingen)

Littré, É. 1861. *Oeuvres complètes d'Hippocrate*, vol. 9 (Paris)

Lobel, E. and Page, D.L. 1955. *Poetarum Lesbiorum Fragmenta* (Oxford)

Lloyd, A.B. 1976. *Herodotus Book II: Commentary 1–98, Études préliminaires aux religions orientales dans l'empire romain* (Leiden)

Lloyd-Jones, H. and Parsons, P.J. 1983. *Supplementum Hellenisticum* (Berlin and New York)

Luria, S. 1963. 'Herondas' Kampf für die veristische Kunst', in *Miscellanea di studi alessandrini in memoria di Augusto Rostagni* (Turin), 394–415

Maas, M. and Snyder, J.M. 1989. *Stringed Instruments of Ancient Greece* (New Haven and London)

Männlein-Robert, I. 2006. '"Hinkende Nachahmung": Desillusionisierung und Grenzüberspielungen in Herodas' viertem Mimiambus', in Harder, M.A., Regtuit,

R.F. and Wakker, G.C. (eds), *Beyond the Canon*, *Hellenistica Groningana* 11 (Groningen) 205–27

Marrou, H.I. 1956. *A History of Education in Antiquity*. Trans. Lamb, G. (London)

Massa Positano, L. 1973. *Eroda: Mimiambo* IV, *Collana di studi greci* 58 (Naples)

Mastromarco, G. 1984. *The Public of Herondas*, *London Studies in Classical Philology* 11 (Amsterdam)

Meister, R. 1892. Review of Crusius, O., *Herondae Mimiambi* (Leipzig 1892) and Crusius, O. *Untersuchungen zu den Mimiamben des Herondas* (Leipzig 1892), in *Literarisches Centralblatt* (1892) 1331–4

Meister, R. 1893. *Die Mimiamben des Herodas* (Leipzig)

Moritz, L.A. 1958. *Grain-Mills and Flour in Classical Antiquity* (Oxford)

Morricone, M.L. 1991. 'Due teste femminili dall'Asklepieion di Coo', in Stucchi, S. and Bonanno Aravantinos, M. (eds), *Giornate di studio in onore di Achille Adriani, Roma 26–27 novembre 1984*, *Studi Miscellanei* 28 (Rome) 181–207

Nairn, J.A. and Laloy, L. 1991. *Hérondas: Mimes*, third edition of 1928 original (Paris)

Oder, E. and Hoppe, C. 1924 and 1927. *Corpus Hippiatricorum Graecorum*, 2 vols. (Stuttgart)

Pack, R.A. 1963. *Artemidori Daldiani Onirocriton Libri V* (Leipzig)

Page, D.L. 1941. *Select Papyri: Literary Papyri: Poetry* (Cambridge, Mass.)

Page, D.L. 1962. *Poetae Melici Graeci* (Oxford)

Parsons, P.J. 1981. Review of Italian original (1979) of Mastromarco (1984), *CR* 31, 110

Paton, W.R. and Hicks, E.L. 1891. *The Inscriptions of Cos* (Oxford)

Pfeiffer, R. 1949. *Callimachus: vol. 1 Fragmenta* (Oxford)

Pickard-Cambridge, A. 1968. *The Dramatic Festivals of Athens*[2] (Oxford)

Pollitt, J.J. 1974. *The Ancient View of Greek Art: Criticism, History and Terminology* (New Haven and London)

Powell, J.U. 1925. *Collectanea Alexandrina: Reliquiae minores Poetarum Graecorum Aetatis Ptolemaicae 323–146 A.C. Epicorum, Elegiacorum, Lyricorum, Ethicorum* (Oxford)

Preisshofen, F. 1978. 'Kunsttheorie und Kunstbetrachtung', in Flashar, H. (ed.), *Le classicisme à Rome aux Iers siècles avant et après J.C.*, *Entretiens sur l'antiquité classique* 25 (Vandoeuvres-Geneva) 263–282

Puchner, W. 1993. 'Zur Raumkonzeption in den Mimiamben des Herodas', *Wiener Studien* 106, 9–34

Quincey, J.H. 1966. 'Greek Expressions of Thanks', *Journal of Hellenic Studies* 86, 133–58

Radt, S. 1977, 1985. *Tragicorum Graecorum Fragmenta*, vols. 4 and 3 (Göttingen)

Reinach, Th. 1891. 'Herodas le mimographe', *Revue des Études Grecques* 4, 209–32

Reinach, Th. 1909. 'La date du mime II d'Hérodas', in *Mélanges offerts a Louis Havet* (Paris) 451–6

Rhodes, P.J. and Osborne, R. 2003. *Greek Historical Inscriptions 404–323 BC* (Oxford)

Ridgway, B.S. 2000. *Hellenistic Sculpture II: The Styles of ca. 200–100 B.C.* (Madison, Wisconsin)

Rist, A. 1998. 'A Fresh Look at Herodas' Bucolic Masquerade', *Phoenix* 51, 354–63

Rosen, R. 1992. 'Mixing of Genres and Literary Program in *Herodas 8*', *Harvard Studies in Classical Philology* 94, 205–16

Rutherford, I. 2001. *Pindar's Paeans: A Reading of the Fragments with a Survey of the Genre* (Oxford)

Rutherford, W.G. 1891. *ΗΡΩΝΔΟΥ Mimiamboi: Herondas, A First Recension* (London)

Schmidt, M. (ed.). 1858, 1860, 1861, 1862, 1868. *Hesychii Alexandrini Lexicon*, 5 vols. (Jena and Halle)

Schmidt, V. 1968. *Sprachliche Untersuchungen zu Herondas*, *Untersuchungen zur antiken Literatur und Geschichte* 1 (Berlin)

Schulze, W. 1893. 'Zu Herondas', *Rheinisches Museum* N.F. 48, 248–57

Schwyzer, E. 1939, 1950, 1953, 1971. *Griechische Grammatik*, 4 vols., *Handbuch der Altertumswissenschaft* II.i.1–4 (Munich)

Sherwin-White, S.M. 1978. *Ancient Cos: An historical study from the Dorian settlement to the Imperial period*, *Hypomnemata* 51 (Göttingen)

Simon, H.-J. 1991. *Τὰ κύλλ' ἀείδειν: Interpretationen zu den Mimiamben des Herodas*, *Studien zur klassischen Philologie* 57 (Frankfurt, Bern, New York, Paris)

Sitzler, J. 1896. Review of Crusius, O., *Herondae Mimiambi* 2nd ed. (Leipzig 1894), in *Neue philologische Rundschau*, 161–6

Skinner, M.B. 2001. 'Ladies' Day at the Art Institute: Theocritus, Herodas, and the Gendered Gaze', in Lardinois, A. and McLure, L. (eds), *Making Silence Speak: Women's Voices in Greek Literature and Society* (Princeton and Oxford)

Skutsch, O. 1985. *The Annales of Q. Ennius* (Oxford)

Smotrytsch, A.P. 1962. 'Gerond i Ptolemej II Filadelf', *Vestnik Drevney Historii* 79 (1962) 132–6

Snell, B. 1986. *Tragicorum Graecorum Fragmenta*, vol. 1 (Göttingen)

Spanoudakis, K. 2002. *Philitas of Cos*, *Mnemosyne* Suppl. 229 (Leiden-Boston-Köln)

Stadtmüller, H. 1894. 'Zu Herondas und der neuen Herondasausgabe von Crusius', *Blätter für das Gymnasialschulwesen* 30, 456–60

Stählin, O. and Treu, U. 1972. *Clemens Alexandrinus*, vol. 1: *Proptrepticus und Paedogogus* (Berlin)

Stanzel, K.-H. 1998. 'Mimen, Mimepen und Mimiamben – Theokrit, Herodas und die Kreuzung der Gattungen', in Harder, M.A., Regtuit, R.F. and Wakker, G.C. (eds), *Genre in Hellenistic Poetry, Hellenistica Groningana* 3 (Groningen) 141–65

Stewart, A.F. 1990. *Greek Sculpture: an Exploration* (New Haven and London)

Taillardat, J. 1967. *Suetonius: Περὶ βλασφημιῶν. Περὶ παιδιῶν* (Paris)

Theodoridis, C. 1998. *Photii Patriarchae Lexicon*, vol. 2 (Berlin, New York)

Treu, U. 1981. 'Herondas 3.24–6 und die Schulpraxis', *Quaderni urbinati di cultura classica* 8, 113–16

Trümpy, C. 1997. *Untersuchungen zu den altgriechischen Monatsnamen und Monatsfolgen* (Heidelberg)

Uhlig, G. 1883. *Dionysii Thracis Ars Grammatica*, in *Grammatici Graeci*, vol. 1.1/3 (repr. Hildesheim 1965)

Usener, H. 1902. 'Milch und Honig', *Rheinisches Museum* 57, 177–95

Ussher, R.G. 1973. *Aristophanes: Ecclesiazusae* (Oxford)

Ussher, R.G. 1985. 'The Mimic Tradition of "Character" in Herodas', *Quaderni urbinati di cultura classica* 21, 45–68

Valk, M. van der. 1976. *Eustathii Archiepiscopi Thessalonicensis Commentarii ad Homeri Iliadem Pertinentes*, vol. 2 (Leiden)

Vanderpool, E. 1959. 'News Letter from Greece', *American Journal of Archaeology* 63, 279–283

Vatin, C. 1970. *Recherches sur le mariage et la condition de la femme mariée a l'époque hellénistique, Bibliothèque des Écoles françaises d'Athènes et de Rome* 216 (Paris)

Vogliano, A. 1906. *Ricerche sopra l'ottavo mimiambo di Heroda (ΕΝΥΠΝΙΟΝ) con un excurso (iv.93–5)* (Milan)

Voigt, E.-M. 1971. *Sappho et Alcaeus: Fragmenta* (Amsterdam)

Wachsmuth, C. and Hense, O. 1884, 1884, 1894, 1909, 1912. *Ioannis Stobaei Anthologium*, 5 vols. (Berlin)

Webster, T.B.L. 1964. *Hellenistic Poetry and Art* (London)

Wehrli, F. 1936. *Motivstudien zur griechischen Komödie* (Zurich and Leipzig)

Weil, H. 1891. Review of Kenyon, F.G., *Classical Texts from Papyri in the British Museum, including the newly discovered poems of Herodas* (London 1891) and Rutherford, W.G., ΗΡΩΝΔΟΥ ΜΙΜΙΑΜΒΟΙ (London 1891), in *Journal des Savants* 1891, 655–73.

Weil, H. 1892. Review of Bücheler, F., *Herondae Mimiambi* (Bonn 1892) in *Journal des Savants* 1892, 516–21

Wendel, C. 1935. *Scholia in Apollonium Rhodium Vetera* (Berlin)

West, M.L. 1978. *Hesiod:* Works *and Days* (Oxford)

West, M.L. 1982. *Greek Metre* (Oxford)

West, M.L. 1998. *Iambi et Elegi Graeci ante Alexandrum Cantati*², 2 vols. (Oxford)

Wilamowitz-Moellendorff, U. von. 1909 *Euripides: Herakles*² (Berlin)

Willcock, M.M. 1987. *Plautus: Pseudolus* (Bristol)

Will, É. 1979. *Histoire politique du monde hellénistique (323–30 av. J.-C.)*[2], vol. 1. (Nancy)

Willetts, R.F. 1967. The Law Code of Gortyn, Kadmos Supplement 1 (Berlin)

Zanker, G. 1980. 'Simichidas' Walk and the Locality of Bourina in Theocritus, *Id.* 7', *Classical Quarterly* 30, 373–7

Zanker, G. 1987. Realism in Alexandrian Poetry: A Literature and its Audience (London)

Zanker, G. 1996. 'Pictorial Description as a Supplement for Narrative: The Labour of Augeas' Stables in *Heracles Leontophonos*', *American Journal of Philology* 117, 411–23

Zanker, G. 1998. 'Genre-Marking in Hellenistic Poetry and Art', in Harder, M.A., Regtuit, R.F. and Wakker, G.C. (eds), *Genre in Hellenistic Poetry*, *Hellenistica Groningana* 3 (Groningen) 225–38

Zanker, G. 2000. 'Aristotle's *Poetics* and the Painters', *American Journal of Philology* 121, 225–235

Zanker, G. 2003. 'New Light on the Literary Category of "Ekphrastic Epigram" in Antiquity: The New Posidippus (col. X 7–XI 19 P. Mil. Vogl. VIII 309)', *Zeitschrift für Papyrologie und Epigraphik* 143, 59–62

Zanker, G. 2004. *Modes of Viewing in Hellenistic Poetry and Art* (Madison, Wisconsin)

Zanker, G. 2006. 'Poetry and Art in Herodas, *Mimiamb* 4', in Harder, M.A., Regtuit, R.F. and Wakker, G.C. (eds), *Beyond the Canon*, *Hellenistica Groningana* 11 (Groningen) 357–77

# INDEX

Numbers in italics refer to notes by poem and line-numbers; non-italicised numbers denote page-numbers.


Abdêra *2.58*
abstracts *1.67*, *4.14*, *6.16*, *7.45*
Adrêsteia *6.35*
adultery, of free women with slaves 138–40, 153–5
*Adultress, The* (second-century A.D. mime) 140, 155
Aiolos *7.96*, *8.36*, *8.37*
Akê *2.16*
Akesês *3.61*
Alexandria 21, 22, *1.28–32*, *1.28*, *1.29*, *1.30*, *1.31*; climate of *1.28*; festivals of *1.29*; Museum of *1.28–32*, *1.31*, *8.72*; philosophers at *1.29*; wine of *1.31*
alliteration 3, *2.28–9*, *2.56*, *3.66–7*, *5.9*
anacoluthon *1.53*
*antilabê* 20, 38, 39
Apelles 106, *4.59–71*, *4.72*; as analogous to Herodas in his subject-matter and artistic programme *4.72–8*, *4.75*, 128–9, 186
Aphrodite *1.9*, *1.26*, *1.62*, *1.82–5*, 29, *5.77*, *6.75*, *7.25*
art, works of 106, 124–8; *agalma* and *andrias 4.20–6*, *4.36*; drawn lines in painting *4.73*, 128; inscriptions on *4.24*; involving the spectator *4.30–4*, 125, 128; in the Koan Asklêpieion *4.1–20*, *4.5*, *4.11*, *4.27–9*, *4.30–4*, 124–8; lifelike quality in 107, *4.27–38*, *4.33*, *4.59–71*, *4.59–62*, *4.71*, *4.72*, 125, 126, 128; 'low' subject-matter in 129; poetic descriptions of 107–8, 124; character expressed by 128; as solitary figures 127; visualised in audience's imagination 124–8
Asklêpieion, Koan 1, 5, 6, 105–6, *4.1–2*, 122; exedra in *4.27–38*; collection-box (*thêsauros*) in 106, *4.90–2*, 122
Asklêpios *2.97*, *4.1–20*, *4.3*; cult-centres of *4.1–2*; hymns to *4.1–20*; cure-tablets dedicated to *4.19*
Asklêpiadai *4.1–2*, *4.27–9*
*askôliasmos* 225, 226, *8.36–65a*, *8.42*, *8.47*, *8.74*
assault *2.41*, *2.46*
Athene: goddess of handicrafts *4.58*, *6.66*, 181
baldness *6.59*, *6.76*, *7.72*
Baukis *7.58*
beeswax *7.28*
Brikindêra *2.57*
brothel-keepers 51, *2.77*
brother and sister gods, temple of 21, *1.30*
Chairôndas (Charôndas) *2.48*
characterization 22, *1.24*, 32–5, 51, 66–71, 79–80, 95–7, 106–7, 153–5, 181–3, 201, *7.56–61*, 215–7; epic allusions in 33–5; 'mosaic' technique in, 32, 67, 95, 153–5
chickens *6.98b–102*, *6.102*, *7.48*
Choirilos of Samos 2
clay in Prometheus' creation of men *2.29*, *2.31*
clepsydra *2.41–5*, *2.42–5*, 66, 70
coinage *2.22*, *7.79*
compensation-money *2.89*

dialect, generally Eastern Ionic 3–4, 7–11; aphaeresis 9; apokôpê 11, *8.1*; artificiality of 2–4; Attic reduplication 10, *4.77*, *5.4*, *5.39*, *5.44*, *6.19b*, *6.44*; compensatory lengthening 9; contraction 8, *1.88*; crasis 9, *1.3*, *4.75*, *8.66*; elision 8; hiatus 9, *1.43*; hyperionicism 10, *2.80*, *3.35*, *4.89*, *5.44*, *6.90*; inconsistency 3–4, 7–8; length of ι in comparison of adjectives *1.87*, *2.90*; metathesis 8, *4.7*, *6.6*, *6.99*; psilosis 3–4, 9; synekphônêsis / synizêsis 9, *2.30*, *2.82*, *3.7–8*, *5.4*

diction, highflown *1.7*, *1.9*, *1.61*, *4.92*, *5.19*, *5.50*, *7.49*, *7.111*; epic *1.9*, *1.33–5*, *2.10–15*, *2.101*, *2.102*, *3.58b*, 95, *4.12*, *4.50*, *5.39*, *5.75*, *6.11*, *6.28*, *6.58*, 201, *7.7*, *7.22*, *7.39*, *8.1*, *8.59*, 235 n.13; liturgical *4.79–85*; rhetorical *2.2*, *2.21–7*, *2.21*, *2.42–5*, *2.60*, *2.62–3*, *2.90*, *2.92–4*, *2.95–100*, *2.100–2*, 66, 69, 70; tragic *3.5*, *3.11*, *3.14*, *3.71*, *5.20*, *5.68*, *7.18*, *7.74*, *8.2*

dildoes 166, 167, 168, *6.19*, *6.51*, 184; in comedy 167, *6.19*, 200; in mime, 167, *6.19*, 181

dildo-stitchers 182

Dionysos, in *Mim.* 8 *8.28*, *8.31*, *8.36–65a*, *8.40*, *8.46*, *8.68*, 233

diptychs, poetic 166, 198, 199, 214–5

distancing 2–4, 185–6

doors, knocking on *1.1*, *2.50*

double-entendres *1.55*, *6.51*, *6.76*, *6.102*, *7.58*, *7.60*, *7.61*, *7.63*, *7.109*, *7.110*, *7.112*, *7.128*, 214–15

dreams, experienced by poets 225–6, *8.9*

eavesdroppers *1.47*, *6.16*

endearment, terms of *1.7*, *1.60*, *2.82*, *3.72*, *5.69*, *6.46*, *6.77*, *7.113*, *7.125*

Erinna *6.20*, 186, *7.58*

festivals *1.29*, *1.56*, *3.53*, 5.80, *6.17*, 225, *8.23*, *8.36–65a*

fines *2.46*

fishermen *3.51*

games, children's *3.6*, *3.7*, *3.19*, *3.26*, *3.64*

geese *4.31*

genitals: male 5.45, *6.51*, *6.69*, *6.76*, *6.102*, 181, 184, *8.4*; female *6.51*, *6.97*, *6.102*, *7.61*, *7.112*, *8.4*

genres, crossing of 2, *8.44*, 234–5

Gerênia *5.80*

goatherds, identity of in *Mim.* 8 226, 233–4

goats, in dreams *8.16*

go-betweens 21–2, 32

gossip *6.16*, *6.27*, *6.41*, 182, 183

grave-robbers *5.57*

grey, of eyes *6.49*

Herakles *2.96*

Herodas, name and life of 1; and Apelles *4.75*, 128–9, 186; and Hellenistic art 127–9; and Hippônax 2, 3, 7, 51, *2.23*, 79, *3.5*, *3.49*, *5.30*, *5.75*, *6.17*, *6.28*, *6.34*, *6.58*, *6.72–3*, *6.101*, 200–1, *7.43*, *7.48*, *7.67*, *7.78*, *7.125*, *8.6*, *8.31*, *8.36*, *8.59*, *8.75*, 233, 234; and Theokritos 2, 4, 21, 22, 36–9, 105, 107–8, 168, 226, 233–5; engagement with his poetry *1.71*, 186, 226, *8.71*, *8.79*, 233–5; as narrator of *Mim.* 8 224–5, *8.9*, 233; political objectivity of 95–7, 184–6

Hippônax 2, 3, 7, 51, *2.23*, 79, *3.5*, *3.49*, *5.30*, *5.75*, *6.17*, *6.28*, *6.34*, *6.58*, *6.72–3*, *6.101*, 200–1, *7.43*, *7.48*, *7.67*, *7.78*, *7.125*, *8.6*, *8.31*, *8.36*, *8.59*, *8.75*, 233, 234

honey *5.85*, *7.43*

Hygieia *4.5*

Isthmian games *1.52*

Kallimachos 2, 4, 7, 8, *1.13*, *1.71*, 225, 226, *8.4*, *8.9*, *8.72*, *8.79*, 233, 235

Kallixeinos of Rhodes *1.29*

Kêphisodôtos 105, *4.1–20*, *4.20–6*, *4.23*, 128
Kerkôps *7.9*
*kinaidoi 2.74*, *2.77*
*kômos 2.35–7*
Korê *1.32, 1.56*
Kos 1, 2, 21, 51, *2.27*, *2.95–100*, *2.95*, *2.96*, *2.98*, 79, *3.59–60*; Korê-cult on *1.32*; Moirai-oath on 21, *1.11*, *1.66*; Soter and Philadelphos' connections with 123
*magoidia*, *magoidos* 21, 32, 140
Merops *2.95*
metatheatre *1.71*, 35, *6.20*, 186, *7.57*, *7.58*
metics *2.10–15*, *2.40*, *2.87*, 69
metre choliambs 2, 6–7, *1.71*, 35; use of in mime 2; caesura 7; diaeresis 7; ischiorrôgic 7, *1.21*; resolution 7; *skazôn* 6
mime 2, 4–6; people of 32, 40 n. 2, 140; *see also under magoidia*, Sophrôn
mice, iron-eating *3.76*
Misê *1.56*
Middle Comedy 51, 66
millstones *6.81*, *6.83*, *6.84*
Minôs *2.90*, 71
Mistress, the deity *5.77*
Moirai 21, *1.11*, *1.66*, *4.30*
monkeys *3.41*
month, days of *3.9*, *3.53*, *5.80*; Taureôn 166, *7.86*
names *3.59–60*, *4.63*, *4.71*, *5.3*, *5.65*, *5.68*, *6.46*, *6.59*, *7.74*; paronomasia in *1.50*, 51, *2.75*, *2.76*, 79, *3.94*, *4.6*, *5.1*, *5.9*, *7.5*, *7.9*; of prostitutes *1.89*, *2.63*, *4.35–6*, 126, *6.50*, *7.5*
Nannakos 79, *3.10*
New Comedy 34, 51, 66, 79, 95, 139–40, 167
nominatives as vocatives, rude *3.84*, *4.42*, *4.93*, *5.8*, *6.99*, *7.67*; neutral, through assimilation *5.55*
Nossis *6.20*, 186, *7.57*
oaths 21, *1.11*, *1.66*, *2.81*, 106, *4.*30, *4.43*, *5.56*, *5.77*, *6.4*, *6.23*, *7.31*, *7.71*
old age *1.15–16*, *1.17*, 32, 38, *2.71*, *3.29*, *3.39*
Olympic games *1.53*
orators, Attic: and Battaros *2.1–10*, *2.2*, *2.16–20*, *2.17*, *2.25*, *2.37–8*, *2.41–5*, *2.41*, *2.42–5*, *2.60*, *2.65b–71*, *2.67–8*, *2.74*, *2.75*, *2.84*, *2.86*, *2.90*, *2.92–4*, *2.95–100*, *2.100–2*, 69, 70
Paiêôn *4.1*, *4.11*
*paraklausithyron 2.37*
paragraphos 20, *3.87b–97* (passim), *4.1–20*, *6.15b–17a*
part-distributions 20, *1.7*, *1.19–20*, *1.81–5*, 51, *3.87b–97* (passim), 95, 104–5, 107, *4.1–20*, 199, *7.64–76*
performance 4–6, *1.7*, *5.1*, *5.48–9*, *5.49*, 157 n. 17, *6.97*, 200, *7.65*
personification *2.71*, *3.14*, *5.23*, *7.72*, *7.94*
Phasêlis *2.59*
Philainis of Leukadia 23
Philetas 123
Phrygian, as a term of abuse *2.37–8*, *2.100–2*, *3.36*, *5.14*
plectrum, of a lyre *6.51*
prices: of a cloak *2.22*; of repairing a millstone *6.83*; of shoes *7.79*; of slaves *5.21*; of tiles *3.45*
programme, literary 4, 225–6, *8.44*, 233–5
prostitutes 34, *2.19*, *2.82*; depilation practised by *2.69*, 66
proverbs *1.37*, *1.32*, *1.54*, *2.9*, *2.45*, *2.62–3*, *2.73*, *2.80*, *2.100–2*, 68, 69, 70, 71, *3.10*, *3.19*, *3.51*, *3.60–1*, *3.67*, *6.5*, *6.12*, *6.16*, *6.18*, *6.27*, *6.39*, *6.60*, *7.47*, *7.49*, *7.63*, *7.115*, *7.119*, 214, 216, *8.10*

Ptolemies: 1 Soter *1.29*; II Philadelphos *1.29*, *6.64*; III Euergetes *1.21*; V Epiphanes *1.28*; brother and sister gods, temple of 21, *1.30*; encomia to in low contexts *1.28–32*, 37–8; Kos, Soter and Philadelphos' connections with 123
punishments *3.60–1*, *3.68*, *3.85*, *4.78*, *5.28*, *5.32*, *5.68*, *5.78*
puns *6.92*, *8.71*
Pythian games *1.51*
realism 184–6; offset by artificiality of dialect 2
recitation 4–6, 200
refusal formula *1.81*
rent *2.64*
respectability, social, concern with *6.56*, 181, 183, 215
Rhinthôn 201
schools: schoolmasters, primary 79, *3.9*, *3.30*, *3.68*; schoolrooms 79, *3.57*, *3.97*, *3.83*; teaching writing *3.14*, *3.22*, *3.24*, *3.28*, *3.30*
shoemakers 182, 200–1
silent parts 5, 200
slaves *2.46*, *2.82*, *5.15*, *5.18*, *5.21*, *5.27*, *5.78*; abuse of *4.39–56*, *4.42*, 168, *6.1–14*, *6.5–8*, *6.10*, *6.16*, 182, *7.6*, *8.4*, *8.5*; free women, relations with 138–40, *5.15*; tattooing of *5.28*, *5.65*, *5.78*; torture of *2.85*, *2.87*, *2.88*, *5.32*, *5.68*
Sophrôn 2, 22, 32, 51, 66, 68, 167, 168
soul, conceived of as a breath *3.4*
staging: details supplemented by audience's imagination 4–6, *1.7*, *4.12*, *4.56b–78*, *4.58*, 122–8, 156–7, *6.99*, 199–200
synekdochê *3.5*
tattooing *5.28*, *5.65*, *5.78*
tax-collectors *6.64*, 181, 185, 186
temple-attendants *4.41*
textual matters 3–4, 20, *1.2*, *2.10–15*, *2.42–5*, *4.51*, *4.57*, *4.61*, *4.94–5*, *5.4*, *5.9*, *5.17*, *5.85*, *6.34b-6*, *6.36*, *6.41*, *6.80*, *6.81*, *6.90*, *6.94*, 199, *7.9*, *7.10–11*, *7.12*, *7.25*, *7.26–42*, *7.29*, *7.33*, *7.54–5*, *7.96*, *7.128–9*, 224, *8.16*, *8.30–1*, *8.79*, 234
Theokritos 2, 4, 21, 22, 36–9, 105, 107–8, 168, *6.37*, *6.55*, *6.71*, *6.98*, 226, 233–5
Timarchos 105, *4.1–20*, *4.23*, 128
tmesis *1.38*, *3.5*, *4.18*, *4.29*, *4.49*, *4.60*, *4.93*, *7.12*, *7.114*, *8.46*, *8.58*
torture *2.85*, *2.87*, *2.88*, *5.32*, *5.59*, *5.66*, *5.68*
Trikkê *2.97*
Tyre *2.18*
visiting, literary motif of *1.9*, 168
women, Hellenistic, increasing independence of 21, *1.2*, 153–4; *see also* adultery
Xouthos *8.79*

Printed and bound by CPI Group (UK) Ltd, Croydon, CR0 4YY

09/06/2025

14685953-0003